Truth and Tension in Science and Religion

TRUTH

and

TENSION

in Science and Religion

by
Varadaraja V. Raman

Beech River Books
Center Ossipee, New Hampshire

BℝB

Beech River Books
P.O. Box 62, Center Ossipee, N.H. 03814
1-603-539-3537
www.beechriverbooks.com

LIBRARY OF CONGRESS CATALOGING-IN-PUBLICATION DATA

Raman, Varadaraja V.
Truth and tension in science and religion / by Varadaraja V. Raman.
p. cm.
Summary: "An examination of the frameworks of science and
religion that provides a multi-cultural view of how they affect
our perception of the truth"--Provided by publisher.
Includes bibliographical references (p.) and index.

ISBN-13: 978-0-9793778-6-0 (pbk. : alk. paper)
ISBN-10: 0-9793778-6-2 (pbk. : alk. paper)

1. Religion and science. I. Title.

BL240.3.R36 2009
201'.65--dc22
2009014978

Cover design by Ethan Marion.

Printed in the United States of America

This book is dedicated to
all men and women of goodwill
who recognize whatever is ennobling
and enhancing in both religion and science,
and choose to discard whatever is not.

Acknowledgments

Like every author of a scholarly work I am indebted to a hundred others who are recognized in the references and bibliography of the text. In addition to them, I should also express my gratitude to a number of fellow thinkers in the field with whom I have exchanged views and insights in discussions and internet exchanges. I prefer not to mention any one by name for fear of forgetting some others, but I am sure they know who they are. In particular, however, I should mention Dr. Jerome Stone for kindly writing a brief foreword for this book, and my wife, M. L. Raman for her meticulous look at the manuscript with suggestions for altering phrases and tone, and rendering passages less opaque. I am also very thankful to my enthusiastic editor, Brad Marion, who assisted me in presenting these thoughts in the format of the following pages, and to Ethan Marion, for the art used on the cover.

Portions of this book have been published as Internet postings or as lectures elsewhere.

Contents

Foreword

This is one of those rare books which has treasures and delights both for the beginner and the old hand in the topic of the relation between science and religion.

Dr. Raman is well qualified for this task with a strong understanding of both science and religion. A practicing physicist, he is also an outstanding scholar of Hindu thought, Indian culture and student of Sanskrit. His book on the Bhagavad Gita is a gem. He is one of the leading teachers of Indian culture to the North American Hindu community. He also had Roman Catholic schooling. He has read deeply in the major religions of the world and been a participant observer in many of their worship celebrations. As a scientist he is appropriately critical, but he also has an appreciation for the spiritual depths to be found in these religions. For years he has been a participant in the intense and intensive discussions on science and religion by the Institute on Religion in an Age of Science.

As a youth Dr. Raman was horrified by the violence between Hindus and Muslims when the Indian subcontinent was divided between Pakistan and India. In his disgust, he rejected all religion. However, his father advised him not to judge religions by what some adherents did. "He told me that religions soothe the heart and uplift the soul, have given rise to great literature, marvelous music and magnificent places of worship. I have seen Hindus meditate, Muslims observe the Ramadan fast, Christians celebrate Christmas, and Jews Hanukkah, all in peace."

One of the great merits of this clearly written book is that it avoids oversimplifications. Rather than speak of *the* scientific view, it will talk of approaches from *different* scientific disciplines. And the author often reminds us that the traditional viewpoint in a religion is not held by all of the adherents of that religion.

Among the topics covered are: the science of spirituality, art, music, poetry, purpose in the universe, intelligent design, pseudo-science, the meaning of numbers, the question of determinism, pseudo-sciences, postmodernism and, of course, love and death.

This book is carefully and clearly written and should be of interest to adherents of any faith or none. As a United Church of Christ minister for eighteen years and a trained philosopher and Christian theologian who has pondered these questions for many years, I find this to be a wise and balanced book. Anyone with an open mind will find in it many pleasures, food for thought and important insights.

Jerome A. Stone, Ph.D.
Meadville Lombard Theological School
Emeritus Professor of Philosophy—William Rainey Harper College
Member of Highlands Institute on American Religious and Philosophical Thought and the Institute on Religion in an Age of Science

Preamble

Whereas the brains of all creatures evolved for achieving social unity and group survival, the human brain also developed the peculiar and unique capacity to interpret its perceptual inputs in ways that give meaning, purpose, rational consistency, emotional satisfaction, and conviction regarding the world of perceived reality. In a more evolved state, with the development of language and concepts, it began to define, describe, and look upon these interpretations as *truths*.

Not all these *truths* could achieve the consensus that individuals and groups crave for. The divergences among the upholders of different interpretations (truths), have given rise tensions as to what constitutes truth, and these became the hallmark of sophisticated human cultures.

This book explores this phenomenon in a variety of contexts.

Ultimate Truth is not grasped by the eye, nor by speech or other sense organs, nor by austerity or work, but when one's nature is purified by the light of self-less knowledge.

—Adapted from Mundaka Upanishad: III.1.8

Chapter 1

Introduction

Science and religion were inseparably intertwined for many centuries in most cultures of the human family. After all, both spring from the same inner urge to understand and unravel the mystery of existence—existence of a world with all its splendor and richness, and of a mind that reflects, a heart that feels, and a spirit that experiences all aspects of life.

With the rise of what is called modern science in the sixteenth and seventeenth centuries in Western Europe, this field began to elaborate worldviews that were at odds with long-held notions as to the nature and functioning of the physical world. More seriously, some of the findings of the modern scientific quest seemed to diverge from various assertions held sacred in religious texts. It was as if twins who had long lived and played together in the same arena were now drifting away because one of them had discovered a richer ground to sport in. Alternatively, perhaps it was like a married couple who discovered at some point that they were too incompatible to stay together, thus wrecking the harmony that had long existed between them.

At least in the Western Christian tradition, astronomy, geology and biology unraveled facts and developed visions that could not be easily reconciled with the Scripture. No matter how persuasive the fruits and format of science are, it has not been successful in meeting some of the deeper needs of the human experience, certainly not as well as traditional religions do. Therefore, many capable and creative scientists remained anchored to their faith, even if it sometimes meant accepting positions that do not conform to Aristotelian two-valued logic.

Even with all that, by the close of the nineteenth century Andrew Dixon White, who chronicled in detail the gory confrontations between science and religion, wrote:

> My conviction is that Science, though it has evidently conquered Dogmatic Theology based on biblical texts and ancient modes of thought, will go hand in hand with Religion, and that, although theological control will continue to diminish, Religion, as seen in the recognition of a Power in the universe, and not in ourselves which makes for righteousness and in the Love of God and of our neighbor, will steadily grow stronger and stronger, not only in the American institutions of learning, but in the world at large. (1896, 1:28)

Indeed, most thinkers understood at the time, as they still do in our own times, that there is much more to religion than cosmology, the age of the earth and anthropogenesis. This crucial truth, though seldom articulated by combatants on both sides, was apparent to generations of creative scientists who, even while practicing technical science, continued to be affiliated to their faith tradition in pious, respectful, and profoundly fulfilling modes.

When the religious establishment persisted in insisting on pre-scientific worldviews about certain aspects of the phenomenal world, scientists generally ignored it because that did not interfere with their practice of science in any important way. Commentators on science and religion, much more than working scientists, were drawn to the divergent claims of science and religion on issues which had little to do with meaning, purpose or divinity. Some of them announced and amplified the irreconcilable differences between scientific results and religious doctrines on matters pertaining to astronomy and zoology, propagating the impression that science and religion are essentially two irreconcilable institutions and an intelligent person simply cannot in good conscience owe allegiance to both.

Thoughtful scientists and scientifically inclined thinkers have often felt that a serious schism between science and religion would not be in the best interest of society and civilization. Einstein made the famous remark that:

> A legitimate conflict between science and religion cannot exist... Science without religion is lame, religion without science is blind. (1940, 605)

The essence of this statement is that as human beings we are incomplete without some science and some religion. This feeling is shared by many. That is why in the twentieth century, serious efforts were initiated to build bridges of understanding and mutual respect between science and religion. Journals emerged, such as *Zygon* and *Science and Theology*, and also institutions such as Institute on Religion in an Age of Science, the Metanexus Institute for Science and Religion, and International Society for Science and Religion. Scores of books exploring the relationship between science and religion began to be published. Countless interesting exchanges and clarifications have ensued from these, and from many conferences and internet groups dedicated to science-religion issues. These have become commonplace in today's scholarly landscape in the Western world. Similar movements have started in other countries and religious traditions as well.

One might think that all these activities would have led to greater understanding and harmony between science and religion in the modern world. However, this is not the case. After more than half a century of such efforts, the subject of the role and relevance of science and religion is still a matter of considerable debate and controversy. If anything, the chasm between science and religion seems to be growing. Jerry Coyne, an ardent admirer of Richard Dawkins expressed this rigid perspective by saying:

> The real war is between rationalism and superstition. Science is but one form of rationalism, while religion is the most common form of superstition. (2006, 15)

Dawkins has compared the current scene to the Nazi threat of the 1930s. In his view, those who are cozy with religionists are like the naïve Neville Chamberlain (*The God delusion*, 2006). Similar views are held by some Islamic extremists about Muslims who hold dialogues with the West. Dawkins' virulence against religion, whether justified or not, reminds us of a statement by a certain T. T. Martin:

> The German soldiers who killed Belgian and French children with poisoned candy were angels compared to the teachers and textbook writers who corrupted the souls of children and thereby sentenced them to eternal death. (1923, 398)

Such rhetoric, besides being off the mark in truth-content, is not helpful in a world wrought with conflicts and confrontations.

One might get the impression from all this that such science-religion disagreement is a uniquely Christian phenomenon, and that it does not occur in other religious contexts. The reason it has become so acute in the Western Christian context is that modern scientific results blatantly differing from traditional religious explanations of human beings and natural phenomena first arose in the Western Christian matrix where religious scholars became aware of, and often contributed to, the advancement of scientific knowledge. As and when this occurs in other frameworks, similar debates, discussions, mutual name-calling, and bridge-building are bound to occur there too. In fact, science-religion debates have already begun in the Hindu (see for example, Meera Nanda, *Prophets looking backwards*, 2003), Islamic (see for example, Mansoor Moaddel, *Islamic modernism, nationalism, and fundamentalism*, 2005), and Buddhist (see for example, B. Alan Wallace, *Choosing reality: A Buddhist view of physics and the mind*, 1996) traditions, though the last of these is gaining ground in the West more than in Buddhist societies. In each instance, the flavor of the discussions is different, but generally there are efforts to establish that the respective ancient texts already embody many of the results and insights of modern "western" science.

It must be pointed out that though one talks about science and religion, in every culture most of the conflicts are between (some) scientists and (some) theologians. The vast majority of the practitioners of religions go about their religious activities and commitments independently of, perhaps even indifferent to, what science and scientists say about these matters. Likewise, practicing scientists in all countries are by and large immersed in their various fields and subfields, indifferent to, and often quite ignorant of, what religious people are saying about science and its limitations. But theologians who are eager to provide props for religion from the latest scientific theories and results, as well as cultural patriots who wish to show the keenness of the minds of their ancestors often write apologetically on the doctrines of their affiliation to attune them to the most recent scientific refrain.

Likewise, a few scientists, and many philosophers and commentators on religion, publish profusely on the congruence or divergence between science and religion, either justifying religion on the basis of scientific worldviews or provocatively propagating their arguments against it. In other words, it appears that science can and does flourish in its own right in its own place, as religion does in its context. Most often, belligerent noises come from those who have either little understanding of science or little sensitivity to religion.

Some feel that religion and science fall under very different categories. They argue that the two fields must be treated as *Non-Overlapping Magisteria*, or NOMA, as the late Stephen Gould named them in his widely read book *Rocks of the ages* (1999). Others go a step beyond and say that one of them (religion) is no *magisterium* (domain of authority in teaching) at all, and deserves to be relegated to the archives of ancient history. For example, Richard Dawkins has been consistently asserting that, if anything, science has discredited religion. On the other hand, some argue that scientific knowledge itself is a grand façade: superficially attractive, but hollow within. Paul Feyerabend, a master in denigrating science and its methodology, went so far as to say, "The similarities between science and myth are indeed astonishing" (1975, 298). Given the growing negative impacts of technology, condemnation of science is a popular theme, and not everyone thinks that this has potential for grave danger for civilization.

No matter what position one takes, science is here to stay for at least as long as the human mind functions, and religion, too, for as long as societies exist as we know them. Moreover, the exchanges between them will continue and serve an interesting purpose of their own, even if extremists on either side are out to destroy the other. Not surprisingly, a number of scholars from various traditions have authored a book entitled, *Why the science and religion dialogue matters: Voices from the International Society of Science and Religion* (Watts and Dutton 2007).

It is an unfortunate fact that, unlike former times, in the context of the truths that the institutions (science and various religions) proclaim and uphold, there is considerable tension. The tensions invariably arise when the adherents of one group encounter those of another. The differing faiths and frameworks are at the root of the tensions.

The human mind is tossed between truth claims by science as well as religion. Each is persuasive in its own milieu, but when brought to an open arena there is more tension than harmony between the two. It is unlikely that this tension will ever slacken, certainly not as long as protagonists for each group hold on to their own perspective with uncompromising tenacity. If faith is the factor in the religious context, framework seems more fundamental for scientific truths. Yet science is not without its faith components, and religions also function within formulated frameworks. In this context, it would seem that the primary criteria for the adoption and furtherance of either perspective should be the impact they have on the human condition: on the individual, on culture, and on civilization. Any quarrel of significance between scientifically-inclined thinkers and religious practitioners should be motivated more by how their opponents' beliefs hurt and harm than by whether they are true or false. Truth and falsehood pertaining to ultimate questions are not always easy to establish to the satisfaction of one and all, but one can hope to find some consensus on what is helpful and harmonious.

The pages to follow are commentaries from the perspective of one whose mind has been enriched by science, and who has derived fulfillment from religious associations. I have tried to present both perspectives on a variety of issues.

The growing field of Science and Religion has to its credit a vast and developing body of literature. In order to make the book more accessible, I have not cluttered it with footnotes, and given appropriate references in parentheses. At the end the reader will find a select bibliography for further exploration and elaboration of the chapters.

Chapter 2
On Science and Religion

Science and religion in history

Science and religion are among the loftiest expressions of the human spirit. Science is the human mind's quest to unravel the workings of the world. It is a collective effort to understand, explain and grasp the perceived world. Religion is the human heart's search for meaning and purpose behind existence, and a yearning to connect with the Whole. It arises from the recognition of the uniqueness of consciousness in the universe. In the traditional framework, religions emerged from the cosmic visions of Vedic rishis, from the covenant of Moses with God, from the enlightenment of the Buddha, from the commitment to non-violence of Mahavira, from the sermons of Jesus of Nazareth, from the revelations to Prophet Mohammed, and from the syncretistic inspiration of Guru Nanak and Bahaullah. Among other things, religions led to the formulation of ethical principles in the Judeo-Christian world, fostered compassion in the Buddhist-Jaina world, inspired sophisticated metaphysics in the Hindu world, and provoked massive scholarship in the Islamic world. When religion is a quest to communicate with the transcendent and the commitment to serve others, it elevates the human spirit to its highest potential.

Once, science used intelligent guessing about how the world was formed and how it ticks. But during the past few centuries, with empirical methodology, ingenious instruments and mathematical analysis, science has made astonishing advances in unveiling the secrets of nature. It has fathomed the deepest core of matter and the depths of space. More important than discovering unseen aspects of the world, knowledge acquired through science has demolished plague and pestilence, and the mindless fears that tormented our ancestors. Before one romanticizes the good old times, it would be eye-opening to read and reflect on the mindset and fears of people in medieval times all over the world. Bad omens, unlucky numbers, goblins, cherubim, dragons, evil spirits, witches, and the like clouded the minds of the common people. Women were held in low esteem, looked down upon as weak and the source of sin, and were exploited. Aspects of that mindset have survived to this day in many parts of the world. The applications of science have enhanced the quality of life, mitigated pain and disease, and accomplished physical wonders bordering on the incredible. Science is a fruitful enterprise indeed. Ironically, science has also brought us to the brink.

The history of human civilization is marked by major revolutions, some slow and some abrupt, some dramatic and some subtle, some of local significance and some of global impact. Among the most important of these are the agricultural revolution, which introduced sowing, harvesting and storage of crops. This was to have long-range effects on the history of humanity. Jared Diamond (*Guns, germs, and steel*, 1997) has shown that by the sheer accident of having several plants (such as barley and wheat) and animals (such as goats and cattle) which could be domesticated, Eurasia managed to forge more powerful and conquering civilizations than most other regions of the world.

The agricultural revolution soon led to the cultural revolution; gradually, language, abstract thoughts, ethical frameworks, writing, and other elements became intrinsic to human societies. All this radically changed us from being another mammal in the plethora of species into something that began to see meaning and significance in existence, to pose questions, and to have an ever increasing impact on the world wherein we live. It was in this setting that philosophies and religious systems arose.

Religion continues to be a potent force in modern societies. It is true that with the success of modern science some of the doctrines of traditional religions are not taken as seriously or literally as they used to be, at least by the scientifically informed. The power and performance of science have weakened some of the traditional claims of religions. Nevertheless, in a great many places all over the world, there is a resurgence of interest in religions and pseudo-religions, in cults and charismatic preachers.

Already in ancient times, some thinkers toyed with the notion that perhaps the earth was not that central in the universe. However, for various reasons, this idea did not attain full credence in any culture until the sixteenth century. Then, as is well known, Nicolas Copernicus elaborated on the hypothesis of a heliostatic universe. He managed to account for planetary motions with reasonable success, more efficiently, and with far less cycles and epicycles than the ancients had done. This was a revolutionary idea at the time, but the religious establishment of the cultural matrix in which it was proposed did not receive it with great enthusiasm. Many scholars have analyzed why this was so. In any event, one root cause for the negative reaction to the Copernican worldview was that it summarily displaced humans from the center of the universe. This had enormous theological implications, for every theology has a God-Man connection, and in that context, Man takes on a special position vis-à-vis other entities in God's entire creation. It is difficult to reconcile a world in which the home of humans is but a minuscule speck in the cosmos with the doctrine that God created the world with all its beauty and abundance intending the pinnacle of His *magnum opus* as its primary beneficiary. The Copernican worldview was the starting point of another major transformation that was to occur in human history: the so-called scientific revolution in the sixteenth and seventeenth centuries.

Ironically, or perhaps symbolically, Copernicus was a canon who served the Roman Catholic Church faithfully for all his life. Perhaps the significance here is that, though they were to differ in the way they interpreted the world, science and religion are intrinsically interconnected, both being expressions of the human spirit.

There is no question but that the Copernican revolution was a jolt to the spiritual sensitivities of humanity. There are two ways of coping with this major crisis in our religious worldview. One is to reject and ignore some of the basic underpinnings of traditional religion. This approach could lead (and indeed has led) to serious impacts on a meaningful and fulfilling experience of life, at least for a vast majority of humankind. The religious dimensions of culture, civilization, and of individual human lives have more than historical and aesthetic significance. In profound ways, they are too precious to relinquish, and perhaps impossible to erase altogether. History shows that attempts to eradicate religion from society have not met with great success. More frequently, one religious paradigm replaces another. Religions are important facets of culture and are here to stay. Therefore, the challenge is to make them benign.

In the second approach, one tries to refine religions by making them more in tune with enlightened values, and to fine-tune theologies to make them more consonant with modern scientific worldviews. This is surely a more worthwhile and realistic goal than the eradication of religions from human culture, without sacrificing the enrichment that religions provide. Indeed, this approach rests on a sensitive understanding of the nature of the human condition in relation to its connections with the cosmos. The visions, as articulated by the religious leaders of past ages in various cultural contexts, have a remarkable universality. When appropriately interpreted, some have even seen in them worldviews that have parallels with some of the deeper implications of certain discoveries of the sciences of our own times. But it is important in such contexts not to mistake insightful visions with arduously and methodologically acquired scientific knowledge.

The industrial-technological revolution arose a couple of centuries later and began to harness matter and energy on the basis of an understanding of the workings of the physical world. Both these revolutions, the Copernican and the scientific, like religions long before them, began with great promise for the betterment and enrichment of the human condition, but have somehow led to more perilous problems to confront than ever before.

It would be a misreading of history to imagine that in earlier times there was neither science nor technology. From the unrecorded dawn of consciousness, when the human mind wondered and human hands turned a stone or a stick this way and that to feel and fathom what it was, science has been there in every community and culture. In periods now long past, scientific creativity and discovery flourished in India and China, Egypt and Mesopotamia, Greece and elsewhere. Devices have been contrived to lessen muscular effort and facilitate manipulation of the world since time immemorial. Wonderment and curiosity about the surroundings, and eagerness to diminish sweat and work are inherent to the human spirit.

Universality of science and ubiquity of technology

Since the emergence of modern science, scientific efforts in various countries and continents have come to be subsumed under a single umbrella, made up of an abstract international body of scientific practice and culture. In our own times, the nations of the world have their own research laboratories and publications, and yet, the works carried out and published in geographically separated places are interwoven into a web held firm by invisible bonds that know no borders, that feel no cultural differences. The meter and the kilogram in any national bureau of standards are precisely the same, no matter what the religion or form of government may be in the country.

Some may think the chief significance of the scientific revolution of the sixteenth and seventeenth centuries is that it led to the discarding of geocentric views. This was important, as was the discovery of elliptical planetary orbits, which opened our visions to hitherto hidden aspects of the universe, and also the formulation of the laws of motion, which led to a deeper understanding of the physical world. But most significantly, the scientific revolution initiated a universality which transformed the very nature of the enterprise into a collective quest.

Science certainly has its local interests, narrow nationalism, and petty fights over priorities too. After all, it is only a human enterprise. There are rivalries and races in the pursuit of knowledge and competition in discoveries. There is national pride when a prize is announced. Yet, the technical work of scientists is blind to nationalities, they overlap and mingle like sounds from different instruments in an orchestra to create and constitute the grand symphony that science is. The true strength and stature of modern science lies in its universality. Science is no longer bits of insights here and there, nor imaginative speculations by keen minds in particular cultures. It surely is not parochial, ethnic interpretations of natural phenomena or narratives from sacred books. Rather, science is a restless drive to eradicate misunderstanding in the interpretation of every occurrence from the micro to the macrocosm, to unravel every mystery and dispel every doubt and darkness from the inquiring mind.

In spite of national differences and cultural diversity, no matter what language one speaks and what creeds one subscribes to, the one common thread that connects the minds of men and women in today's world is international science. The commonalties in the towns and cities of the modern world are electric lights and communication systems, automobiles and computers.

Modern science is characteristically transnational in nature, and modern technology is ubiquitous. There is no member state of the United Nations organization where science is not taught or planes do not land. Whether one understands science or decries it, no serious thinker or leader in the twenty-first century can ignore science or function efficiently without its technological offshoots. The primary contribution of science has been to quench curiosity through disinterested search, to provide intellectual satisfaction through its explanatory successes, and to enhance creature comforts through ingenious technology.

We live in a world where science and technology hold sway. If we look around any spot on earth that has found its way into the mainstream of human history, we cannot escape the presence of wheels and wires, gadgets and generators, vaccines and pills. The material impacts of science, the magic and madness of machines are omnipresent and inevitable. Science and technology are here to stay, and their influences are likely to grow even more in times to come.

In no other context—not in art, music, sports, much less in politics—do men and women of all races, languages and religions, hold hands as comrades in a common pursuit. This speaks as much to the glory of science as an enterprise as all its technological triumphs do. It is important to realize, whether one is from the East or the West, from the North or the South, that modern science is not Western any more than that the zero is Hindu or that gunpowder is Chinese, except in the accident of their geographical origin. For better or for worse, the scientific revolution merged diverse streams of search into a single surging river, as it were.

Separateness of religions

However, nothing of the kind happened in the realm of religion. Here the ancient roots have stayed separate and sturdy, and the trees grew taller and vigorous, too, shooting out branches along different directions, but the branches of a tree drew nourishment primarily from their respective roots. Different sects and schools arose within Judaism, Buddhism, Hinduism, Christianity and Islam , but in each instance, a core remained safe and secure.

Unlike science, there arose no common religious institution to embrace all faiths and form a single superstructure unto which all would come and pray. True, there have been efforts to repair old divisions, attempts to heal historical wounds, even movements to bring out the best from all religions. However, Din Ilahis and Unitarians, Baha'is and Brahmos have been elite groups, rather than major religions with mass followings. If anything, over the past few centuries, newer groups have come and gone, new prophets and cult leaders have forged additional movements.

One reason for this is that science is concerned with the external world of cold reality, whereas religion is linked to inner warmth, local moorings, trusted traditions, and close community. Every religion is affiliated not only to ancient prophets and personages, but also to time-honored rites and rituals, which have acquired the weight of centuries. To reject all this and embrace a global network is more difficult than to switch from a geocentric to a heliostatic model. To find resonance with prayers from alien faiths is more difficult than to use telescopes and microscopes to explore the world. It is a fact of cultural irony that on the issue of Divinity, which so many religions worship as omnipresent, the local variations are unable to merge.

In schools everywhere, we find the same laws of nature and the same mathematics taught, the same facts of anatomy and the same genetic structures explained; whereas in places of worship, we find different symbols venerated, different kinds of eschatology expounded, and different days prescribed for fasting and feasting.

In their convictions as to the nature of the Divine and on who represents God here below, religions differ in profound ways. When a belief-system encounters a competing worldview, spokespeople for religions tend to regard others as astray or evil. Left to itself, no religion recommends anything harmful towards others. However, when faced with people of a different faith or symbol, the zeal to convert emerges, and all the caring and submission to God tends to transform into big-brotherliness (at best) or into hate and hurt (at worst). Human history is replete with ugly memories of mutual massacres, rampages, burnings at the stake, inquisitions and holy wars—all perpetrated in the name of God and religion. True believers do not have the slightest doubt that their own religious, moral, and cosmological worldviews are the only correct ones. Where and when they acquire power over others, they can be far more dangerous than pious theists, cocksure atheists, or narrow fundamentalists in non-theocratic societies.

On monodoxy and AGA

We interact with the world in different modes. One of these is through concepts and ideas. At a sophisticated level of this mode, we try to understand and interpret the world in terms of certain broad categories. This approach is commendable as a goal, insightful in its formulations, and fruitful in its results. But it can also lead to a mindset that I call *monodoxy*: single belief.

This term can mean two things. Monodoxy regards a framework, mode, or system of ideas as the only acceptable orthodoxy (literally, *right belief*), such that, those who hold differing views (and even adherents to one's own system who suggest significant changes to it) are frowned upon or penalized severely. Furthermore, the validity of its framework is taken so seriously that those who disagree are vilified, dismissed, or when possible, actively oppressed. Thus, monodoxy is a deeply felt conviction that one possesses the right answers to all fundamental questions, while others do not. Often monodoxy is also a reflection of the conviction in one's own (or one's group's) intellectual and moral superiority vis-à-vis others.

Monodoxy is fairly universal in human societies. It has been present all through human history, and in all cultures. It is difficult to avoid, especially in epistemological, religious, social, and political contexts where it is most prevalent, because it is necessary for the practice and furtherance of a system, and sometimes, even for its survival. There are different types of monodoxy:

(a) *Methodological.* A particular methodology for the interpretation of the world is taken to be the only valid one. In our own times, scientific methodology tends to be monodoxical. As Mikael Stenmark puts it, in this view, "there is nothing outside the domain of science nor any area of human life to which science cannot successfully be applied" (2001, 18). According to Merriam-Webster's Collegiate Dictionary, *scientism* is: "an exaggerated trust in the efficacy of the methods of natural science applied to all areas of investigation (as in philosophy, the social sciences, and the humanities)." It is important to recognize that it is possible to adopt the principle that a particular methodology is the most effective one in a particular field of inquiry, without claiming that anything that is investigated in other domains is without merit. What is ignored in such a perspective is that other methodologies could lead to no less satisfying results, if the goal is not just explanation. Those who wish to adopt other modes also claim there are aspects of experiences— usually called paranormal—which may be better understood through other methodologies.

(b) *Criteria for Truth.* In the view of some, the scientific criteria for validating or rejecting propositions tend to be monodoxical. The scientific community brushes off as unacceptable systems that spell out other criteria for truth (see above), such as experiential verifiability, emotional satisfaction, scriptural compatibility, etc. It does not grant that there are categories of truth that are intensely personal, and can carry considerable weight to the individual.

(c) *Transcendental.* William Scott Green noted, "religions exhibit a tendency to totalize, to extend their reach to all dimensions of experience.... Overtly and covertly, religion influences political structures and activity by encouraging and enforcing some attitudes and behaviors by discouraging and disparaging others" (2003, x). No less seriously, they also have an urge to impose their values and visions on people of other religions. This is often the root cause of interfaith conflicts. Assertions to the effect that there is only one Savior for all humankind, only one last Prophet, only one vision of afterlife, etc. are examples of this kind of totalizing. It seems to be difficult for religious systems to accept that God could have given rise to different means and symbols for recognizing His presence in the universe. It is important to distinguish between orthodoxy, which stipulates correct belief, and monodoxy, which claims one's beliefs to be the only right ones. Religious monodoxy has resulted in much ugly behavior, ranging from sectarian persecution to the desecration of the religious symbols of other faiths.

(d) *Socio-economic.* This type of monodoxy occurs in political ideologies. Every political party, philosophy, and economic school tends to proclaim that its prescriptions for solving societal and national problems are the only right ones. Monodoxy in these contexts leads to polarization of views, and inhibits cooperation and accommodation, which are essential for collective benefit. Since this is a theoretical position, it is more common among people who think, reflect and write on issues than among business people, and much less among the common folk.

There may be several causes for monodoxy. Economic or political self-interests may not always be the primary ones, at least at the conscious level. The monodoxical attitude is a deeply felt conviction, a state of mind that results from a genuine belief that one has the solution to all the problems related to a particular sphere, while others do not. It is a reflection of the belief in one's own (or one's group's) intellectual and moral superiority vis-à-vis others, without any intent to exploit others.

There are two elements in Indic thought that may serve as antidotes to monodoxy. One is in the Rig Veda where it says *"ekam sat viprat bahudhà vadanti* [truth is one and the learned refer to it in different ways]" (Hymn 164). The other is in the Jaina doctrine to the effect that truth and reality cannot be apprehended from just one perspective. Known as the doctrine of multiplicity (*anekanta-vàda*), it may also be called epistemic relativity. It asserts that all our views and opinions on issues are functions of our perspective, as in the following poem:

> It was six men of Indostan
> To learning much inclined,
> Who went to see the Elephant
> (Though all of them were blind),
> That each by observation
> Might satisfy his mind.

[Each blind man, groping different parts of the elephant, formed an idea of the elephant from his partial perspective: that it was like a wall (broad and sturdy side), spear (round and smooth and sharp tusk), a snake (squirming trunk), a tree (above the knee), a fan (ear), and a rope (swinging tail))].

And so these men of Indostan
Disputed loud and long,
Each in his own opinion
Exceeding stiff and strong,
Though each was partly in the right,
And all were in the wrong!

(from "The Blind Men and the Elephant" by John Godfrey Saxe, 1873, lines 1-6, 43-48, pp. 135-36)

We may have to accept this as the human condition: Truth in its totality is beyond our grasp.

Many level-headed thinkers in this day and age would agree that a certain degree of intellectual arrogance, if not bigotry and fanaticism, is associated with monodoxy. However, in one's eagerness to avoid this, one may also let oneself slip into its flip side, which may be called *Anything Goes Attitude* (AGA). In a classic work attacking the scientific framework Paul Feyerabend said: "All methodologies have their limitations, and the only 'rule' that survives is 'anything goes'" (1975, 296). AGA arises from a number of factors. First, there is the conviction that it is intrinsically impossible to affirm on purely logical grounds that one mode of looking at things is necessarily more valid than another. If God created the world, who is to say if the Creator had two arms or a hundred? Over the ages, different cultures have developed different approaches to life and reality. It is naïve and ethnocentric to assume that what one's own culture has developed is the best. The growing power and dominance of science renders ineffective and helpless religious and other modes of describing or recognizing reality. This epistemological hegemony seems to be unfair.

A feeling of guilt on the part of some Western thinkers that their own civilization has behaved shabbily towards many other civilizations during the past few centuries has also induced AGA. Feyerabend said that one reason he is against science is that other worldviews need to be given a chance.

An enthusiasm for respecting every explanation of natural phenomena in every culture, past and present may not always be the most enlightened way. At an international conference I was attending a few years ago in South Africa, a speaker from New Zealand reported that some cultures believed that their island had been created in the dawn of time by a deity just for them. She went on to say that Westerners there were now teaching about plate tectonics and the formation of land masses in mid-oceans in the schools, and were thus demolishing the traditional and sacred history of the islanders. This was, she said, Eurocentric arrogance, for it had no respect for the belief system of other cultures.

I rather doubt that teaching people, whether Westerners or Southerners, about current scientific findings and worldviews is a display of arrogance. What is arrogant is to assume that only the Western mind can understand modern science. If we saw an ancient religious rite involving human sacrifice, would we be ethnocentrically haughty if we were to make an effort to have them modify the practice by substituting a symbolic vegetable in lieu of the human?

AGA can also have the effect of shaking faith in one's own cultural, religious, and philosophical framework, since nothing is taken as having any intrinsic or absolute merit. It can dissolve distinctions between science and superstition, between astronomy and astrology, between magic-mongering and medicine, between UFO-logy and SETI, etc. Some thinkers in the scientifically-developing societies have been lulled by AGA into believing that medieval worldviews are as valid as modern scientific. When this is applied in the context of diseases, male superiority, and fear of eclipses, the results can be both ridiculous and devastating.

Monodoxy must be avoided, and also AGA. To hold on to absolutes on the moral plane on purely logical grounds is difficult, but if it is abandoned altogether, society could degenerate to a savage free-for-all with no mooring or maturity. In some contexts, a certain degree of monodoxy is appropriate. On the other hand, to accept every world picture as valid can land us in fantasies and superstitions.

The Jaina doctrine known as *anekânta-vâda* or many-perspectives-thesis can help one avoid falling into the trap of totalizing (Shah 2000). According to this, truth and reality are too complex to be apprehended in their totality from a single perspective. Only facets of the truth can be recognized each time and from different perspectives.

It is important to note the difference between honest conviction that a particular path is more effective than others in arriving at one's goal, and repudiating all others as silly or meaningless. Eventually, the more appropriate one will win. This is the assumption on which free societies function.

The demon-haunted world

One of the ironies of the last quarter of the twentieth century was that there began a steady revival of the mindless beliefs of ages past. There still are millions who are convinced that winged angels hover over their homes, that the stock market is affected by Jupiter's position in relation to Mars, that names which add up to certain numbers will bring good health and high-paying jobs, and that weird witches are floating around everywhere. Dark age worldviews are successfully raising their horrible heads.

We live in an age that is rich in its knowledge of the world around us. We have come to know a good deal more about mute matter, throbbing life, measuring mind, and the expansive universe than ever before in human history. Nevertheless, even as we probe deeper into the mysteries of the universe, our sciences are becoming so specialized and complicated that only a handful of experts in any field are fully informed and understand what their fellow workers are talking about. Large sections of society may hear about a few spectacular discoveries or breakthroughs, such as the detection of planets in other solar systems or the development of a new drug for a disease. However, by and large, there is widespread illiteracy as to the nature and goals of science, its framework and methodology.

Science has no doubt imparted its benign impacts through medicine and technology to enhance public health and prolong life spans, and it has added much to our creature comforts and entertainment modes. Science has also caused some drastic jolts through environmental disasters and a capacity for overkill of the human race.

We have charted distant stars and galaxies, penetrated into the remote recesses of space, uncovered fantastic entities in the cold expanses above, measured the very limits of the universe, and surmised how this world of ours came to be. We are tempted to feel sorry for generations past, who had no inkling of how vast our universe is, and how old, and how it all began. They were unaware of quasars and pulsars, or of an expanding universe. They were constrained by mythological lore and insufficient data in their appraisal of the cosmos. But what excuse do moderns have for living in the conceptual framework of ages past?

With all that, science's contributions towards elevating the human spirit, endowing us with intellectual joys, and ridding the mind of stifling superstitions have not exactly permeated the masses in any society. Instead, there is a vast body of pseudoscientific literature that is appealing, understandable and cheap, that entertains and deludes. Countless books, websites, and internet postings on distorted science are out there to satisfy their curiosity. For one thing, much of this is more intelligible than technical science, even more so than some of the better popularizations of modern science, because no matter how watered down, understanding current science requires serious study, conceptual thinking, and more than a passing interest in the matter. On the other hand, pseudosciences (such as astrology and numerology) make everything easy and understandable. They do more; they tend to satisfy our innermost craving to believe in the fantastic and the illogical. Perhaps because for eons our ancestors groped in the dark and dreamed up mythologies rather than rigorous mathematical explanations, tales rather than theories, our brains resonate more easily with the weird and the way-out, and our hearts experience greater thrill with the obscure and the arcane. Robert Park coined the term voodoo science to cover "pathological science, junk science, pseudoscience, and fraudulent science" (2000, 10).

The undeniable fact is that people with a scientific and skeptical bent on the one hand, and the rest of the decent people in society on the other, are attuned to different standards of thinking, analysis, and criteria for truth. Whether this happens through genetic coding, proper education, or early brainwashing, it is hard to tell. Even among scientists, our cultural sensibilities and spiritual penchants are unevenly developed.

Many scientists lament the dismal state in which twenty-first century finds itself as regards the appreciation and understanding on the part of the general public of what science is all about, and the related intellectual consequences for society at large. In his book *The demon haunted world* (1996), Carl Sagan gives painful portraits of intelligent people harboring the most unscientific beliefs: be it about Atlantis or Nostradamus. He refers to tabloids which spread canards like the discovery of temple ruins on the Martian surface. He mentions periodic reports about aliens: the illegal ones who come without green cards but with green bodies sometimes. He refers to UFOs, of whose existence, like that of a reincorporated Elvis Presley, so many people do not have the slightest doubt. He analyzes the nature of apparitions and visions. He discusses obstinate assertions about spirits. He talks about popular mystery-mongering, such as the Bermuda Triangle, Big Foot, and the Loch Ness monster. Together with other scientifically-enlightened minds that care for the sanity of civilization, he points to the anti-science forces that are becoming more and more assertive in our society. Many devotees of science feel that only minds that have been enriched and illuminated by the scientific spirit can see through the dangers that are lurking in this gradual degradation of society into a medieval mind-set.

Many in the no-nonsense hardcore school of scientists have forcibly articulated a lament about the demon-haunted world of scientific darkness into which, they fear, humanity is fast plunging. Such moaning, however eloquently and reasonably articulated, has not been very effective thus far. One reason for this is that many scientists, rationalists, and empiricists adopt different criteria for truth-acceptance than the rest of the decent people in society.

In this context, it is important to realize that science education does not mean, and it should certainly not be confined to, revealing to students, whether they are interested or not, all the great results and achievements of science. Rather, it should involve more systematically the teaching of the methods and framework of science, the instruments that enable science to unravel so many mysteries of the universe, as also the lives of some eminent scientists like Louis Pasteur, Madame Curie, and Michael Faraday. Respect for, interest in, and understanding of science will occur only when one appreciates the routes and rules by which scientific knowledge is acquired.

At the same time, science courses must refer to the larger society, deeper values, and cultural settings in which science functions. And here one must treat with sensitivity religious beliefs in so far as they are meaningful, uplifting, and non-hurtful. People affiliated with religions feel that, with all its probing and penetrating instruments and fertile formulas, science has not proved, and may never be able to prove, the non-existence of entities and principles that transcend the spatiotemporal world to which we are dimensionally and physically condemned. Science may rule them out as highly improbable and even irrelevant to its own pursuit. Though it may define, for its own purposes, reality as only that which is subject to detection through physical means, it lacks the final authority, and cannot confine actual reality by fiat to only that which is tangible and instrumentally detectable. Spokespersons for science must allow that there are matters that lie beyond logical proofs, mathematical formulas, and repeatable experiments, and extra-scientific existence does not make them any less significant for individuals and to groups.

Uncertain science

Most scientific thinkers have little faith in palmistry, numerology, or astrology. These are categorically characterized as pseudo-sciences by science. However, there are still large numbers of people all over the world who not only believe in some of these , but pursue them in what they regard as a scientific framework. It may be noted in passing that Islam is the only major religion that explicitly rejects any kind of soothsaying. Ironically, it was Arab and Persian scholarship that introduced astrology into medieval Europe. The Hindu world has a rich and ancient astrological tradition. Some have claimed that it has its roots in the Vedic tradition, although there is a recent movement to deny this. There is even an American College of Vedic Astrology. B. V. Raman, a prolific author of articles and books, and founder of the American College of Vedic Astrology, has done perhaps more for the cause of astrology than anyone else in modern time. David Frawley, described as "an Indian in an American body," has expounded Vedic astrology in several of his writings (see for example, his *Astrology of the seers: a guide to Vedic/Hindu astrology*, 1990). After the scientific revolution and the rise of modern astronomy, astrology gradually lost credibility in the Western world, certainly among the scientifically awakened, but it continues to thrive in the West largely through daily predictions and charts in newspapers.

Then there are the so-called paranormal experiences and phenomena which range from poltergeist and premonition to telekinesis and telepathy. These have been reported and even scientifically investigated for many years, but with no conclusive evidence acceptable to the scientific framework. As of now, the scientific establishment roundly rejects them, some interested investigators continue to explore them, while a goodly number of the public is persuaded that they exist. Significant monetary rewards have been offered by skeptical groups for clear and substantial evidence of such phenomena, but there have been no takers thus far. James Randi, who has offered a million dollars for scientific proof of paranormal phenomena, is reported to have said:

Acceptance of nonsense as mere harmless aberrations can be dangerous to us. We live in an international society that is enlarging the boundaries of knowledge at an unprecedented rate, and we cannot keep up with much more than a small portion of what is made available to us. To mix our data input with childish notions of magic and fantasy is to cripple our perception of the world around us. We must reach for the truth, not for the ghosts of dead absurdities. (1992, 80)

But propagators of such worldviews have enough followers without any vindication from scientists and other unbelievers. One reason for this is that not everyone is familiar with, let alone practices, the rigorous rules by which science evaluates the truth-content of claims. Another reason could well be that paranormal experiences are very personal. They are also anecdotal, and may not always be the result of hallucination or mendacity. It may well be that the human brain gives rise to random events and experiences that cannot be, or have not yet been, tracked down by the order-searching channels of scientific methodology.

Then too, in the view of some serious thinkers, there are apparently phenomena that cannot be related to as-yet-unknown features of the physical universe, and to the as-yet-not-fully-understood capacities of the human mind, brain, and consciousness. Even from the perspective of physics, it has been argued that superluminal communication may be possible by the use of faster-than-light particles *(tachyons)*. John Gribbin suggested that "Perhaps tachyonic link even provides a clue to such mysteries as poltergeists" (1977, 194), although he later said that such ideas were meant to be jokes. Well-respected scientists, some with Ph.D.s and at least one Nobel prize winner in physics, have expressed full confidence in ESP and telekinesis. Arthur Koestler, a superb writer and careful scholar, was convinced that there was something to phenomena like clairvoyance, and that the prejudice of scientists is keeping these away from mainstream science (*Roots of coincidence,* 1972). Such writings have goaded a number of good scientists, even physicists, into the conviction that there are aspects of the world that transcend the essentially matter-energy based physics. Some were inspired by off-the-cuff comments of eminent physicists, and went on to elaborate their own conviction on the matter, conveniently quoting from the works of distinguished scientists. At least one physicist of renown, John Wheeler, is known to have been quite annoyed by such appropriation, describing parapsychology as a "pretentious pseudoscience" (1979, 189). In the contexts of all this, there is a Committee for Skeptical Inquiry which publishes an internationally circulated magazine, *The Skeptical Inquirer,* as a counter to facile beliefs, but it may be long before its message permeates into the psyche of the people at large.

Dissonance, bi-sonance, and consonance

Countless people conduct their lives while simultaneously holding on to incompatible worldviews. Isaac Newton and Leonard Euler, Augustin Cauchy, Michael Faraday, Srinivasa Ramanujan, and many other clear thinking individuals have had deep religious convictions which, when brought under the microscope of logical rigor and empirical demands, might simply crumble down.

Even after the rise of modern science, many creative scientific thinkers have been deeply religious. Indeed, practically every scientist from the seventeenth to the nineteenth century expressed, in one way or another, his belief in some kind of God. Vladimir Vukanovic, summarized it this way:

> Behind the orderly pattern in nature, behind the direction
> of cosmic evolution, many scientists see God. Their
> understanding of nature may be partial, insufficient,
> unclear, but the feeling that God is closer because of their
> research, brings a wonderful excitement and has deep
> religious meaning. (1995, 7)

It is difficult to insist that these people could not think or reason. Indeed, to this day there are good thinkers and creative scientists who are meticulous in their scientific methodology when they are arguing, observing and theorizing, but are no less committed to some of the doctrinal dimensions or spiritual visions of their faith community, which outsiders might regard as of dubious validity. In the particularity of form and terms, these are vestiges of early indoctrination, but in spirit and worldview, they carry significant trans-denominational weight.

This should lead any reasonable person to conclude that the call of religion has little to do with the appeal of science. Religions have several dimensions that have nothing to do with science. Many of the doctrines of religions relate to God and the hereafter, often to matters that lie beyond the realm or reach of science. Religions have a communal dimension, which is manifest in the prescription of days of feasting and fasting, specification of places of pilgrimage, and so on. Above all, religions have an ethical dimension that formulates rules of right conduct. Religions have symbols that soothe the heart and modes that uplift the spirit.

Equally important, religions enable us to perceive or conceive of dimensions of the human experience that transcend logic and rationality. Like the aesthetic joy from listening to glorious music or beholding a magnificent work of art, the religious experience endows us with an ineffable ecstasy that, no matter what its cerebral-neural origins, is a profoundly fulfilling human experience. None of these has anything to do with gravitation or speed of light, with electricity or molecules. One may learn about the heliocentric nature of the solar system, and still subscribe to the doctrine of the Trinity. One may accept plate tectonics, and still fast during Ramadan, feast on Divali day, or light candles for Hanukkah. One may agree with Darwin's theory of evolution, and still visit holy shrines with reverence for the associated symbols. One may attach credence to space-time curvature and yet be kind to one's neighbor and faithful to one's spouse.

Thus, religious involvement is not just a possibility; in many instances, it is an inevitable part of being fully developed. Even those who disparage traditional religions and proudly proclaim themselves to be atheists, materialists, agnostics, or whatever, have some source, implicit or explicit, to quench their spiritual thirst. Even nations that prohibit public religious expressions organize impressive parades and celebrate national heroes with great fanfare. Thus, in the view of some, God is no longer a beautiful *hypothesis* as the First Cause, but a plausible, if not compelling *conclusion* from measured parameters. Some have contended that an intelligent principle is the root cause of everything and this now seems to be more than just a religious dogma.

All this reveals the fact that the yearning for spiritual experience is not an abnormal or trivial quirk of the mentally challenged, as some would contend, but a deeply felt component of the healthy human heart. Naturalist thinkers have tried to explain this in terms of neurochemistry and Darwinian adaptation tricks. Persuasive as some of these suggestions may be to some, they are not universally established truths. From the religious perspective, this yearning is implanted by the heavens above, by the Divinity that creates and sustains us. William R. Stoeger S.J. expresses the view of many religious people when he says: "God does, in some sense, intervene or reveal God's self in a special way in nature and in history..." (Murphy and Stoeger 2007, 243). If one insists, the religiously inclined would say that evolution and adaptation are themselves rules spelled out by the Almighty.

Whatever the source, whether it expresses itself as relentless search for super symmetry, as poetic mysticism, or as faith in God, the thirst for an Abstract Beyond is part of thinking entities, unless they are chip-based. From the purely scientific perspective, as Steven Weinberg pithily said, "the more the universe seems comprehensible, the more it also seems pointless" (1977, 154). Though much has been made about this, it is as much a truth as that the more we Fourier-analyze a Beethoven symphony, the more it seems music-less. It is a simple and incontrovertible fact that cosmic meaning and purpose will not be found when sought through mathematical equations and physical theories. It does not follow, however, that meaning and purpose are irrelevant to human existence any more than food and exercise. If meaning and purpose cannot be found through physics, then, as Voltaire said of God, they have to be invented in the interest of sanity.

In the view of many people, any system that denies these is more foe than friend to the human condition. Science as a belief system may not concern itself with these, but if it belittles religion as a source for significance to life, it is not likely to win much adherence or applause.

Psychologist Leon Festinger (*A theory of cognitive dissonance*, 1957) introduced the notion of cognitive dissonance: a state in which people sometimes hold contradictory or irreconcilable opinions, which could create internal tension and affect one's behavior. Festinger elaborated on the thesis that there is a tendency for individuals to seek consistency among their cognitions (i.e., beliefs, opinions). When there is an inconsistency between attitudes or behaviors (dissonance), something must change to eliminate the dissonance.

He went on to say dissonance results when an individual must choose between attitudes and behaviors that are contradictory.

Note that, in many instances, when one describes a situation as being cognitively dissonant, it is so only for the external observer. To the individuals so categorized, their views often seem complementary rather than contradictory; sometimes one even reinforces the other.

What must be recognized in this context is that, in order to understand something, we use our mind: thinking, reasoning, logic, etc. However, this is only one aspect of conscious living. In many instances, we feel rather than analyze, whether it is a beautiful sunset, a lovely rose, a magnificent piece of music, or love for a dear one.

One result of the enormous successes of rationalistic science is that we have come to attach far greater significance to whether one thinks correctly than how deeply one feels. Though interconnected, thinking and feeling often reign separately. Blaise Pascal was only restating an ancient truth when he wrote that "*Le coeur a ses raisons que la raison ne connaît pas* [The heart has its reasons that reason does not know]" (1670, 277).

Most normal humans oscillate between the two modes of experience: thinking and feeling. While one is in the feeling mode, logic and analysis may recede. It is only to the observer that behavior prompted by feeling alone is not in consonance with the rational dimension. We are bipedal, bimanual, binaural, and binocular. We are also experientially *bi*-sonant creatures: responding to the voice of the head *and* of the heart. This has been our boon and blemish: to be feeling creatures *and* erring from impeccable syllogism. It is our capacity to deviate from the path of rigid reason that enables us to imagine, create, be inspired and be religious. Those who optimize their thinking and feeling modes, who are deeply religious and sharply scientific (in the best meanings of the word), enjoy experiential bi-consonance. From the purely analytic perspective, this may seem to be cognitive dissonance, just as for those constrained only by feelings, scientific understanding of the rainbow might appear to be heartless vivisection.

Michael Ruse summarized the matter in the context of Darwinism this way:

> Can a Darwinian be a Christian? Absolutely! Is it always easy for a Darwinian to be a Christian? No, but whoever said that the worthwhile things in life are easy? (2000, 217)

We may replace the word Darwinian by a scientifically inclined person, and Christian by a religiously-committed person, and I think Ruse's statements will still hold. There are a good many scientists in all religious traditions who would concur with John Polkinghorne when he says:

> I am both a physicist and a priest and ... I believe that I can hold these two aspects of me together, not only without compartmentalization or dishonesty, but also with a significant degree of mutual enhancement. (1998, 64)

Cultural claims for scientific origins

William Whewell (*History of the inductive sciences,* 1857) extolled ancient Greek science very eloquently, and added that it was superior to Arab science because of the political institutions and national education. Pierre Duhem (1906) distinguished between the ample English mind and the abstract and theoretical French or Continental logical mind: logical, *esprit de finesse* in doing science. He also wrote a book (*La science allemande,* 1917) in which he analyzed a third type, the German mathematical mind *(esprit de géometrie).* Though such analyses may be interesting, they have the danger of splitting science into cultural subdivisions with potentially unhealthy consequences. In the 1930s, for example, under the leadership of Phillip Lenard and Johannes Stark, there arose the notion of a German (Aryan) physics and a Jewish physics to which Einstein belonged. This was one of the low points in the history of German science.

One may detect similar tendencies in other cultural settings also. Interestingly enough, the awareness of significant scientific thought in the non-West arose from academic explorations by Western scholars. Aside from archaeology, which brought back to life Mesopotamian and Indus Valley civilizations, and many submerged Afghan-Islamic and Buddhist relics, these scholars dug deep into ancient manuscripts, interpreted and misinterpreted them and brought them to the knowledge of even the local peoples who had all but forgotten their own ancient heritage. Thus, Joseph Needham's monumental work (*Science and civilization in china,* 1954-59) on Chinese science brought to light aspects of that great civilization that were not as universally known before his labors.

Likewise, the founding of the Asiatic Society (of Bengal) by Sir William Jones in 1784 instigated an abundance of research and discoveries on ancient Indian history and wisdom. It was soon discovered that there were treatises on mathematics and medicine, astronomy and chemistry in the Sanskrit world that had been unnoticed and unrecognized. Since then countless Indian scholars have contributed richly to the exploration of these ancient treasures. Several scholarly books on the history of science in India have been published (see for example, Bose and Subbarayyappa 1971). There have also been scientists galore from Indian universities. Starting already by the close of the nineteenth century, countless scientists and mathematicians from India have joined hands with their colleagues in the rest of the world, and have been contributing significantly to world science and mathematics. Some of them have achieved international renown and prizes. However, in recent decades, thanks again to promptings by some modern writers, genuine scholarship has often turned into narrow nationalistic claims. There are books and pamphlets, internet postings and sensational articles today, embarrassing to Indians who know better, that claim that all the findings of quantum mechanics and nuclear physics, all the insights of modern mathematics, and all the accomplishments of modern technology, were implicit in ancient Sanskrit texts, only to be rediscovered, perhaps stolen, by the West. The goal of such writings is, in the phrase of one cultural patriot, "Modernization without Westernization."

As early as in 1600, David ben Solomon wrote:

> The Egyptians received mathematics and geometry, together with astronomy, from Jacob and his sons when they sojourned in Egypt, in addition to what [the Egyptians] had already received from Abraham or forefather.... The Greeks received this science from the Egyptian magi. (quoted in Efron 2007, 18)

In the Islamic world too, serious Western scholarship brought to light the works of major scientific and philosophical thinkers. We are indebted to Seyyed Hossein Nasr (*Science and Civilization in Islam*, 1968) for a systematic account of the field. But here too, narrow ethnic nationalism has sometimes taken over, as we see in a book published by a gentleman in Malaya who tries to convince the world that all the results of modern science (such as the big bang and the big crunch, the oscillating universe, particles smaller than atoms, fine-tuning (by Allah) for the creation of the universe, very speedy spacecraft, and more) may be found in the Holy Qur'an. One Muslim cleric, Youssef al-Qaradawy, has declared that:

> Modern science had at last provided evidence that Mecca was the true centre of the Earth; proof, he said, of the greatness of the Muslim *qibla*—the Arabic word for the direction Muslims turn to when they pray. (Abdelhadi, *BBC News*, April 21, 2008)

In the perspective of what is called *Ijaz al-Koran* [miraculous quality of the Qur'an], the Holy Book enshrines scientific truths.

There is no question but that most scientists explore the world because human beings are endowed with intelligence so that they might better comprehend, and thus better appreciate and admire the world. From a religious perspective one could argue that science is somewhat of a moral responsibility. From a historical perspective one may wonder why modern science arose in the West. In a ten volume opus published between 1913 and 1959 (*Le système du monde*), Pierre Duhem developed the thesis that modern science had its origins because of the Catholic Church. Stanley Jaki, building on that idea (*The savior of science,* 2000) has argued that the civilizations of Greece, China, India, and the Islamic world, great as they were, failed to usher in modern science because of their erroneous notions of God. He states that science emerged in the West because it accepted Christ as the only begotten Son of God. It is unclear why it took 1500 years after Christ was thus accepted for science to be born, and in a region distant from where the people first embraced Christianity, rather than in Eastern Christendom. On the other hand, the Marxist historian Christopher Hill (1965) made a good case for the role of Puritanic insistence on first-hand religious experience and science's call for empirical evidence in the success of science in England. Similarly, Robert K. Merton credited the virtues of German Pietism and English Puritanism for the rise of experimental science. Not many Catholics accept this thesis. Merton (1973) also listed the criteria for the emergence of science anywhere: communism (the results of science are common to and belong to one and all), universalism (scientific truths are universal), disinterestedness (selfless dedication to science), and originality (organized skepticism).

In our world of global economy and parochial scholarship, thinkers from practically every major religion have expounded on the importance, relevance, and uniqueness of specific traditions for modern science. Perhaps every tradition has elements of scientific thinking implicit in it. But none is unique to the point of declaring itself to be indispensable for the rise of science, although practically every tradition does that.

Contextual relevance of science and religion

In science-religion dialogues, one often discusses the validity and the claims of the two expressions of the human spirit, and argues for their respective methodologies in the quest for knowledge and understanding of what human beings experience and value. But one may adopt another approach: to recognize the relevance of science in one set of contexts and that of religion in another.

To illustrate this, consider this international news item. In the thick of the war in Iraq, a spokesperson for the Iraqi government appealed to the God of his faith and assured his listeners that the infidels would soon be crushed and that their evil souls would be promptly dispatched to the dark depths of Hell. Even as he was speaking, the enemies were blasting away brutal bombs and they overcame the people who were understandably indignant. Without passing judgment on the appropriateness of the unfortunate war, we may note that, in the context of exerting physical might, scientific knowledge and know-how are generally more relevant than heartfelt prayer. Even if religion is invoked, blessings may be inspiring, but curses tend to be pathetically ineffective.

On the other hand, when the hostile parties were burying their dead, of no matter which faith, and sought consolation for the bereaved, prayers and religious feelings soothed the hearts of countless people in ways that are beyond the scope of science, technology, and mathematical formulas. Or again, when the mob in Baghdad riotously looted artifacts and hid them in their homes, harsh orders for their return and threats of penalty were quite fruitless. But when a religious head warned the looters of punishment from an angry God, many returned the stolen goods in a hurry in repentant fear. Here, too, we saw the role and relevance of religion.

When we see a fragrant flower and admire its beauty, when we pick up a shell from the shore and marvel at its pleasing symmetry, or when we read about the tardy tortoises on Galapagos Islands, we are intrigued by how all these came to be. We may convey our wonderment to a biologist, and she will explain in fascinating detail the emergence of the biodiversity that is splashed all over the planet. Similarly, when we see the diamond sparkle or the rainbow in the sky, when we wonder at the stars or notice a dry plastic sheet sticking to our clothes, physics can tell us how the range and variety of perceived reality arise. Science becomes relevant in such contexts.

But most of us also experience a mystery that is beyond cerebral grasp. There is the pleasure of poetry, the joy of music, and the ecstasy of meditative merger. Love and compassion move us, hope and goodwill light up our hearts, and sometimes we feel the pang of sorrow and bereavement. In such contexts, suspending intellectual reflections and acknowledging our finitude can be more fulfilling, meaningful, and relevant than equations, theories, and experiments.

It says wisely in Ecclesiastes 3:1: "To everything there is a season, and a time to every purpose under heaven." It would seem that, in like manner, there is a time for science and a time for religion. Of course, the two cannot be totally separated, for life is to be lived as an integral whole. Yet, there are times when one aspect of living comes to the fore rather than another. Unless we recognize the contextual relevance of science and religion, we could well be in states of confusion and conflict. Fourier-analyzing a sonata while the pianist is playing the second movement may not be wise. It is easy to ruin a dinner by mixing the dessert with the entrée. The physicist-psychologist Helmut Reich studied conflicting situations empirically and formulated his findings in a book. In it he tersely wrote:

> When applying (partial) theories, one may find that one or the other theory has more explanatory power under some conditions, and less under others. In other words, one may find that the context affects the explanatory efficacy of a partial theory. (2002, 3)

Divisions and subdivisions in religion and science

Every religion, historically considered, had its origin in the visions, sayings, and preaching of individuals who are said to have had extraordinary spiritual and mystical experiences. However, every religion has also spread far and wide in the course of centuries through the commitment of countless followers who have been propagating the messages of the original masters. In the process, both consciously and otherwise, the evangelists have been giving their own interpretations of the messages embodied in the sacred writings of the religions. Sometimes there are significant differences in these interpretations. This gives rise to sects within religious systems. Sometimes, the sects branch off into independent religions.

The longing to connect with the cosmic whole finds expression in various religions. The founders of religions were historical personages who provided frameworks for channeling this profound yearning. In many instances, they and their followers were convinced that they had discovered the one and only way to achieve spiritual fulfillment, which is the goal of all religions. In that conviction, they feel/felt that it was their moral/religious responsibility to persuade/force others to their own modes. Some within the fold rebelled against the orthodox interpreters of their religion and formed different schools, which became the various sects.

Invariably, there is a main body of the religion, which is like the trunk of a tree, of which the sects are like various branches. Sometimes, the main body is powerful enough to regard the sects as deviant modes of scriptural interpretations. This phenomenon has been especially so in the Abrahamic religions. There was a time when various Christian sects had little mutual regard. Sectarian persecutions and wars were not uncommon. By and large, Christianity has moved away from internecine acrimony. Now, there are even efforts to come together in ecumenical ways. In the classical Hindu world, there used to be claims of superiority by worshipers of Shiva, Vishnu, and Shakti for their respective Divinities, as reflected in various Puranic episodes. But there was seldom the kind of sectarian bloodshed that once characterized Christianity and Islam. In modern Hinduism, as in modern Christianity, Hindu sects live, by and large, in harmony. The dysfunctional caste system is not based on sectarian divisions.

In some instances, a breakaway sect may itself become a full-fledged religion. In a sense, Christianity may be regarded as one such: for Christ was born a Jew and a new religion came to be named after him. This is true of Buddhism in the Hindu world, for Buddha was born in a Hindu family, and of Baha'ism in the Islamic world, whose founder was born a Muslim. Guru Nanak, the founder of Sikhism was born Hindu too, but the independent and syncretistic religion he forged did not come to be named after him.

Religious sects which depend heavily on the worship of a particular sage or saint or divine form or name are sometimes known as cults. The term often has a pejorative connotation, especially when used by the followers of one religion describing the practices of another. Sociologists and scholars of religion have defined terms like sect and cult in a variety of non-uniform ways in their attempts to classify and understand religions.

From a larger point of view, the various religions of the world may be regarded as particular sects of a pan-human religious longing that is the characteristic common to all religions.

For almost two centuries, there were only two or three major branches of science: those dealing with life and related phenomena (biology), those dealing with the properties of matter (chemistry), and those exploring the laws governing the physical and astronomical world (physics). Mathematics was often intimately linked to the last of these. But investigators were not restricted to one discipline or another. Galileo was physicist, mathematician, and astronomer. Newton was physicist, alchemist, and chronologist. D'Alembert was physicist, mathematician, philosopher, and man of letters. Leibniz was lawyer, statesman, and mathematician.

It was only in the nineteenth century that specialization, such as we now have, began. Fields within fields arose: physiology and cytology within biology, electromagnetism and optics within physics, physical and organic chemistry within chemistry, and so on. New disciplines also emerged: geology, anthropology and archaeology, for example.

In the twentieth century, specializations became even deeper. For instance, genetics, neuroscience and microbiology became independent sciences within biology. In the field of chemistry, there are quantum chemistry, analytical chemistry, material science, and more. Within physics, we have a whole range from atomic and nuclear physics to solid state and high energy physics. Astronomy is sub-specialized into observational astronomy, cosmology, astrophysics, and such. These divisions and subdivisions reflect two features of modern science. First, scientific knowledge has been growing in range and depth at an enormous pace. Second, the vast knowledge acquired by scientific workers in the various fields is not within reach of any single individual. We need real specialists in the various sub-sciences who can explore the field further. Often such specialists may be unaware of developments in sister fields under the same large umbrella. Thus few microbiologists may know about developments in neuroscience and vice versa. Much of solid state physics may be unfamiliar to an elementary particle physicist, and so on. One simply does not have the time to know everything.

Corresponding to the sectarian conflicts in the religious world, sometimes there are rivalries and mutual lack of respect among scientists dedicated to different approaches in specific fields. The mathematical modelers and physiologists among neuroscientists may not care much for one another's work. The same may be said of string theorists and others in fundamental physics, or proponents of a steady-state and the big-bang in cosmology.

Interestingly, while super-specialization has been going on (where—as one wit put it—one comes to know more and more about less and less until one knows everything about nothing), there have also arisen synthetic scientific fields. Like religious ecumenism and interfaith encounters, this occurs when different disciplines merge to form newer disciplines. Such, for instance, are physical chemistry, bio-physics, and DNA-anthropology. Another fine example of such a new field is AI (Artificial Intelligence) which combines physics, biology, psychology, electronics, and more.

Loyalty and caste in religious convictions

One of the important requirements for being a member of a religious community is faith in the tenets of the religion. Such faith should be deep enough for the adherent to be unmoved by evidence to the contrary. This is not an imposition but an involuntary conviction. It is important that the adherent to a religion have respect and love for its symbols, and regard its sacred history with reverence. Also, in the face of enticements to join another sect or system, one should resist the temptation and remain steadfast in one's faith at no matter what cost. All this is part of what may be called religious loyalty.

All religions expect loyalty, and some also demand it. Religious loyalty is a reflection of the depth of faith one has for the religion of which one is part. It can be fulfilling, uplifting, and comforting too. Though one cannot with certainty trace the roots of religious loyalty as a *general* aspect of the human experience, the origins of its *particular* manifestations are not hard to recognize. Invariably, specific religious loyalties arise from upbringing in the family, systematic education, communal indoctrination, cultural conditioning, and other such local factors. Sometimes, religious loyalty erupts all of a sudden in the heart of someone who has for long been ignorant of, indifferent or even opposed to a given religious tradition. The conversion of Saint Paul and the change of heart of Saint Augustine in the Christian tradition come to mind. There have been similar transformations from doubt to devotion in the lives of many less famous individuals in every religious framework.

Not all religions have authorities who explicitly demand loyalty. In our own times, not all such authorities wield power over individuals. People who are under the iron hand of religious rulers are fine as long as they sing the assigned songs, repeat the required credos, and attend the prescribed places of worship. If, for whatever reason, whether from conviction or from conscience, one is derelict in the stipulated expressions of affiliation, and more seriously, if one openly declares opinions contrary to the tenets of the god-men in power, the plight of the dissenter could become pitiable.

There is also, in the framework of most traditional religions, what may be called *religious casteism*. By this I mean the implicit or explicit belief that there is a hierarchical gradation of the religions of the world in which one's own religion occupies the pinnacle. There is perhaps nothing experientially wrong in considering one's own as a high expression of religious truth. But to proclaim the faiths of others as intrinsically wrong or inferior is what makes religious casteism both morally and logically unacceptable to the modern mind. In many substantial and significant ways, the religions of the world have contributed, and continue to contribute, to the ethical behavior and spiritual enrichment of countless people in all the cultures of the human family. However, aside from its moral arrogance, religious casteism prompts many practitioners into objectionable, intrusive behavior towards people of other faiths. This has also provoked countless cases of religious persecution and forced conversion.

Religious loyalty is like love for one's own parents. Religious casteism is like the conviction that others are deluded in their equally intense love for their own parents, and the demand that they abandon their filial love and transfer it elsewhere. At the family level, this seems obviously absurd, but it is not uncommon at the interfaith level.

The bad and good of religion and science

Aside from the spiritual fulfillment they give to billions of human beings, religions have also enriched human culture in countless ways, through art and poetry and music. They have served the emotional needs of people in unbearable situations in life by giving them consolation, courage, and hope. And religions have stirred many people to acts of love and kindness, caring and compassion.

But then, from practically every healthy and helpful initiative, unintended degenerate features invariably emerge. Many well-meaning scholars like David Martin (*Does Christianity cause war?* 1997) and Keith Ward (*Is religion dangerous?* 2006), and others have argued that it is a mistaken view to regard religions as a negative force in history. On the other hand, scholars such as George Hamilton Smith (*Atheism: The case against God,* 1974), Richard Dawkins (*The God delusion,* 2006) and others, have argued eloquently that religions have caused more harm than good.

It is an unfortunate fact that recorded histories of world religions are sprinkled with many unhappy episodes. Sufferings and deaths have been instigated by strongly held religious beliefs and confrontations between groups holding opposing views on God and the hereafter. Aside from the superstitions and irrational beliefs that still linger as vestiges of ancient worldviews, there have also been ugly instances of mindless cruelty associated with religions. Perhaps the most pernicious of these relate to the way in which religious orthodoxy has sometimes treated its own. In the classical Christian world, the supreme Catholic Church instituted the Holy Inquisition whose victims—mostly God-fearing Christians—were imprisoned, tortured or burnt at the stake for blasphemy and heresy. The Protestants engaged in their own kinds of persecutions. In the Hindu world, the treatment of the so-called lower castes and untouchables (referred to these days with some euphemisms) has been among the most abominable practices in social history. The treatment of women in many societies, based on theocratic laws, continues to be less than human.

The scriptures of some religions prescribe death to those who go against their religion. In the Bible, it says that if any member of one's own family were to suggest that they go and serve "other gods" then "thou shalt surely kill him; thine hand shall be first upon him to put him to death, and afterwards the hand of all the people. And thou shalt stone him with stones, that he die..." (Deuteronomy 13:9-10). Fortunately for Judaism, the Jewish world no longer takes such injunctions seriously. A Hadith *(Sahih Bukhari)* recommends explicitly that whosoever changes his religion must be killed. This, too, is not taken seriously anymore.

It cannot be denied that religions have also provoked bitter interfaith wars. Aside from the Crusades between Christians and Muslims in the Middle Ages, and the Thirty Years War between Catholic and Protestant nations in Europe, in modern times we have seen violent conflicts between Hindus and Muslims, Muslims and Jews, Catholics and Protestants, Shiites and Sunnis, and in Sri Lanka between Hindus and Buddhists.

The Christian zeal to save non-Christian souls wiped out old Norse religions and Amerindian cultures, just as the spread of Buddhism in Southeast Asia obliterated the earlier pristine cultures there. Islamic onslaughts decimated practically all the faiths in lands where Muslim conquerors were victorious, except in India and Southern Europe.

The terrible things perpetrated in the name of religions have often come from bigotry, fanaticism, and clinging to narrow visions of God and spirituality. These passions, with enormous potential for harm and hurt, are often instilled from an early age.

It is fair to insist that none of this is an indictment on religion, but rather of how religions have been twisted and turned to perpetrate horrific deeds on the basis of some select passages from sacred texts, while ignoring a hundred others which preach compassion, love, charity, and understanding. Religions soothe the heart and uplift the soul, have given rise to great literature, marvelous music, and magnificent places of worship. Hindus meditate, Muslims observe the Ramadan fast, Christians give charities, Jews remember their history, and all celebrate festivals in peace and joy.

Left to themselves, religions are seldom injurious to others. When the illustrious personages of great spiritual standing initiated the religions of the world, they could never have imagined the kinds of absurd and atrocious outgrowths that have resulted from their teachings. But faced with a rival, often at the instigation of charismatic bigots or know-it-alls, all the caring and submission to God can be transformed into hate and hurt. History is replete with ugly episodes of mindless massacre, ruthless rampage, heartless burning at the stake, and horrendous holy wars, perpetrated by people who believe they alone hold the Key to the Kingdom. Religions have surely been dangerous. The unpardonable hurtful excesses that have resulted from religious zeal deserve to be condemned, but it is religious leaders who must be held responsible for how a religion is practiced. Religious leaders have also guided and inspired men and women to noble and commendable acts. Any God up there must be furious and shedding tears of pain witnessing the horrors His children have been perpetrating in His name.

Science began as a quest to understand and explain the world around us, and has been enormously successful in this enterprise. Some scientists of former times were also convinced that the knowledge thus acquired would benefit humankind in important ways, as many still are. Though some philosophers of former times had warned that knowledge could lead to more confusion and even catastrophe, little did anyone seriously suspect that someday scientific knowledge would turn out to be quite dangerous.

Today we know that human destiny is in peril, and this is related to scientific advances. Our understanding of the human body, of the causes of diseases, and of medications and inoculations have considerably enhanced public health, brought down infant mortality, and extended our longevity. This in turn accelerated the rate of population grown. Within a century, our numbers increased from two billion to more than six, putting enormous stress on our resources of matter and energy.

At the same time, quality of life has been steadily increasing on the material plane by adding countless creature comforts, which become accessible to larger numbers of people by providing them with remunerative work. Jobs are created largely through manufacturing and industries, which sustain technological societies.

But factories and industry spew out toxic chemicals into the biosphere. And the mismanagement of economics has resulted in labor shortage in some parts of the world and joblessness in others. Moreover, every material convenience arising from scientific technology is based on energy production and utilization. But energy consumption and utilization invariably and inevitably result in some impact on the environment. This means that the more we consume, the more we affect the environment in negative ways. Also, the greater the number of people, the more severe and serious the damage to the environment becomes. This has led us to an awful predicament: either arrest economic growth and development of the vast majority of people on the planet, or face the most terrible consequences on the ecosystem that keeps all life forms functioning in good health. Advances in genetic engineering have had current and potential benefits in fields ranging from food production to the cure of deadly diseases. At the same time, they can also ruin our current basis of agriculture and individuality.

Computers and internet communication that weave the whole wide world into a web have created a global village with its own unhappy outgrowths. Great risk of identity theft, loss of privacy, alluring unwitting young to dangerous liaisons, transmission of techniques for manufacturing deadly weapons, as well as of lurid pornography, widespread dissemination of misinformation and literature instigating contempt and disgust against one religion or another—all these have come within easy reach of countless perverted minds, evil-doers, mischief-makers and hate-mongers. Karl Peters (*Dancing with the sacred,* 2002) has analyzed at length other aspects of the peril in the global village.

While scientific knowledge by itself may be enriching and mind-expanding, it can invariably be put to good as well as to bad use, and it is not clear that as a species we have developed the wisdom to always distinguish between the two, or foresee the implications and future effects of new technologies. Also, knowledge of inevitable disaster (such as the melting of the polar icecaps or the certain collision of an asteroid with our planet) is hardly helpful, if we can do little to prevent them. If anything, knowledge of any impending doom can only fill the human heart with paralyzed terror.

All through the ages, thinkers have been warning of such possibilities. In the sixteenth century Cornelius Agrippa wrote presciently:

> All sciences are only the ordinances and opinions of men,
> as injurious as profitable, as pestilent as wholesome, as ill
> as good, in no part perfect. But doubtful and full of error
> and contention. (1526, 154)

Our respect and enthusiasm for science rest on the recognition that, with its empirical methodology, ingenious instruments, and mathematical analysis, science has made astounding advances in unveiling the secrets of the phenomenal world.

Religious fanaticism, despicable as it is, may be subdued some day. Sure, there still are large pockets of religious perversity, but there are also places where the destructive passions of true-believers are restrained by enlightened laws. Some day, sectarian cleansing and killing for creed may become mere embarrassments of history for all peoples. The dangers of religions can perhaps be tamed in the future.

The social, moral, and environmental impacts of technology have not always been very benign. Malcolm Muggeridge, in a famous essay, painted the paradoxes in a technologically impacted world:

> As the astronauts soar into the vast eternities of space on
> earth, the garbage piles higher; as the groves of academe
> extend their domain, their alumni's arms reach lower; as
> the phallic cult spreads, so does impotence. In great
> wealth, great poverty; in health, sickness; in numbers,
> deception. Gorging, left hungry; sedated, left restless;
> telling all, hiding all; in flesh united, forever separate. So
> we press on through the valley of abundance that leads to
> the wasteland of satiety, passing through the gardens of
> fantasy; seeking happiness ever more ardently, and
> finding despair ever more surely. (1970, 624)

We have reason to be more frightened by the dangers lurking in the tentacles of technology which are wrought with doomsday devastation. They seem like the mean-spirited might of an evil genie, unleashed and uncontrollable. The decimating possibilities from scientific knowledge could result in more havoc than what can be caused by all religions, now and of the past, without the material support provided by technology.

Science and religion: theory and practice

There are many official spokespersons for various religions who wield authority and proclaim correct knowledge. Many of them are rote repeaters of ancient texts, with little acquaintance with astronomy and biology. They continue to preach and practice in the mind-set of bygone eras, from which modern science has emancipated large sections of humanity. The positive aspect of their work lies in that they serve to safeguard humanity's various religious legacies from disappearing altogether. However, sometimes they also contribute to the persistence of ancient superstitions.

It would be good to emphasize that the goals of the Science-Religion Dialogue should be:

— To underscore the emotional, spiritual, ethical, and inspirational enrichment that religions provide.

— To recognize the positive contributions that modern science has made to human civilization: such as providing an understanding of the limitless range of the phenomenal world, enhancing our capacity to probe into the microcosm and also to measure the universe, unraveling the mysteries of matter, life, and mind, eliminating diseases, exposing the superstitions and pseudo-sciences, etc.

— To spread an awareness of the negative human impacts of modern science, and find out how these may be diminished by adopting values enshrined in religious traditions.

— To explore how some of the no longer acceptable aspects of the traditional religious framework may be changed, modified or rejected so as to bring religions in harmony with rationally acceptable criteria for explaining physical phenomena and with the spirit of social/humanistic enlightenment. This includes respecting other religions (in so far as they are non-hurting) as much as enjoying deep devotion to one's own.

All of us function in a framework of values and worldviews. Religions furnish us with a grand backdrop for life, which provides meaning and purpose. From this perspective, all of us are religious one way or another. It has been rightly said that in a deeper sense human beings are more religious than rational. Huston Smith wrote a book entitled *Why religion matters* (2001). It might be no less important to write a book on *What kind of religion matters*. Since the vast majority of people in the world are affiliated to one religion or another, it may be that it is not being religious that matters, but how one is so. There are different ways of being religious.

There are many ways in which being religious can be enriching, comforting, and meaningful. Some of these include accepting the revelations of a prophet, regarding a historical personage as the embodiment or messenger of the Divine, considering a body of writings as holy and beyond question, engaging in periodic worship of the sacred symbols of a tradition, taking part in the sacraments of time-honored rituals, participating in the celebrations of a community, abiding by the moral injunctions of a religion as best one can, subscribing to a doctrinal framework as to the hereafter. These are some of the ways in which one may be religious in a denominationally determined way. Not everyone attaches the same degree of weight to these, but millions also adhere to them in the various religions of the human family, deriving significant fulfillment.

There is another mode of reacting to religions, provoked by the ugly manifestations of religions over the ages: persecution, perversity, bigotry, casteism, intolerance, inquisition, and superstitions. Here one derides all faiths, writes off God as a product of misled minds, rejects everything whose origin is in organized religious traditions, regards those who subscribe to a religion as deluded souls, is suspicious of those who preach a religion, is opposed to all religious symbols, treats religious inclinations as anti-secular, cannot see even aesthetic value in rituals, and keeps reminding the world of the danger of religious fanatics. Though its practitioners imagine themselves to be non-religious, this mode is no less religious in fervor and conviction.

There is a third way. This includes recognizing the unique potential of the human spirit and experience, affirming our finitude in the face of unimaginable grandeur, looking upon personal achievements with humility, regarding consciousness as among the unfathomable mysteries, experiencing awe at the magnificent universe, seeing something good in every tradition that has brought meaning and solace to countless people, respecting all faiths and facial features, having reverence for what others hold as sacred, but condemning and eschewing all aspects of religion that harm and hurt, caring and being compassionate to weaker creatures, rejoicing in the observance of happy events, considering humanity as a single family and all life as marvelous manifestations of extraordinary complexity, being touched by the piety of prayers and moved by the magic of music, meditating on an Unknown Wholeness in an effort to connect with it, conducting one's life and profession with due regard to one's responsibility towards others and the environment, doing whatever one can to alleviate pain and suffering, and reckoning "Thou shalt not hurt" as primary ethics.

There are also other ways of being religious, some combining elements from all the above. Ultimately each of us decides how to be religious in one's own way. Most of all, any mode that does not hurt others would be the most enlightened of all.

The power and prestige of science is so great that even those who would decry science or remind us of its limits like to claim they are scientific. But what exactly is being scientific? Like being religious, there are different ways of being scientific too.

To keep abreast of developments in science from news reports and popular articles, to respect science and its theories about the phenomenal world, to reject pseudoscience which flourished in the past and has not yet died away, to be literate in basic mathematics, to be able to read graphs and interpret numbers written in the form of ten to the power of something, to differentiate facts of observation from theories that account for them, to be able to distinguish between explanations from the scientific community and those from stray outsiders who propagate their ideas through books rather than as papers in respectable journals—these are among the ways of being *intelligently* scientific.

There are also ways of being, perhaps well-meaning, but *loosely* scientific. These include: presenting weird theories in scientific jargon or in deceptively technical frameworks, with scant attention to evidentiary rigor, talking about supernatural phenomena or the distant future, insisting that numerology and astrology are valid sciences and using computers to caste horoscopes, arguing that aliens brought civilization to earth and that UFOs are wreaking havoc on us, seeing modern science couched in ancient books, and not distinguishing insightful poetry from scientific propositions, trying to prove the existence of God from thermodynamics and quantum mechanics.

One is professionally scientific when one collects data for systematic study, measures, calculates and analyzes, explores how scientific knowledge may be applied for practical purposes, acquires all the available knowledge pertaining to a particular field and tries to contribute to a discipline through papers in journals and in conferences, probes into specific aspects of natural phenomena to uncover underlying simplicity and natural laws, and communicates regularly with fellow workers in the field.

When one respects reason and carefully acquired data, demands coherence and consistency in explanations, recognizes the importance of instruments and mathematics in science, and knows that attempts to understand the world require systematic study of complex interconnections; when one considers the truth-claims of propositions from dispassionate and critical perspectives and realizes that the goal of science is to explain the phenomenal world in ways that are consonant with the results of carefully conducted observations, and concedes that it is neither the business nor within the competence of science to prescribe or proscribe human behavior, but only to describe the world, one is *epistemologically scientific.* An epistemologically scientific person is aware that no scientific theory can claim to be the final and never-to-be-changed explanation of any phenomenon, but that it is merely the best one available in the context of all the information one has at a given time.

To claim that there is nothing more to life than seeking scientific explanations for everything, to imagine that every aspect of the human experience can be fully understood only when brought under the dissecting microscope of science, to look down upon those who derive personal fulfillment and collective joy in other than scientific modes—these are examples of being *mindlessly scientific.*

One is not religious merely because one puts on religious garb or mutters mantras. Some insist they are scientific merely because they use technical jargon and extrapolate from meticulously derived knowledge, but that is not being scientific.

Religion bashing

Religious visions and doctrines have flourished in all cultures since ancient times. But there have also been skeptics and atheists who have challenged and rejected many of these. When Lucretius moaned the superstitions of the age and exclaimed how many horrors had been perpetrated in the name of religion, he was echoing the thoughts of many in the ancient world and of later generations too.

Atheist thinkers have included poets, philosophers, scientists and common people. They openly reject any belief in the God or in the doctrines of their tradition.

Whereas in ancient and even in modern times until recently, rebels often spoke and wrote against their own religion, and scientists with no belief in traditional religions tended to clothe their skepticism in neutral or euphemistic language, in the past few decades the new field of *generalized religion bashing* has been emerging. Books trivializing, ridiculing, and condemning everything religious are becoming *à la mode.*

The religion bashing sport is of three different types. The first rests on the *unscientific charge thesis.* Here, the foundations of religion are attacked on the basis of the latest scientific findings and worldviews, in order to demonstrate how untenable religious doctrines are. A subset of this is the analysis of religions in psychological and evolutionary terms, and to suggest that religions really have no intrinsic truth content.

The second type of religion bashing rests on what may be called the *muddled-mind thesis*. Here religions are attacked by explaining that those who accept them are simply deluded. Once they are properly educated, it is said, their minds will be cleansed of the religious beliefs and superstitions that cloud their understanding of the world.

The third mode of religion bashing is through *demonization*. Here the goal is to list and elaborate on all the terrible things that have been done in the name of religions: sectarian persecution, cruel caste system, medieval inquisition, shameful slavery, subjugation of women, killing the infidel, etc. It assumes that objective reflection on the charges brought against religions in the context of the harm they have done should prompt the right-minded to reject all religions.

Able religion bashers use one or more of these approaches when they deprecate and denigrate religion. Among the many illustrious and successful religion bashers of our times (in the English speaking world) must be mentioned Richard Dawkins, Christopher Hitchens, Daniel Dennett, and Sam Harris. Their books are widely read and appreciated by the millions who share their disregard for religions.

Many practicing physicists may not show much interest in topics like the physics of consciousness or immortality, but such subjects have been growing in significant measure in recent years. A related phenomenon is that some scientists have become overtly anti-religious in their expressions. In former times, unbelieving scientists generally kept their atheism to themselves, primarily because they did not wish to offend others. But in recent years, some have come out of the closet, as it were, and have become quite vocal, not just in arguing for atheism, but in condemning traditional religions in explicit ways.

One of the more articulate thinkers of this category is Richard Dawkins. His virulence against religion may be seen in one of his articles where he stated that child abuse, though unpleasant, "may do them less lasting damage than the mental abuse of bringing them up

Catholic in the first place" (2002, 9-12). Dawkins is a distinguished zoologist, brilliant mind, and man of erudition, but he is no less a passionate advocate of no-nonsense science. In his plea for basic scientific common sense as well as in his piercing critique of religion, he continues the tradition of Bertrand Russell. In *Unweaving the rainbow* (1998) he explodes the myth that science is bereft of poetry. In the *Blind watchmaker* (1986) he resolves the puzzle of an ordered universe by saying that we need no Creator for this, for mindless laws of the universe constitute the watchmaker who creates stars and planets, oceans and life. In a collection of his superb essays, provocatively entitled *A devil's chaplain* (2003), one can see the sharpness of his intelligence when he tries to discredit religion and mysticism. Peter Atkins (*Creation revisited*, 1993), another scientist who has only contempt for religion, states that:

> Reconciliation [between science and religion] is impossible. I consider that Science is mightier than the Word, and that the river of religion will (or, at least, should) atrophy and die. (1997)

But it is not clear how effective these have been in arresting the persistence or growth of religions. If anything, the opposite seems to be happening. Ironically, along with the rise of religion bashing, religious fundamentalism has also been growing. This leads to a vicious circle. It is not easy to see which of these prompts the other. The attitude and behavior of some religious extremists certainly call for public outcry and strong condemnation. However, the intemperate pronouncements of some eminent religion bashers seem to be pushing a good number of moderate religious practitioners even more staunchly to their religious framework. A scholarly work psychoanalyzing religion bashers would be interesting as a scientific study.

A very effective instrument of religion bashing is the cinema. Movies depicting the immorality of priests and the superstitions of the ages are not uncommon these days. A powerful Bill Maher documentary, *Religulous* (2008), became quite popular. It is a caricature of the Abrahamic religions: their extreme versions, the absurdities that some of their more ardent followers utter, their parochial persistence and historical vacuity exposed in scathing interviews and sarcastic snippets, which at the same time chuckle and cry at the human condition. There is nothing in the movie that atheists and skeptics would consider new. People might discuss similar things in casual conversation. But by bringing together so many pathetic expressions of religiosity from the major Abrahamic faiths, giving special exposure to the more extreme wings of Christianity and the mindless mobs in the Islamic world screaming "Kill the infidel," the movie paints it all as one horrible heap of anachronistic nonsense with hardly an iota of grace or goodness.

Maher makes no reference to the great art, glorious music, or grand poetry that has been created by deep religious attitudes. Nor is there any mention of the solace and peace that religions have brought to countless millions in moments of despair and sorrow. But then, one may argue, this movie is intended to show the inanity of religious beliefs, not the genuineness of religious feelings, let alone the now-past capacity of religions to create some of the most beautiful aesthetic expressions of human culture.

Perhaps it would have been a better movie if, after exposing the ridiculousness of some of the archaic beliefs and making every religious person look foolish, Maher recognized that if we all appreciate the positive contributions of religions, honor our ancestors for the cultural richness they have left behind, continue to enjoy and share the great art and music of various religions, adhere to the core message of love and service implicit in all religions of the human family, we could hold hands together as members of the same human family to resolve the myriad problems we are facing as a planetary species.

It is important for the practitioners and devotees of science not to be carried away by the intellectual triumphs and material potency of science to the point of looking down upon other sources of insight and fulfillment for other people on earth. Condemning evils that have arisen from religion is one thing, but condemning religions as a whole would be like wanting to destroy a garden because weeds have disfigured it.

Science bashing

A number of factors have also come into play to diminish the respect that science once enjoyed from the public at large. For starters, science has not turned out to be a blessing without a blemish. Not all the outgrowths of science have been benign. Scientific knowledge has given rise to germ warfare, chemical weapons, and nuclear holocausts. Then there are countless side effects of technology, from environmental pollution and population explosion to rain forest depletion, and global warming. We live in a world polluted by poisons spewing from the industrial age, which many see as a direct consequence of the scientific worldview. Just as religion has been harmful through its doctrinal arrogance, science has had impacts that endanger health and survival.

Moreover, science paints a purposeless universe. At least from the perspective of human consciousness, this is a universe replete with majesty and mystery, where awe and beauty, love and laughter are more immediate than leptons, hadrons, and field bosons. Consider also the catastrophic pessimism into which thermodynamics and astrophysics dump us; and the fact that scientists keep changing their explanatory models like cars from Detroit or Osaka, making theories of past generations approximate, obsolete or downright wrong.

Then again, to understand the technical jargon of science, mounds of sophisticated mathematics, abstruse terminology, and exhausting analytical techniques are needed. Given that high school algebra is hard enough to master, not many are eager to buy into inscrutable science when rosier pictures are available for far less. Moreover, the benefits of science, like antibiotics, television, planes, computers, and hurricane prediction, can all be had without taking an oath of allegiance to scientific rationality and empiricism.

It would seem that science as an intellectual quest is above reproach. But this is far from being the case. Right from its inception, science has been regarded by some as an arrogant intrusion into God's secrets or as a dangerous quest for knowledge that could lead to disastrous effects.

In modern times, there have been at least three kinds of attacks on science. The first rests on what may be called the *disastrous consequences thesis*. It is based on the idea that if a little knowledge is a dangerous thing, too much knowledge can be downright fatal. This view has resulted primarily from some of the applications, actual and potential, of science. In particular, the impact of technology on the environment, the threat of global warming and species annihilation have led some people to call for a total ban on further research, at least in some fields.

A second motivation for science bashing is based on the *amoral thesis*. It is contended that since scientific knowledge is morality-neutral, it enables its practitioners to engage in some highly immoral behavior. However noble their ultimate goal may be, many scientists are engaged in researches that call for cruelty and the wasting (sacrificing) of animals, and of fetuses. This is sometimes presented as an argument against some sciences.

Then there is the *anti-religion thesis*. Science tends to dilute faith and question the existence of heaven, hell and even God. Indeed, it tends to reject everything supernatural. It reduces love to glandular secretions and altruism in the genes. The popular writings of many science-informed atheists, naturalists, and religion bashers make it clear that science is an avowed enemy of religion. Supernatural entities—and they include not just angels and goblins, but the gods of religions also—are considered mere fantasies, whether or not they serve any practical purpose. What to make of book titles like *The God delusion, God is not great,* and *God: the failed hypothesis?* It is a historical fact that, in societies where scientific knowledge is dominant, affiliation to traditional religions tends to weaken, certainly among its scientifically-alert population. These are good enough reasons for rejecting science, say the science bashers.

Chapter 3
Epistemological Aspects

Facts, perspectives, and truths

That you are reading this line now is a fact. That there is some light in the place where you are reading is also a fact. Things and events of whose existence or occurrence there can be no disagreement among people with normal modes of perception and basic reasoning constitute the world of facts. Every fact is an aspect of perceived reality, for it is through our doors of perception that we recognize the world around us. However, there are two stages in this process: one is the direct recognition of the existence of a thing or an event; the other is the conscious processing and interpretation of the perception. This interpretation may be called one's perspective on a fact.

Our perspectives on facts depend on many complex factors, such as time and place, cultural and linguistic background, philosophical and scientific training, influences from previous inputs and experiences, subscription to particular ideologies, etc. Because these are not the same for all people, disagreements arise, even among well-meaning individuals, as to the interpretation of facts. For example, in political or international confrontations, opposing parties may agree upon some incontrovertible facts, but their interpretations of these are often in conflict.

The concept of truth has been explored by philosophers since time immemorial. Whereas there may be little disagreement about facts, truths are viewed differently in different religious contexts. K. A. Krishnaswamy Iyer said:

> Vedantic truth...springs from our intimate experience of
> life verifiable at all times by introspection under the
> guidance of intuition. (1930, 57)

John F. Haught says:

> By truth I mean what is sought out by the desire to know
> as distinct from what other desires seek. (2006, 38)

Philip Hefner gives a more nuanced definition of truth in the
context of Christian theology:

> Even though the Christian faith purports to be truth
> from and about God,...the appearance of that faith is an
> event within the processes of the world and its unfolding,
> and the faith presents a truth about the world. (1993, 14)

This perspective is valid in all religions. Holmes Rolston III
considers religious and scientific truths, not so much in terms of their
content, as of the commitment of the seeker when he writes:

> Scientist and theologian alike seek what is called universal
> intent, a setting aside of private interests so as to promote
> the single-minded discovery of public truth, what is true
> at large and for all persons. (1987, 17)

In the Islamic perspective, Seyyed Hossein Nasr explains there is:

> The Law, contained in essence in the Qur'an..., the Path,
> dealing with the inner aspect of things....The Law is as
> the circumference of a circle, of which the Path is the
> radius, and the Truth the center. (1968, 28)

In Buddhist thought, human suffering is the fundamental truth.

In common parlance, truth is intimately related to facts. In most
everyday situations where immediate perception rather than abstract
reasoning or indirect evidence alone determines the validity of
propositions, there is generally no distinction between fact and truth.
Because of this, one often uses the words almost synonymously. In

such situations, it really does not matter if we say it is true that Paris is the capital of France or it is a fact that Paris is the capital of France. In certain other contexts, however, such casual use may not be appropriate. Is it a fact that Religion A is better than Religion B, or is this a truth? For millions of people this may be a truth in the sense of a correct belief. For millions of others, this may not be so. However, it is not a fact in the sense of the existence of something objective. Indeed, not all truths are also facts. That Krishna actually spoke the Bhagavad Gita is truth for millions of people; that Moses received the Commandments directly from God is truth for millions also; that Christ is the Savior who resurrected is truth for millions of people; that Mohammed was the last prophet is truth for millions of people also. Nevertheless, it is not evident to everybody that these are all facts.

Truth, though often associated with facts, is closely related to perspectives. One may establish the factuality of a claim, but one cannot as easily dispose of the truth-content of a claim. This is because the existence of facts is independent of the human mind. Truths, however, are formulations by the human mind, and are often interpretations of facts. In other words:

> Facts are what there seem to be,
> Truths are how they seem to me.

In many instances, as in the example of the capital of France, there is no more than a trivial difference between facts and truths. However, there are significant instances in the context of religion and other matters pertaining to the human condition, where what are proclaimed to be truths are often one's own or one group's interpretations of facts. When we regard the contents of a sacred book as truth, we are describing a perspective as truth. Even in science, what one calls truth is often an interpretation of facts in the framework of certain universally accepted principles. Thus, when one says that human life has no ultimate purpose, this is only a valid interpretation of known facts from certain scientific perspectives.

Religion takes its truths to be facts. Meaningful and fulfilling interpretations of the human origins as given in many religious texts do not always stand up well to a meticulous scrutiny of their factual content. On the other hand, science sometimes takes its interpretations of facts to be verities that reflect the totality of experience. There are more interpretations of a set of recognized facts than may be seen in the equations and theories of physics.

Criteria for truth content in science and in religion

In dialogues between science and religion, controversies often arise as to claims of the validity of scientific and religious propositions. Philosophers have delineated truth criteria in various ways. According to the correspondence theory of truth, for example, truth is a structural correspondence between a statement and an observed event, fact, etc. There are other technical philosophical theories of truth, like the consensus theory, the pragmatic theory, the coherence theory, the redundancy theory, etc. Without going into technical discourses, one may still be clear about the criteria on which the enterprises of science and religion appraise the validity of their respective truths. The two systems—science and religion—have generally different sets of rules when they operate in their well-defined spheres of concerns.

The following are seven criteria for scientific truths:

(a) *Logical consistency.* Science is a rational enterprise. It is wedded to reason, logic, proof, inner consistency, and the like. Nothing that violates these will be admitted as a scientific truth.

(b) *Concordance with carefully observed and meticulously collected facts.* At the same time, science is not a purely logical system of thought, like pure mathematics, metaphysics or speculative philosophy. It is very much concerned with the world of experience and reality as perceived by the normal human brain. To be of interest or validity in science, propositions must conform to every detail of empirically derived data, both qualitative and (when possible) quantitative.

(c) *Scientific results are not one-time experiences.* Scientific results need to be confirmed and reconfirmed over and over again. This means that facts interpreted as scientific truths must be verified and repeatable. It is important to understand that repeatability may be actual or only in principle. There are many domains of science where the results are not repeatable in actuality. This is so, for example, in the fields of planetary formation, archaeology, and of course, cosmogony. In these contexts, what one means by repeatability is that similar/parallel phenomena may in fact be repeated or reproduced experimentally.

(d) *Consistency with related phenomena.* No scientific result stands by itself. Every proposition is, or should be, related in some way or another with some other phenomenon.

(e) *Actual or potential consensus among experts.* Propositions in science have to be subjected to careful and critical examination. Unless this is a possibility, a proposition presented to the scientific community is usually ignored or rejected.

(f) *Confirmation or rejection by independent searchers.* Scientific results must stand the critical scrutiny of others who are working in the field. Only when the body of experts in a field is persuaded of the correctness of a proposition, not by voting but by confirming it in various ways (extending it, elaborating upon it, and relating it to other well established results) does a proposition become a part of the general body of science. As Claude Bernard said, "*L'art c'est moi, la science c'est nous* [Art is me, science is we]" (1865, 38).

(g) *Agreement that even the most reliable evidence is only provisional.* Though seldom explicitly stated, no scientific result, law, theory, or principle is taken as the last word. The scientific community always leaves open the possibility that further evidence that might arise at a future time could question, change, or throw out what has thus far been considered true. This is an important difference in perspective between science and religion. It does not make scientific truths more or less valid. This is how they are considered.

These criteria for truth are held by scientists and by the scientific establishment as a whole.

Religious truths, that is to say propositions accepted as truths in the religious context, are also governed by certain criteria. These include the following:

(a) *Source is a higher authority.* Religions are based on the teachings and revelations of personages who are regarded as spiritually awakened. These teachings are generally accepted as conveying higher truths from a supernatural source. Every religious spokesperson traces or rests his or her religious truths to sayings and writings in one or more sacred books. Not all the members of a fold may accept the same authority. Thus the Pope is authority only for Roman Catholics. In the Islamic tradition, Shi'as and Sunnis appeal to quite different authorities, as Shaivas and Vaishnavas do in the Hindu tradition.

(b) *Conviction at the innermost depths of one's heart.* Religious truths are felt to be valid in the deepest core of one's being, beyond cerebral analysis and reasoning. As long as this conviction is there, the associated statement is taken as a religious truth. Such a conviction is, as it says in Hebrews 11:1, "the evidence of things not seen."

(c) *Profound personal experience.* Notwithstanding its community dimensions, i.e. though religions are invariably practiced in a group-cultural context, religion is often a very personal experience for the individual. Like art and music, religious truths are felt and internalized rather than critically dissected and logically proved, except by theologians. One has only to read some mystic poets to recognize this. Here, for example, is a passage from St. Teresa of Avila:

> I threw myself down in despair before an image of the Mother of God. With many tears, I implored the Holy Virgin to become my mother now. Uttered with the simplicity of a child, this prayer was heard. From that hour on, I never prayed to the Virgin in vain. (Vogt 1996, 33)

(d) *Potential for ecstatic states.* Most religious frameworks can lead the practitioner to a heightened state of consciousness arising from communion with the cosmos at large. This may range from a simple experience of inner peace, as during prayer or meditation, to the ecstasy of mystical experience and trance. Religious ecstasy, unlike the thrill that comes from scientific knowledge, does not need the understanding of complex concepts. To give but one example, consider the following utterance by the poet Kabir:

> What a raging fire of love has burst forth!
> See how its sparks shoot into the Void
> To join with the source of all light.
> Ah, what a joy! (Kumar 1996, 81)

(e) *Attested by historically revered personages.* All religions rest on the attestation of spiritual masters who have confirmed the proclamations of the initial authorities. No traditional religion is without spiritually-inspired commentators, the saints and sages of the tradition. Indeed, interpreters and commentators have done more for the preservation and propagation of religious truths than the original religious founders themselves.

(f) *Meaningful even in the face of apparent contradiction with some facts.* Religious truths are meaningful, i.e. they provide purpose and meaning to the life of the individual, and to human existence more generally. Logical consistency is not banned from, but is irrelevant for, religiously held worldviews. The Latin phrase "*credo quia absurdum* [I believe because it is absurd]," derived from Tertullian's phrase "*credibile est, quia ineptum est* [credible, because it is ridiculous]" (*De Carne Christi,* ca. 200), only partly expresses the idea. In fact, it should be *credo quamvis absurdum*: I believe even though it is absurd (to others).

(g) *Capable of transforming a person's life.* In principle, if not always, religious affiliation and practice have significant impact on the psychological, emotional, and spiritual life of the practitioner. Some of those impacts may seem positive and some negative to an external observer, but they are always taken to be fundamentally positive by the practitioner. This is one of the important factors for the persistence of religions. In the Christian tradition, the classic example of this is the conversion of St. Paul who Luke says was blinded by a dazzling light before he was fully awakened to the message of Christ (Acts 9:1-22). The theologian Wolfhart Pannenberg is said to have had a "light experience." In the Hindu world, Sri Aurobindo was a scholar of stature who, with a profound understanding of traditional Hindu visions, formulated its essence in the context of modern views, such as evolution. Like Pannenberg, he, too, had experienced mystic vision which transformed his life.

These criteria hold mainly for traditional religions. Non-traditional religions, such as religious naturalism, humanism and Unitarianism, formulate rules that reject or alter some of the principles enunciated above. Their goal, impact and practice are different from those of traditional religions. The newer religious visions, often products of modern science and enlightenment, try to discard beliefs that diverge from scientific findings, attach less weight to ancient authorities, and do away with some of the negative side effects of traditional religions on humanity at large. They tend to be more accommodating of divergent views. However, such religions have the potential for diminishing some of the positive elements of traditional religions. In the reduction of everything to facts and figures and provable propositions, some of the poetic aspects of the traditional religious experience are diluted, while the solace and comfort that the magic of traditional religions provide are all but erased.

Johan Huizinga (*Homo ludens,* 1938) introduced the notion of Man the Player: many aspects of human culture may be seen as playing. Some of the plays are serious games: participants are expected to be engaged in collective activities in accordance with well defined rules. From this perspective, we may look upon science and religion as games that a community of participants agrees to play based on certain rules. One reason for conflicts between science and religion is that the two do not accept the same criteria for ascribing validity to propositions, i.e. do not play by the same rules. It is not a question of which set of criteria is right and which is wrong, or which is better and which is worse. It is rather a matter of adopting whichever set one chooses. Disagreements are inevitable when people who play together follow different sets of rules. It would be unrealistic and frustrating if people played together with a ball, some imagining they are paying soccer, and the other that they are playing volley ball. The problem is not with the ball, but with how it is treated by the different groups. The same person can sometimes play one game, and sometimes another. Likewise, it is not impossible, from this perspective, to do science and also be a religious person, as we see in many instances. Our goal should not be to ban all games, but only those aspects of games that are hurtful.

Why in science and *why* in religion

The question "Why does something happen?" often arises in science as well as in religion. It is important to recognize that the meanings attached to the question are quite different in science and in religion. Suppose someone asks you, "Why are you reading this now?" You might give two types of answers: (a) "Because I like to read discussions on science and religion"; (b) "Because I wish to find out what is said here." Both are perfectly valid answers.

However, we notice that the first answer refers to the past, to a built in system in which the event takes place, the rules by which the phenomenon (your reading) occurs, etc. Generally speaking, science interprets *why* in this way when it tries to answer *why*-questions. Answers of the second kind refer to something that is yet to happen, actions directed towards a goal, etc. Generally speaking, religions interpret *why* in this way when they try to answer fundamental *why*-questions. This is explicit in many European languages, where the word why is expressed as *for what:* French *pourquoi,* Spanish *porqué,* Italian *perchè,* German *warum.* The second meaning, (for what, to what purpose) is quite clear here.

Sometimes, when religion also tries to respond to *why* in the first sense, it comes into conflict with science. Normally, modern science does not interpret *why* in the second sense, except when some biologists hold on to entelechy, intelligent design, etc. Most physicists feel that interpreting *why* in the second sense, as Aristotle did, has generally been a fruitless exercise. So they conclude—rashly, some would say—that the question is meaningless, useless, silly, etc. Nevertheless, since the formulation of the Anthropic Principle in the mid-1970s, some physicists are also trying to find a second type answer in cosmology.

Why is the sky blue? Why does water boil when heated? Why do planets go around the sun in elliptical orbits? Why does hydrogen emit those particular wavelengths? Why does a projectile follow a parabolic path? These and a thousand other *whys* are addressed routinely by science in the first sense of the word, and not in the second sense.

Why did the world emerge? Why should one be kind? Why is monogamy a virtue? These questions are taken up by religion in the second sense of *why.* Science normally does not take up such questions.

If religion recognizes that science can be quite successful in answering *why*-questions with the first meaning, and science recognizes that religion, philosophy, and poetry can meaningfully answer some questions in the second mode, then that would avoid many conflicts. But not all protagonists of science and of religion are willing to concede that.

Determinism and levels of reality

Determinism (more exactly, nomological determinism) refers to a particular feature of the world by which every event that occurs is the inevitable outcome of precisely operating physical laws on simple and complex systems. In debates on determinism which have gone on during ages past, and are likely to continue for ages to come, one needs to distinguish between varieties and levels of determinism. The classification below attaches epithets to the variety of determinism:

(a) *Macroscopic determinism.* Here, as far as we know, perfect determinism reigns. We may understand this by means of an analogy. If a marble is let to slide through a slanted narrow tube (whose windings would correspond to the laws to which it is subject), then we can say precisely where the marble will land at the other end of the tube. In this system determinism occurs at the *classical physical level,* and is most useful in tracking down phenomena such as the motions of planets and pendulums, the path of projectiles and rockets, and such. In a famous essay Pierre Simon de Laplace (*Essaie philosophique sur les probabilities,* 3rd ed., 1820) stated:

> An intelligence knowing, at a given instant of time, all forces acting in nature, as well as the momentary positions of all things of which the universe consists, would be able to comprehend the motions of the largest bodies of the world and those of the smallest atoms in one single formula, provided it were sufficiently powerful to subject all data to analysis. (quoted in Kline 1985, 238)

This was perhaps the first universal philosophical principle enunciated by physics, and the first dream of a theory of everything. This Laplacian determinism is a direct consequence of the classical laws of motion (how motion occurs as a result of external forces) which can be expressed as mathematical equations. The theoretical possibilities from this type of determinism are immense. They have enabled the human mind to predict eclipses and discover new planets. The idea itself is not very new. Already in the eleventh century, the Persian poet Omar Khayyàm wrote:

> With Earth's first Clay They did the Last Man's knead,
> And then of the Last Harvest sow'd the Seed:
> Yea, the first Morning of Creation wrote
> What the Last Dawn of Reckoning shall read.
> (Fitzgerald 1859, 53)

In the eighteenth century, thinkers like Voltaire and Schopenhauer expressed similar ideas.

(b) *Statistical determinism.* A special variety of this determinism occurs when a system consists of an enormous number of constituents. Thus, for example, though the molecules of a gas in a closed jar move in accordance with classical deterministic laws, they can never be tracked down individually. This leads to the *statistical mechanical level,* in which the motions of the entities comprising a system consisting of a very large number of component parts can be analyzed only in terms of probability. Statistical mechanics is another fruitful branch of physics, but it has not given rise to interesting metaphysical speculations, perhaps because there are not too many popular (non-mathematical) versions of it. But it has much potential for it, given that it is linked to irreversibility and the arrow of time.

(c) *Microscopic indeterminism.* One of the findings of quantum physics is that in the microcosm, only imperfect determinism reigns. This is referred to as quantum mechanical indeterminism, by which one means that there are calculable margins within which microsystems evolve. As an analogy, if a marble is let go on a fairly broad slide, then we may know roughly where it will land, but the exact point of landing will not always be the same. [This is only an analogy. In the case of the marble, one can calculate precisely where it will land, if we knew certain parameters.] At the *quantum mechanical level* of reality, the intrinsic indeterminism allows for a small margin within which alone events occur with calculable probabilities. The quantitative aspect of quantum mechanical indeterminism is expressed through Heisenberg's uncertainty principle. It results from the wave aspect of microcosmic (atomic and subatomic) entities. In essence, it simply states that unlike the motions of pebbles and planets, the precise motions of electrons and protons can never be predicted. This gave rise to more philosophical and speculative literature than perhaps any other physical theory. It has been used to give scientific status for free will, and also for justifying metaphysical positions as to the nature of reality and consciousness. In the 1930s Bernard Bavink wrote:

> There is today within the circle of natural scientists a willingness to restore honestly the threads from these sciences to all higher values of human life, to God and Soul, freedom of will, etc.; these threads had been temporarily all but disrupted and such a willingness had not existed for a century. (quoted in Frank 1957, 233)

Extrapolations, sometimes interesting and often imaginative, of the latest findings of physics into philosophical and religious realms, which have little to do with the measurable, calculable, physical world, have been part of science ever since it began to diverge from traditional religions. In this context, there is seldom any consensus. As Percy C. Bridgman pointed out long ago in the context of quantum mechanics:

> There is, then, no disagreement about the experimental situation: disagreement begins with our interpretation of the significance of the experimental facts. (Hook 1961, 59)

This should remind us of the definitions of fact and truth given earlier.

(d) *Chaotic unpredictable determinism.* It turns out that macroscopic determinism is the result, not just of the basic equations of motion, but because these equations are *linear* (a technical term in mathematics). If and when an element of non-linearity is introduced into a system, the deterministic pattern is strongly affected. Analysis shows that some fantastic things can emerge from it. This phenomenon is known technically as chaos. Crudely stated, there is a level of complexity at which, even at the classical physical level, slight perturbations can lead to enormous consequences in the long run. To use the now famous picturesque metaphor:

> The equations that governed the flow of wind and moisture looked simple enough, for example—until researchers realized that the flap of a butterfly's wings in Texas could change the course of a Hurricane in Haiti a week later. (Waldrop 1992, 66)

Such effects cannot be calculated in any simple way. Other examples of chaotic indeterminism may be seen in weather patterns, population growths, evolution of species, and the like. We may call this the *chaos level* of reality.

(e) *Psychological (human context) indeterminism.* This relates to the age-old problem of free will: Do human beings have the freedom to think/do what they wish, or are they constrained by the rigid determinism of classical physical laws? According to one (now not so widespread) school of thought, macroscopic determinism should apply here also. It is the complexity of the situation that creates the impression that the outcome is not precisely determined, even as it seems impossible to predict which coins would land as heads and which as tails when a billion coins are thrown randomly. One of the eloquent exponents of this view was an essay "On the Freedom of the Will" presented to the Royal Norwegian Academy of Science in 1839 by Arthur Schopenhauer. He believed that human beings do not have any free will. Our actions are conditioned by how our bodies respond to external stimuli. The impact of Laplace is evident here.

In this context, it may be useful to distinguish between experiential indeterminism and submerged determinism. By the first, I mean how a system of experiences in the mind is involved when a step is taken in a sequence of events. External factors could influence this decision, but, in principle, the mind can envisage different courses, weigh their respective consequences, and then act. Human beings who deny having any choice whatever in their individual actions under all circumstances (i.e., who have no experiential indeterminism whatever) may need psychiatric help. Even philosophers who argue for the absence of free will may admit that they choose their position freely. Citizens under the most oppressive dictatorial regimes cannot *act freely* at their will, but they can choose to do one rather than another *in their minds*. The so-called compatibilist view is that both physical determinism and psychological free will are possible.

By submerged determinism, I mean the neuron-basis of our actions and attitudes. It is entirely possible that the laws of physics and chemistry alone determine, very subtly, the actions (decisions) of the doer. Benjamin Libet's work in the 1970s suggested that unconscious neuronal processes occur prior to any so-called conscious decision (*Mind time: The temporal factor in consciousness*, 2004). This indicates that free will is not as free as it seems to be.

Although, from a philosophical/ethical perspective, submerged determinism may be an interesting issue, only experiential indeterminism can be of any practical interest. To say that neuron firing is what made me decide to use abusive language against my neighbor is not, in essence and in outcome, any different from saying that the devil made me do that. But then, we can never be consciously aware of this. Note, however, that even if this were so, it is certainly possible to affect the neuron factor in behavior. After all, what else is obedience to an order or following an injunction? This could even occur without our being conscious of it, as when a person is under hypnosis.

We can see that psychological indeterminism has a lot to do with ethics, while we may never be able to connect submerged determinism with ethics. That is why the former would interest philosophers and ethicists, while the latter would interest physicists and neuroscientists.

(f) *Hypercomplex level.* Beyond the various shades of determinism in physical phenomena, there is another level that governs our lives and also affects the physical world in subtle ways. This is the world of thoughts and ideas which have their origins in the human brain. This is different from the realm of atoms and molecules, of quarks and leptons from which the world has emerged, even as a painting by a master artist is different from the paints and brushes from which it arose. Thoughts differ in their essence from the neurons that give rise to them, as a landscape differs from the cans of paint whose blobs lead to it. The level of reality including thoughts and ideas may be called the hypercomplex level. Science has yet to investigate the nature of the hypercomplex level of reality. Indeed, as of now, it does not even recognize it as a separate dimension of the real world.

The relevance of hypercomplexity becomes apparent when one considers the course of one's own or any individual's life. A little reflection will reveal that the current situation in which one finds oneself arose from countless factors. If there had been even a slight change or replacement in one of them, one's entire life could be different. Anyone can do the *Gedankenexperiment* (thought experiment) of imagining what circumstance(s) led to one's meeting a friend or a life-partner, or to one's choice of education or profession, and reflect on what might have happened if that circumstance been different ever so slightly. The course of any individual human life, as of human history, is the result of countless choices, but instigating those decisions are thoughts and circumstances over whose emergence we have little control.

The ways in which thoughts, ideas, and chance occurrences influence the course of individual human lives, of society and civilization, and of history should become obvious to any student of biography or history. Imagine for a moment what might have happened if the Buddha had not been protected by his father from every pain and suffering, if a different Roman governor had sent Jesus in exile rather than crucified him, if there had been no slave-mongering in Africa when the Europeans came there, or if Hitler had succeeded in his efforts to become a good painter. Imagine what might have happened, or not happened, if photography and other recording devices had not been invented. The world in which we live would have been significantly different.

The hypercomplex level has also had impacts on the physical world. The entire face of the earth has been modified, with roads and bridges and towns and train tracks as a result of human activities. But all these activities had thoughts and ideas at their foundations. Human industry and technology have affected the earth's physical and biological environment in many ways. But what are ultimately the sources of industry and technology? They are the sciences and values which are enshrined in thoughts and ideas in the hypercomplex realm. The planet Mars had for eons existed without an object from the earth landing on its surface. And this changed because of human science: a dramatic instance of hypercomplexity influencing the physical world.

The most important feature of the hypercomplex realm is that occurrences in it are utterly unpredictable. The predictability in the classical realm can, in principle, be perfect. The predictability in the realm of systems with large numbers of components is statistically constrained. The predictability in the realm of quantum systems is law-wise constrained (the Heisenberg principle). The predictability in the realm of chaos is enormously complicated, but still subject to physical laws. But the predictability in the hypercomplex realm is zero. That is why any prediction of human events, whether individual or collective, will most likely be plain wrong.

This does not mean that one cannot or should not project future possibilities on the basis of current situations. Such intelligent conjecture can even be helpful in inspiring us to intelligent, fruitful, and less destructive actions. However, it is important to bear in mind that a single unexpected event arising from elements at the hypercomplex level (such as a new idea, discovery, individual behavior, or perspective) could alter significantly the course of human events.

Free will implies that the next move by a conscious entity is as yet undetermined, and could be one of many possibilities, depending on the free exercise of judgment by that entity. If the capacity for free exercise of judgment prior to an action (which is what free will is) has been given to the human being by God, then God cannot and should not know what the actions of humans would be prior to their performance, especially if God is to judge and reward or punish human beings on the basis of their actions based on their own free will. If God is aware of this, how can we then regard God as having given us real freedom?

One solution to this paradox may involve recognizing the hypercomplex level of reality. At the hypercomplex level, events occur, not simply by the operation of the usual physical forces, but also from thought processes. Thus, whereas the motion of a projectile is governed solely by physical forces, the initial magnitude and direction of motion of a football are determined by a decision on the part of the ball player. Events of this kind occur only in the hypercomplex level in which thought and decisions come into play. As a result, events at this level are totally unpredictable.

From a theological perspective, the omniscience of God refers to knowledge and phenomena at the usual physical (classical and quantum) levels, but not at the hypercomplex level: not because God is ignorant, but because God chose to create a hypercomplex level, perhaps because it is far more interesting and has great potential for unlimited creativity.

On knowing the future

Precognition is knowledge of what is going to happen. It is easy to imagine an all-knowing God who, by definition, knows the future also. However, do or can human beings have precognition? Even if there is predestination, normally, in the phrase of a popular song (*Que Sera, Sera*), "the future's not ours to see." While we have footprints on the sands of elapsed time, there is no trace of events yet unborn, especially of events in the world of human beings. To be told that one recognizes marks which will be left by future events sounds like psychic mumbo jumbo, unacceptable to rational modes, but not to all, nor at all times.

Knowledge of the future has ranged from the magic of mythology, through foretelling of royal undertakings, to journalistic astrology, which dishes out occurrences in individual lives based on birthdays in relation to zodiacal signs.

There are, or used to be in the ancient world, literally hundreds of objects, creatures, and events for divination: from abacomancy (divination from dust) and bolomancy (from the flight of arrows), to scatomancy (from excrement), xylomancy (from the burning of wood), and zygomancy (from the tilting of a balance), which were used for divination. Sometimes specific techniques were spelled out for knowing the future. For example, Kjeld Nielson (*Incense in ancient Israel,* 1984) tells us about Babylonian libanomancy: divination from smoke. The Baru (magician) could predict who would prevail in a battle by observing the direction along which smoke moved.

In the Hindu world, aside from divination which are sometimes based on lizard sounds (as practiced in some other cultures also, such as the Polynesian), horoscopes still play a role in giving approval to marital matches (see for example, Gayatri Devi Vasudev, *The art of matching charts,* 2004), although, with an increase in "love-marriages," star charts are losing their importance in serving as guides. There is also a system of variable prediction: undertakings (such as travel, weddings, laying the foundation stone for a building, etc.), which are initiated in certain months, on certain days, at certain time intervals, etc., will meet with success. Thus, the period between winter and summer solstices is regarded as more auspicious, as are the weeks from new to full moon.

While prophets foretell catastrophes, there are also some people who report flashes of recognition of events that have not yet transpired. Many folks have had dreams that seem to have materialized or vague feelings that something was going to happen, before it actually does. According to Shakespeare, Caesar's wife, Calpurnia, dreamt that he was going to be assassinated, and she warned him of it in advance.

Nostradamus is the best-known non-religious prophet. His clever quatrains (*The prophecies,* 1555) are vague enough to be interpreted as different events of later centuries. Enthusiasts have seen in his lines prophecies about Napoleon, Hitler, Khrushchev, Kennedy, and more. Nostradamus had predicted major upheavals: pestilence, long famine, wars and floods, to occur on June 22, 1732. Nothing of the sort occurred. There never was a more pessimistic prophet or one who let his frightening fancies run wilder: earthquakes, plagues, pillages, poisons, rapes, wars, tyrants, deaths, and such (Leoni 1982).

In the last quarter of the twentieth century, panic raged in California because Nostradamus had written:

> A very mighty trembling in the month of May,
> Saturn in Capricorn, Jupiter and Mercury in Taurus.
> Venus also, Cancer, Mars in Virgo,
> At that time Hail will fall larger than an egg.
> (Century 10, Quatrain 67)

The stated planetary configuration will occur only in 3755.

Many skeptics have written against all this. James Randi made a collection of many such predictions and published a not very sympathetic volume entitled *An encyclopedia of claims, frauds, and hoaxes of the occult and supernatural* (1995). Obscurantism has an appeal that the rational might of science cannot easily extinguish. There is more thrill in the game of groping in the dark than in the impeccable proof that *pi* is a transcendental number. Nothing is more unwelcome than the killing of a fanciful dream by the rude awakening wrought by science and reason. Therefore, people who speak or write against clouded beliefs are generally not welcome.

Prediction: religious and otherwise

Another technical meaning of revelation is the unveiling of a momentous event which is to occur in the future. The term is used in this sense in the Book of Revelation. Here it is declared that there will come a time when people of evil nature "shall have their part in the lake which burneth with fire and brimstone..." (Revelation 21:8). But God will wipe away all tears from the eyes of the good. There is an ancient notion that the world would be periodically consumed by a deluge, only to be reborn, fresh and fertile. These thoughts have their echoes in the Hindu prophesy (Horace Wilson, *Vishnu Purana*, 2001) to the effect that Vishnu will appear as the stupendous Kalki, riding a mammoth white horse, effulgent as a comet in our vicinity. With his sword and axe and a roaring rumble he will put an end to the world filled with sin and evil, and reestablish a reign of order and righteousness.

Passages in the Holy Qur'an suggest that there is a preordained time when, unbeknownst to man, Allah will ordain the *qayaamah* (Day of Judgment) to start. It is stated:

> When there comes that great overwhelming Event, the Day
> when man shall remember all that he strove for, and Hell-
> fire shall be placed in full view for all to see, then for such
> as had transgressed all bounds, and had preferred the life
> of this world, the Abode will be Hell-fire. (Sura 79:34-39)

In 992, when Good Friday and the Day of our Lady coincided, astrologers were let loose to interpret this simultaneous occurrence in terms of global disasters (Vulliaud 1952). Vesuvius erupted soon thereafter, an epidemic occurred, and the Huns and the Normans were rampaging all over Europe. It was not difficult to see forebodings of the imminent catastrophe; all the more so, since the round number 1000 CE was fast approaching. Panic struck whole townships in Europe, crowds thronged to places of worship, communal prayers became more than a habit, and a terrified population genuflected with more terror than hope. But the fateful year came and went without any noticeable global catastrophe. The sun and the moon rose and set; seasons changed, flowers blossomed in spring and birds chirped in peaceful indifference. World and man were here to stay.

In 1179, John of Toledo predicted (Lewinsohn 1958) that within the next seven years the planets would all align themselves with the constellation Libra. From this he concluded that the earth would experience some of the most devastating earthquakes which would crush sinning mankind underground. Again the dismal news spread far and wide, and the panic-stricken reactions were no less intense than two centuries earlier. Underground shelters were dug up, days of repentance were declared, palaces closed their doors tight, and people fasted and prayed. One might argue that all this proved to be very effective, for even though the planetary conjunction did occur in 1186, nothing terrible happened to mar the normal life in Europe or beyond. In 1524, according to expert astrological insights, the world was going to be submerged in a massive deluge. There is reason to believe that this dire prediction did not come to pass.

Invoking planetary influences for terrestrial mishaps was not the prerogative of astrology. John Gribbin and Stephen Plagemann, in *The Jupiter effect,* predicted that there would be a devastating earthquake in Los Angeles in 1982 because all the planets would align themselves on the same side of the sun; their combined gravitational pull would spell disaster on the crust of California.

> The unusual alignment due to occur in the early 1980s will affect the sun. This in turn shakes up the planet earth. But we realized while studying the repercussions in the area of earthquakes that the link works through the atmosphere. What we are really talking about is an effect of the sun on the circulation of the atmosphere. This determines weather pattern shifts. (1974, 261)

Sensational predictions, being a variety of yellow journalism, sell very well when presented as books and magazine articles. According to a Mayan Indian prediction, as advertised in some websites, the world, or at least the calendar will come to an end on December 21, 2012.

A hundred years ago, most scientifically enlightened people might have thought the ends of the world as envisioned by traditional religions were mere fantasies of a darker age which would soon disappear with the spread of scientific knowledge and enlightened thinking. They were very mistaken indeed. For today, thanks to the instigative writings of people like Hal Lindsay (*The 1980s: Countdown to Armageddon,* 1981) and his followers and imitators in other traditions, and the chaos and impasse in global problems, the idea of an impending planetary catastrophe is gaining ground. Its religious underpinnings are often virulently ethno-centric and xenophobic, and tend to wreck any effort to find common ground among the competing and often confrontational races and religions of humankind. The ancient authors of the Doomsday idea in the New Testament and Islamic scripture probably never imagined that one day their dire predictions would be used for political ends and to sow hatred for rival religions and claimants for land in the Middle East.

Types of faith

Faith may be looked upon as the implicit trust one places in a person, thing, or idea, often without asking for or requiring any proof of its validity. In this sense, it is not quite true that the scientific enterprise does not rest on any faith. Let us consider the following examples:

— When we are told by our mother that such and such a man is our biological father, we generally accept it as true.
— When we are young, we take our teacher's word for granted and trust that she has right knowledge of what she is teaching.
— We drink fruit juice and milk from the carton we buy at the store, trusting that no one had added cyanide to it.
— We board a plane, quite convinced of the pilot's skill and sobriety.

It is impossible to go through life without accepting certain matters to be true without getting first hand confirmation about their correctness or veracity. We may describe this type of faith as quotidian faith or q-faith. Q-faith is the unquestioning acceptance of a statement on the assumption that the probability of its being wrong is extremely small. Q-faith is not rationally or empirically fully justifiable, but the probability of its being correct is so high that we are willing to take a risk in adopting it. Its truth content can be verified in principle by appropriate investigation. Without q-faith it would be impossible, in terms of time, to go through life. This idea is expressed in the New Testament: "We walk by faith, not by sight" (2 Corinthians 5:7).

Next consider the following beliefs:

— The workings of every aspect of the world are, or will eventually be intelligible to the human mind. That is to say, every phenomenon in the physical world can and will some day be explained fully in rational and coherent terms.

— There is order and harmony underlying the physical world.

— Nothing happens all by itself, i.e., every observed event has a cause.

— What has been observed to occur again and again an enormously large number of times will occur again: for example, one of the reasons we are so sure the sun will rise tomorrow is that it has been doing so for many years of our life. (Trust in induction.)

— The only right way to answer the question of the origin of the universe is, in the words of Steven Weinberg, "by the methods of science, by theory-aided observation and observation-governed theory" (2001, 54).

None of these statements can be proved on logical grounds to be unassailable. There is no obvious reason why the laws of physics that are currently observed to be operating in the world should have been the same ten billion years ago, or in a galaxy three billion light-years away, nor why the ultimate truth about the origin of the universe can only be arrived at by the methodology of science.

Yet, the scientific enterprise accepts these propositions as true. These also fall under the category of faith. We may describe these as examples intelligibility-faith or i-faith. I-faith is at the very foundation of the scientific enterprise. It is adopted for at least three reasons: one cannot do any science without it, some of it seems most reasonable even to an unprobing mind (intuitively true), and it has served the scientific quest extremely well thus far. However, if circumstances necessitate, the world of science would give up, however reluctantly, one or more elements in its faith foundation. Thus, for example, the notion of strict causality had to be modified, though not given up, as a result of the discovery of radioactivity.

Finally, consider the following beliefs:

— The Vedas have existed all through eternity.
— Moses received the Ten Commandments directly from Yahweh.
— Christ, the Son of God, came to save all humankind.
— Mohammed received God's message from Archangel Gabriel.

Implicit acceptance of the undemonstrated validity of these propositions is required of adherents of the corresponding religious tradition. Acceptance of a proposition on the basis of its scriptural authority constitutes religious faith or r-faith. R-faith is not something that one will readily abandon even if there are demonstrable indications that it might be invalid. It is embraced, not because it conforms to what is generally regarded as common sense or because it is useful in understanding something, but because it is a fundamental tenet of a religious system. When it says in the Old Testament, "I know that my redeemer liveth, and that he shall stand at the latter day upon the earth" (Job 19:25), it is an expression of r-faith. When Nârada declares in the opening chapter of the first book of the *Ramayana*: "Whoever shall read the saga of Rama which purifies the mind, will be freed of all sins" (Bala Kanda 1:97), it is also an example of r-faith.

Thus, r-faith is very different from the q- and the i-types of faith. Its roots are in revelation, cultural upbringing, and religious traditions. In some traditions, it is believed that r-faith is given to a select few as a blessing. Biologists might trace it to particular genes. Whatever its cause or source, r-faith is often associated with the spiritual dimension of an individual. Some type of r-faith is essential to be a wholehearted member of most organized religions and to be committed to the spiritual quest. R-faith is the spontaneous, voluntary and cheerful acceptance, arising from deep inner conviction, of something that one may or may not be able to prove on logical grounds. Pope St. Gregory the Great is said to have declared:

> *Fides non habet meritum ubi humana ratio praebet experimentum* [Faith has no merit where human reason supplies the proof]. (591, 76:1197C)

Usually, but not always, r-faith refers to unquestioning belief in a transcendent principle, most often called God. Even in the so-called atheistic religion of Buddhism, one talks of various Bodhisattvas who have trans-corporeal existence. Some important elements that give meaning and relevance to life are also associated with r-faith, such as hope for the future, possibility of post-mortem persistence, and the intrinsic value of goodness. Thus, r-faith is implicit belief in something that is not material and obvious, tangible or easily recognizable. When Bhaktivedanta Prabhupada states that "the Gita can only be perfectly understood by devotees" (1968, 439), it is also an expression of r-faith. In the Bible, it is written: "faith is the substance of things hoped for, the evidence of things not seen" (Hebrews 11:1).

In the scientific realm, seeing refers to recognizing all the convincing data one can get through sensory faculties, and through reason. In religions, it means recognizing meaningful and fulfilling truths through intuition and deep conviction. It has been observed that there is this important distinction between science and religion:

in science, one believes what one sees, whereas in religion one sees what one believes in. St. Augustine asked rhetorically:

> *Quid est enim fides nisi credere quod non vides?*
> [What is faith if not believing in what thou seest not?].
> (ca. 400, 7:228)

Countless people have benefited from, and been enriched by r-faith. People with r-faith are fulfilled in their spiritual longing and religious commitment, whether they be churchgoing Christians, Makka-going Muslims, bhajan-singing Hindus, or of whatever other tradition. According to Harold Koenig:

> Systematic research indicated that in some parts of the United States, 90 percent of persons with serious medical illness use religion at least to some degree as a coping resource, and approximately 50 percent of those persons report that religious faith is the most important factor that enables them to cope (i.e., it is more important than family, friends, work, or any other known coping resources). (2000, 107)

This is equally true in many other parts of the world.

In the following statements from the scriptures of three major religious traditions, it is of r-faith that one speaks:

> But those who with faith, holding me as their supreme aim, follow this immortal wisdom, those devotees are exceedingly dear to me. (Bhagavad Gita 12:20)

> Be thou faithful unto death, and I will give thee a crown of life. (Revelation 2:10)

> Those who believe and work righteousness, their Lord will guide them because of their Faith. Beneath them will flow rivers in Gardens of Bliss. (Qur'an 10:9)

Some have wondered how faith, which serves religion well, happens to be inappropriate in Science. Thus, when Robert Ingersoll declared that "investigation is better than unthinking faith" (1877, 395), what he had in mind here was r-faith, and not i-faith. It is not always recognized that the r-faith of religion has little to do with i-faith, hence with science.

When one fails to make the distinction between the nuances of faith, arguments and impasses are bound to arise. Then, we will have difficulty differentiating between fundamental science and metaphysical theology. Referring to some of the challenging problems of modern cosmology, John Barrow says categorically:

> If our methods fail, then any boundary between fundamental science and metaphysical theology will become increasingly difficult to draw. Sight must give way to faith. (1990, 373)

It is not clear that in the context of a puzzled science, r-faith is really helpful for scientists. If anything, in such contexts science generally reconsiders aspects of the i-faith on which it rests and functions.

Types of doubts

Doubt is a state of mind, some would say an affliction of the mind. It refers to a condition in which one is unable or unwilling to accept, on the face of it, a given statement as true. When we say we are in doubt, what we mean is that we are not altogether certain about the truth or correctness of a proposition, the reliability of a person, the existence of something, etc.

Like the word *faith*, the word *doubt* is also used in a variety of contexts with varying shades of meaning, resulting in some avoidable misunderstandings between science and religion. Here again, controversies tend to arise when one ignores the variety of doubts that might arise in the mind. To clarify this, we may consider three different situations where doubt could arise.

First, consider a salesperson who extols a product that he or she is eager to sell. One may not be prepared to accept everything that the person says. Or again, if a doctor were to tell a close relative of a seriously ill patient that there is a good chance of recovery, one may have some doubts about what the physician says. Finally, when a very probable suspect who is questioned by the police asserts that he or she is really innocent, one may not accept the statement as absolutely true. These are instances of what may be called quotidian doubt or q-doubt. In q-doubt, there is reason to suspect that the proponent of a proposition is probably not telling the truth. Usually, the individual has an ulterior motive for this. The opposite of q-doubt is not faith, but credulity or gullibility.

Next, consider a preacher who tells the audience that those who commit sins are bound to suffer one way or another, here in this world or in the hereafter. Or again, there may be an expert in economics who says that if certain steps are taken, certain economic problems will be solved. Finally, let us take up the assurance that one will attain salvation if one accepts Jesus Christ as the Savior, or Mohammed as the last Prophet, or an equivalent proposition in another religion. In these instances, too, one may doubt that the proposition is 100% reliable. The doubt arising in these cases is different from q-doubts. Here, those who make the claim are honest and sincere in what they say. They have no intention to cheat, fool, or take advantage of others. Doubt may arise in these cases, not because one distrusts the credibility or integrity of the source, but rather because the proposition in question strikes the doubter as somewhat improbable. This type of doubt may be called skeptic's doubt or s-doubt. S-doubt is not necessarily associated with disregard or lack of respect for the source, or with suspicion of dishonesty.

When it says in the New Testament "He that doubteth is damned" (Romans 14:23), it is of s-doubt doubt that one is speaking. When it is declared that there is no doubt in the Holy Qur'an (32:2), what is implied is that one should not approach it with s-doubt. When the Bhagavad Gita (4:40) says that for the doubting person there is happiness neither here nor in the next world, it is again of s-doubt that Krishna speaks. S-doubt is the antithesis of r-faith, and is not religion-friendly. Over the ages, many thinkers have recognized this. Thus, the poet Tennyson reminded us in his "In Memoriam A. H. H." (1849)

that sowing doubts in times of prayer would spoil the richness of the experience:

> Leave thou thy sister, when she prays
> Her early heaven, her happy views;
> Nor thou with shadowed hint confuse
> A life that leads melodious days.

Suppose there is an announcement that some chemists have produced nuclear fusion reactions at ordinary temperatures. Upon reading this report, the general public may be impressed and excited, but the scientists who know something about nuclear fusion, and especially those who are working in the field, will have serious doubts about the correctness of the report or the claim of the chemists. They will immediately set to work to reproduce the reported result. If an astronomer says that he or she has spotted a comet or a new galaxy at such and such a celestial location, then other astronomers will direct their instruments towards the reported coordinates to check if this is indeed true. This gesture, from a truth-content point of view, is also an expression of doubt in what one has been told.

Consider the case of a student who is performing an experiment in a physics laboratory to verify a certain law of physics which was enunciated in a lecture. Why should the student do the experiment? Does he not trust the professor or the text book? The point is, a student learning the methodology and techniques of science must not, in principle, trust (i.e. accept unquestioningly as true) whatever the teacher says. The act of doing an experiment in a science course is a scientific ritual in which the student implicitly says: "Yes, my teacher may be right in what he told us in class, but unless I do the experiment myself and verify it to be true, I really cannot accept its validity."

These are all examples of what may be called confirmatory doubts or c-doubts. A c-doubt arises, not out of distrust in the integrity of the source (q-doubt), or even necessarily from the implausibility of what is stated (s-doubt), but from two other considerations. First, scientific results need to be validated by people beyond and away from the first source through independent observations and repeated verifications.

This has nothing to do with the unreliability or untrustworthiness of the source. In fact, if a reported result is not pursued by others to verify or modify it, this would be an insult to the scientist who first presents it to the community. Secondly, no matter how reliable the scientific authority may be who proposes or tries to propagate a scientific proposition, unless his or her claim is tested independently by as many different people as possible, using all the available resources, it is not regarded as scientifically valid. Thus, c-doubt is a necessary component of the scientific enterprise; it is an important element in scientific methodology, just as r-faith is a necessary ingredient of religion.

Just as it is simplistic to say that there is no faith component in science, it is not quite true that there is no doubt component in the religious context. Many deeply religious people experience s-doubt when they encounter a religious system other than their own. Indeed the rejection of the doctrines of a different religion is an emphatic expression of s-doubt. St. Thomas Aquinas did this explicitly with respect to Islam (*Summa contra gentiles,* 1264). Likewise, a religious person may also have some s-doubt with respect to certain doctrines in one's own religion. Indeed, this is the starting point of any new religious sect. Buddhism and Protestantism, the Arian heresy in Christianity and the Shiite versus Sunni sectarianism in Islam, are examples of sectarian movements within religions that arose from the s-doubts of religious thinkers.

Even devout believers have sometimes experienced s-doubt. "Doubting" Thomas the apostle, St. Paul, St. Augustine, and C. S. Lewis from the Christian tradition, and Vivekananda from the Hindu tradition, had all entertained serious s-doubt before becoming profoundly religious. Though some religious people have held that r-faith whose validity is logically demonstrated is not true religious faith, many religious thinkers who have been touched by science, tend to argue that, at least at some stage, s-doubt is a necessary precondition for faith. Thus, Michael Corey says:

God might actually prefer the critical-thinking agnostic, who eventually comes to Him through a word-won battle of conflicting beliefs, to the mindless subservient "believer" who hasn't even bothered to examine his or her belief structure. (1993, 289)

Though one may wonder how this author and others seem to know about God's preferences, the point made here is that honest s-doubt is not necessarily incompatible with religious seeking.

Contextual relevance of faith and doubt

The value in distinguishing different types of faith and doubt lies not only in clarifying these important mental states, but also in recognizing that both doubt and faith are indispensable in science and in religion, and that both are relevant in different contexts. Thus, for example, singing a devotional hymn in church is a great thing to do, but doing this in a physics colloquium may be inappropriate, if not laughable. Telling a joke at a party may be appreciated, but not during a funeral service. In like manner, no matter how fulfilling it may be to an individual, r-faith will not be very helpful in the formulation or elaboration of a technical theory in science or mathematics; just as doubting the sanctity of scripture becomes inappropriate, if not offensive, during the performance of a sacrament or religious ritual.

Generally speaking, q-faith and q-doubt come into play in personal attitudes, decisions, and actions. They are irrelevant in the public (science) domain. That is to say, they come to the fore in our attitudes and behavior towards others, in interacting with people we know, when we are buying things, etc. Sometimes, however, q-faith also arises in the minds of scientists when they are in the midst of developing a theory. For example, Einstein and others spent many years trying to formulate a unified theory of gravitation and electromagnetism, goaded by the conviction that the two must be different manifestations of one and the same deeper reality. This conviction is an instance of q-faith. No element of i-faith is violated if there are two fundamental forces, rather than one, governing the universe. Contrary to the normal undertaking in science, which is to try to explain an observed phenomenon, attempts at unifying the two fields is an intellectual struggle to formulate a theory that has no immediate observational basis whatever. This q-faith-based effort did not bear any fruit. On the other hand, the hypothesis of wave-particle duality, proposed by Louis de Broglie on the basis of his q-faith in symmetry in nature, turned out to be successful. Similarly, an observational quest to detect an aspect of nature that is predicted by a scientific theory is often inspired from c-faith in the theory. This may or may not lead to success.

Failure to see the difference between i-faith and r-faith leads to statements like the following:

> Whereas religions normally make a clear statement on their articles of faith, science introduces its assumptions more surreptitiously. (Wallace 1996, 12)

Contrary to what is implied here, science does not try to sneak anywhere surreptitiously. It just marches on, with its triumphs and errors, letting the rest of the world benefit from, and be enriched by, its fruits, or discard its worldviews as per one's taste and talent, inviting all, but compelling no one to accept its findings.

Religiously-inclined scientists—and there are many—do not like to compartmentalize their scientific and religious dimensions. They wish to be religious and scientific in every aspect of their life, and live a fully integrated life. This is a valid position to take, and for some it is perhaps the only meaningful way of being religious as well as scientific. However, in this context it is important to be clear about what one means by an integrated life. To most people, it would be difficult to bring one's faculty for c-doubt in the presence of a sacred altar during a religious participation, and equally hard to bring in one's r-faith while doing a scientific experiment or elaborating a scientific theory. As long as it is recognized that c-doubt and r-faith are reserved for different categories of experience, it is certainly possible to ignore or keep aside one mental state while being engaged in another. This is neither disloyalty to science nor disrespect for religion. What is important is to take into account the contexts appropriately. To be religious and scientific does not mean that one has to bring into action both c-doubt and r-faith in all contexts, much less simultaneously.

Gnosis and sciencis: apará and pará

The clear bifurcation of human knowledge into that which can be intellectually grasped and that which can only be spiritually experienced is an ancient realization. In practically every religion and tradition, one makes this distinction. It may be said to correspond roughly, in the modern secular world, to the distinction between technical theoretical physics, which can be known only through thorough acquaintance with higher mathematics, and other types of knowledge which do not call for that.

Gnosticism refers to certain worldviews and practices in the ancient Christian world. Its pre-Christian roots had components like mysticism and esoteric practices. It was built on the conviction that by these means the human soul could pierce through the intervening opaque walls between us and the realm of the Divine, and ultimately reach the heavenly world beyond. The word Gnosticism is derived from the Greek for knowledge: *gnosis*. This Greek word refers to practices which lead to r-faith based knowledge, whereas the Latin world for knowledge, *scientia,* gave us the word for practices that are based upon s-doubt—science—an entirely different kind of knowledge. Both types of practices claim to lead to the acquisition of knowledge.

One of the tenets of Gnosticism was that it embodies higher knowledge which has come down to the practitioners from God Himself. Moreover, this knowledge is to be accepted without proof or demand for proof, as all revealed knowledge ought to be. Then again, this knowledge is about God and the Divine Realm, about transcendence, about the esoteric origin of the world according to which the world is the result of some corruption of the divine. Gnosticism is also about ways of finding our way back to where we came from, and about the ultimate dissolution of the world.

Though the word and practice of Gnosticism per se, in the technical sense, are no longer as widespread as they once used to be, the underlying Gnostic view of an unfathomable mystic undercurrent, the concept of higher knowledge, and an indescribable transcendence are still very much in the framework of discourse, implicitly or explicitly, often in transformed language and modes, in all r-faith based systems.

In the Hindu tradition, too, there is a clear-cut difference between esoteric knowledge of the beyond which cannot be grasped through ordinary perception, the intellect and worldly knowledge. In one of the Upanishads it says:

> *Dve vidye veditavye iti ha sma yad brahmavido vadanti,*
> *parâ caivâparâca*
> [Two kinds of knowledge are to be known, as the knowers
>   of Brahman declare: the *pará* (higher) and the
>   *apará* (lower)].
> (Mundaka Upanishad 1:4)

The Vedas, phonetics, rituals, grammar and the like belong to the lower category, while that which cannot be grasped, "which is eternal, omnipresent, and super-subtle" is the undecaying.

If we coin a word *sciencis* to refer to knowledge gained through the mode, methodology, and framework of (modern) science as an enterprise, then it may be said that science-religion dialogues are exchanges between *sciencis* and *gnosis*.

On exopotent and endopotent truths

Most people benefit from the fruits of science, and they have great respect for the knowledge that science has brought to humanity. Most people are also enriched by the religious experience: communal fellowship, joyous celebrations, meaningful sacraments and ceremonies, magnificent art and music, spiritual peace, and much, much more. And yet, there have often been conflicts and confrontations between science and religion. What exactly brings this about?

Various answers have been given to this question. Generally, anti-religious scientists point to the atrocities committed in the name of religion, and theologians point to the arrogance and totalizing claims of some scientists who are unwilling or unable to grant that there are mysteries that lie beyond human comprehension. Also, some scientists adopt the attitude that the religiously inclined are a little less intelligent; and some of the religious adopt the attitude that the anti-religious are evil.

But in most instances, at the intellectual level, science-religion disagreements tend to arise from the claim of each party to have the truth on one's own side.

At this point it is useful to recall the distinction between facts and truths. All our knowledge about the world around us arises from our sensory perceptions. Facts may be looked upon as elements in our cognition on which all people who enjoy normal sensory perception can agree. There are both direct and indirect facts: that is to say, facts that we directly perceive, and those that we recognize through indirect, reliable means.

Given a fact, different people may give it different interpretations. Though it may be a fact that there is a table in this room, some may say that it is hard, big, brown, etc., and others may say it is beautiful, awkwardly placed, meant to serve us, etc. All these interpretations of facts are what we call truths.

The essential difference between scientific and religious truths is that they are two fundamentally different kinds of interpretations of the human condition.

Scientific truths have two characteristics. First, a scientific truth can have consequences (impacts) on our understanding and manipulation of the world. So we will describe them as *exopotent*. Exopotent truths are fruitful, i.e. they lead to useful and practical applications. The word *useful* does not necessarily mean something of practical utility. It could also be relevant in the context of understanding a natural phenomenon. It is important to realize that even mistaken interpretations of some aspect of the physical world may constitute scientific truths. Thus, at one time, the phlogiston theory of heat and the corpuscular theory of light were scientific truths, because they were useful in certain contexts.

The second important characteristic of exopotent truths is that they are locality-culture-invariant, their validity does not depend on where one considers them or the cultural perspective from which they are considered. At any given time, exopotent truths are universal.

A characteristic of religious truths is that they have significant consequences (impacts) on our internal experience of life as individuals. We say that religious truths are *endopotent*. Endopotent truths are fulfilling, i.e. they lead to psychologically and emotionally satisfying states. It must be realized that even atheism and other philosophical systems that do not belong to particular religious traditions, or that may be a synthesis of several, are endopotent truths.

Endopotent truths are also interpretations of facts. The geocentric model is an interpretation of observed facts. To replace it with the heliocentric model leads to an exopotent truth. Clinging on to it, in spite of evidence to the contrary, would be an example of an endopotent truth. It must be noted that neither the statement that the sun is the center of the universe nor the statement that the earth is the center is a fact (or a truth as one is accustomed to say). However, post-sixteenth century, one is clearly exopotent and the other is clearly endopotent.

Three things must be said about endopotent truths. First, inner peace, psychological satisfactions, and emotional security (endopotent factors) are more important than practical additions to creature comforts (exopotent factors). It is, therefore, not surprising that religion has always been a major factor in human culture and civilization. This is why, contrary to the recommendation or desire of some rationalist, atheist, and scientific thinkers, religions can never be completely eradicated from human culture. What one may try to accomplish and succeed in doing is to modify religious institutions and doctrines so as to make them more satisfying and less harmful than they have been. Secondly, unlike exopotent truths, endopotent truths are often locality-culture-variant. Indeed, in the context of art, music, and poetry (all furnishing endopotent truths) they could even be individual-variant. Finally, the impression that, because endopotent truths seem subjective, they are less valid or important than exopotent truths may be somewhat mistaken. Ultimately, every individual holds as truth only what is meaningful and important for him or her. The idea that one is loved by one's family or friends may be a far more significant truth to a person than the fact that the universe is more than ten billion years old.

It has been said that what matters is not what we believe in, but what we do with our beliefs. This is an important observation in the context of science and religion, if only because arguments have been made for and against both with reference to their impacts. Both science and religion have had positive as well as negative impacts. A positive impact is one that enhances the quality and experience of life, whereas a negative impact is hurtful or harmful, physically, emotionally, or psychologically. We may refer to these as beneficent and maleficent impacts.

All truths have *impact potential* (i.e., each is capable of provoking actions of one kind or another). In every case, the impact itself could be exopotent or endopotent or both. Whereas religious truths by themselves are only endopotent, the actions stemming from them could be endopotent or exopotent. For example, engagement in prayer is an endopotent action, and an act of charity or kindness towards a fellow human being is an exopotent action. Both are beneficent in nature. On the other hand, a superstitious fear arising from a religious belief is maleficent and endopotent, while religious persecution of heretics is maleficent and exopotent. Some actions may be beneficent in an endopotent way and maleficent in an exopotent way. The actions of religious bigots in holy wars are of this kind.

In science, chemical weapons and their use are instances of maleficent exopotent actions, whereas the use of vaccines is beneficent exopotent. In some instances it is difficult to foresee whether scientific knowledge will lead to beneficent or maleficent actions. As we increase our understanding of the human genome, there is potential for both beneficent and maleficent use of this new knowledge.

This analysis enables us to spell criteria for the retention or rejection of truths, both scientific and religious. Those who argue eloquently against religion stress the maleficent exopotent potential of religion, and those who argue for science stress its beneficent exopotent potential, and conversely.

From these considerations we may list the following set of principles for understanding the relevance and importance of science and religion:

(a) One must recognize that religion and science embody essentially different categories of truths: one is endopotent and the other is exopotent.

(b) To ignore either of these would diminish the human experience. However, endopotent truths (provided by religion of one kind or another) are a deeper human need than exopotent truths (provided by science). Here it is important to distinguish between exopotent *truths* and the material aspects of reality with which they are concerned. We need food and shelter; however, these are not truths, but materials.

(c) The validity of endopotent truths is a function of one's cultural background (upbringing) and the consequent intellectual framework, but that of exopotent truths is not.

(d) The significance of truths is related to their potential impact.

(e) Individuals and societies may accept or reject truths on the basis of whether the potential impacts are beneficent or maleficent. This is not to say that they always do this. All too often, unwholesome choices are made.

(f) Science and religion, considered without reference to these factors, could lead to sterile and even dangerous interpretations.

Chapter 4
Explanatory Dimensions

Explanations in science

A principal aim of science is to offer explanations for all that is happening in the world. What does one mean by the term explanation? Indeed, some have argued (Stephen Gaukroger *Explanatory structures: Concepts of explanation in early physics and philosophy*, 1978) that the very notion of explanation could change from age to age. To clarify the notion in simple terms, let us consider the following situations:

> A very small child in front of a television that has been turned on will be totally indifferent to it. If a little older, she may be watching it happily, and the question may not even arise in her mind as to how this is possible—people talking, cars moving, music playing, etc.—all on a screen in a box. Even some adults do not bother to concern themselves about such things. At this stage, there can be no science, since a need for explanation has not been felt.
>
> At a more advanced stage, the child may begin to wonder and ask someone about the matter. If an adult were to say that there are live people and things in the box who show up every time we turn the television on, the child might simply say, "Oh!," and be quite satisfied. As far as she is concerned, the matter has been explained.
>
> Next, consider the fact that an object that is hurled into the air always falls back. This was once explained

thus: "Just as a child who goes away from home eventually returns, objects moving away from earth's surface return to the ground, which is their home."

Finally, consider the boiling of water when sufficiently heated. To explain this, we may be told that the effect of heat on any substance is to change its state from solid to liquid or from liquid to gas. This explanation may also be satisfactory to many.

A mature person will regard the first example of explaining television as ridiculous, the second as unscientific, and the one about water as partly acceptable. In all instances, whether or not the person seeking the explanation is satisfied is what matters. If satisfied, as far as that person is concerned, an explanation has been found. Explanations are satisfactory or unsatisfactory, rather than right or wrong. On final analysis, explanation is creating the impression that one understands what gives rise to an observed fact or event. In addition, an explanation often calls for a general principle in terms of which an observed occurrence can be understood.

How can one be sure that the impression of having understood a phenomenon is no more than an illusion? Let us go back to the adult's answer to the child concerning the television. We may not find that explanation satisfactory at all, but the child does. This is because of two different but interrelated factors. First, the child's mind is not yet developed enough to recognize the impossibility (not to say the absurdity) of the explanation. This is because she is not sufficiently familiar with the world. Thus, two conditions are necessary in giving or evaluating an explanation: intellectual maturity and familiarity with the complexity of the world.

Explanations often involve cause-effect connections. Moreover, when we trace the cause of a phenomenon, we may inquire into the cause of that cause, and so on and on. In the scientific search, such quests lead to fundamental laws and principles. All scientific explanations are based on the discovery or formulation of laws, principles, and constants in terms of which occurrences in the phenomenal world may be understood.

However, in this framework, one often needs to assume the existence of entities and processes that are not directly perceptible. Such assumptions are implicit or explicit in the realm of scientific explanations and are part of scientific theories. Scientific explanations invariably involve abstract concepts, logical connections and invisible things. This is not surprising, because explanation is the uncovering of order and logical consistency through the mind's eye. The mind manipulates, not things and stuff, but ideas and relations, concepts and consistencies.

Explanations in religion

There are basic differences between explanations in science and those in religion.

Science and formal religions began with efforts to answer questions of origin. Whether humans, animals, languages, or ethics, one can always inquire into how it all started. Every religion has a genesis story. The seven-day creation of the Abrahamic tradition is one of the better known, but there are other views: Hindu, Chinese, Babylonian, ancient Greek, and more. What religions say on the matter are not just blanket statements, but an explanation of how the world began.

Over the ages, science, too, has come up with answers to origin-questions. However, whereas religious explanations assume a prenatal state for the universe in the mind of God, scientific ones do not. Most religious explanations of the origin of Man make him special in the scheme of things, and almost coeval with the birth of the universe. Science explains anthropogenesis as a much later and non-special occurrence in the universe.

In ancient times, religions tried to explain natural phenomena too. Thunder and lightning were explained as gods expressing their wrath; epidemics were explained as resulting from the presence of witches in a community; eclipses were explained as caused by celestial dragons temporarily devouring the sun or the moon; diseases were explained as caused by this goddess or that; and so on. However, wherever modern science came to the fore, the credibility of such explanations suffered considerably.

Aside from explanations as to origins, which were often majestic and poetic, and those of natural phenomena, which were often mythological and fanciful, religions have also tried to explain phenomena that do not ordinarily come under the purview of science. For example, consider the unequal distribution of good fortune and ill luck in the world. Why is one child born in a wealthy family where it receives every comfort and another in a poor and struggling one?

Why do innocent people suffer and the guilty often get away with impunity? The Hindu explanation for this involves both the immutable law of action and consequence *(karma)* and rebirths (reincarnation). Our current circumstances have resulted from actions in a previous birth. Others give up on such tough questions and say, "God works in mysterious ways."

Why is there evil in the world? Why are earthquakes and volcanoes inflicting untold suffering on innocent people? Why do people engage in wrongful actions, inflict pain and cold cruelty? One school of Hindu thought says that all this is part of divine play; the cosmic mind is thickening the plot, as it were, to make it all more interesting. Christianity explains this as punishment for Adam's original sin of disobeying God and trying out the apple that had been expressly forbidden.

Why do people suffer, and why is there pain? Buddhism explains pain as resulting from attachment to things and to sensual pleasures. Be balanced in behavior, cut out your cravings, and you will find that life is less painful. Those who have experienced this would say that there is empirical proof for the Buddhist explanation. On the other hand, Islam would explain pain as another instance of the Will of God.

On such issues science has very little to say, except through extensions of biological evolution into the cultural context. But here there is seldom unanimity, even among scientists.

There are many dimensions of the human experience where religions have served us well. However, wherever modern science assumes the role and responsibility of explaining natural phenomena, religions are often put on the defensive, because scientific methodology leads to more consistent and coherent explanations of natural phenomena. Conflicts between science and religion will persist whenever and wherever religion competes with science in the explanation of physical occurrences, and science competes with religion in offering matter-energy explanations for profound human experiences.

Theories in science

The word theory is derived from the Greek *theoria:* speculation or view. It is used in a variety of meanings. Thus, one speaks of Plato's theory of ideas, Kant's theory of knowledge, Cantor's theory of sets, Hobbes' political theory, the impressionist theory of art, and music theory. In each of these instances, the word has a slightly different meaning; the only common feature in all of them is the conceptual framework involved. Similarly, in common parlance, simple beliefs are sometimes referred to as theories. A detective might say, "My theory is that it is Mrs. Jones' paramour who ate up all the cheese." Likewise, the once popular belief that the right ovary produced male children and the left ovary female ones is sometimes called a theory (Dawson 1917). "According to the Aristotelian theory," writes one author, "heavier bodies fall faster than lighter ones."

In scientific literature, and especially in physics, theory has a clear meaning and function. It is certainly not a simple belief, nor just another way of looking at things. It is meant to serve the explanatory goal of science. Efforts to explain physical phenomena and their generalizations (laws of nature) lead to the formulation of theories. A theory in science is the conceptual development of a set of basic ideas and interrelationships concerning the physical world, in terms of which observationally authenticated phenomena and empirically derived laws may be clearly understood.

For example, Johannes Kepler's First Law of planetary motion stated that all planets move in elliptical orbits with the sun at one of the foci. We may ask why planets follow such orbits rather than, say, circular or square ones. Isaac Newton's *theory* of gravitation is based on some fundamental assumptions about forces between masses in the physical world. It involves a whole body of mathematical development in terms of which the empirically derived laws of planetary motions can be explained. Similarly, Niels Bohr's *theory* of the hydrogen atom is based on the model proposed by Ernest Rutherford a couple of years earlier. It rests on certain basic assumptions, and its function was to account for the empirically observed results pertaining to the spectral lines of hydrogen. A theory must explain, not simply describe, some aspect of the physical world. Postmodernist trivialization of a scientific theory as simply "a way of looking at the world" totally misses the point of the power of a good theory to explain, to the last detail, every aspect, both qualitative and quantitative, of a given phenomenon. A poet and a painter can also look at the world, as does a philosopher. Their creative expressions do not constitute a scientific theory by any means because they are not meant to explain anything.

Sometimes, two rival theories may explain the same set of phenomena. In such situations, it is hard to decide which one to accept. A classic case during the eighteenth century involved the ultimate nature of light: the corpuscular and the wave theories. Either one could successfully explain all then-known optical phenomena. However, it followed from the corpuscular theory that light should travel faster in water than in air; whereas, according to the wave theory, it should be the other way around.

The experimental resources of eighteenth century physics were not sufficient to test out which of these two consequences is actually the case. In the course of the nineteenth century, Jean Foucault and Armand Fizeau (Whittaker 1951, 1:100) succeeded in doing the appropriate experiments that determined the velocity of light in air and in water, and found that light travels faster in air than in water. The corpuscular theory of light had to be abandoned. An experiment of this kind, which decides between two competing and, until then, equally valid theories, is known as a crucial experiment.

There is an anecdote about the merciless physicist Wolfgang Pauli. He once complained about a scientific paper with minimal merit, "It is not even wrong" (Peierls 1997, 17), meaning it is most uninteresting. As a matter of fact, however, a scientific theory is never right or wrong. It is only good or bad, satisfactory or unsatisfactory, successful or unsuccessful, acceptable or unacceptable, because the goal of a theory is to explain some aspect of perceived reality in terms of certain concepts and models, rather than to uncover ultimate truths.

Theories in religion

The role of a theory is to explain observed phenomena. This sometimes involves entities that are not directly perceived. From this perspective, it is fair to say that there are also theories in the religious framework.

Perhaps the most intriguing phenomenon in the physical world is its very existence. So is the presence of human beings, not simply as biological entities that come and go, but as feeling and reflecting creatures that engage in love and hate, create and destroy, formulate and follow moral injunctions, seem to know the difference between right and wrong, beauty and ugliness... and then are transformed into cold and inert bodies, bereft of the consciousness that kept them alive and kicking.

Religions attempt to explain these interesting phenomena: cosmogenesis, biogenesis, and ethicogenesis. Their answers, though seldom described as such, may well be looked upon as theories also. For example, the Vedas, the Bible, and the Koran—all revered texts in major religious traditions—tell us about the creation of Man and Woman. From an epistemic perspective, these are different theories to explain the presence of humans on the planet. But in the religious framework one avoids the word theory for such efforts to explain because they are usually part of religious doctrines.

In cultural history, these theories are embodied in texts that have acquired sanctity. As a result, they have a degree of invulnerability and infallibility within a given religious framework. Scientific and religious theories differ, not in the goal of their proponents, but in the attitude of their adherents. It is important to recognize (assuming human and historical origins to scriptural writings) that the authors of scriptural texts were keen intellects who sought to solve the perennial mystery of origins in what seemed to them at the time to be the most reasonable terms. It is quite possible that, if the thinkers who wrote those texts were to come back in our midst, they would be the first to want revised editions of their theories in the light of current knowledge and understanding, for they were extraordinarily intelligent people. In a new version of Genesis, one might read, for example, "God said, 'Let there be electromagnetic waves,' and there were electromagnetic waves."

Traditional religions have offered theories about the nature of ultimate reality. In the Hindu view, ephemeral reality is a mere illusion, while ultimate reality is never-decaying and eternal, not unlike Aristotle's celestial world. Though these are usually presented as philosophy, theologians in many traditions also explore them. Science is concerned with aspects of reality such as they appear through our faculties of perception, and not with the nature of ultimate reality, whatever that may be. Philosophy and religion develop theories about the nature of reality per se. Philosophical theories of reality seldom enjoy universal assent.

Another important difference between scientific and religious theories involves how they are evaluated. The successes of religious theories are judged, not so much by their resilience in the face of logical and empirical scrutiny, but by the reverence associated with their sources. Since religious theories do not depend on verification of their logical consequences, competing and mutually contradictory religions, resting on mutually incompatible worldviews, have flourished all through history. In so far as each group is content with its own pictures, there is no serious problem, because it is not unlike different readers preferring different novels. However, when one's enthusiasm for one's own version prompts one to impose it on others, often in a spirit of arrogance and condescension, then troubles start. This is one of the refrains of this book.

On instrumentalism

In the foreword to Copernicus' treatise *De revolutionibis orbium coelestium [On the revolutions of the heavenly spheres]* (1543), which ushered in modern science, we read the following statement:

> For it is the duty of an astronomer to compose the history of the celestial motions through careful and expert study. Then he must conceive and devise the causes of these motions or hypotheses about them. Since he cannot in any way attain to the true causes, he will adopt whatever suppositions enable the motions to be computed correctly from the principles of geometry for the future as well as for the past. (Osiander 1543, xx)

Some historians of science regard this as one of the first formulations of what is known as the instrumentalist philosophy of scientific truths. Newton expressed similar views. However, gaining confidence from their continuing successes during the eighteenth and nineteenth centuries, most scientists began to feel that science was, in fact, the only accurate revealer of the nature of reality, an idea that is still held by many practicing scientists.

However, in the late nineteenth century, an interpretation of scientific truths developed, inspired by John Dewey's general view that every thought and idea has significance only in so far as it has any tangible effect, especially on the human condition. The ideas and concepts that arise in the human mind, he argued, are not unlike the tools and instruments developed by human ingenuity. Their purpose is to solve present and pressing problems.

The instrumentalist perspective has sometimes led to the assertion that scientific truths are only useful descriptions, their validity resting only on their fruitfulness, and that, though they may be applied for constructing bridges and gadgets, they cannot be seen as correct descriptions of Reality. Steam engines were constructed based on a scientific theory of heat that has been completely discarded. The first electric batteries were put together with an erroneous view of electricity, and so on.

Moreover, quantum physics has modified significantly our notion of reality. All that science does is to develop concepts, theories, and calculations by which we arrive at numbers that tally extraordinarily well with pointer readings. As Paul Dirac put it, "The only object of theoretical physics is to calculate results that can be compared with experiment" (1930, 7). Some have interpreted this as science's inability to describe reality per se. They argue that all that science does is to provide a consistent framework from which we can interpret Nature. It has been said that this is also precisely what religion does, and that therefore science has no greater claim to correct knowledge about Reality than religion. Since Truth is essentially a correct comprehension of Reality, there is no difference between science and religion, except in the matters they investigate.

Let us look into this further. Unlike tools, which are usually meant for particular tasks, a scientific theory, though initially formulated for a particular phenomenon, soon gains a universality which makes it relevant in many other contexts as well. More importantly, even if one grants that scientific explanations are accepted as truths only because they work (i.e., they seem reasonable and can be applied to produce devises), this does not in any way diminish their intrinsic worth. There does not seem to be any better mode of explanation the human mind has come up with for the task of providing consistent, coherent, and logically acceptable interpretations of carefully authenticated, experimentally verified, and precisely measured phenomena. It is reasonable to claim that religions approach *other* dimensions of the human experience, but the assertion that, in the context of explanation of *natural* phenomena, religious worldviews are as valid as scientific, has given rise to some serious disagreements. Instrumentalism does not mean a relatively weaker epistemic standing for science, given that there is no alternative strategy that is even remotely as effective in the goal of reasoned understanding.

On the mechanistic world model

The mechanistic worldview regards the world as a huge machine, operating in accordance with precise and well-defined laws, routinely and ceaselessly, utterly unaware of, and quite indifferent to, why it is doing what it is doing, and irrespective of whether its functioning has any impact on anything whatever. Underlying the mechanistic view is the notion that, ultimately, the world can be reduced to bits of matter, which are endowed with intrinsic properties like mass and electric charge, which bump and bounce, instigated by inter-bit forces, rearranging themselves endlessly in countless patterns, causing all the changes and events in the phenomenal world.

The mechanistic framework for describing and manipulating the physical world is ancient. Archimedes, in old Greece, and others in other traditions, had toyed with devices and gadgets, and wondered about the whole world functioning in routine regularity, just like star movements in the skies. During the European Renaissance, investigators like Niccolò Tartaglia and Leonardo da Vinci gave mechanism a boost. And later, the dissection of the human body by Andreas Vesalius, the formulation of planetary laws by Johannes Kepler, and above all, the quantitative analyses of motion by Galileo Galilei, the Cartesian philosophical framework, and the successes of Newtonian physics made the mechanistic worldview a most appealing framework for science. Some of the major founders and propagators of the mechanistic paradigm, like Marin Mersenne and Robert Boyle, were men who were deeply committed to religion. The gradual erection of a mechanistic paradigm for the explanation of natural phenomena, which has become so much part of our current thinking about the physical world, was described as *The mechanization of the world picture* (Dijksterhuis 1950-61).

It was only a small step to extend the model to animals, and then to human beings. If creatures were automata for Descartes, to his compatriot Julien Offray de La Mettrie, man was no different. In his provocative book *L'homme machine* (1748), La Mettrie developed the idea that the human being is nothing more than a complex and intricate structure which functions in accordance with the laws of physics and chemistry. He wrote that "soul is but an empty word of which no one has any idea," that "the soul and the body fall asleep together," and that death was merely "the end of a farce" (1748, 128).

From the seventeenth century up until the middle of the nineteenth century, the mechanistic model generally implied the equivalent of cogs and wheels, a clockwork functioning of carefully crafted material subunits working everywhere as per immutable laws. However, with the discovery of the electromagnetic field and waves through immaterial space, it became more and more conceptually difficult to adhere to strictly materialistic mechanism (Kearney 1971).

Two points may be noted. Every machine is constructed by intelligent beings. Therefore, this enormously complicated and stable machine could well have been designed and created by a super-intelligence. This opens up possibilities with which those who deny things of that sort feel intellectually uncomfortable. They would rather believe that this cosmic machine arose all by itself. Secondly, practically every machine has a purpose. Unlike a painting or a poem, machines are meant to do or accomplish something very specific. It would thus seem reasonable to extrapolate that this grandiose machine called the universe probably has some ultimate purpose. This again is generally unacceptable to many no-nonsense scientists because it, too, has an undercurrent of traditional religion.

In any event, the view of the universe as a giant machine whose many parts can be analyzed in terms of their various components and guiding principles has been an immensely insightful framework yielding more harvests than most other models of the world. However, increasing knowledge of the microcosm calls for much refinement here.

On the organismic world model

Organisms require component parts to constitute their structure, but there have been profound differences of opinion as to whether an appropriate combination of materials (molecules/chemicals) is sufficient to create an organism without another organism. We can construct an automobile or a television set by using the same materials as in a prototype of the thing; we do not need another automobile or television set to make a new one. With living organisms, the situation is significantly different.

According to one scientific picture (the so-called chemical evolution hypothesis), the first living organisms arose from the combination of chemicals (molecules) under appropriate conditions. However, since then, organisms formed through reproduction and gradual evolution from other living organisms.

Another important feature of organisms is that their activities (functions) are always governed primarily by the need to survive and propagate. Their individual and collective goals are self/group-centered. Furthermore, there does not seem to be any long-range goal in the millions of species that have emerged and perished. Human beings are unique in that they are concerned about their individual long-range status (life insurance, after-death status, etc.). This is very unlike any human-made machine.

Some have tried to extend the organismic view to natural phenomena as well. Intrinsic to the organismic view is the idea that phenomena occur in order to accomplish something. From this perspective, the propagation of light is governed by a need to take the shortest path from one point to another, as most animals would. In physics, one speaks of the principles of least action, of least path, etc., which are successful in accounting for many phenomena. These have sometimes been interpreted as reflecting goal-oriented behavior in nature. In much of ancient science, there was the belief that the human body was in many ways a microcosm: a miniature version of the universe at large. It was seriously believed at one time that there are seven apertures in the face because there are seven (astrological) planets, seven days in the week, and because God had created it all and rested in the course of seven days. Thus, the world was regarded as functioning much like an organism. From religious perspectives, nature and the world itself behave like organisms with purposes. Much of post-seventeenth century science has regarded the world (including organisms) to be functioning like machines. The popularity of the anthropic principle notwithstanding, most physicists still cringe at the notion that the big bang occurred with us in mind. The idea seems to go counter to the Copernican discovery, which decisively removed us from the cosmic center. Generally, physicists are more inclined to describe the universe as mindless, non-goal-oriented routines, subservient to the fundamental interactions and to their macroscopic manifestations like molecular bonds. They do not like to look upon the universe as a well-planned process propelled by some sort of inherent intelligence.

The mechanistic model is fruitful in its explanatory potential and in the grand sweep of results it has achieved. The organismic model is tantalizing in certain contexts, and many find it far more beautiful and meaningful. Perhaps the universe, like humans, is an extraordinarily complex machine with a purpose that we cannot ever fathom.

Hypotheses in science: the *so-what* criterion

Corresponding to doctrines and dogmas in religion, science has its theories and hypotheses. Dogmas and doctrines define frameworks that make religions meaningful. Hypotheses and theories provide frameworks which make science successful.

The purpose of a theory is to explain an observed phenomenon. There are no hard and fast rules for the construction of a theory. Many factors may give rise to theories, such as: analogy (as in Hantaro Nagaoka's model for the atom resembling the planet Saturn), *flash of insight* (as in Kekulé's theory of the benzene ring), *solving a mathematical puzzle* (as when Max Planck tried to modify the formulas for black-body radiation and initiated quantum theory), *resolution of an experimental anomaly* (as in one account of Albert Einstein's theory of relativity in the context of negative results in efforts to detect the ether-drift). The genesis of a theory is a supremely creative event, constrained only by the condition that its conclusions must accord with observed or potentially observable facts.

Practically every scientific theory is based on one or more fundamental assumptions. These assumptions constitute the hypotheses underlying the theory. A hypothesis is thus the starting point of a theory in science. The term is derived from the Greek, *hypo* (under) and *tithenia* (to put), thus meaning "that which is put under."

A hypothesis is usually succinct in expression, concise as a formula, and quite general as a statement. In physics, it often has a mathematical component. By itself, a hypothesis is of no interest in science. It is only when one explores its consequences that its significance, if any, will become apparent. The exploration of the consequences of a hypothesis is what constitutes a theory in science.

A hypothesis in science refers to an aspect of the physical world that is not directly amenable to observation. Thus, the wave theory of light is based on the hypothesis that light consists of undulatory disturbances in space. This is not a property of light that can be directly perceived, but its consequences have been observed. The kinetic theory of gases rests on the hypothesis that a gas is made up of extremely small billiard-ball-like molecules that move and collide at random. It may be impossible to observe molecules directly, but the theory brings out several observable consequences of such a state of affairs, and these have been amply verified. That is why the theory is accepted.

The validity of a hypothesis depends on the verifiability of its consequences as brought out by the theory based on it. Consider a sheet of paper with several dots. Let the dots correspond to data from observations pertaining to a phenomenon. A hypothesis would be like proposing what sort of curve would fit into those dots. The theory would be the drawing of the curve as per this proposal. If the curve passes through all the dots, and furthermore, if new dots (observational data) are discovered that lie on the curve, the theory will be called good, satisfactory, successful, etc. However, there is no guarantee that the proposed hypothesis and the curve drawn are the only ones that could connect the dots (i.e., that they truly reflect the reality of the situation). That is why we say that observations can only falsify a theory, not verify it, for we can never be 100% sure that the line drawn is *the* right one.

Hypotheses are subject to the *so-what* criterion. What this means is that a hypothesis becomes interesting in science, if, and only if, it can provide verifiable answers to the question, "So what?" A hypothesis about some aspect of the physical world that has no verifiable consequence will be of no interest in science. In this matter, it is different from a religious dogma. As Ernst Mach said in *Erkenntnis und Irrtum [Knowledge and error]*, (1905), "the theoretician in science experiments with hypothesis" (Hiebert 1970, 188). It was in this context that Mach introduced the term *Gedankenexperimente:* Thought Experiments.

Nature and supernature

As we look around wherever we are, we see bodies, objects, things, people, animals. There are cars and houses, plants, trees, and birds, clouds in the sky and sun on high, and on and on…we can make an endless list. All these constitute the world around us, and they extend from the center of the earth and dust bits to the very ends of the universe and the most distant galaxies imaginable. All this is part of Nature.

Is there anything more than what we see and feel as tangible entities? Yes, there are: beauty, music, notions of truth and justice, love, hate and thought.…What are these intangible, insubstantial items that are no less real in our experience as sentient beings? They too are part of the natural world, one could argue, for none of these would have arisen without the materials that constitute the universe. Love and lunacy are surely not material things, but they could never arise in a world without neurons, and that means electrons and protons, sodium and calcium, and all the rest of it. Thus, ultimately, there is only Nature—so proclaim many in the scientific establishment.

But this is not all that obvious to many who wonder about and reflect on this mysterious universe where, by some magic mode, we enjoy and suffer for a brief span of eternity. I do not mean just the bone and flesh and blood that embody us, and the skin and skull that encase it all. I mean, rather, this individual entity that thinks and reasons, computes and creates in its own fantastic mode: symbols, equations, and all. The universe, with all those twinkling stars and grandiose galaxies, spouting endless energy and whirling and wandering, all in accordance with perfect mathematical laws....How did all this come to be, and with such balance and elegance, culminating in a mind that knows right from wrong and good from bad, or at least thinks it does?

It arose in the hearts and minds of many ancient visionaries that there is something beyond nature: a supernature, as it may be called in Latin-derived languages. The ancient Greeks coined the word *metaphysics* (beyond-nature), because they believed it to reside far beyond the stellar dome (Another derivation of the word is that this was because Aristotle's work on the subject was kept on the shelf after his works on physics.) Hindu thinkers described it as *alaukik* (not of the world). Their word for Nature assumed its existence, for Nature is *srishti* in Sanskrit, meaning "that which has been created." That supernatural something must be powerful enough to create the world and oversee it too. Being beyond nature, it must also be intangible, and not subject to any of the laws and rules that govern the world, and hence can cause occurrences (miracles) that do not conform to the laws of nature. Every traditional religion accepts some kind of supernatural entity. It seemed reasonable to many thinkers to imagine the supernatural entity to be in some ways very like us, and so this all-powerful, all-knowing creative principle came to be envisioned as God. Some Hindu seers pictured the world as the play of the Supernatural *(bhagvaan ki leelaa)*.

It is generally assumed in the religious context that God is a supernatural agent. Once this is granted, many religions also assumed the existence of other supernatural agents: ghosts, goblins, angels, djinns, asuras, apsaras, and more. Indeed, they were very much alive in centuries prior to the rise of modern science, and are still alive in the hearts and minds of people who have been shielded from the methods and results of modern science. From the scientific perspective, there are not persuasive reasons to believe that such beings actually exist, except in the virtual mythic realm. Some have concluded from this that sooner or later, as and when scientific education and knowledge permeate the vast majority of humankind, belief in the supernatural will also dwindle and disappear. Others rather doubt that this will ever happen.

Supposing that the supernatural does exist, how can we recognize it? One may believe, postulate, or recognize that there are modes of perception beyond the ordinary sensory channels. Through such extrasensory perception (ESP), and only through it, one can affirm the existence of supernature. From this perspective, religious visions and revelations are instances where supernature is recognized. Some believe there are supernatural processes in which humans can participate. One accepts all this on the basis of intense personal experience, or because one is convinced that the world is richer and more complex than has been painted by naturalistic science.

Then again, theologian Alvin Plantinga (*Warranted Christian belief*, 2000) has suggested that since there are a number of basic questions which cannot be answered on the basis of a purely naturalistic universe, it is perfectly legitimate and scientific to postulate supernaturalism. Unfortunately, this is not an idea that can be presented as a paper in *The Physical Review*, although it may be accepted by *The Christian Scholar's Review*. And yet, in this matter, Plantinga is closer to the theological goal than others who want to erect a theology without a supernatural element in it. At least one Nobel Prize winning neuroscientist, John Eccles, expressed a similar sentiment when he wrote:

> Since materialist solutions fail to account for our experienced uniqueness, we are constrained to attribute the uniqueness of the psyche or the soul to a supernatural spiritual creation. (1984, 237)

Nature and subnature

Science gives a very different answer to the question, "What gave rise to nature?" Whereas religion (in its inspiration) speaks of something above nature, science (in its quest) has found a good deal below nature in terms of which the features of the world can be explained in minute details.

Thus, instead of supernature, science unveils *subnature:* a world in the core of palpable matter. Physics has penetrated into the substratum of perceived reality and discovered a whole new realm of entities there, beyond the imagination of the most creative minds of the past. Through sophisticated labyrinths of theory and mathematics, aided by an array of experimental ingenuities, science has uncovered a microcosm that is abundant in minute bits which are not like sand grains, but are smeared out mini-clouds of electric charge and other properties. That unseen world is dense with a plethora of particles: hadrons, mesons, leptons, and field-bosons. Hadrons and mesons are complex, made up of quarks, while leptons are of two kinds: electrons and neutrinos. These ultimate bricks of the substantial world are subject to fundamental forces, transmitted via field-bosons called photons, gluons, W & Z, and gravitons.

From all these subnatural splendors arise the atoms of a hundred elements, where negatively charged electrons whirl around positively charged nuclei. There is a cosmic culinary complex, as it were, by which nature concocts an incredible richness from atomic ingredients. These are the molecules of compounds, forming salt and sugar, wine, water or whatever. All the substances we see and feel (and a multitude that we do not) are made up of molecules, mostly with two or more atoms.

A molecule barely stretches to a few millionths of a millimeter. The number of molecules in a teaspoon of water is of the order of a trillion trillion—more than there are stars in the entire universe. Some molecules are mammoth and magical: Deoxyribonucleic acids or DNA are stupendously large, nearly 120 million times as massive as a hydrogen atom. With variations here and there, they get intertwined in pairs, which spiral, often in a few thousand turns, forming a structure known as the double helix. These are among the most precious formations in the universe, for they encode every bit of information pertaining to the throb of life. The combined mass of all DNA molecules on earth is minuscule compared to that of all ocean water, but they are like the libraries of the world: in them lie all the knowledge and information relevant to life.

Thus, science has uncovered that the nature we see and feel, admire and enjoy is like a complex building, constructed from invisible foundations with specific properties. Some of the molecular configurations at the basis of life have blossomed into myriad patterns of beauty and complexity. In one of them is the miracle of the human brain from which emerge the associated wonders of mind and thought and creativity. But at the root of it all are only quarks and leptons and field particles. And yet, it is important to remember that this is not the last word of science. As all working physicists realize, we are nowhere near the solution to all the mysteries of the physical universe.

The religious vision of supernature has instigated great art, glorious music, epic poetry, colorful festivals, magnificent architecture, and more. Scientific understanding of subnature has led to some of the most fantastic wonders of technology from solid state electronics and lasers to computer chips and much more.

Whether the notion of supernature emerges from subnature or supernature creates and sustains subnature, is the crux of the science-religion debate.

Notion of laws

Laws, as we understand the term in everyday parlance, are constraints to which all the members of a group or nation are subject. Restrictions on individual actions and behavior have existed in all cultures and societies, if not always with rigidity, at least as custom. When stated and written down more formally, these become the *statutory laws* of the land. Breaking such a law could lead to prescribed penalties, should the culprit be caught. Laws, in the sense of injunctions and rules prescribing good and proscribing hurtful behavior constitute what may be called *moral laws*. Moral laws have also been there in all religious traditions and cultural settings. Punishment for dereliction in obeying a moral law is assured in religious systems, one way or another, one day or another.

The question that arises is: Are there laws to which the phenomenal world is subject? Yes, and these are the so-called *laws of nature.* What this implies is that nature, or the inanimate world, also functions in accordance with rules and regulations.

This idea has taken on specific interpretations in the world of modern science, but it is not altogether new. Laozi in China spoke of the Dao: the Way which is the principle of harmony in the world of nature (Li 2001). The Dao is present in mountain and meadow, in sun and star, in wind and water and everywhere. It is the source of peace and harmony and ought to be emulated by humans. A core idea in Daodejing is that things change, but the laws underlying the changes remain unchanged. If one understands these laws and regulates one's actions in conformity with them, one can turn everything to one's advantage.

Hindu vision spoke of *rita,* the regulating principle that keeps the universe going. Here, Man is also placed in the Cosmic Order, and he is expected to be in harmony with it. In Vedic mythopoeia:

> [Varuna] represents the inner reality of things, higher truth *(rita),* law and order in their transcendent aspects, beyond the understanding of man. His absolute power is felt during the night and in all that is mysterious, while man-made laws, represented by Mitra, rule the day. (Daniélou 1964, 118)

In the ancient Greek mythological tradition (Brown 1953), *chaos* was in the vast emptiness, pervaded by darkness (Erebus) and night (Nyx) These two primordial principles engendered upper air (Aether) and day (Hemera). The ancient Greeks contrasted Chaos with the Cosmos that is the world, disorder from the order that reigns. In the Buddhist tradition one speaks of *dhamma-dhâtu* which is the so-called Law-doctrine which is taken to be the reality behind being and non-being. It is said that this is all-inclusive, even as the earth's rotation happens day and night.

Sometimes such universal order implied a balance. The principle of balance in turn gave rise to the notion of justice and moral law also. The injunction to give "life for life, eye for eye, tooth for tooth, hand for hand, foot for foot, burning for burning, wound for wound, stripe for stripe" (Exodus 21:23-25), such as we read in the Bible, may be seen as a transformation into the ethical place of this universal balance.

Likewise, we read in the Qur'an: "We shall set up scales of justice for the Day of Judgment, so that not a soul will be dealt with unjustly in the least, and if there be (no more than) the weight of a mustard seed" (Sura 21:47). The Arabic word for scales is *mîzân,* which is also taken to be an eternal and essential feature of Heaven. It has been pointed out that "the allegorical interpretation of the Koranic balance" (Plessner 1973, 63-65) played a role in the development of Arab alchemy.

The ancient visions of laws that govern the world were general rather than particular, and holistic in their descriptions rather than specific in their explanations. They recognized an overarching framework under which the totality functioned, but did not give the details which made each part function.

Laws of nature: modern science

The notion of laws of nature, such as we use in today's science, began with the emergence of modern science in the seventeenth century. In its earlier phases, there was the notion that these laws were ordained by the Almighty Creator of the physical universe. This idea gave way when a more mechanistic interpretation of the world emerged, but it came back with the affirmation of natural theology.

The first law of nature to be discovered in the modern use of the term was Kepler's law of elliptic planetary orbits. Kepler's laws not only formulated universal aspects of a particular phenomenon (planetary motion), but, in the process, they changed our approach to the study of celestial bodies, transforming astrology into astronomy.

Careful and systematic observations suggest that all natural phenomena arise from specific patterns of behavior of various parts of the world. That is to say, the physical world at large, of which whatever we see and experience are only small parts, functions in methodical and uniform ways. Even when there seems to be apparent irregularity in behavior, one has been able to discover underlying regularities. Recognizable patterns in nature that have universal validity are referred to as laws of nature. Heinz Pagels refers to them picturesquely:

> What they [scientists] find is that the architecture of the universe is indeed built according to invisible universal rules which I call the cosmic code. (1984, 156)

When these relate to the physical world, one is also able in most instances to uncover a quantitative or mathematical dimension.

As with other fundamental concepts, there are no universally accepted definitions or even views among philosophers on what a scientific law is. Philosophers of science have given a variety of definitions for a law of nature. Whatever definition one adopts, at any given point of time it would be difficult, if not impossible, to assert whether a given statement, in spite of all its concordance with observed facts, is in fact a law or not. Take, for example, the relationship between the pressure and the volume of a given amount of gas at a specified temperature. This relationship, generally known as Boyle's law, was taken to be true until more careful observations at high pressures revealed discrepancies between the law as stated and results of observations. Later it was found that this is only an approximate description of how gasses behave, and was accordingly improved upon. Similarly, the so-called law of Dulong and Petit of specific heats of solids was accepted as true for many decades until precise experiments at very low temperatures proved it to be invalid there. Examples of this kind may be found in many contexts throughout the history of science. In many instances, one way out of the difficulty is to state right away that the experimentally observed (or deduced) law in question holds only within a well-specified range of observations. In the case of laws that are not derived directly from experiments, this would be impossible.

In view of this, one may adopt the following cautious definition: a law of nature is a suspicion of a certain *pattern* of behavior in a certain aspect of nature. It must be recognized that we are talking about a pattern of behavior and not behavior as such. What this means is that a law of nature is a general statement, not a particular one. The statement that Mars moves in an elliptical orbit is not a law. But the statement that all planetary bodies move in elliptical orbits around their central star is a law. The statement that copper expands on heating is not a law, but that all metals expand on heating is a law. As long as there is no reason to believe that a suspicion about a general pattern of behavior about some aspect of the physical world is mistaken, it is considered as a law of nature, i.e. as reflecting an intrinsic feature of the world. With this understanding, a law may be exploited for theoretical as well as for practical purposes.

This definition raises an important question: "Is scientific knowledge, much of which is condensed in the statements of the various laws of nature, merely a subjective matter, as seems to be suggested in this definition?" For the word suspicion implies what we think, rather than what is out there. Science seems to lose its great virtue of objectivity in this view. In answer to this, we simply note an important lesson from the history of science: No law of nature, as stated by humans, can be regarded as the final unalterable truth. As illustrated above, many laws, once categorized as being inexorably true, have been found to be either only approximations or even totally wrong in the long run. It is therefore wise to be cautious in our assertions. Also, a suspicion of a state of affairs does not necessarily deprive that state of all objective existence. It is quite possible that the suspicion is right.

Logical limitations of physical laws

One may speak of some general characteristics of all laws. Paul Davies summarized them as universality, absoluteness, eternality, and omnipotence (*The mind of God*, 1992). Though this is taken for granted in the scientific framework, one may always raise philosophical objections to the assumption that laws do have these features. We have only become aware of these physical laws we hold to be true through our experiences on this planet and, even more recently, in some other sections of our solar system. However, this is only an infinitesimal part of a grand universe that is known to be stretching to billions of light years. Moreover, the experiences on which we base our understanding involve a very short time span in the long history of the cosmos: a few thousand years compared to the billions of years during which the universe seems to have been existent. The question that then arises is: "Are we justified, on the basis of very limited spatio-temporal data, in asserting that these laws have operated all through time and are valid in every nook and corner of the universe?"

Before the rise of modern science, there used to be a clear cut distinction between the physics of the terrestrial plane and the physics of the heavens. It was believed that in the celestial sphere entirely different laws operated: there, for example, all motion took place only in perfectly circular orbits, no changes ever occurred, and matter never decayed. We no longer hold these views. Indeed, a necessary step in the development of modern science was the recognition of the universality of the laws of nature here and beyond. Although the Copernican Revolution is generally looked upon as removing humans from the coveted center of the universe, thus humiliating their ego, one could just as well regard it as resulting in the merger of our abode with the heavens.

On the other hand, one could also argue from a purely logical point of view that the older Aristotelian world view was more sound: for according to it, extrapolation of our limited experiences into the domain of the totally unknown and (apparently) unreachable was not justified. For example, suppose that we had known in precise quantitative terms that all falling bodies accelerate at a certain rate here on earth, but were unaware of the law of gravitation. Could we have concluded from this that bodies on Jupiter or on the moon would also fall down with the same acceleration? Yet, in a sense, this is precisely what we do in certain contexts of modern physics.

Thus, at least at the quantitative level, things do not behave in quite the same manner everywhere in the universe. We now know that the explanation for this lies in the fact that the rate of fall depends on the mass of the planetary body: the greater the mass, the faster the fall. But there is also another parameter which determines the rate of fall. And that is the gravitational constant G. We believe that this has the same value on the moon, on Jupiter, and everywhere in the universe. Indeed, the gravitational constant is one of many other such *universal constants* that play a fundamental role in determining the general features of the world we live in.

There are a number of physical laws whose quantitative aspects involve what are called fundamental constants: such as the velocity of light, the charge on the electron, etc. We do not know why these constants have the specific values they have. The situation could well be compared to pre-Newtonian physics when the acceleration due to gravity was known, but one did not understand why it had that particular value. If it turns out that these fundamental constants have the observed values because of some local properties of the galaxies, it is conceivable that we may have to restrict some of our ideas as to the universality of physical laws.

The second law of thermodynamics, for example, has no meaning in the context of a very small number of particles and at very small dimensions—a fact which was not as apparent when the law was first formulated in the middle of the nineteenth century. Likewise, for extremely short time intervals, the principle of energy conservation may be broken. More generally, we know that the laws governing the microcosm are in many ways different from those at the much larger scale. And if the universe is indeed oscillating (expanding and contracting, only to be re-formed and to re-expand) it could well be that in each phase of its existence it is governed by an entirely different set of laws.

There are at least two reasons why physicists believe in the spatio-temporal universality of the laws of nature. The first is that there is no evidence to the contrary. From spectroscopic analyses of the nature of matter in distant stars and observations of their motion there is little reason to suspect that they are governed by different laws. More importantly, the whole enterprise of a rational coherent science would be impossible without the assumption of uniformity in the universe at large.

We may still grant that science can never be absolutely certain about the eternal and universal validity of physical laws. However, two things must be borne in mind while considering these imperfections of science. First, that they arise from the human being's inherent limitations as an organism in the physical universe, and thus they are part of every other competing effort to interpret the world of experience. Secondly, humans have been able to accomplish much, both intellectually and practically, in spite of these constraints.

Law and ultimate explanation

Kepler's laws of planetary motion were arrived at by a generalization of the data of observation. Boyle's law of gases, which enunciated the relationship between the volume and pressure of a given quantity of gas at a certain temperature, was derived from the results of careful experimentation. So was Ohm's law, which states the relationship between the current through a wire and the potential difference between its end points. Laws of this kind, which follow directly from observational or experimental data, are called empirical laws. They are essentially insightful generalizations from a series of particular observations.

But this is not how Newton's law of gravitation was discovered. Newton did not collect experimental data to arrive at this law. His discovery resulted from his attempt to account for Kepler's laws. His goal was to explain, rather than to generalize. The law of gravitation is thus a concept-derived law. The notions of force and attraction are concepts that were introduced into a theory, in terms of which the law is formulated.

Empirical laws generalize. They do not tell us what makes nature behave in a particular manner. Concept-derived laws often explain, in terms of entities and principles that are not directly observed or perceived, what empirical laws state. Experimentalists discover empirical laws. Theoreticians hit upon concept-derived laws.

Empirical laws may be explained by concept driven laws, but how are we to explain concept-derived laws? Why, one may ask, do bodies attract each other? If told that this is the property of all masses, one may still ask why is it a property of all masses. Clearly, one can continue asking such questions at every step. Newton did not pretend to know the cause of gravity.

Often, a concept-driven law is taken to be the ultimate answer to such questions, for it gives the most fundamental reason for nature's behavior regarding a particular property. This is the reason why some have maintained that, on final analysis, science describes, rather than explains the physical world. And yet it is important to recognize that the description of natural phenomena through the scientific mode is different in essence from a description in the language of art or poetry. Scientific description endows us with the power of prediction of a course of events, and of manipulation of an aspect of nature, which other kinds of description do not and cannot.

In the theological context one speaks of God as the first cause, meaning that every cause has a cause, and ultimately the one cause of all causes in God. In science, the law becomes the first cause of a set of phenomena. The law itself cannot be accounted for, except by saying that nature behaves that way. This is what prompts many theologians to say that God is the cause of the laws governing the universe. Though this does not explain anything, it is as valid a perspective as the one which says that the laws just happened by themselves.

Reductionism

An important element in the scientific effort is the idea that much of what we observe is the result of the ultimate entities and processes that undergird the world. What this means is that by delving deep into the core of matter and the processes obtaining there, one can explain practically everything in the phenomenal world. This is essentially an elaboration of the Thales' paradigm that everything has sprung from water.

With the rise of modern science in the seventeenth century, physicists introduced certain key concepts like mass, velocity, acceleration, force, and momentum in terms of which they could describe and explain a whole range of natural phenomena. In the eighteenth century, this framework developed into the enormously powerful and fruitful field of classical mechanics. In the nineteenth century, it was extended to electromagnetic phenomena. By introducing the notions of electric charge and field, many other phenomena could also be explained. A significant result of this framework was the discovery, on paper, of electromagnetic waves: perhaps the most spectacular achievement in all of history.

For more than three centuries, science—especially physics—kept reaping astounding successes, and unwittingly developing not only an enriching worldview, but also a philosophy of nature and a framework for explanation. This is the reductionist paradigm in science. Reductionism states that by analyzing a system to its ultimate component parts we can unravel it at its deepest levels. In the process, one reduces any feature of the perceived world to its component elements with the hope of exposing all the secrets about the phenomenon. Reductionism holds that the world and its workings can *only* be understood in terms of the ultimate constituents and forces which give rise to it.

The physics paradigm, when applied to living organisms (including the human body), was very fruitful also. Some biologists thus reduced biology to a branch of physics, and this evolved into the thesis that every aspect of the experienced world can ultimately be reduced to its constituent parts.

There is no question but that the reductionist method has been enormously successful, not only in physics but in biology too. But then, it is legitimate to ask if it can be applied universally, not to say doctrinally, to all aspects of life and mind. And what about culture and poetry and all the other aspects of life that give meaning to existence. Can all these be reduced to fundamental particles and forces that have given rise to the physical world?

Some eminent biologists of the twentieth century, like Ernst Myre (*What evolution is,* 2001) rejected reductionism which traced all the characteristics of organisms to genes. He believed that evolutionary pressures act on the organism, and not on individual genes, in biological evolution. So have other scholars and commentators on science. Mary Midgley, the patron saint of anti-scientism and fearless polemicist, summarily called for a rejection of reductionism. In *The myths we live by* (2003), she calls for a scientific pluralism, pointing out that reality can be viewed through many maps and many windows. While this is an enlightened humanistic perspective, it fails to say that each map or window serves a different purpose. The scientific window has explanatory prowess as the artistic window has aesthetic virtues.

Among the many illustrious physicists who have turned against reductionism we may mention Freeman Dyson who feels that reductionism tried "to reduce the world of physical phenomena to a finite set of fundamental equations" (1995, 1-11). Another is Robert B. Laughlin. He says that the addiction of physics to reductionism reminds him

> ...of a hospital where no one ever dies but instead experiences "negative patient care outcome" or "failure to achieve wellness potential." In either case the confusion is ideological. The death of a patient is an unthinkable failure of the hospital's mission to preserve life. The subordination of understanding to principles of phase organization is a similarly unthinkable failure of one's mission to master the universe with mathematics. (2005, 113)

It is important to note in this context that scientific reductionism is not the reduction of every phenomenon to quarks and leptons, but rather to a framework of inexorable laws and principles, and these include probabilistically tractable events. Steven Weinberg clarified the matter this way:

> Grand reductionism...is the view that all of nature is the way it is...because of simple universal laws, to which all other scientific laws may in some way be reduced. Petty reductionism is the much less interesting doctrine that things behave the way they do because of the properties of their constituents. (2001, 111)

Theory of Everything (TOE)

Since ancient times, from theological monotheism to philosophical monism (whether Shankara in India or Spinoza in Europe), the view has been expressed that underneath the diversity and multiplicity we see all around there is a basic unitary principle from which everything has emerged. The idea of unity in diversity *(In varietate concordia)* is an ancient insight. Its cultural manifestation may be seen in a country such as India, where a variety of languages and religions blend into a single nation held together by laws and loyal bonds. The European Union has adopted this as a motto. A similar motto, *e pluribus unum* (from many, one) is etched on the currency in the United States.

In the modern context and beyond the metaphysics, physicists have been formulating a similar principle. *The Theory of Everything* (TOE) is a conceptual climax of the reductionist quest. The incentive for the modern attempts to formulate a theory of everything comes from Einstein's life-long quest to find a unified field theory of gravitation and electromagnetism. Unlike Maxwell's theory of electromagnetism, Einstein's effort was based on no empirical evidence whatever. It was perhaps the first instance in the history of science when a physicist attempted to construct a theory with nothing really to explain. It was based on the aesthetic prejudice that there must be a single unifying principle from which everything would follow. Einstein wrote in a letter to a school friend, Marcel Grossman, in 1901:

> It is a wonderful feeling to recognize the unifying features
> of a complex of phenomena which present themselves as
> quite unconnected to the direct experience of the senses.
> (Pais 1982, 57)

Its goal is to reduce the entire phenomenal world to a single all-embracing principle of which the range and variety of the entire universe are but inevitable consequences. Most physicists recognize, like Paul Davies, that "the search for such a TOE is to a certain extent an act of faith, motivated by the deep belief that nature ought to be simple" (Davies and Brown 1988, 6). Attempts at formulating a TOE are based on considerably sophisticated mathematics (of group theory, in particular). General comments on it by non-experts and in the media are usually based on popular non-technical versions of the theory. It is seldom recognized that the goal of TOE is lofty and its framework is one of the more spectacular ideals which the human mind is striving to achieve.

Terms like M-theory, string theory, and loop-gravity are examples of struggles to achieve a TOE. Unfortunately, its deeper aesthetic and conceptual triumph—if and when it does occur—will be (like the proof of Fermat's Last Theorem) within reach of only a handful of people who have entered the sanctum sanctorum of theoretical high energy physics. It must be emphasized that, as Murray Gell-Mann pointed out:

> [TOE] is a misleading characterization unless "everything" is taken to mean only the description of elementary particles and their interactions. The theory cannot, by itself, tell us all that is knowable about the universe and the matter it contains. (1994, 129)

It is important to emphasize this, because much of the visceral antipathy to reductionism on the part of philosophers comes from the impression that reductionist physics tries to reduce every aspect of human experience, including love and hate, war and peace, to quarks and leptons and fundamental force fields. Thus, for example, Phillip E. Johnson, lawyer-critic of Darwin (*Reason in the balance,* 1995) noted that fundamental physics and cosmology tended to make their devotees religious, except that, in their religion, only a creation story that can, in principle, be subject to scientific analysis would be acceptable.

Reductionism and holism: two sides of the perception of reality

While it is easy to break down a system into its component parts, it is difficult to see how those parts add up to what one observes. Two atoms of hydrogen and one of oxygen are very different in properties from the aggregate of water molecules resulting from many of them proportionately combined. The bonds and structures of molecules give rise to properties not found in their component atoms. Reductionism reveals what *are* underneath everything, much more than how they converge into something very different. It reveals the *being* part of the world, but not always the *becoming* aspect.

Holism is the view that, by considering the whole picture, one gets a more complete view than by analyzing something into its component parts. This is because a system consisting of several parts has properties which are not present in its components. Aristotle wrote, as it is commonly rephrased, that "the whole is more than the sum of its parts" (350 BCE, 8.6, 1045a: 8-10). This was perhaps the earliest expression of emergentism. There is hardly a system without holistic properties. What we experience is often the holistic aspect of a system.

This is why the recent trend has been to criticize reductionism as inadequate, not to say pretentious. While reductionism may seem reasonable at one level of the physical world, its application to the biological and the human world is far less effective. Some philosophers, theologians, and even scientists think that often people embrace reductionism with the same zeal as other systems embrace scriptural infallibility. The critics do not realize, however, that reductionism has an appeal for only one reason: it has given rise to a rich harvest of significant results. Most molecular biologists and neuroscientists who write technical papers in peer-reviewed journals, and contribute to new breakthroughs in their fields still work from this perspective. If and when a non-reductionist approach turns out to be useful in providing explanations of observed phenomena, science will surely adopt it.

The term holism has been used with a variety of connotations. According to one interpretation, articulated by Nancey Murphy:

> Holism rejects the distinction between analytic and synthetic truths because meanings can always be adjusted to fit beliefs to experience in preference to rejection of the

beliefs.... Furthermore, it does away with the long-lived distinction between fact and value. (1990, 8)

But we may consider the concept from other perspectives. The first is *experiential holism*: an all-embracing view of a system. The grand view of a forest as a whole is different from the view of single trees. This kind of holism is interesting and meaningful. It plays a part in art, literature, and philosophy. But since it rarely explains anything, we do not find it in science. Walt Whitman's poem, "When I Heard the Learned Astronomer," beautifully contrasts the reductionist and the experiential holistic modes:

> When I heard the learn'd astronomer;
> When the proofs, the figures, were ranged in columns
>   before me;
> When I was shown the charts and the diagrams, to add,
>   divide, and measure them;
> How soon, unaccountable, I became tired and sick;
> Till rising and gliding out, I wander'd off by myself,
> In the mystical moist night-air, and from time to time,
> Look'd up in perfect silence at the stars.
> (1855/1892, 214)

Experiential holism is essentially what mystics have reported, and described as unitary experience.

The second type of holism may be called *biological holism*. An intrinsic feature of biological systems is that they are interconnected. No organism can live by itself, and no species is completely independent of every other. *Biological holism* arises from the fact that not only is the evolution of every creature affected by its environment, but its very survival depends on it. This idea was articulated by Jan Christiaan Smuts when he wrote:

> At the start the fact of the structure is all-important in wholes, but as we ascend the scale of wholes, we see structure becoming secondary to function, we see function becoming the dominant feature of the whole, we

see it as a correlation of all the activities of the structure and affecting new syntheses which are more and more of a creative character.

There is a creative activity, progress and development of wholes, and the successive phases of this creative Evolution are marked by the development of ever more complex and significant wholes. (1926, 105)

One version of biological holism is the Gaia hypothesis propounded by James Lovelock (*The ages of Gaia: A biography of our living Earth*, 1979; Lynn Margulis, *Symbiotic planet: A new look at evolution*, 1998). Though the hypothesis has been severely criticized by some eminent biologists, the essence of the hypothesis is that, in some ways, the earth with its biosphere constitutes, or behaves very much like, a whole living organism that maintains itself through several mutually balancing and feedback processes.

The third kind of holism refers to the fact that when A and B are combined, the resulting C has more properties than what each of the components bring, that it may have properties which neither of them had when they were separate. We may call this non-linear holism. One of the tasks of science is to account for this. Current efforts to explain this are through the notion of emergence. *Non-linear holism* may also be described as emergentism.

When we focus on the reductionist and separateness aspect of the phenomenal world, we get one vision of reality. When we focus on its holistic feature, we experience another, sometimes very different, vision. For instance, considering states or provinces in a country is a reductionist mode, while taking a nation as a whole is the holistic mode. Each is relevant and important in its own context.

The more we focus on one, the more the other becomes blurred. This complementarity, in the Bohr sense, between reductionism and holism is illustrated in the microcosm where the particle aspect of an entity like the electron appears as a particle in its reductionist aspect and as a wave in its holistic mode. Thus reductionism and holism are two modes of apprehending reality. Each meaningful and satisfying in its own way, but neither is a complete description of the world. From this perspective reductionism and holism are somewhat like the microscope and the telescope, two powerful instruments to explore the world: one revealing the smallest constituents of what makes up the world, while the other is sweeping the cosmic grandeur and makes us aware of the unity behind the diversity.

It is fair to say that, if science makes us understand the world through its methods of analysis, religion should make us see the human experience as a grand, rich, and unifying tapestry. When science focuses uniquely on the reductionist mode it can miss the grander vision of reality. When religion is without a grand holistic vision that sees the commonalty among the peoples of the world, it is reduced to a narrowness that is petty and can be dangerous.

To assert either that reductionism alone leads to understanding, or that it is mistaken in its efforts to understand, would be a slanted view. Likewise, it would be a distortion to claim either that holism is what brings us true awareness or that it is merely old-fashioned metaphysical poetry.

Chapter 5
Belief Systems and God

Theology

Religion has its experiential aspects and its intellectual aspects too. The latter is reflected in a time-honored discipline which approaches religion in ways similar to the scientific enterprise. Known as theology (etymologically, a systematic study of God), its goal is to analyze, understand, and formulate in a reasoned framework the doctrines and worldviews of a religion.

Theology is a rational enterprise: it is based on logic and reason, exactly as science is. Pursued by keen thinkers in practically all classical religious systems, it takes into account the facts of experience vouched by religious people, and gives cogent interpretations to the statements and texts from religiously recognized sources. As a discipline, theology is quite old. In Greece and Rome there were theologians. There have been theologians in the Judaic and Islamic traditions also. Shankara and Ramanuja were among the foremost theologians in the Hindu tradition, as Abelard and Thomas Aquinas were in the classical Christian world.

Until the twentieth century, theologians generally considered their discipline as separate from science, essentially different in scope and concern, but no less systematic and analytical in its approach. Theology was concerned with cosmogenesis, ethical behavior, goal and ultimate salvation, and other questions of profound significance to the human condition. In the words of Paul Tillich:

> Theology formulates the questions implied in human
> existence, and theology formulates the answers implied in
> divine self-manifestation under the guidance of the
> questions implied in human existence. This is a circle
> which drives man to a point where question and answer
> are not separated. (1951, 1:61)

During the twentieth century, as science began to investigate
issues relating to the origin of the universe, the genetic roots of human
tendencies, the neurophysiological origins of human behavior, the
psychological dimensions of unethical desires, and the like,
theologians could not remain indifferent to advances in the sciences.
Many of them became interested in physics, astronomy, biology and
psychology, and weaved the results of science into their discussions.
From these emerged the view that theology must be integrated with
scientific knowledge. John F. Haught put it this way:

> Theology cannot rely too heavily on science, but it must
> pay attention to what is going on in the world of
> scientists. It must seek to express its ideas in terms that
> take the best of science into account lest it become
> intellectually irrelevant. (1995, 18)

In this same context, Arthur Peacocke listed the following five
criteria

> ... for deciding on a best explanation: comprehensiveness,
> fruitfulness, general cogency and plausibility, internal
> coherence and consistency, and simplicity or elegance.
> They would be as valuable for science as for
> theology .... The web of beliefs and knowledge, including
> those about God and God's relation to humanity, will be
> susceptible to revision and even replacement as new
> experiences, new experiments, and new knowledge,
> impinge upon its outer edges. (2002, 28)

Such views have led to another approach to theology: to consider it as another branch of science. A good example of this approach may be seen in Kevin Sharpe's book, *The science of God: Truth in the age of science* (2006). Sharpe goes even further. He argues that theology should be in the pursuit of new insights rather than wedded to tradition. Its concern should be with humanity at large rather than affiliation to denominational churches. Spirituality should be a major concern of theology. There is little doubt that this book will create a stir in the theological community while enriching the landscape of science-religion dialogues. Sharpe also suggests that theology should be set in a framework similar to that of science. Just as biology, the science of life, is the systematic, methodological study of life; geology is that of the earth, dendrology is of trees, and so on, so too theology should be the science of God, a systematic, methodological study of God. Though Sharpe does not put it in these terms, this in effect is the goal of his book.

In this context, we may note that there are two dimensions in the human experience of reality: the external and the internal. One the one hand, there are aspects of the world that we consider, study and speculate upon, whose impact on us as beings with feelings, emotions and culture is minimal or nothing. On the other hand, there are aspects whose consideration, study and speculation have significant impact on our feelings, emotions and cultural identities. The scientific enterprise deals, by and large, with matters of the first kind, whereas theology is concerned with matters of the second kind.

We may look upon theology, then, as a sophisticated, rational enterprise that analyzes issues related to those aspects of human existence that touch us profoundly as beings situated in a cultural/religious framework with a history and spiritual sources. To tie it to our interpretation of the physical world is not necessary, and may not always be effective.

Every theology is based on some doctrines. In fact, a set of doctrines is sometimes referred to as a theology. Doctrines are statements that one is expected to accept and believe in, without any or sufficient proof. Often there are advantages to accepting doctrines.

In the religious context, the acceptance of doctrines permits membership in a group, and it may lead to positive feelings and certain types of enhanced experiences as a human being.

Thus, the notion of Trinity is a doctrine in one version of Christianity. The Law of Karma is a doctrine in Hinduism; and *ahimsa* (non-violence) is a Jaina doctrine.

Theologians analyze the doctrines of their faith, and provide persuasive arguments for their validity in a rational framework. Theological explanations and argumentations are generally related to the fundamental dogmas of the religion to which the members of the faith community must avow explicit or implicit assent. This calls for acceptance of scriptural, revelatory, priestly, or some authority.

In the scientific world, too, there are some basic doctrines, though they are seldom acknowledged as such. For one thing, the statement that every feature of the experienced world is intelligible to the human mind and can be adequately explained by the exercise of reason and through the scientific methodology is an indispensable doctrine on which the scientific community works. The statements that every occurrence has a cause, or that, of a set of possible explanations for a phenomenon, the simplest is the correct one, are also universally accepted and implicit scientific doctrines.

The most compelling argument for accepting some of the doctrines of science is that, on their basis, science has been able to obtain an impressive body and range of significant and consistent results pertaining to perceived reality.

The search for theoretical unity, in the absence of any experimental indication to the effect, may be described as scientific theology, in that it is based on a doctrine for which there is no observational evidence, only an aesthetic imperative. To say that there is a theological dimension to science is not to belittle it, but to recognize that, like religion, this enormously powerful enterprise rests on some unproven, but immensely rewarding fundamental assumptions. We do not know where these assumptions come from, but we do know that they have in many ways enriched and enhanced the human experience.

Dogmas and doctrines

Meanings of words change with time. In the Greek world of the distant past, the word dogma meant whatever appeared to be good or true. In the political context, it also referred to the collective decision of an assembly whose goal was the welfare of the people. In another epoch in the ancient Greek world, dogmatism had little to do with religion. Edward Grant points out:

> The Dogmatist school emphasized reason but also regarded direct observation of the internal organs as vital to a proper understanding of the ailments that afflict the human body. The Dogmatists became the first physicians in history to dissect and even vivisect the human body. (2004, 65)

The meaning has changed drastically since then. With the rise of Christianity, the meaning changed. Generally speaking, dogma refers to a basic belief of a religious system that is propounded by a religious authority: institutional or scriptural. Dogma is a technical concept in theology with variations in its meaning. The connotation in a religious context is a basic belief in an established religious system, which is required of those who claim membership in the fold. A dogma is described in the Catholic context as:

> A truth appertaining to faith or morals, revealed by God, transmitted from the Apostles in the Scriptures or by tradition, and proposed by the Church for the acceptance of the faithful. It might be described briefly as a revealed truth *defined* by the Church...(Herbermann 1913, 89)

Darwell Stone (*Outlines of Christian dogma*, 1903) stated that the existence of God, the reality of revelation, the trustworthiness of the Bible, and the divine guidance of the Church would be examples of Catholic dogmata.

It is also a dogma of Christianity that Christ, the Savior, was the Son of God; of Islam, that Mohammed was the last messenger sent by Allah. Traditional Hinduism, though it has several beliefs, such as that the Vedas have non-human authorship, has no explicit dogma with which all adherents are obliged to concur. The recitation of the Shema, which begins with a declaration of monotheism, is said to be a dogma of Judaism. It is no longer a dogma of Judaism that the Jews are a chosen people. A dogma of Communism is that the root causes of all changes in society are economic, etc. In each instance, the entire conceptual framework rests on the respective dogma. In societies where traditional religious authorities hold the power base, unpleasant consequences would follow if one refused to accept the dogmas of the state-proclaimed authorities. Among the healthy things that have happened where modernity has taken hold is that ardent enforcers of dogmas who inflict harsh penalties on dogma-dissenters do not have control.

In the nineteenth century, one could proudly proclaim the dogmas of one's faith. Thus, John Henry Newman frankly wrote: "From the age of fifteen, dogma has been the fundamental principle of my religion" (1866, 61). Today, few people define their religion in terms of its dogmas. Politicians are afraid to say in public that they subscribe to specific religions: if they do, the consequences are not always pleasant. Perhaps this is because more and more people who do not subscribe to organized religions speak out openly, without fear of persecution, and the term *dogma* has acquired a pejorative tinge, especially its adjectival form *dogmatic,* which usually connotes mindless obstinacy in the face of evidence to the contrary, and even intolerance sometimes. This negative characterization also comes from the post-Enlightenment framework in which a proposition is not accepted solely on the basis of its source. However, dogmas are the creedal framework for an organization; they are like the rules of a game. If one refuses to subscribe to the rules, one should refrain from the game, not complain about it.

There is no religion without basic doctrines. But it should be remembered that, in a phrase Benjamin Disraeli used in an 1861 speech to the House of Commons, a religion is not just "a depository of doctrines" (Corfield 1995, 14-21). Dogmas and doctrines constitute the backbones of established religions: without them, religions would collapse. But their interpretations could change with time. Inter-religious and inter-sectarian conflicts are often struggles between competing doctrines and dogmas. Of all the doctrines that need revision in our own times as a result of changes that have occurred in recent history, perhaps the ones that claim religious truths to be enshrined only in their own sacred works, and the ones that prompt people to disrespect and desecrate others need urgent reformulation. This is difficult to accomplish, given the deep conviction that one has been taught to feel about the verities of one's own religion. But if we wish to live in a more harmonious world, it is not clear that we have an alternative.

Theism

The idea or the conviction that there is a supernatural, all-encompassing, all powerful principle constitutes theism. The term is derived from the Greek word for God: *theos*. Theism pictures God as one with infinite good and noble qualities. Belief in God or the doctrine of the existence of God is part of most religions. However, the vision and nature of God, as propounded by various religious systems, is not the same.

Not all traditional religions are theistic. In the Jaina framework (Aidan Rankin, *The Jain path: Ancient wisdom for the West*, 2006.), for example, the material world has always been there, and will always be there. In other words, the conservation of matter principle is literally time-invariant. This means there was no beginning, no origin, hence no creator. It is also argued that God cannot be perceived, and therefore, from an operational point of view, there is no God, as far as we are concerned. However, Jainism holds that every soul is potentially omniscient, making it divine. Thus, in the Jaina worldview, divinity is everywhere, without there being a God.

Long before the logical positivists of the twentieth century, Gautama Buddha, who taught compassion and modes of freeing oneself from pain, attached little weight to metaphysics of any kind. In the famous parable, entitled "Arrow Smeared With Poison," we read:

It is as if a man had been wounded by an arrow thickly smeared with poison, and his friends and kinsmen were to get a surgeon to heal him, and he were to say, I will not have this arrow pulled out until I know by what man I was wounded, whether he is of the warrior caste, or a brahmin, or of the agricultural, or the lowest caste. Or if he were to say, I will not have this arrow pulled out until I know of what name or family the man is—or whether he is tall, or short, or of middle height…Before knowing all this, that man would die. Similarly, it is not on the view that the world is eternal, that it is finite, that body and soul are distinct, or that the Buddha exists after death that a religious life depends… (Majjhima-nikaya 1:426ff, see also Bodhi 1995, 231-32)

As to whether there is God or soul or reward in heaven, we are told that he considered such questions "the jungle, the desert, the puppet-show, the writhing, the entanglement, of speculation" (Rhys Davids 1899, 188). Thus, at the very least, Buddhism avoids the issue of God.

In its ethical humanist framework, Confucianism (Yao 2000) finds no need for a metaphysical God either. Men are classified as superior and inferior, as moral and immoral. The question of an absolute or almighty God does not arise.

With its pluralism in worship and doctrine, Hinduism is perhaps the only religion that permits both atheists and theists in its fold. There are powerful branches of Hinduism that proclaim the existence of a personal God with a variety of forms and names and sacred history, while other schools of Hindu thought, called the *nâstikas,* openly declare there is no God, not even the abstract divinity of yet other schools.

Theism is more than belief in a Creator. It is belief in a Creator-God who is very much interested in the well-being of his Creation, and most of all, in the Creator's concern for human beings. One may reasonably maintain that a Creator was responsible for the genesis of a world with law and order, and even of humanity, and leave it at that. This view of a Creator-God who, somewhat like a clockmaker, manufactured the machine and let it tick away indefinitely, came to be known as deism (derived from the Latin *deus* rather than the Greek *theos*). In the Christian world, it emerged in the sixteenth century and gained attention in later centuries in various versions. Though deism does not sound as heretical as atheism, it had its severe critics, opponents and persecutors in Christendom during many years. In the Hindu world, deism would be equivalent to a belief only in Brahmà, the Creative Principle, who simply creates the world and lets it play itself out, while theism would also include Vishnu, the Sustaining Principle, who is deeply interested in human welfare. In other words, both kinds of God are part of Hinduism. The non-God view (atheism), the Loving-God view (theism), and the Indifferent-God view (deism) may all be found in different phases and frameworks of traditional religions.

In traditional cultures, the quest for understanding the world was often associated with the conviction that the world was created, not just formed accidentally. It is also believed that the Creator of the world was supremely intelligent and powerful. Thus the existence of God was taken for granted in the scientific framework of many peoples in former centuries.

When one reflects on the human condition, on our folly and pettiness, on the hurt that we inflict on one another, and what nature inflicts on us all, it is difficult to believe that an Almighty with love and compassion would permit such things. This is one reason why, since ancient times, many philosophical thinkers have held the atheistic position more commonly than practicing scientists. Thus Socrates the philosopher was an atheist, but not Aristotle or Archimedes, the scientists. Reflective Lucretius was an atheist, but not Marcus Terentius Varro, the precursor of microbiology. The free thinker Charvaka of India was a die-hard atheist, but not the astronomer Aryabhata, and so on. Likewise, in the nineteenth century, the philosophical writers Herbert Spencer and Thomas Huxley were doubters, but not the physicists Michael Faraday and James Clark

Maxwell. When one is involved in the discovery and discernment of the marvelous laws and symmetries that shape the phenomenal world, one cannot but be struck by the silent and unfathomable intelligence that seems to pervade the Cosmos.

The No-God Thesis

There have been countless individuals in all cultures and religious frameworks who have not shared the belief in the God that their fellow-religionists are so sure about. But not all who deny belief in God are godless in the same way. Some, at a later age, reject the religion into which they were initiated when they were young. So they withdraw from their church or synagogue, and lead a perfectly happy life without the religious belief that gives meaning to so many of their former co-religionists. Sometimes, they become atheists in that they explicitly and openly announce their rejection, not just of their religion, but of belief in any God whatever. Upon thinking over the question of God's existence, they sometimes become genuinely angry.

This may happen because of at least two factors. First, they feel that it does not take much to recognize that contradictions and inconsistencies arise when the specific God picture of any religion is subjected to critical analysis. In the vast majority of instances it is not belief in God in the abstract that is common to all who deny religion, but belief in the particular type of God to which one has been conditioned since early childhood. They see some incongruity between the picture of a compassionate and merciful God on the one hand, and all the injustice and suffering one sees in the world. Then again, they reflect on all the horrors that have occurred in human history in the name of God and religion.

Recognizing this, these atheists speak out against God, religion, and believers. Sometimes they write books to show that there is really no God. At one time, it was difficult to find a publisher for such books. Today, if one can write well expounding the atheistic position, preferably with a provocative title, one can get handsome royalties.

Going even beyond atheism there is anti-theism, being virulently against belief in God. In Hindu and Norse mythologies there are characters who hate God. They have sometimes been described as misotheists.

In the last decades of the twentieth century a new form of atheism developed. Imitating the evangelists, it is a movement to spread the good news of atheism. Dan Barker who coined the word, said:

> Freethought is worth sharing with the world. If the conditions are right, it is possible for a freethinker to successfully evangelize a believer. (1993)

However, no matter how well intentioned, the Evangelical zeal carries with it the risk of overselling the merchandise even if it means sacrificing the truth. David Sloan Wilson, an eminent biologist and evolutionist, and a clear-thinking atheist himself, does not have high regard for the new atheists. He writes in his blog:

> The authors associated with the new atheism movement begin with a deep antipathy toward religion and select their examples from the text of science like so many parables from the Bible. Not only do they ignore, misrepresent, and selectively report the facts of religion, but their practical recommendations for solving the problems associated with religion are ineffective, silly, and worse. (2008)

Effectiveness of both theism and atheism

What debaters in ivory towers often fail to realize is that when it comes to achieving well-defined goal, both theism and atheism can work, depending on how able a leader is.

First consider Martin Luther King Jr., a Baptist minister who became an enormously successful civil rights leader. His oratory and commitment served the cause of freeing African Americans from the racial discrimination and marginalization that were their plight. King, one of the founders of the Southern Christian Leadership Conference, was a deeply religious person who believed man to be "a free being in the image of God" (1959, 16). His theism not only enriched him in his personal life, it inspired him to lead a great historical movement, which had the most dramatic impact on his nation. Herein, we see the power of deep religious belief.

At the other end of the world, in India, there was E. V. Ramasami Naicker (Gopalakrishnan 1991). He was a powerful orator in his native Tamil language. But, unlike King, Naicker was not only an avowed atheist, but virulently anti-religious. He rejected the religious narratives of his own religion (Hinduism) as superstitions and lies which had been fabricated to exploit the weak and the powerless. He pitied those who believed in religion. Long before Richard Dawkins, this anti-Brahmin leader declared: "He who created god was a fool; he who spreads his name is a scoundrel, and he who worships him is a barbarian" (Sorenson 2005). He tore to pieces the sacred works of his religion. Like King, he too was outraged by the treatment that the so-called lower castes were getting at the hands of the Brahmins in his native Tamil-Nadu. He founded an organization for the advancement of the Dravidian people. By his commitment to his people he earned the title of *Periyar:* The Great One. He achieved the goal of emancipating his people with his intensely atheistic stance, though his followers continue to cling on to their traditional worship modes.

While it is interesting that two great leaders, one a theist and the other an atheist, achieved the same result, there has been one important difference: Periyar's message of rationalism and anti-religion has had little impact on the masses. Members of the caste for whose social and political liberation he fought and won are no more scientifically enlightened today than in his heyday. More seriously, his work has resulted in more hatred than understanding between Brahmins and non-Brahmins in the Tamil country. On the other hand, Martin Luther King's legacy has been one of love and non-violence, which has brought the blacks and the whites in America closer, and engendered greater understanding and mutual respect.

Perhaps these stories do not establish the superiority of theism over atheism, but rather that those who preach the more refined aspects of human behavior do more for society and civilization than those who strive to accomplish their goals through hate and hurt.

Both the Marxist-Leninist atheistic ideology and the fanatically theistic Jihad movement in certain sectors of the Islamic world show how pernicious either position can become.

Problem of evil

The word *evil* has several meanings. It is invariably associated with something unpleasant, unwelcome, and unfortunate. Pain and suffering, disease and death, creatures killing other creatures for survival: all this is evil. The destructive forces of nature—earthquakes, hurricanes and volcanic eruptions—can sometimes be seen as evil. There are also moral evils, such as lying and lust, rampage and rape, as well as evils associated with the human condition, such as poverty, hunger, and paralysis. There is no end to the evils we see in the world around us.

To those who regard our planet and life as having arisen from sheer chance, there is no such thing as the problem of evil. However, if one accepts a God Who is merciful, compassionate, and loving, one may wonder why He created a world where such states come into play. If that God is almighty, it is legitimate to ask why the power is not used for eliminating evil.

This question has troubled reflective thinkers from the most ancient times. The keen thinkers of the ancient world came up with a variety of defenses for God, the merciful and the omnipotent. In the Hindu world, whether you belonged to the monist or the dualist school, there were philosophers who explained that God had nothing to do with human suffering: it is all our *karma* (consequential deeds). The French philosopher Pierre Bayle (1695) wondered about God's omnipotence and goodness in such contexts, and suggested that this showed the limitations of the human mind in trying to understand God. Gottfried Leibniz retorted with *Essays on theodicy: On the goodness of God, human liberty and the origin of evil* (1710), in which he introduced the term *theodicy* (the justification of God) to express the problem of evil. He argued that, in spite of all the evil, this is still the best of all possible worlds (similar to what Churchill said about democracy).

On November 1, 1755, All Saints Day, a terrible earthquake rocked Lisbon in Portugal, killing tens of thousands of people. Many thinkers in Europe were shocked by the event. The Catholic people interpreted it as an expression of God's anger at human misbehavior, which included allowing Protestants to live among them. On the other hand, many Protestants thought the earthquake was because Portugal had remained Catholic (Braun and Radner 2005). It would be wrong to think that these were irrationalities of a darker age. Similar sentiments have been expressed in the twenty-first century when there was an earthquake in India, a tsunami in Southeast Asia and the hurricane in New Orleans.

The Portuguese earthquake prompted Voltaire to write a *Poème sur le désastre de Lisbonne* [*Poem on the Lisbon Disaster*], in which he asked rhetorically:

> Will ye reply: "You do but illustrate
> The Iron laws that chain the will of God"?
> Say ye, o'er that yet quivering mass of flesh:
> "God is avenged: the wage of sin is death"?
> What crime, what sin, had those young hearts conceived
> That lie, bleeding and torn, on mother's breast?
> Did fallen Lisbon deeper drink of vice
> Than London, Paris, or sunlit Madrid?
> (1756, lines 15-23, 255-258)

There have been a hundred earthquakes and disasters before and since, and thousands of others have wondered thus. Many have rejected God precisely because we find so much evil, cruelty and injustice in the world.

Some theologians have tried to explain the situation as God's wish to test our faith. Others have tried to argue that, in many contexts, what we perceive as evil may be the alternative to something even worse of which we may be unaware. One may still wonder how a merciful God, even to test us, could inflict pain on helpless children and innocent people.

We may define evil as that which causes one any kind of pain: physical, psychological, or emotional. The experience of such pain, as Phil Hefner once remarked, is a jolting intrusion into one's sense of meaning in life. Each of us experiences physical pain only when it comes to our particular body. But we can—and do—experience psychological and emotional pain when we see others suffer. This may be called hetero-evil. Our sense of hetero-evil arises from cultural upbringing, which is of two kinds: universal and local. By universal, I mean that which is generally applicable to all normal human beings. Thus, all normal human beings will cringe at the sight of a blind infant in agony when mangled by a beast. This would be an example of hetero-evil of the universal kind. The reckoning of hetero-evil must have something to do with human cultural/biological evolution.

On the other hand, the sight of a dying cow would be an evil for a Hindu, and that of a living Hitler might seem an evil for someone of some other faith. These are instances of evil of a local kind. The recognition of evil of the local kind may be traced to the historical religions that have emerged in various regions of the world, and the ideological/memetic cloning that is a characteristic of all belief-systems.

Perhaps it is not appropriate to associate the existence of evil to the God of any religion. Indeed, if one views God as that principle in human existence which awakens us to our best potential, then the religious dimension should compel us not to be indifferent to any hetero-evil, and to exert a little to alleviate the evil that we see around us, sometimes even at a cost to ourselves. In the context of hetero-evil, it is more important to act than to try to explain.

When there was a terrible earthquake in Gujarat on January 26, 2000 (India's Republic Day), I wrote the following poem:

When Disasters Strike

When lightning strikes a praying crowd
And the pious burn and die;
When earthquakes bury decent folk
And orphaned children cry;

When sick and old are abandoned too
And people lose their mind:
Try not for these and disasters such
Answers clear to find.

There are times to ask if God is just
A thought or indeed a fact.
There are times at which we need to go
And begin to act.

With loss and pain and intense grief
We don't have much to gain
From arguments on heaven and hell.
They'll all be just in vain.

Let's search and see what we can do
For those who are in need,
How we can console and heal,
How we can clothe and feed.

It does not matter if we do not know
Why there's pain around.
What we need are helping hands,
Not learned views and sound.
(Raman 2002)

The problem of evil arises perhaps because it ignores its own expectation. How can mercy be shown or good done if there is no suffering and only good to begin with? The problem of evil arises when we picture God as a friendly figure, out to do only good and show mercy. This is probably a simplistic view. If one admits that God is kind and loving sometimes, then one must also allow Him to be sadistic at other times. After all, we find both joy and sorrow in the world. What this means is that if we choose to believe in a God with anthropic features, then we must be prepared to grant Him/Her, on a grand scale, the capacity for immense good, and also immense evil: that is how a God, created in the human age, will and can be.

Or, if one chooses to accept only a good-natured God, then one will have to admit the existence of a bad-natured counter-entity, one no less powerful. When the good-natured God wins, we have joy and blessings; when the other one wins, there is pain and suffering. On the other hand, if we prefer the indifferent, cold, logical-mathematical God of the physicist, or the silent substratum of the Hindu Brahman, then we might as well stick to equations, logic circuits, and mute meditations without all the magic and poetry of the God of traditional religions. Or, we may reject the notion of God as irrelevant, irrational, and full of contradictions.

Proofs of God

Philosophers and theologians over the ages have been giving proofs for the existence of God. There are many Hindu, Christian, Jewish, and Muslim thinkers who have demonstrated to their satisfaction and to fellow members of their faith system that God does exist. In the Christian tradition, one of the earliest ontological arguments for God was given in the eleventh century by Anselm. Let us suppose that G is the greatest thing the mind can conceive of. If G does not exist, then another, which is exactly like it, must be greater. Therefore G must exist. Or else, something greater must be possible. Muslim and Jewish scholars have also been trying to prove God's existence.

There is a pseudo-historical story (De Morgan 1872) that in Catherine of Russia's court in the eighteenth century, during an argument with the French philosopher Denis Diderot on the existence or otherwise of God, the mathematician Leonhard Euler said something to the effect that $[a + b^n] / c = d$, therefore God exists. Unable to decipher the sophisticated symbolism of the eminent mathematician, the nonplussed atheist Diderot left the court in embarrassment and humiliation. Historians of science have established that this was merely a story. In any event, that scene has been repeated in different variations by many people (scientists/ mathematicians) since, but with more seriousness than Euler. Bernhard Riemann tried to establish divine matters through mathematics. Tippler, in his provocative book, *The physics of immortality* (1994), proved to the satisfaction of most who could not fathom his learned quotations from world-scriptures and technical physics that the soul's immortality had finally been established beyond a reasonable doubt.

More seriously, the keen mathematical thinker Kurt Gödel, who had been baptized as a Lutheran, believed he had found an irrefutable mathematical (symbolic logical) proof for the existence of something God-like, which he first circulated in 1970, basing himself on the ontological proof of Anselm.

Ax. 1. $P(\varphi) \wedge \Box \, \forall x [\varphi(x) \rightarrow \psi(x)] \rightarrow P(\psi)$

Ax. 2. $P(\neg\varphi) \leftrightarrow \neg P(\varphi)$

Th. 1. $P(\varphi) \rightarrow \Diamond \exists x [\varphi(x)]$

Df. 1. $G(x) \Leftrightarrow \forall\varphi[P(\varphi) \rightarrow \varphi(x)]$

Ax. 3. $P(G)$

Th. 2. $\Diamond \exists x G(x)$

Df. 2. $\varphi \, ess \, x \Leftrightarrow \varphi(x) \wedge \forall\psi \, \{\psi(x) \rightarrow \Box \, \forall x [\varphi(x) \rightarrow \psi(x)]\}$

Ax. 4. $P(\varphi) \rightarrow \Box \, P(\varphi)$

Th. 3. $G(x) \rightarrow G \, ess \, x$

Df. 3. $E(x) \Leftrightarrow \forall\varphi \, [\varphi \, ess \, x \rightarrow \Box \, \exists x \varphi(x)]$

Ax. 5. $P(E)$

Th. 4. $\Box \, \exists x \, G(x)$

("Ontological Proof," 1995, 403-404)

This should strike those who are uninitiated in symbolic logic as more of a mumbo-jumbo than mantras in archaic Sanskrit. One can see the translation of that ontological proof in everyday language in Clifford Pickover's *Wonder of numbers*:

Axiom 1.   (Dichotomy) A property is positive if and only if its negation is negative.

Axiom 2.   (Closure) A property is positive if it necessarily contains a positive property.

Theorem 1.   A positive property is logically consistent (i.e., possibly it has some instance.)

Definition.   Something is God-like if and only if it possesses all positive properties.

Axiom 3.   Being God-like is a positive property.

Axiom 4.   Being a positive property is (logical, hence) necessary.

Definition.   A property *P* is the essence of x if and only if x has *P* and *P* is necessarily minimal.

Theorem 2.   If x is God-like, then being God-like is the essence of x.

Definition.   NE(x) means x necessarily exists if it has an essential property.

Axiom 5.   Being NE is God-like.

Theorem 3.   Necessarily there is some x such that x is God-like.

qed.

(1976, 83)

In this context, one may refer to Francis F. Clooney S.J.'s book, *Hindu God, Christian God: How reason helps break down the boundaries between religions* (2001), which discusses with much erudition how thinkers in various faith traditions have exerted similar efforts to establish rationally the fact that God really exists. What is interesting in this book is that, unlike most Western interpreters of Hinduism, Clooney mentions not only Sanskrit, but also important Tamil texts of relevance to the topic.

In traditional theology, various thinkers have metaphysical and rational proofs for the existence of God. But in the age of science, empiricism is what determines the truth content of propositions. This has inspired some writers to formulate the idea of God, and establish His existence, through the *methodology* of science, rather than through the traditional rational framework. Russell Stannard published a whole book entitled *The God experiment: Can science prove the existence of God* (1999).

What all this shows is the immortality of the debate and the urge to *prove* God's existence among religiously-inclined scholars. It has been said that "were theologians to succeed in their attempt to strictly separate science and religion, they would kill religion" (Tippler 1994, 10). This is equivalent to the declaration that if a person forgets his/her spouse's birthday, that would end their marriage. This may be true in some cases, but cannot be formulated as a general proposition. The future of religions lies not in hanging on to the coattails of empirical science for proof, respect and recognition, but in appreciating the value and significance of trans-rational experiences and insights in matters spiritual, and in conceding the fallibility and finitude of the human mind when confronting the Infinite.

Proofs of God carefully elaborated by the likes of Spinoza, Tippler, and Gödel may be interesting for a handful of thinkers acquainted with logic, mathematics, cosmology or quantum physics, but they really become laughing stock in the reckoning of those who have experienced God through love or Nature, scripture or compassion, and above all, through the faith that resonates in the heart. One should root for reason and rationality, but when one waves axioms and theorems, Heisenberg and quantum electrodynamics to prove that Moses received the Commandments from the Almighty out there somewhere in the Middle East, that Brahmà is the one who keeps making the universe periodically, that Jesus was indeed the Son of God, or that the Archangel Gabriel spoke in Arabic to the Prophet, some people are amused, if not made uncomfortable. The aesthetic beauty and spiritual grandeur of mathematics are like the soul-uplifting magnificence of Art, Music, and Poetry. To contrive proofs of God through them is like using the piano to prove a Euclidean proposition.

To trace Omnipotent God through Einstein's equations or vacuum fluctuations may be more than muddled mixing of metaphor and mathematics: it may be plain wrong. Moreover, the vast majority of the truly faithful do not understand Fritjof Capra, Frank Tippler, Victor Weisskopf, and others. Nor do they feel the need for the approval of such authors to believe in the Almighty God of their tradition. They are not hankering for the sanction and support of esoteric equations to derive inner peace from meditation. The Bhagavad Gita, the Torah, the Dhammapada, the Bible, the Holy Koran, the Guru Granth Sahib, and other such texts offer much to spiritually-inclined souls, even if they lack knowledge of quarks or quantum field theory.

It does not follow from any result of science that the universe could not have emerged from the creative Mind of an omnipotent principle. When it comes to a discussion of science and religion, it may be useful to bear in mind that there is more to the human experience than *explaining* the world. Many matters of significance (such as love, compassion, kindness, justice, aesthetics, and the relevance of the human spirit in a cold and apparently value-less cosmos) are beyond the purview of science. Science may explain how these come about, but that is irrelevant to the thrill we derive from them. There is more to life than verifiable and refutable propositions.

But not all scientists have been theistic believers. In former times, atheistic scientists used to be secretive because, like homosexuality in some societies, it was a socially and culturally unacceptable stance. Sometimes they modified traditional theism into deism, an inoffensive mode of rejecting the God of religions. But in our times, there are scientists who openly reject the existence of God, even speak out and write eloquently against all religions.

Theistic scientists generally keep their religion and science in separate compartments. Though he championed heliocentrism, Galileo was no less religious than his Inquisitors. Isaac Newton delved deep into Biblical Chronology, but he kept it away from gravitation and optics. Though he formulated a theory of genetics, Mendel was not an atheist. Einstein said some nice things about God and religion, but kept Relativity and the photoelectric effect on the purely physical plane.

The God pictured by physicists is, to use a phrase of one of them: "mathematical thought, the order and harmony that make the world tick." For many thoughtful minds, there seems to be something creative in the immutable laws undergirding the universe; somehow these bring about unexpected changes and evolving transformations even amidst the routine regularity of precise lawfulness. There seems to be enough leeway for creativity even in a framework of rigid laws. But there are also scientists who feel no need to imagine cosmic intelligence, infinite power or an all-knowing principle behind all the drama in the space-time arena. For them, technical terms and concepts like emergence, information, Higgs boson, and mutation, are enough to explain away the awesome splendor stretching from the minute to the magnificent.

No matter where science takes us, it may never be able to prove or disprove the existence of a transcendent principle. And as long as the human mind is alive and active, there will always be irreconcilable debates on its existence or non-existence. That is why many theists would resonate with the following verse I composed:

> God is in the lepton's core
>> In galactic stretches too.
> The cosmic birth: He's been long before.
>> Yet, for ever fresh and new.
>
> Some prove a God, some disprove,
>> With logic as their art.
> But no one can ever move
>> God from the faithful's heart.
>
> Let mockers mock, and scholars say
>> Whatever they decide.
> The God to whom most people pray,
>> Isn't proved, but felt inside.
> (Raman 2002)

Negative theology

Those who have had profoundly convincing experiences as to the existence of something beyond the physical world have often said that at the highest stages one simply cannot talk about God. In the

Brihadaranyaka Upanishad there occurs a dialogue between a seeker and Yajñavalkya in which the sage describes the ultimate principle as:

> Neti, neti: not this, not that. It is incomprehensible, for he has never been comprehended, is indestructible, for he cannot be destroyed, he is unattached, for he does not attach himself... (BU 4:22).

Known as apophatic theology or *via negativa,* this view also finds expression in the Christian tradition where the Divine is described in negative terms. It says in the New Testament that "no man hath seen God at any time" (John 1:18). We also read: "Who only hath immortality, dwelling in the light which no man can approach unto; whom no man hath seen, nor can see" (Timothy 6:16).

Such passages reflect the wisdom of thinkers who understood that while the divine may be a deeply experienced aspect of being fully human, it is not something that can be described adequately in tangible terms. There are occasions when the names and visions of the divine that have been inculcated into our psyche enrich us in meaningful ways and elevate us spiritually, but to translate all that in the words of common language would at best be like the papier-mâché replica of a sculpture by Michelangelo: a pathetic, if not blasphemous imitation of the original. But many such have been attempted, and understandably only with marginal success.

The *via negativa* fosters a sense of humility, for God is not something that anyone can aspire to know while in the mortal frame. Equally, this view reminds us of the finiteness of the human mind and its incapacity to comprehend that which is a multi-splendored infinity. In other words, the negation is equivalent to surrender in order to bring the limitless totality within reach of a human mind that is restricted in a thousand ways to meet the needs of physical existence, and cluttered by mutually contradictory ideas and views that are often engendered by temporal and parochial visions.

What is surprising, therefore, is the cocksureness with which many people talk about the attributes of God, and as if this is not enough, have tried to impose their images of the unfathomable on the worship modes of others. If there be a God who judges human behavior and misbehavior, it is perhaps this aspect of forcible imposition of one's own version of the Almighty on others that would be reckoned as the most unpardonable.

On the virtues and vices of atheism

Atheism is the emphatic affirmation of the non-existence of God. It has a long history. From Diagoras and Anaxagoras in ancient Greece to Veer Savarkar and M. N. Roy in modern India, along with countless more all over the world, there have been many atheist thinkers over the centuries. There have been various shades of atheism in China, Greece, India, and the West.

Often atheists have had to pay a price. They have been ostracized, made to drink hemlock, burnt at the stake, and verbally abused also. In the Soviet Union and Communist China, it has been just the opposite: Belief in God was/is the crime. In classical India, atheists were not looked upon with much respect. To a degree, this is true in modern India and in the United States as well. However, Hinduism is perhaps the only theistic religion that tolerates atheism within its fold. In other words, Hindus can be atheists, and a great many are. No acharya or Baba or Hindu organization can boot an atheist Hindu out of his or her inherited religion. In this matter, the Hindu world is as enlightened as the modern secular West where atheists can live in freedom and speak out boldly.

In history, there have been two kinds of influential atheists: To the first belong philosophical atheists. Some of them have been enlightened humanists. Charvaka and Brihaspati in ancient India, Lucretius of Rome, Karl Marx and Bertrand Russell in the modern world come to mind. On the other hand, Stalin, Mao Zedon and Phol Pot are among the notorious monsters who were also rabid atheists. This goes to show that there is nothing intrinsically good or evil in being an atheist.

Many atheists in the West are disillusioned Christians or Jews. Not surprisingly, in a book on atheist perspectives, *Philosophers without Gods: Meditations on atheism and the secular life* (Anthony

2007), the chapter headings are "From Yashiva to Secular," "Overcoming Christianity," "On Becoming a Heretic," "Divine Evil," and such. There is also an implication there that atheism is somehow superior, more rational, and less prone to fanaticism, and that faith automatically leads to fanaticism. This last assumption ignores the facts that billions of religious people are not automatically fanatics and that non-religious fanatics have done no less havoc than religious ones.

The fact is, when we are born, we are neither theists nor atheists, but *ignoro-theists,* (i.e., individuals who have never even heard of God). Belief and disbelief in God arise from one's upbringing. One reason why many people are theists is that they have grown up in families affiliated to a theistic religion or live in a religion-friendly community. Atheism is the erasing of a belief that was inculcated (like love of parents or respect for elders) in an individual at a pre-reasoning stage. All our ancestors some 50,000 and more years ago were most likely ignoro-theists (not something to be either proud of or ashamed about). There are probably pristine ignoro-theist cultures still in the world.

The central point of atheism is that God is a human concept, useful perhaps to some, but quite unnecessary for the important things in life. One can be moral, respectful, reverential, caring, and compassionate and all the rest without believing in a supernatural, punishing God. Enlightened atheists are generally intellectually honest and meticulously rational. They can be as caring and compassionate as truly religious persons. But now and again they can become as rabid in their non-belief as some religious fanatics. Atheist extremists are not only unbending in their denial of God, sometimes they have the same kind of passion for converting believers into their fold. This in itself may not be bad, but in this context some of them display unwarranted arrogance and speak with contempt about theists. Many atheists equate belief in God with affiliation to religions. They also regard religion as a competitor to science in explaining origins and ends. As a result, they think that all religious people are misguided or ill-informed. This is like saying that music-lovers are misguided because they do not understand that musical notes can be Fourier-analyzed.

Atheists can be as fired up in proselytizing as evangelists of any denomination. The brilliant philosopher Daniel Dennett sounds like a general in an army that is out to free humanity from the fetters of religion. He takes up his mission with the zeal of a preacher, declaring his penetrating appraisal of religion: "I say unto you, O religious folks who fear to break the taboo: Let go! Let go! You'll hardly notice the drop!" (2006, 20). Such language is appropriate, given that (as he sees it) religion is an unfortunate spell to which we are bound, and he is out to break it. In 2006, Dennett published a provocative essay in which he described people who had rid themselves of all traditional religious beliefs as *brights,* without using any epithet for those who have not. His book, which offers some generous, if sarcastic-sounding suggestions for how the *non-brights* might call themselves, is an expansion, elucidation, and defense of the *brights'* position. The book says little that is entirely new to reasonable skeptics, informed atheists and unreligious scientists, but it says it all with great wit, intelligence and persuasiveness.

In a "I-come-to-bury-Caesar-not-to-praise-him" style, Dennett says he is not out to decry, degrade, or destroy religion, but only to analyze it from scientific perspectives. All he wants to explain is that religion is just another human invention to serve human needs, and is no revealer of truths, much less a vehicle that gives us a post mortem ride unto a grander or more terrible world beyond space and time. His analysis of religion and its emergence is sharp and insightful, and as informative as that of a master anthropologist about an exotic culture. In an age in which mindless religious fanaticism does havoc the world over, and sometimes tries to distort or usurp science, philosophers like Dennett do serve a purpose.

However, what escapes Dennett's analysis is that we are all under the spell of something or other. It could be fanatical religion or unadulterated rationality. Redemption for the *brights* consists in breaking the spell of religion, and in coming under the spell of pure rationality in the appraisal and experience of everything human. As to whether thinkers such as Dennett will transform millions into *brights*, it is difficult to say. It may be generations before that goal is achieved. Some, after recalling Stalin and Mao, may even wonder if it is a safe goal to strive for.

Consider Christopher Hitchens' book on anti-religion: *God is not great: How religion poisons everything* (2007). This is an eloquent, powerful and (by and large) intelligent articulation of the atheist's manifesto on religion. It is replete with instance after instance of how religion-inspired behavior and scriptures have been embarrassments to rational thinking and common decency all through human history. Its litany of absurdities and horrors should make any atheist jump in ecstasy while theists may be provoked to exclaim that it is the devil who is not great.

Most of Hitchen's narratives are well-reasoned, his arguments are incisive, and his anecdotes are telling. Unfortunately, some of them are marred by *ad hominem* attacks, with words like *fraud, hypocrite, fool,* and *idiot.* Thus, Malcolm Muggeridge is *silly* (p. 212); Pascal reminds him "of the hypocrites and frauds who abound in Talmudic Jewish rationalization" (p. 212); Pascal's "theology is not far short of *sordid*" (p. 211). Mel Gibson is an *Australian fascist* (p. 110). But his favorite epithet is *stupid.* Bishop Heber's hymn is *stupid;* the "gruesome laws of the Pentateuch are *stupid*" (p. 104); the notion of intelligent design is *stupid;* the factions which took an interest in native-American burial grounds were *stupid;* the magazine in honor of Osho is also *stupid* [Italics added above].

Hitchens speaks bluntly about the evils perpetrated by religionists, and also truthfully about the inconsistencies inherent in religious doctrines. But the way he presents his case is like that of the man who, because of a major car accident in his childhood which left a permanent scar on his psyche, was inspired to write a treatise called: *Automobiles are not great: How cars kill people and pollute the atmosphere.* Such a book might say it all very well, but then the automobile industry has manipulated the public into believing that they cannot live without the vehicle. Also, the public has grown so accustomed to its more useful aspects (especially if they can avoid

DWI and invent effective catalytic converters) that they are not yet ready to set all cars on fire. That is the situation with religions in the world. At this point, their usefulness outweighs their negative impacts. This is why it is not likely that this book will displace religions from human culture any more than that a mosquito will move a mammoth. Practically every horrible thing detailed in the book is valid, but its merciless denigration of religions is like the unsophisticated report of the garbage collector who imagines that households generate only trash and filth.

Hitchens claims to have visited many religious congregations all over the world, of all faiths and denominations. I, too, did exactly that for a whole year, and was greatly enriched by participating in the spiritual richness and beautiful music that the services offered, and touched by the genuine caring and the charitable impulses that they fostered. But Hitchens does not seem to care for any of the aesthetic dimensions of religions, much less been moved to lofty heights by the visions, real or imaginary, poetic or promised, of any religion. It appears that, as one who has only observed them as an unsympathetic outsider, he has not been able to taste any aspect of religion the way practitioners do. This is fine, but on that constrained basis he may not be entitled to insist that others should not or cannot taste them either, or that those who do are mindless. Indeed, sometimes he writes like postmodernists who blurt out inanities about science without ever having done a laboratory experiment, peered through a telescope, or done a complex calculation.

In making his case for why religions ought to be dispensed with, Hitchens lists a series of charges against them, all of which are valid up to a point, and none of which is taken literally by countless practitioners of the major religions in this day and age. The first of these, "presenting a false picture of the world to the innocent and the credulous" (p. 205), reveals his bias: the pictures are not *false* (which implies intention to cheat), but *mistaken* (like the eighteenth-century phlogiston theory), formulated centuries ago by thinkers who did not have the benefit of the knowledge and insights we possess today. We can in fairness blame the folks who adopt them today, but not the originators of the ideas.

He lists the doctrine of blood sacrifice as another evil, (p. 205). But not all religions subscribe to this: Christianity, Buddhism, Sikhism, Jainism, and Vaishnava Hinduism have generally become against this practice, and they include vast numbers of deeply religious people. Another charge, "the imposition of impossible tasks and rules," is perhaps the least tenable. Such rules have always existed in civilized societies. True enough, most of them have their roots in religions, and border on the ideal. Celibacy, refraining from promiscuity and pork, loyalty to spouse and the like are not as terrible as they are made out to be. More often than not, they are secretly violated, maybe with an occasional feeling of guilt.

In his scathing analysis, Hitchens spares no sacred book. In his rebukes he gives not an iota of respect to anything remotely linked to a traditional religion, not even to the Beatitudes. In his judgment on prophets and saints, he does not mince any word: The Dalai Lama's pronouncements are *absurd;* Martin Luther became a *bigot;* Muhammad is a *mammal* [Italics added above]; Augustine was "a self-centered fantasist and an earth-centered ignoramus" (p. 64); all he can say about Abraham is that he agreed to murder his son (p. 206).

It is easy for enlightened minds to resonate with the harsh comments on the dark sides of religion that Hitchens paints in profusion and with great passion. At the very least, any fair reader has to be empathetic to the understandable anger and frustration that so many feel about the madness and mayhem that still emanate from many mindless practitioners of religions. Sadly for human civilization, in the context of the atrocities and abominations that have been, and still are, perpetrated in the name of God and religion, a book like this is inevitable, perhaps even necessary. That may be why ours is an age in which treatises on atheism are doing well in the marketplace.

Books like this can certainly serve as valuable eye openers for the uninformed and the uninitiated, even if they anger many of those who are wedded to ancient worldviews and sadden those who wish to see more balanced portrayals of one of the most persistent and meaningful institutions in human civilization. With appropriate refinements, such books could serve as a good antidote to naïve and extremist exaltations of the outworn doctrines and dangerous incitements to fanatical behavior that are very much part of today's world.

A serious drawback with atheism is that unwittingly or otherwise, it deprives people of a metaphysical source for hope in despondency, consolation in bereavement, and joy in celebrations. This is one reason why it fails to draw many adherents. Philosophical atheism is intellectually sophisticated, just as philosophical theism is, but it has little practical value. Atheism is allied to modern science, just as theism is allied to spiritual life. Atheists do not always realize that one can be decent and caring even if one is a theist. Belief in God also gives inner peace to countless people who feel that this is more significant, relevant, and important for sane living than being right or bright. Most philosophical atheists tend to be insensitive to the deeper emotional and cultural needs of people and groups.

It is good to remember that most traditional religious theists are *proprius-theists* (believing in their own God) and *allus-atheists* (rejecting the gods of other religions).

The agnostic approach

I once witnessed a heated debate between an ardent Christian and a devout Hindu as to how we will be rewarded or punished in the end by the Almighty. The Christian spoke about the day of reckoning and eventual entry into heaven or elsewhere, while the Hindu argued for successive reincarnations as paybacks until one finally merged with the Source. I was more impressed by the certainty with which the participants argued their tenets than with the arguments that each presented. I must confess that neither one persuaded me. Though both made passionate cases for their respective positions, the strengths of their arguments lay mainly (it seemed to me) in how ably they revealed the weaknesses in the opponent's position. They both did this very well.

Then again, both were merely repeating what they had been taught, and there was not much indication that either of them would convince the other by reasoning and logic. It occurred to me that views on these matters form from an early age, in keeping with the religious framework that has been drilled into a person, or perhaps from books one reads later in life, but not because of empirical evidence.

Though the vast majority of people accept without much thought or questioning the assertions of traditional religious texts and preachers regarding transcendental reality, quite a few have also doubted its existence. In other words, many have had s-doubts about some of the details in the r-faith of religions, but they have either not pursued the matter, or simply accepted it so as not to rock the boat.

However, all through the ages and in all societies, some have wondered aloud about the contents of r-faith. They reject outright all the religious narratives about the distant past and religious prognostications about what is to come in the very distant future, let alone about God, angels and such. More in realization of the limits of the human intellect than in frustration or antagonism, some of them say that they really do not know about these matters. These are the *agnostics*. The term was coined by Thomas H. Huxley at a meeting of the Metaphysical Society in 1876. In his own words:

> I took thought and invented what I conceived to be the appropriate title of "agnostic." It came into my head as suggestively antithetic to the "Gnostic" of Church history who professed to know so much about the very things of which I am ignorant, and I took the earliest opportunity of parading it to our society, to show that I, too, had a tail like the other foxes. (1889, 183)

Huxley's agnosticism incorporates an element of confirmatory doubt, for he said:

> In matters of the intellect, follow your reason as far as it
> will take you, without regard to any consideration....Do
> not pretend that conclusions are certain which are not
> demonstrated or demonstrable (1889, 170).

For millennia, keen minds with admirable qualities have been enunciating the most divergent theses as to the nature of God and the hereafter, and argued about their respective contentions intelligently and voluminously. Their followers have been so convinced of the correctness of the views of the masters that they have often engaged in mutual verbal (and even sometimes physical) abuse. Corporal punishment for wrong doing, however unpleasant, is understandable. But to burn fellow beings on the stake, sever their heads or maim their bodies because they had different notions of what constitutes God and afterlife, arises from mindsets that, one would hope, might soon become things of the past. In this context, to say, "I'm afraid I don't know," seems more modest and reasonable, and less prone to provoke vehement attacks.

In principle, an agnostic must respect the convictions of atheists and theists. She is not to tell anyone, "You are wrong," but only, "I don't know for sure." The agnostic is impressed, but not offended, by the certainty with which people proclaim their *truths* about ultimate questions. She believes that it is enriching to ponder these and to accept some non-hurtful conclusions that she feels are fulfilling, even if it is only "I don't know." Acceptance of some mysteries for the agnostic can be as satisfying as its resolution is for others.

Like the words *faith* and *doubt, agnosticism* has also been often misunderstood. It is rejected because it hesitates to affirm a reality beyond the concrete world of appearance (commonsense reality) in which we normally function. Some have argued that consequences of agnosticism range from meaninglessness, because it adamantly refuses to attach long-range significance to anything, to hopelessness, because it confesses that one is totally lost as to what life is all about, and of course, to atheism, because it says, directly or indirectly, that there is not sufficient evidence for one to believe in the existence of God. This view was succinctly expressed by Enrico Cantore: "Science leads to agnosticism, and agnosticism breeds desperation" (1977, 172). It has also been argued that agnosticism could lead to paralysis of action, meaning perhaps that if one is not sure of Heaven or Hell, of a punishing or a rewarding God, one cannot choose between moral options. It is not clear that uncertainty about the aftermath should necessarily lead to naughty behavior, or that honesty, decency, truthfulness and other such virtues should be necessarily linked to, or hinge upon, receiving a bonus sooner or later.

Agnosticism arises from at least two factors. First, there is the conviction to the effect that ultimate questions are interesting to speculate upon but impossible to answer unequivocally: such as, questions relating to the nature of God, the relevance of humans, slime and slugs in the larger cosmic scheme, and the long-range meaning of life, love and laughter, let alone the possibilities of post-mortem personal experiences. To say that it is difficult to formulate unshakable views of these matters does not mean that one cannot or should not work within frameworks that can be meaningful and uplifting during one's lifespan. It is somewhat like saying that, because marital love may at some time slip and lead to divorce, one should not get married.

Roots of belief systems

Geneticists, psychologists, evolutionists and philosophers have all given various explanations for the rise of religious belief. However, irrespective of these theories which apply to us generally as a species, we can still look into the roots of our own individual beliefs. We all hold certain views and opinions about the world and about life. If we pause to trace the origins of these, we will find that they have resulted for the most part from our interactions with others through our personal and cultural environment. The molding factors include our parents, teachers and friends, as well as the books we read, the movies we see, the places we visit, etc. From a general perspective if one traces the origins of human beliefs and worldviews, it will be found that, leaving aside our genetically acquired traits and tendencies, they arise from three distinct factors which may or may not interact with one another. These are:

(a) *The logical framework of the human mind.* Because of our biological evolution, the normal human brain functions in a particular way. There are clearly recognizable laws of thought that conform to what we call basic logical principles. Logical reasoning is a capacity of the human mind, *not* its unfailing characteristic. Practically all systems of thought, i.e. philosophies, opinions, and sciences that reflect a worldview, have a logical basis.

(b) *Our own experiences in the world around us.* Clearly, any worldview is a function of what we experience. Indeed, science tries to explain these experiences. In speculative systems where one goes beyond one's immediate perceptions, one still takes these into account, whether consciously or otherwise. Thus, for example, Thales of Miletus said that everything is made up ultimately of water, because he had seen the river-based civilizations of Egypt and Mesopotamia. When a Hindu sage-poet described the *hiranya-garbha* (golden egg) that emerged from water, he might have been inspired by the sight of the rising of the morning sun from the sea. Likewise, our views on political, moral, or religious questions, for example, are governed by our own personal experiences in these matters.

(c) *Emotional and psychological factors.* We are creatures, not only of the mind, but of feelings and emotions as well. Indeed, feelings and emotions are more fundamental to our being than pure logic and reasoning. Consequently, these factors play a role in the ideas we develop, the beliefs we hold, and the worldviews we accept. Just as in the application of the logical principles we are not always consciously aware of them, so too we seldom recognize the psychological and emotional undercurrents in our thoughts and behavior.

The views of modern science regarding the nature of the world are distinguished from those of pre-modern science by several of these factors.

In the pre-modern scientific outlook, the logical framework of our minds is as fully exploited as in the modern scientific stage. Many Greek thinkers, the authors of the Nyaya-system in India, Arab philosophers and medieval scholastics were keen logical thinkers. However, their thoughts were purely *rationalistic:* reasoning with little reference to facts of observation.

In the pre-modern scientific stage, experiences had a smaller role. There was relatively less conscious effort to reconcile one's worldviews with the facts and data of experience. Thus Aristotle could say that men have more teeth than women, although it would have been easy for him to check out if this statement was correct. Even if blatant contradictions were recognized between a firmly held belief and observed facts, one was not greatly perturbed by such discoveries. Thus, even when comets appeared and disappeared without causing any great catastrophes, people continue(d) to believe that such correlations exist(ed). In the modern scientific framework, however, factor (b) is of the utmost importance.

The third factor, the emotional and psychological component, played a major role in pre-modern scientific outlook. But often one was totally unaware of its influence. In the modern scientific context too, this factor sometimes comes into play, but there is every effort to minimize and eliminate this as a determining element in the scientific worldview.

Many pre-modern scientific views arose from the same urge to understand and explain the world that inspires modern science. But that urge is satisfied more easily at a less sophisticated stage, often by relatively simplistic answers. The most superficial impressions of experience are likely to be accepted without further examination. Thus, from the observed impression of the rising and setting of the sun and the stars, it was concluded that the earth stands still while the firmament revolves around it.

At that stage, one also tends to make unreasonable extrapolations from observed facts. Thus, because there are seven apertures on the human face it was once argued that there could be only seven planets in the heavens. In the ancient framework, there was also a general indifference to verifying claims that were propounded to be true, especially by authorities. The requirement that statements must be subjected to observational tests before they are accepted is quite natural to the modern scientific mind. But it was rarely taken as seriously by people, even the more enlightened, in pre-modern scientific times. In matters beyond technical science, one can still find modern examples that ignore this criterion.

Chapter 6
Spiritual Aspects

Spirituality: religious perspective

Since the dawn of self-awareness, human beings have gone beyond the biological urgencies of food and procreation, shelter and security as they created art and poetry, music and philosophy. They have wondered about the world and the reason for existence. These are expressions of what we call the human spirit.

Is there, or is there not, more to human beings than matter and energy, than molecules and metabolism? Are we, or are we not, endowed (as most religions tell us) with a non-material aspect, called soul, spirit or whatever? What about spiritual experiences? Are these for real, or are they simply non-normal modes of brain activity? Is the mystic in a heightened state of awareness or is she just hallucinating? Is there more to consciousness than the highly complex networking of zillions of neurons firing away in the frontal lobe, or is it the result of some kind of a resonance with something out there in the universe?

Over the ages such questions have been, using a crude phrase, beaten to death by philosophers, skeptics, yogis, mythmakers, scholars, theologians, and scientists too. But the issues continue to be very much alive. If anything, they are taking on fresh energy and momentum, even as traditional religions are making a grand comeback all over the world.

There are several reasons for this. First, the growing surge of the rationalist-scientific framework has called into question religious truths, and it attempts to exile God from human culture. At the same time, the materialist stance on human life has the potential for trivializing moral values and human worth. Then again, science itself has become far more complex and sophisticated now than in the eighteenth and nineteenth centuries when the grand achievements of celestial mechanics, electromagnetism and thermodynamics made people assert with more confidence than now that there is nothing beyond matter and energy in the world. Finally, we have recently come to understand brain and biochemistry much better. Just as our knowledge of quantum mechanics revealed to us aspects of the physical world never before imagined, it is entirely possible that a deeper knowledge of neurons and their properties might reveal aspects of thought and spirit that seem as yet to be only emergent properties of the brain.

But on this issue there is a great divide. Most neuroscientists, cognitive scientists, and molecular biologists cling on to the traditional scientific view that all talk of soul and thought of God are sparks from the complex brain, like so many other fantasies and fairy tales which emerge from the same brain: all interesting, but just that, and not revelations of hidden dimensions of physical reality. As they see it, soul and spirit are sprouts from the fertile soil that the brain is, and not subtle silent entities embedded therein. It is only a matter of time, they say, before we account for the perennial propensity of the brain to engage in God-talk. Already there are numerous books to that effect.

There are serious thinkers, and among them some scientists too, who are not persuaded. They are convinced that there is more to the mind than macromolecules, more to mysticism than muddled thinking. They are convinced that the brains of mystics experience an aspect of the world that ordinary brains just let go unobserved. They work on the conviction that the spiritual dimension is somewhat like Pluto, whether planet or not, of pre-telescopic astronomy. It has always been there, but one not equipped with the appropriate mode of detection (spiritual outlook and discipline) simply cannot know about it.

Religion is an important dimension of this spiritual potential of *Homo sapiens*. It enables us to experience the world apart from the natural needs of hunger and thirst. It elevates us to levels that transcend our physical constraints. Religions are like lofty peaks rising high above the surrounding plains of our physical being, merging, as it were, into the distant domain of heaven itself, beckoning the human spirit with their grandeur. Some think religions are only as real as mirages; others that they lead us to a grander realm.

The spirituality thesis is that there is a trans-physical cosmic principle that sustains and stirs the physical world of which humans gain a partial and fleeting awareness during an all-too-brief terrestrial sojourn. It cannot be grasped by the probes of the mind, nor made to conform to the paradigms of logic. Its essence can only be inadequately conveyed through words and symbols. It can be realized through meditative disciplines, or as a result of some extraordinary vision. It is there for sure, proclaim the mystics, because they have had glimpses of that subtle web that weaves the world of space and time, of matter, energy and causality.

The poet William Blake wrote:

> If the doors of perception were cleansed everything would
> appear to man as it is, infinite. For man has closed himself
> up, till he sees all things through narrow chinks of his
> cavern. ("The marriage of Heaven and Hell," 1790, 39)

The inner recognition of the spiritual dimension involves gaining awareness of an aspect of the universe that is not normally available to us. This awareness constitutes mystical experience. In this sense, mysticism is not necessarily associated with any religion or even God in the sense of a belief system based on prophetic revelations, but is essentially one in which we come to grasp an aspect of the universe that is hidden from our usual perceptual cognitions. It is somewhat like the scientific grasp of atomic structure or the hidden dimensions of string theory which are of course there, but whose appreciation calls for some serious commitment and study, as well as a certain level of sophistication.

Human beings have always sought to get a glimpse of that realm, to try to connect ever so slightly to the ethereal Beyond, of which we are, perhaps, pale reflections. The spiritual quest is the expression of the deepest longing to connect with the Whole. In Michelangelo's Sistine Chapel masterpiece, we see the tip of Adam's finger barely touching that of God, as if created Man is moving away from the Creator. It could also be interpreted as the human spirit trying to get in touch with God.

Jack Miles reminded his readers that the vision of God as gathered from the Bible should remind his Western (Judeo-Christian) readers of their cultural heritage:

> We are all, in a way, immigrants from the past. And just as an immigrant returning after many years to the land of his birth may see his own face in the faces of stranger, so the modern secular...reader may feel a tremor of self-recognition in the presence of [God]. (1995, 4)

A very similar idea is expressed in the ancient Hindu framework by which the human spirit, in its quest for its source, will recognize that it is but a fragment of the eternal cosmic whole from which it has emerged.

Spirituality: nineteenth-century instigation

Science tends to have a different view of spirituality. For more than a century after its emergence, Galilean-Newtonian science was generally indifferent to spiritual matters. For the most part, it tended to regard spiritual experiences either as religiously significant, deserving respect, or as simply delusionary, requiring treatment.

In the 1840s, two young sisters, Margaret and Kate Fox, who lived not far from Rochester, New York, said they heard raps on the walls of their room (Stuart 2005). People were amazed, and a continuous stream of visitors came to examine the mysterious phenomenon. The girls now began to provoke the sounds, often in meaningful answers to questions; and claimed, much to the bewilderment of their mother and close friends of the family, that spirits were communicating with them.

The matter drew wider attention, and the young women were brought to Rochester for public demonstration for a modest fee. Investigators were called in, committees were set up to report on the sounds, and a theory emerged to the effect that the source was in fact the restless spirit of an individual who had been murdered in the farmhouse where the sisters lived. The reputation of the Fox sisters grew, and Mary Todd Lincoln (the President's widow) asked for their services to communicate with the spirit of her assassinated husband. After decades of such feats, one of the sisters admitted to cheating: they had been causing the sounds by cracking their ankles!

But long before their confession, other (similar) departed spirits had gotten into the act in other parts of the country. A number of people soon managed to establish contacts with disembodied individuals with ease and expertise. And so began the science of spiritualism, with séance boards and all. Spirits, after centuries of relative indifference, suddenly began to show an extraordinary eagerness to establish contacts with humans in Europe and in North America from the middle of the nineteenth century onwards, mercilessly ignoring millions in those parts of the world where nobody had heard of the Fox sisters. The ankle-cracking of the little women played no small role in the emergence of such sciences as ESP and telepathy.

Ever since the Fox sisters fooled the world and provoked the modern spiritualist movement in the Western world in mid-nineteenth century, spooks and goblins have been revived with gusto, and even the scientific establishment has been forced to open up its closed mind and search for fairies and the levitation potential of humans. What the world needs is surely more knowledge and education, more caring and compassion, more love and peace. But a little diversion now and then is perhaps not all that bad. So, when the obscurantism of darker ages, such as numerology and tarot cards, Ouija boards and palmistry join hands with astrology in a chorus of occult sciences, it should be an amusing rather than a sorry spectacle for those who have grown up beyond the sixteenth century, were it not for the fact that the popularity of these matters is also an index of how little impact science education has had on society.

It is a fascinating, even incredible fact of human history that, as a result of a couple of pranksters, spiritualism became a fad, and diverted attention from spirituality as a religious mode. It attracted some eminent scientists, and instigated the formation of the Society for Psychic Research. Enthusiasm for this gradually fizzled out, and physicists returned to their customary indifference to spiritual matters.

Then, some decades later, with the propagation and popularity of LSD and other hallucinogens in the second half of the twentieth century, spiritual experiences came to be taken seriously by some investigators, but not in the traditional religious framework. Chemicals were regarded as tools for opening up the "doors of perception" (title of a book by Aldous Huxley, 1954) to other levels of consciousness, like yoga in traditional Hindu spiritual quests. This inspired investigations of spiritualistic claims. In certain religious rites, intoxicants are shared, whether chewed as a pulp, imbibed as a potion or inhaled as mind-numbing fumes. Soma juice, opium, incense, and mescaline are not recent inventions or discoveries as instruments for spiritual excitation. Or again, an unwitting victim might consume a mushroom in the wild, which may contain chemicals that work wonders on the brain, kindling it to mystical modes. Harvard psychologist and spirituality-via-drug guru Timothy Leary co-authored *The psychedelic experience,* in which he said:

> A psychedelic experience is a journey to new realms of consciousness. The scope and content of the experience is limitless, but its characteristic features are the transcendence of verbal concepts, of space-time dimensions, and of the ego or identity. Such experiences of enlarged consciousness can occur in a variety of ways: sensory deprivation, yoga exercises, disciplined

meditation, religious or aesthetic ecstasies, or spontaneously. (1964, 11)

Leary spread his Gospel through an outfit called the League for Spiritual Discovery which he founded, and he lectured in many college campuses to convert the young. He was successful in this endeavor in that it opened up the new drug culture in the United States, which spread all over the world, as have other things good and bad.

Puffing and sniffing for soaring into hallucinatory heights is an age-old practice, often indulged in with religious fervor, or simply for fighting boredom. But somehow such experimentations with our consciousness tend to become risky and self-destructive in the context of modern life. Marijuana and opium could very well be innocuous intakes in a carefree existence in a remote, somnolent village with little responsibility and no machines and motors to manipulate. But in a complex technological society, where our behavior affects others, and every accident prompts alert responses from everybody around to relieve the pain or save the life of a victim, such indulgences cost money and effort to society. This, rather than any system of ethics, is the reason why heroin, cocaine, marijuana, and the rest of the addictive kicks are listed among society's problems.

Drug-based spirituality may be interpreted in two ways. Spiritual experiences are in fact states of heightened awareness: they enable glimpses of higher levels of reality. They can be achieved with drugs by cracking open the barriers which have arisen in the evolutionarily developed normal brain. In other words, drugs (whether from an external source or synthesized via yoga) alter brain chemistry, producing spiritual experiences. But this also suggests possibilities, such as: Vedic hymns arose from imbibing soma juice; Moses' godly encounter was due to a theotoxin; the voice of Gabriel that the Prophet Mohammed heard was due to altered brain states; and the saintly visions of Virgin Mary arose from unwitting consumption of entheogenic mushrooms. Traditional religionists, therefore, feel that spirituality thus degenerates into hallucinatory ravings. Charismatic drug-gurus write books, address dissatisfied folks hungering for something beyond cheeseburgers and soft drinks, and offer instant ecstasy with a pinch of some potent powder, potion or perfume. All this is fine, except that so many of them end up in hospitals where they need the care and attention of more normal brains.

Mysticism: religious perspective

One thread that connects all the religions of the world is mysticism. Hindus and Buddhists, Jews and Christians, Muslims and Baha'is, Confucians and Zoroastrians—all have had their mystics. However, since God is viewed differently in different traditions, religious mystics tend to obtain knowledge, not of God in abstraction, but of personal God as envisioned in their respective religious worldview. Tamil Shaiva saints experience one type of mysticism, seeing the Shiva principle everywhere, whereas Sri Caitanya of the Bengali tradition recognized Krishna everywhere. For Tulsi Das, it was Rama and Hanuman, whereas in the mystical vision of St. Francis of Assisi, he saw the stigmata of Christ. Bernadette of Lourdes had a vision of Virgin Mary. Jewish Kabala and Islamic Sufis experienced yet other mystic modes, and so on.

To the religious aspirant, spirituality is thus linked to a profound and ineffable experience that enriches life by revealing possibilities in existence and features of the tangible world that are not as obvious when we are in the thick and thin of daily chores.

The person of faith, in ritual or worship, while reciting a prayer, singing a psalm, and invoking a mantra, feels deep within a communion that, like the philosopher's stone of alchemy, transforms the lead and copper of animal existence into the silver and gold of divine delight. There have been saints and sufis in every tradition who have moved beyond the prayers of the day and season, and felt a communion with the Mystery, making them extraordinary beings. They are the mystics who are venerated in the religious traditions, for in them one sees spirituality attain its noblest heights. The rest of us are like amateur climbers who walk the carved out tracks to reach a modest plateau, or play in the plains; the saints are like arduous Alpinists who have scaled the loftiest peaks.

From the religious perspective, spirituality implies two fundamental things. First, it refers to an aspect of the world that is beyond the material-energetic, a realm that is too subtle for scientific instruments to measure or detect. Secondly, it refers to an innate capacity of human beings that enables us to become aware of the transcendent through a variety of means that are recommended by the religions of the world. Furthermore, in order to utilize this capacity, one needs to embrace a religious mode, be initiated into some religious practice, and undertake the quest with serious intention. In other words, from the perspective of religion, spirituality is an attribute and a potential of the human condition. In some religious systems it is regarded as resulting from grace from the Unfathomable Mystery. Like rationality, it is the capacity to raise our awareness to a non-material plane of reality. Our spiritual dimension provokes us to love, kindness, caring, compassion, truth and beauty.

Mystical experience is an ineffable phase of consciousness which has been reported over the ages by people from all cultures and traditions. There is a paradox in this statement since what is ineffable (i.e., not expressible in words) cannot be reported. The paradox may be clarified if we grant that such reports are invariably inadequate, imperfect and vague, and that verbal descriptions do not convey the full nature and measure of the experience.

Mystics report a feeling of oneness with the world around, a dissolution of the boundaries between things, including one's individuality as a separate self. Most of all, the mystic experience generally puts one in an ecstatic state.

Vedic rishis, Buddha, Moses, Christ, Mohammed, and many saints have had mystical experience. Their episodes and associated phenomena gave credibility to the founders of religions, including the Pythagorean brotherhood of ancient Greece and some cults in our own times. This is one reason why it may be difficult for Religious Naturalism to become a religion with mass-following.

Mystical experiences are often culture-specific. Christian mystics have visions of St. Mary and the stigmata of Christ. Hindu mystics see Krishna and Kali. In the Islamic world, especially among Sufis, mysticism is *ma'rifa* (knowledge of Allah). In Religious Naturalism, the basis is rational understanding of the phenomenal world. This can lead to awe and reverence for the laws and processes governing the origin and functioning of the universe, but not to visions.

Like knowledge and understanding, mystical experience can occur at various levels or depths. The concept may be extended to similar, though not as intense and heightened, modes as saints and prophets have had. Practitioners of religions have mystical experience, in however rudimentary a level, when they pray or participate in hearty religious music with deep faith. So do people who engage in serious yogic meditation. Even contemplation of a star-studded sky or ocular interaction with a giggling infant may be loosely described as mystical.

Prayer and meditation are two different kinds of mystical experience: exo-mysticism and endo-mysticism. In the first, one achieves a mystic state by focusing on something external: stars, God, or divine symbols. Here, the vision is revelatory of an aspect of the world that is not ordinarily apparent. In the latter case, the focusing is inward. This leads to recognition of an aspect of consciousness, of the innermost core of one's self of which one is not ordinarily aware. Meditative mysticism was experienced by yogic and Upanishadic seers in the Hindu tradition.

Mysticism is usually associated with religions, and yet some have maintained that it has little to do with institutionalized religions, ethics, or scriptures. Agehananda Bharati, in *The light at the center* (1976), claimed that even an atheist, agnostic, or immoral person might get a "zero-experience," as he called it.

We may consider mystical experience by means of an analogy. Consider the letters of the alphabet: they may be scattered on a sheet at random in a jumble, they may be in groups of simple words and ordinary sentences, or they may be strung into magnificent poetry. When they appear as disconnected clutters, we experience dreams; as simple words and sentences, they constitute usual reality to which we are accustomed; as grand poetry, it gives us the experience of mystical merger.

Neurotheology

In the scientific paradigm of matter-energy-natural-processes, every experience, whether normal, abnormal or supernormal, may be traced to the state of brain chemistry. So the idea of a neurotheology is not new. In the nineteenth century, William James wrote:

> To posit a soul influenced in some mysterious way by the brain states and responding to them by conscious affections of its own, seems to me the line of least logical resistance. (1890, 1: 181)

Today the matter has been raised to its empirical exploratory level, and the buzz-word is neurotheology (a term coined by Aldous Huxley). As Laurence O. McKinney foresaw (*Neurotheology: Virtual religion in the 21st century,* 1994), it has become virtually a religion among scientists. It develops a framework, based on experiments on the brains of patients and volunteers, which tracks down various spiritual and religious experiences to specific parts of the brain, and tries to establish in systematic and reproducible ways what materialist science suspected all along: that spiritual experiences, like alcoholic intoxication, is essentially an abnormal cerebral state.

Eugene d'Aquili and Andrew Newberg pointed out (*Mystical mind,* 1999), on the basis of their experimental findings, that the region of the brain called posterior superior parietal lobe is responsible for enabling us to orient our bodies in three-dimensional space. It also helps us recognize our individual selves as distinct from the external world. If, for some reason, this lobe is affected or damaged in certain ways, the differentiation is erased, and one experiences the oneness of which mystics speak.

V. S. Ramachandran and Sandra Blakeslee demonstrated that divine visions are closely related to the functioning of the left temporal lobe (*Phantoms in the brain: Probing the mysteries of the human brain,*

1998). Ramachandran has called it the God-module. One of his epileptic patients is said to have confessed that during some of his episodes he felt "Oneness with the Creator." In principle, it is possible to excite this lobe and make anybody "see God." There seems to be more than poetic truth in Johann Paul Richter's words:

> *Gott ist ein unaussprechlicher Seufzer,*
> *im Grunde der Seele gelegen*
> [God is an unutterable sigh,
> placed in the core of the soul].
> (1807, 14)

Others have suggested that physical factors in the environment, such as emanations from solar flares and changes in the ambient electromagnetic field, could trigger disturbances in the brain and cause epilepsy and mystical oneness.

Like the relentless quest of dedicated detectives to corner a criminal, the scientific search, especially its neuroscientific wing, is in hot pursuit of uncovering what exactly is behind this extraordinary experience that some individuals have had in such heightened intensity, and which is at the root of practically every religion in the world. Their investigations and theories invariably characterize the most lofty and long-revered aspect of human experience into an unusual state that may potentially arise in any human brain. In other words, science tells us that, unlike the sun and stars, God and angel are not out there, but are fantasies of the brain under abnormal conditions. It may be that mysticism could be the brain's resonance to something out there, but this idea is not taken as an option by the scientific establishment. And yet, it is a thesis of evolution that eyes developed because seeing is possible on our planet on terra firma, while creatures in the depths of the sea have no ocular mechanism. It could well be that the human brain developed in ways which enable it to recognize the spiritual aspects of the universe in peculiar ways.

Another interpretation of mystical experience is from psychiatrists who describe it all as arising from a deranged mind. In doing so, they fail to differentiate between sickness and vision: whereas a sick mind is pathetic and erratic, a visionary mind experiences what is not accessible to minds in their normal states. Transrational is not the same as irrational.

As with other matters of religious import, modern science has intruded into the mystery of mysticism by trying to explain it in various ways. Eighteenth-century physics had the effect of unweaving the rainbow, as the poet Keats called it: reducing the beauty and grandeur of the celestial arc to Snell's law of refraction operating in water droplets in the atmosphere. Likewise, in the view of some, mescaline-mysticism is dismantling the spirit. This is an even greater intrusion into the human experience. Millennia of culture and civilization have arisen from firm belief in a transcendent principle. In that framework, saints and scriptures have been teaching us to relate to something Beyond through prayer and penitence. Now all this is reduced to properties of complex molecules that modify neuron firing and create weird images. All the poetry and potency of prayer is reduced to brain chemistry. Religious ecstasy is relegated to the hypothalamus and the frontal lobe, and traced to orgasmic bliss that was triggered somewhere along the evolutionary chain.

To the practitioner of religion and the person of faith it really should not matter, but it does put the theologian on the defensive. It also detracts from the goal of the spiritual aspirant: which is not so much to figure out what causes the experience of entanglement with the Whole, nor even to get an indescribable kick from feeling high or spaced-out or whatever the jargon of drug culture might be, but to be immensely enriched and meaningfully transformed as a human being by the spiritual quest. The religious approach to spirituality is like delighting in a gourmet meal; the scientific approach is like studying the recipes or chemically analyzing the ingredients of the menu.

Consciousness: religious and scientific perspectives

From the merger of a microscopic sperm and an egg in the darkness of the uterus arises an entity that gradually acquires self-awareness and an identity all its own. This embodied consciousness reflects and rejoices, creates and communicates, and engages in countless activities for a brief time-span. Then, after a final puff, its non-physical attributes vanish. No thinking mind can remain unimpressed by this remarkable phenomenon, which, as far as we know, is unlike any other in the silent stretch of space and time. If anything is mystery, then human consciousness is. Of all the wondrous elements in our vast and complex universe, there is perhaps nothing more spectacular, certainly nothing more intriguing, than consciousness.

Each one of us carries within a totality that is more than the sum of our body's material substrate. Many of the atoms and molecules that make up our anatomy at this hour were not part of us until only recently. Millions of microorganisms thrive and perish in our saliva and alimentary canal. With all that, there is a subtle self, or at least the non-trivial illusion of one such, that has been illumining every one of us, something that etches the identity of a separate existence even within a hugely interconnected whole. This self has been with us since the first utterance of *I* and *me,* and it will be part of us until the dusk of life when, gradually or suddenly, our individual memories will falter and fade away for good.

Consciousness breathes awareness into inert matter. From the religious perspective, the capacity for awareness and experience, for logical analysis and joyful interaction, is an attribute endowed by the Creator upon some of His creatures. In other words, consciousness is a special gift to humans beyond the material components of the body and their proper functioning. It is a gift of God that has not been given to other animals. This is the Abrahamic vision.

The puzzle of consciousness has been tackled by philosophers since the most ancient times. The authors of the Upanishads have much to say about it. In India, sophisticated meditative techniques were developed to apprehend, rather than comprehend, consciousness. As Ravi Ravindra put it:

> From the perspective of yoga... the deepest self, to which alone belongs true seeing and knowing, cannot be known; but it can be identified with. One can become

that self (*Atman, Purusha*) and know with it, from its
level, with its clarity. (2004, 101)

It is quite satisfying to many to regard love and laughter, acts of
kindness, and the quest for truth as among the peak performances of
neuron firings, as evolutionary upshots of cerebral chemistry, as
readable scripts from a genetic programming. It may well be that we
are essentially sophisticated carnal robots which compose music, write
poetry, and make jokes. But it is also plausible that some kind of
transcendence is at work in the context of value and meaning and
whatever else goes with what we loosely call the human spirit.

From the perspective of one Hindu vision, if there is splendor in
the perceived world and pattern in its functioning, and if this can all
result in the grand experiences of life and thought, then even prior to
the advent of humans, there must have been an *experiencer* of a vastly
superior order. As A. N. Whitehead recognized, "consciousness
presupposes experience, and not experience consciousness" (1929,
53). This Cosmic Experiencer spans the cosmic range in space and
time. This universal undergirding principle is known as Brahman. Just
as the expanse of water in the oceans is scattered all over land in ponds
and lakes and rivers and bottles, all-embracing Brahman finds
expression in countless life forms. Every living entity is a miniature
light. We have emanated from that primordial effulgence, like photons
from a glorious galactic core, destined for the terrestrial experience for
a brief span on the eternal time line, only to re-merge with that from
which we sprang.

The Hindu vision paints individual consciousness on a cosmic
canvas. It recognizes the transience of us all as separate entities, yet
incorporates us into the infinity that encompasses us. It does not rule
out the possibility of other manifestations of Brahman, sublime and
subtle, carbon or silicon-based, elsewhere amidst the stellar billions.
It recognizes the role of matter, and the limits of the mind, but sees
silent spirit at the core of it all. It does not speak of rewards and
punishments in anthropocentric terms, or of a He-God
communicating in local languages. Yet, it regards the religious

expressions of humanity as echoes of the Universal Spirit, even as volcanic outbursts reveal submerged powers of far greater magnitude.

In the vision of the *advaita* school of Hinduism: the abstract quality-less divine principle (*nirguna brahman*), which is the root cause of everything, appears as divinity with qualities (*saguna brahman*) such as goodness and mercy, compassion and grace, which is personified as the gods we worship in various forms and with various names. This is not unlike the fact that one section of the all pervasive electromagnetic radiation impinges on the human brain as light and provides it with the joys of color, form, and beauty.

The scientific, philosophical, and religious quest for transcendence may well be more than imaginative fantasy. Even as a heliotrope is drawn to light, the evolved brain may be reaching out for transcendence. This thirst could well be the yearning of the human spirit to remember its own pre-physical origins.

Science has revealed a good bit of the mechanism of heartbeat, kidney function, digestive process and of practically everything going on in the human body. It has traced the roots of perception in the brain, even a little of the connections between thinking, dreaming, and brain states. It seems to be just a few more layers of mystery before we uncover the core of consciousness: such is the conviction of scientists who probe into the secrets of the self with models, meters, and microscopes. Since the 1990s, more than a couple of millennia after Patañjali and other explorers of yogic experiences in India, we have been seeing books, journals, and conferences on consciousness-science.

Science looks for the source and nature of consciousness, tries to trace its emergence to molecular matter. It is not interested in reaching higher levels of consciousness. This is left to practitioners of meditation and experimenters with psychedelic drugs. The assumption in the scientific perspective is that consciousness is ultimately a brain-engendered phenomenon, and not, as religions generally view it, indicative of some intangible entity like soul or spirit. Science's tenet is based on the observed fact that even tiny amounts of extraneous chemicals can significantly alter normal consciousness. Anesthesia does it all the time in hospitals. Intrusive molecules create perceptions of reality that have little correspondence with what nature-fashioned brains recognize.

Francis Crick asserted that our identity is "no more than the behavior of a vast assembly of nerve cells and their associated molecules" (1994, 3). But to many, this hypothesis is only as persuasive as the assertion that an epic poem is just a mix of letters and spaces on pages.

Science has to figure out what transforms sensory inputs into consciousness, what converts pressure waves into the joys of glorious music. Reaction to stimuli is not consciousness. Responding to light like a photographic film is not the same as appreciating the beauty of the rainbow. The transformation of stimuli into experiences is what David Chalmers (*The conscious mind,* 1966) famously called the *hard problem,* and argued, contrary to some current thinking and provoking much opposition, that reductive explanations of consciousness just will not work.

Efforts to explain consciousness reductively in the scientific framework have been largely through neuroscience and/or quantum mechanics, or a combination of both. There have been quite a few theories in this regard. Stuart Hameroff, in his essay on "Consciousness, neurobiology and quantum mechanics" (2006), and Roger Penrose (*Shadows of the mind,* 1994) have talked about microtubules in the brain giving rise to consciousness. The most recent attempt to link quantum physics with consciousness is due to Stuart Kauffman who opines that:

> A conscious mind is a persistently poised quantum coherent-decoherent system, forever propagating quantum coherent behavior, yet forever also decohering to classical behavior. (2008, 209)

Daniel Dennett wrote a book with a somewhat presumptuous title: *Consciousness explained* (1991). He spoke of the brain as made up of a bundle of agencies, which are loosely independent, wherein content-fixation occurs, and he bluntly rejected the existence of what

Clarence I. Lewis (*Mind and the world order,* 1929) called *qualia:* the qualitative experiences that the brain turns physical inputs into. In his view, we are not just descendants of apes, but are zombies. Needless to say, some critics suggested that Dennett's book should be called "Consciousness Explained Away."

The subject of consciousness is open to investigation and reflection from a variety of disciplines. Ken Wilber suggested in a paper (1997, 71-92) that it can be approached from at least a dozen different perspectives, ranging from cognitive science and introspection to quantum mechanics and subtle energies.

Science has constructed machines that do muscular work more efficiently than hard-working laborers. It has devised systems that compute and classify more rapidly than the most gifted humans. Man-made machines compose music, draw graphs, and play chess better than brainy mortals. There seems to be no limit to what technology can fabricate. Gerald Edelman and Giulio Tononi (*A universe of consciousness: How matter becomes imagination,* 2000) say there are two levels of consciousness: primary and higher-order. The sense of self is associated only with the latter. They trace consciousness to what they call the dynamic core in the neurophysiology of complex organisms. Edelman also gave a four point recipe which led to the development of software agents that live, eat, mate, and play. Artificial Intelligence scientists are convinced that silicon-based conscious entities will be with us some day.

The scientific interpretation of consciousness as an emergent property of the cerebral system suggests that our own visions of reality are no more than pictures resulting from evolutionarily developed sub-cranial biochemistry. Birds and beasts function in different realms of reality. Objective descriptions become species-dependent.

This need not trivialize reality. Through evolution we have managed to resonate with aspects of reality that are of relevance to our survival. From this perspective, there may be other levels of our perception of reality. Through other means, the human brain may be able to extend its capacities for becoming aware of further dimensions of reality: perhaps that is what the mystics of the world manage to achieve. One may argue that alteration of neural chemistry through yoga or other practices helps reveal or develop these awarenesses.

Which view of consciousness is correct: the religious, the scientific, the mystical, or whatever? One might as well ask which view of music is correct: enjoyable melody or superposition of discrete frequencies?

Consciousness in the future

Merlin Donald (*A mind so rare: The evolution of human consciousness*, 2001, 178ff) suggested that there are at least three levels of consciousness. In Level One there is "sensory binding and selective attention." In Level Two, there is also short term memory. At the highest Level Three, awareness is long-term, where there is also governance and actions are controlled voluntarily. This shows that consciousness can evolve to higher levels.

The Buddha means the Enlightened One. This refers to a person who has achieved the highest level of consciousness. Perhaps there were others, too, of that stature: maybe Pythagoras and Zoroaster, Moses and Jesus, and all the rishis and saints of the world. In other words, it is possible, in principle, for any human being to reach a heightened level of consciousness. In the tradition of the Mahayana Buddhism, there are numerous individuals on the way to becoming Buddhas. These are the Bodhisattvas of the tradition. As Étienne Lamotte explains:

> The Buddha is already possessed of Supreme Enlightenment, while the great bodhisattvas... are merely "close to enlightenment." Apart from this difference, the Buddhas and bodhisattvas... convert the beings in the universes which are theirs and often appear simultaneously in manifold forms and in different universes. (1984, 92)

This notion that eventually all humankind will reach a higher level of consciousness is in consonance with Darwinian evolution.

After all, if we have come this far from our simian state in a few million years, who is to say that we cannot evolve even farther?

In the nineteenth century, Friedrich Nietzsche (*Also sprach Zarathustra [Thus spoke Zarathusa]*, 1885) gave his own vision of a future state of man: the *Übermensch*, Overman or Superman who will go beyond religions and morals and dominate the world. He disparaged Man because he is fettered to Christianity and other religions, and women for various other reasons. He made such provocative statements as "Man shall be trained for war and woman for the recreation of the warrior." Nietzsche declared that man will be a laughing stock or a painful embarrassment in the eyes of the Superman. It turns out that Nietzsche's version of Superman is the one who is a laughing stock and a painful embarrassment, and even served as an unwitting hero for Nazis.

In the twentieth century, there were at least two visionaries who spoke of the future state of human consciousness. The first was Sri Aurobindo. Referring to the current elevated status of human beings in the animal world, he wrote, in complete contrast to Nietzsche:

> But what he [Man] gets of this higher state in his normal mind is only an intimation, a primary glimpse, a crude hint of the splendour, the light, the glory and divinity of the spirit within him. A complete conversion of all the parts of his being into moulds and instruments of the spiritual consciousness is demanded of him before he can make quite real, constant, present to himself this greater thing that he can be and entirely live in what is now to him at the best a luminous aspiration. (1920, p. 754-55)

Again, in his *The life divine* (1914-1920), he wrote that Man "cannot be the last term of this evolution. He is too imperfect an expression of the Spirit" (p. 1009). He also stated:

> The transition from mind to Supermind is a passage from Nature into Supernature. For that very reason it cannot be achieved by a mere effort of our mind or our unaided

aspiration. Overmind and Supermind are involved and hidden in the earth-nature; but, in order that they may emerge in us, there is needed a pressure of the same powers already formulated in their full natural force on their own superconscient planes. The powers of the Super-conscience must descend into us and uplift us and transform our being. (p. 921)

Here we see a bold and bright vision for humanity.

Likewise, Teilhard de Chardin (*Le phénomène humain,* 1955) expressed the view that evolution is unidirectional, moving from molecules to mind towards higher levels of complexity, and that we humans are not its end-point. He suggested that there is an eventual Omega Point, which is personal, transcendent, and autonomous, towards which we are irreversibly drawn. Here again is an expanding vision that blends the physical with the spiritual, and which is in sharp contrast with the nihilism of Nietzsche.

A more recent version of this prediction for the future has been given by Ray Kurzweil (*The singularity is near: When humans transcend biology,* 2005) in whose vision there is a step by step by step progression in the evolution of the universe, from the first physics/chemistry epoch to the final sixth one in which the human-machine civilization will spill into the very limits of the universe. Then inanimate matter would become "substrates for computation and intelligence." At this time, a universal super-intelligence will emerge.

The world as illusion: Maya

Classical Hindu philosophy propounded a vision of reality, according to which the essence of ultimate reality is normally veiled from our apprehension because of a number of constraining factors that are imposed on matter and mind. The result of all this is the creation of *maya,* a world of illusion to which normal human experience is inevitably subject. Maya is a technical term with a variety of interpretations. In the Shetâsvatara Upanishad it says pithily:

Mayâm tu prakritim viddhi mâyinam tu mahesvaram;
tasyâvayaiva bhûtais tu vyâptam sarvam idam jagat
[Know then that the world is illusion, and the wielder of the
    illusion is the Great Divine.
This whole world is pervaded by beings [aspects] that are
    parts of Him].
(SU 4.10)

In modern terminology, the world is essentially virtual reality. In the computer-generated virtual reality, as Howard Rheingold explains (1991, 112), there is the *immersion*, "the illusion of being inside a computer-generated scene," and *navigation*, which is the power to "move around, as if inside it." It could well be that our own real world is but another virtual world. As Richard L. Thompson suggests, "this world is an illusion created by something else. We don't know what that something else is, but we can simply call it Ground Reality" (2003, xiii). Or, to use the sophisticated quantum mechanical jargon of Alex Comfort (1984, 164), perceived reality is made up of the *eigenstates* of the *aum* operator.

In so far as *maya* is a veil that screens the true nature of reality from our apprehension, it may be regarded as something negative. But leaving aside the logical difficulty that the notion of *maya*, in so far as it is entertained by the human mind, may itself be *maya*, it need not be regarded as necessarily evil or hurtful, but enlightening and revelatory. Indeed, it serves us well in the course of our lives, and is at the root of many of our enjoyments, institutions, intellectual exercises, and societal interactions. Certain aspects of *maya* have even helped us gain a deeper understanding (or visions of higher categories) of reality. Let us consider some of these.

Art is *aesthetic maya*. A great painting is an illusion which transports us to an aesthetic experience, as indeed is any work of art. It is the illusion that creates the artistic experience. Goethe said:

> The highest problem of every art is, by means of appearances, to produce the illusion of a loftier reality.
> (1811-14, 2:35)

Literature may be regarded as *emotional maya*. It paints imaginary people and events in moving ways, it kindles our longing for justice, it allows us to express our capacities for anger and compassion, and it helps us in our search for the deeper truths regarding human nature. We know that not one page in a novel is true, yet great literature moves us profoundly, it touches our feelings and stirs our emotions.

Democracy, in principle, is a form of government in which every citizen has a say in the affairs of the nation. Communism is supposed to endow power to the people, it is touted as the end of oppression, and the absence of exploitation. But we know only too well that these are not quite so in actuality. When examined through the microscope of critical analysis, political institutions are *maya* too. And yet, such *political maya* makes millions of people feel they truly enjoy freedom and economic security.

History is supposed to be a record of major events that occurred in the past. In most instances, however, it is a narration of events that did not happen the way they are reported. The goal of history often is, intentionally or otherwise, to make a people feel good about their past. History has often served as a *patriotic maya*. It serves the important purpose of making a people feel good about themselves. It is necessary for a healthy self-image of a people.

Mythology is another grand *maya* that has played a role in human history. It speaks of gods and demons who never existed, in terms and language that are inspiring and fascinating. But mythologies also make a people feel good, creating in them, like history, the impression that their past was graced by majestic beings, by all powerful heroes and heroines who fought for the good and defeated the evil. Myths are thus *inspirational maya*.

Mathematics is *logical maya*. It gives us impeccable demonstrations of theorems, reveals the consistency of concepts, and takes us to abstract domains of sharp analysis. Yet, it has been shown that at the ultimate level, it is impossible to logically prove the basic propositions (the inner consistency) of mathematical systems. It is somewhat like proving the validity of logic by using logic.

Religion may be regarded as *spiritual maya,* for it creates in us the impression that we truly know about the nature and attributes of a divine principle. Yet, it gives meaning and purpose to life, and more importantly, it has been, and continues to be, the source of solace and psychological comfort to countless millions. When Sigmund Freud (*The future of an illusion,* 1927) described religion as an illusion he explained that illusions arise from our deepest wishes, and are to be distinguished from errors which result from simple misapprehension of facts. Illusions could also arise from cultural necessities.

In mystical experience one sees visions of a reality that is probably the result of abnormal brain biochemistry. Mystical experience then becomes a powerful *psychological maya* which has nevertheless instigated affirmations and utterances that have transformed the lives and world views of many individuals and groups.

Philosophy is essentially *speculative maya,* a play with concepts and ideas, creating systems in terms of which one tries to interpret in broad terms the nature of human thought, condition, and world views. With careful analysis and argumentation, however, every system of philosophy crumbles down.

Finally, we have science. Its goal is to reveal the true nature of physical reality. But science too is *maya.* The history of science shows that many past theories, explanations, and convictions of the scientific world were totally wrong. Science is *fruitful maya.* Its framework provides us with intellectual satisfactions, and with its results we are able to concoct a great many things to satisfy our need and greed.

Thus, not just individual lives but civilizations and institutions are based upon *maya* of all kinds. We are condemned or blessed to lead a life guided and inspired by ideas and ideals which are both distorted and enriched by a variety of maya.

The philosopher Loyal Rue wrote a whole book (*By the grace of guile,* 1994), expanding on this, though it is not clear that he was familiar with the Hindu *maya* doctrine. In his book, Rue argues that there are no absolute truths or values, and that admitting this will make us too uncomfortable. What we need, he says, is a *noble lie.* He goes on to show that both nature and human society are based on deception. He asserts that we need deception and self-deception for our very survival, as it were, which is why we color and distort reality.

What Rue calls the noble lie is what I have called endopotent truth. These are not lies, but rather interpretations of experiences that bring sanity, peace of mind, and a sense of security. They also enrich our lives and make them meaningful. We do not regard art and literature, movies and poetry as lies, but as important modes of recognizing the human condition. Perhaps the same may be said of many aspects of religious truths. Sometimes this is equally so of scientific truths. It is only in retrospect and by a later generation that the mistaken notions implicit in past scientific worldviews are revealed.

Mystery: religious perspective

Most ancient cultures accepted occult principles. Mysteries were associated with Isis and Osiris in ancient Egypt, with Demeter and Kore in ancient Greece (Eleusinian and Orphic mysteries), with Indra and yajnas in India, and so on. These were the *mysteries* of religions.

In the temple at Chidambaram in South India, built between the tenth and the fourteenth centuries, there is consecrated an ethereal *rahasyam* or mystery. It represents formless divinity which is regarded in the tradition as the grand mystery of all.

Religions try to articulate the inexpressible; they help us experience the unfathomable. Through these efforts, sooner or later, we are confronted with Mystery. In the solitude of wilderness, during a gaze at the starry heavens, or in silent contemplation of life, we encounter mystery in our different ways. In the metaphor of Omar Khayyàm (Fitzgerald 1859, 389), mystery is a door for which we find no key, the veil through which we might not see. Sometimes it is wiser to accept that there are mysteries, rather than to strive to comprehend them. The recognition and surrender to Mystery can be more fulfilling than refusal to acknowledge it or awkward struggles to unravel it.

Many cultures guard(ed) higher truths from easy reach of the common people. Wielders of wisdom have often practiced secretive possession and transmission of what they regard(ed) as knowledge of mysteries. Egyptian priests, Vedic chanters, members of the Pythagorean brotherhood, Jewish kabala were among the practitioners of the knowledge-for-the-initiated-men-only school. Pythagoreans called it esoteric knowledge. To people outside of the brotherhood, what they were engaged in was mysterious.

Mystery is not confusion in the face of complexity, or puzzlement at a problem, or magic-mongering. It does not call for abandonment of efforts to answer worldly problems. Mystery is the profound response of a sensitive mind to the awe provoked by the magnitude and majesty of the perceived universe and the intractable events and human encounters that causally quilt the web that is the world. Mystery is a feeling of reverence and humility in the face of deeply felt experience that at least some humans experience, it is wonderment at the ultimate source of joys and sorrows in the interlude of human consciousness. It is a reflection on the marvel of the ephemeral flicker of terrestrial existence, an irrepressible why and wherefore of it all.

Machines manufacture and computers calculate, but only humans experience mystery. If we do not wonder about origins and ends at least once during life's journey, we are but biochemical blobs that devour matter and energy for a time-span, sport and make noise, and then go into eternal extinction. There is fulfillment in the experience of unuttered awe, enlightenment in the recognition that there are question marks with nothing to follow. Mystery is like the blanks that frame the printed page: they surround much that conveys matter and meaning.

The eerie aspects of mysteries have somewhat faded, but their vestiges are still very much with us, in every rite and ritual of religious praxis. Mystery may provoke deep silence. In the religious framework, mystery is unknown and unknowable, but one can get glimpses of it. When we pray or worship, when we light a candle or wave a flame to a divine symbol, when we prostrate, bow down or kneel, when we sing a psalm or chant a mantra or proclaim in faith that God is great, we are acknowledging the Mystery that eludes us.

Mystery: scientific perspective

In the world of science there are several types of mysteries. First, there is mystery as the as yet unknown: the range of phenomena that cry out for explanation. What is unknown may be not the phenomenon, but its explanation. However, unlike in the religious framework, in science, the unknown is not regarded as unknowable.

In the last quarter of the nineteenth century, for example, when the most meticulous experiments by A. A. Michelson and E. W. Morley did not reveal the existence of an all-pervading ether which was expected to be there, it was a mystery. It remained so until Einstein's theory of special relativity revealed that there is nothing at absolute rest; hence, no ether. The erasing of this mystery revolutionized the physicist's worldview. When the graphs for black-body radiation did not conform to what was expected, and led to conceptual catastrophes, it was a major mystery. Max Planck's hypothesis cleared up that mystery and inaugurated quantum theory. There are many such examples in science. The removal of a mystery is invariably related to a fundamental discovery.

Because science has been consistently successful in transforming every mystery into new understanding, scientists do not like the word mystery. They would rather call it an unsolved problem. Mysteries, to most scientists, are metastable states of non-understanding, often like darkness before dawn. Like the morning dew, they evaporate away by the light of new knowledge, causing an euphoric eureka.

Aside from the puzzles of nature that tease the human mind, there are other types of mystery that one may experience in the scientific mode. One is the congruence of aesthetics with truth. Nature is orderly, for sure, and understandably so, or else it is difficult to have a stable universe for a long stretch of time. But why should so much beauty be associated with order? Precise and inexorable laws are enough to keep the cosmic clockwork ticking away for eons. But why on earth (some pun intended) should they also be so beautiful? Anybody who has reveled in the equations of Maxwell, Dirac, or Einstein, and contemplated the diagrams of Feynman must be touched by their aesthetic dimension no less than by their explanatory prowess. As we behold the rich patterns and coloration in the landscapes and life forms that have evolved, whether of birds or butterflies, mountains or lakes, we sense endless visual delights. On purely rational grounds, these are quite uncalled for. This could strike one as mystery too.

The scientist discovers; the artist creates. Whether music or painting, poetry or play, story or dance, the artist's work involves the creation of something that did not exist in the universe before. Artistic creativity may someday be traced to the subconscious, to genes, to evolutionary psychology, or whatever. But as of now—the creativity of a Mozart or a Mutthuswami Dikshatar, of a Michelangelo or a Jamini Roy, and the mathematical genius of an Euler or a Ramanujan—all creativity is truly mysterious in that it defies any causal explanation, and may have to do with extraordinarily complex properties of the brain.

"The goal of science," wrote Karl Pearson, "is nothing short of the complete interpretation of the universe" (1892, 14). Following this view, psychologists, behaviorists, neuroscientists, evolutionists, cognitive scientists and many other specialists in the sciences have taken up the challenge of trying to explain how creativity *emerges* in the human brain. I have seen at least one essay entitled "Creativity explained." Not all intelligent people realize that certain aspects of the human experience can never be fully explained, but can be no less a fulfilling personal experience or matter for observing and enjoying as such. This is not to say that scientific efforts should not be expended to figure out how such things as laughter and love, compassion and creativity arise in humans, but it is likely that such theories will have only passing appeal, without enhancing or diminishing their intrinsic wonder.

Finally there is mystery in a mind that reflects, sees the world in a grain of sand and scribbles eternity on a scrap of paper. Intelligibility of phenomena to the human mind is a great mystery, for it is as if the whole universe becomes aware of itself through neuronal sparks in the human brain.

While religious vision sees Mystery as existing beyond perceived reality, science is a mystery in itself: for it is a palpitation of the entire universe in a cerebral network under the human skull! This, to me, is the most mysterious of all mysteries.

Anthropic insignificance

The materialist view leads us to the idea of anthropic insignificance in the universe. From the scientific perspective, the importance of the human species is by no means obvious when viewed in terms of physical dimensions. No planet, star or galaxy, if they could judge, would attribute to puny humans greater esteem than to icebergs or volcanoes. The relative smallness of the human frame is beyond question, even to the most superficial observer. The Earth itself, in comparison to Jupiter, the sun and the stars, is like a pulverized particle in relation to the Pacific Ocean. As the poet William Watson said: "Man and his littleness perish, erased like an error and cancelled" (from "A Hymn to the Sea" in *The Father of the Forest and Other Poems*, 1895, 32).

Furthermore, when it comes to sheer physical power, our bodies are but flimsy structures susceptible to instant decimation by nature's fury. Lightning can kill anyone in a brief thunderous flash. In the words of Shakespeare, "Diseased nature oftentimes breaks forth in strange eruptions, and shakes the old bedlam earth and topples down steeples and old moss-grown towers" (*King Henry IV Part 1*, Act 3, Scene 1, ca. 1597). Hurricanes and tornados, earthquakes and tsunamis can annihilate thousands without a moment's notice. Even tiny life forms in the microbial realm causing plagues and pestilences can spell disasters, ruining cities and wiping out civilizations. In the face of all this, in physical terms we humans are no match for many forces and factors that often arise in the blind fury of nature.

When we compare the age of our species to that of the universe, and reflect on the ephemeral nature of individual lives, our significance shrinks even further. What are a few million years of human survival compared to the more than twelve billion years during which the universe has survived and evolved? What is a century of longevity compared to the age of mountains, glaciers, stars and galaxies? It is clear from such perspectives that if one evaluates significance in terms of size or superior strength, of longevity or persistence, *Homo sapiens* is all too frail, a very recent and vulnerable entity in the grand arena of space in the endless stretch of time. As it says in *The Kasidah of Haji Abdu El-Yezdi*:

> The world is old, and Man is young,
> The world is large and man is small.
> We are but atoms of a moment's span,
> And can't hold ourselves as an All-in-All.
> (Burton 1880, II, Stanza 20).

Even when we acknowledge that at the purely physical level humans do not have a special place in the universe, it would be but a partial vision if we fail to recognize that we play an unusual role in it. To see this, all we have to do is to imagine the auditorium of a theater that is stark empty while a most magnificent performance is on stage. What a wasteful expenditure of artistry that would be! The universe without the human brain in it would be much like this. It would be dark and dismal while it is throbbing with the most fantastic occurrences.

In this context, we may consider a different paradigm which is not unreasonable in our understanding of consciousness. Let us reflect a little on the nature of light and color. We know that light is made up of electromagnetic waves of various frequencies and wavelengths. These waves in the world beyond our brains are not split into a spectrum of colors. But those very waves, upon interacting with the human brain, create the impression of color. This raises rather important questions. Is color an aspect of the physical universe? Would there be such things as color in the universe in the absence of an evolved brain? The mechanisms of color vision are described at the level of the retina in terms of tristimulus values. The exact nature of color perception and the status of color as a feature of our *perception* of the world, is a matter of complex and continuing scientific research and philosophical dispute. So the answer to the question—Is color an intrinsic aspect of the universe?—is, as far as science can tell, No.

Anthropic uniqueness

This brings us to the notion of anthropic uniqueness. It is insightful to reflect on the fact that all the light and beauty, all the grandeur and majesty of the universe are unraveled only in the tiny retinas of human beings which can accommodate pictures of the star-studded expanse with multiple galaxies in them. Neither the golden sunset nor the pattered wings of butterflies, neither the fragrance of flowers nor the taste of honey would emerge as aspects of the physical world without the highly complex human brain. The human brain has the unique capacity to interact with atoms and molecules and pressure waves and photons to metamorphose a bleak jungle of dust and rocks and fire and fury into a magnificent universe studded with the glorious sun and stars and the poetry of silvery snowflakes.

Consider the extraordinarily wide range of art created by humankind over the ages. All the beauty and symmetry, inspiring illusion and aesthetic complexity reflected in them, let alone the fascinating symbolism they embody: all these have emerged from human consciousness. There would be no art without our presence. Indeed, it has been said that painting and sculpture are glorious expressions of the artistic spirit, as are music, poetry and dance. And many thoughtful people have experienced art as a bridge to something beyond. In the words of the poet Elizabeth Barrett Browning:

> What is art
> But life upon the larger scale, the higher,
> When, graduating up in a spiral line
> Of still expanding and ascending gyres,
> It pushes toward the intense significance
> Of all things, hungry for the Infinite.
> (from *Aurora Leigh*, Book 4, 1856, 79)

The world without humans would be plunged in an eerie silence where there would be waves for sure, but no transducing receptacle to transform them into sound and music. Through the magic of our vocal chords and the marvelous resonating devices with strings and wind, and our limitless capacity for creativity we fill the atmosphere of our planet with magnificent music such as is found, as far as we know, nowhere else in the universe. Let us also remember, as Joseph Addison wrote that:

> Music religious heat inspires
> It takes the soul and lifts it high,
> And wings it with sublime desires,
> And fits it to bespeak Divinity.
> (from "A Song for St. Cecilia's Day," Stanza 4, 1694, 1:21-22)

And what about those magical mathematical truths, from the properties of primes and of the exponential, the ubiquitous *pi* and other transcendental numbers, infinite series and transfinite numbers, which seem to have an objective existence, and yet are nowhere to be detected with the most powerful instruments. A mathematician once said that one of Ramanujan's formulas in the theory of numbers was of such pristine beauty that it was the best proof for the existence of God. More exactly, it is the best proof that human consciousness is a mirror on which the highest truths are reflected by some unfathomable process.

Consider the world of ideas, with concepts and abstract principles, perspectives and notions of truth, all of which constitute philosophy. Philosophy, as Emerson reminded us, is the account that the mind gives itself of the constitution of the world. This is another subtle dimension in the universe that has become explicit as a result of human consciousness. But again, could it be that philosophy is also a reflection, blurred or clear, faithful or distorted, in the ocean depths of consciousness of the countless forms and modes in which the kaleidoscopic world can present itself?

Then, of course, there is science, a rational and coherent interpretation of phenomena which is essentially a product of human consciousness. Right or wrong, such interpretations are parts of human thought which constitute a realm of intangible reality, more subtle than the strings of string-theory, and they, too, have arisen from consciousness. Associated with science is technology, with its countless tools and creations which have transformed the face of our planet in ways that Nature by herself could never have even imagined. More than *Homo sapiens* (the Wise Man), we are *Homo faber* (Man the maker), even *Homo creator* (Man the Creator).

Human consciousness has also had significant impact on the world around us. We have intruded in a thousand ways into the domain of nature, often to our advantage, sometimes in ways injurious to our fellow creatures on the planet, and now at peril to our own selves. The planets Mars and Jupiter and Venus had never been viewed in much detail by humans, nor had their images been captured as photographs, before the advent of human science and technology. More dramatically, as far as we know, no nuclear fusion has ever occurred anywhere but in the core of stars. The one exception has been here on earth, and it was instigated by human ingenuity. This is an event of extraordinary import in the context of what nature does and cannot do. But most significantly from a cosmic perspective, all the stories of stellar birth and death, of galaxies and expansion, remained untold for eons until humans verbalized them in words and equations. None of the glory and splendor of the universe would ever have come to the surface, if there was only mute matter and no measuring mind in the cosmos.

Thus consciousness is the map on which the subtle aspects of the physical universe, such as mathematics, music, and the laws of nature, become manifest. We may imagine a universe that subsisted tirelessly since the first big blast from which it all came to be. We may compute and conceptualize symmetry breaking and the separation of the fundamental forces, gravitation and radiation pressure, nuclear fusion and the formation of stars, but it was all like the wandering of a blind man in a vast wilderness: for there was no light before the evolution of the rods in the retina, there was no green grass or blue skies, which are but responsive descriptions of noumenal states.

This then is the role of the human spirit in the world. The emergence of consciousness which led to an awareness of what has been transpiring since cosmic birth was as great an event in cosmic history as the first big blast of its material creation. Aside from uncovering beauty and symmetry, that awareness injects meaning into a mechanical and mindless world. It is as if by our presence we have lit up the whole universe which, until our emergence, had been plunged in a dismal depth of darkness. We are reminded of the poem:

TRANSCENDENCE

Beauty and colors so pleasing to the eye,
Stars and planets in the dark sky,
The ratio in the circle denoted by *pi*,
The surging of the seas and the marvel of the fly

The splendor of the flowers that blossom and die:
All these were there as eons rolled by.
But the plants and the trees, the beasts and the birds
Described not these in rhymes or in words.

Nature and her laws were occult in the dark,
Till consciousness came, and lit them with its spark.
How did this happen, for what purpose and whence?
Could the answer for this be in Transcendence?
(Raman 2002)

A perspective from information theory

A key concept of twentieth century science is *information*. Wherever there is structure, there is information. Information enables one to decide upon a course of action for a particular purpose. Information also serves other purposes in the functioning of the world. In information theory, the term is used in a technical sense with mathematical formulas for negentropy [negative entropy].

We may consider three orders of information which are operational in the universe, qualitatively speaking.

First order information furnishes the codes by which matter-energy is stirred or guided into ordered activity. The basic codes are the laws of physics, from gravitation and electromagnetism to those of elementary particle decay and gluon cementing. These are the rules by which electrons swing around nuclei and planets around stars, by which fire burns and proteins sustain life. We cannot see or touch these laws: they are not located here or there; they pervade the whole universe. They are silent as the informational substratum of the universe. At higher levels, such natural-law information is responsible for valence bonds and chemical structure, and they lead to double helices and neuron firings. Science deals with the details of this kind of information.

Second order information is more subtle. This information transforms sensory inputs into experience in complex cerebral structures. This is the so-called hard-problem of consciousness science. All life is an accumulation of experience of sights and sounds, of tastes and feels and smells, passing by ever so swiftly on the consciousness plane. Furthermore, second order information extracts meaning out of sounds and scribbles. When we hear a spoken word or read a written note, they become intelligible only if there is the framework (linguistic familiarity) necessary for this information. As far as we know, second order information comes into play only under the human skull, though it is not improbable that there could be other such systems elsewhere among the stellar billions. It has not as yet been fully analyzed with the tools of modern science.

Third order information furnishes the human brain with knowledge about the world that is not directly derived from experience and carefully collected data. Third order information is given to but a few. It could range from scientific insights and mathematical theorems to spiritual revelations and knowledge about the beyond. Because of its extreme rarity and subtlety, it is not easy to be sure if third order information is always reliable. But it plays an important role in scientific breakthroughs, and even more so in the religious context. In fact, the initiators of all religions have relied on third order information for whatever they have preached.

There is a way in which the notion of revelation may be incorporated into the framework and terminology of current science. Consider the room in which we are. It is bathed in information-carrying electromagnetic waves from everywhere on earth, but of which none of us are ordinarily aware. However, if we are armed with appropriate electronic gadgetry we can decode all these million messages. That is what our radios, televisions and cell phones do. Or again, consider the photons that pervade all space. Those that enter our eyes reveal the presence of things, their colors and shapes and relative distance.

It requires all the complexity of electrical circuits to decode the radiations from the antennas of the radio and television stations of the world. It requires the complexity of the human ophthalmic system to transform photons into the rainbow hues. Likewise, our universe may be submerged in a sea of a million meanings, which remain couched in their undetected silence. Like neutrinos that can pass through miles of matter without the slightest interaction, *meaning-bits* may be crisscrossing the lengths and breaths of the universe, but if and when they encounter that highly evolved system called the brain, they are deciphered. From this perspective we can understand why it took all these eons before the meaning component of the universe began to be recognized. This view explains revelation, insights, and the other discoveries made by human beings. Just as intense gravitational pressure of enormous magnitude was necessary for instigating nuclear fusion in the core of stars and the synthesis of heavy elements in the bowel of supernovas, the evolution of the human brain was a necessary pre-condition for the manifestation of an all-pervading consciousness in individual entities.

Chapter 7
Ethical Aspects

The religious roots of ethics

Human life is directed not only by worldviews, but also by values. The values are of two kinds. First, there are the abstract and impersonal ones (for example, that we must seek the truth and we must be honest to ourselves). The other kind of values relates to interpersonal behavior. Science provides worldviews based on observation and analysis. But science does not *prescribe* rules for interpersonal interactions, which are an important part of being members of a society.

Traditionally, the principles of ethics were formulated by religions and inculcated by elders in a community. Thus, in ancient Greece, whether it was Socrates or Aristotle, the Epicurean or the Stoic school, reflections on the matter gave rise to different ethical philosophies.

In the Judaic tradition, the Ten Commandments were given to Moses on Mount Sinai. It says that in the third Hebrew month (Sivan) "Moses went up unto God, and the Lord called unto him out of the mountain" (Exodus 19:3). The Talmud is more specific and says it was on the third day of this month, when the Israelites were at the foot of Mount Sinai that the Lord appeared "midst thunder, billowing smoke, fire, and huge blasts of shofar." Such was the setting in which *aseret hadeverim* (the ten utterances) were given to Moses. It is also said that the Ten Commandments were inscribed in stone tablets (*luchot ha'even*). The Judaic world celebrates this event as Shavuot: the season of the giving of law. Aside from announcing Himself as "Adonai, thy

God," one is asked not to have any other God but the one who gave the Commandments: perhaps what was demanded was loyalty to the enunciated principles. Then there was the commandment to keep the Sabbath day as holy: meaning, perhaps, that one should remember God and reflect on the basic ethical principles at least once a week. One was asked to honor one's parents, a guiding principle for gratitude and family ties. Then there were injunctions against murder, adultery, stealing, bearing false witness against a neighbor, and coveting whatever belongs to others. Many of the ethical principles spelled out here can be relevant to all peoples. What makes the reading interesting is the eerie and majestic setting in which it is reported to have been delivered.

Christians derive their moral inspiration from the Biblical life of Jesus; in particular, from the Sermon on the Mount (Matthew 5:3-12). It is not in the form of a commandment, but rather of the benefit from adhering to certain thoughts and behavior. One becomes blessed in so many ways when one is meek, when one hungers for righteousness, when one is merciful and is pure of heart. Blessed too are the peacemakers and those who are persecuted for the cause of righteousness. Indeed one is blessed when one is reviled and persecuted (for upholding a right cause). Of this, St. Augustine wrote:

> If any one will piously and soberly consider the sermon which our Lord Jesus Christ spoke on the mount, as we read it in the Gospel according to Matthew, I think that he will find in it, so far as regards the highest morals, a perfect standard of the Christian life....The sermon is brought to a close in such a way that it is clear there are in it all the precepts which go to mold life. (394, 3)

Of the Sermon on the Mount, again, Fulton J. Sheen wrote:

> When he [Christ] said "You have heard" he included the Mosaic Law, Buddha with his eightfold way, Confucius with his rules for being a gentleman, Aristotle with his natural happiness, the broadness of the Hindus, and all

the humanitarian groups of our day, who would translate
some of the old codes in their own way and call them a
new way of life. (1958, 116)

Values in the Hindu world are enunciated in various sacred texts.
The Bhagavad Gita recommends specifically the following essential
virtues to be cultivated:

> Fearlessness, purity of mind, determination in pursuit of
> knowledge and austerities, charity, self-control, and
> performing prescribed rituals, recitation of the Vedas,
> meditation, rectitude; non-violence, truthfulness, being
> without anger, self-sacrifice, peace of mind; not
> criticizing, compassion towards beings, non-coveting;
> gentleness, modesty, steadfastness; courage, forgiving,
> fortitude, purity, freedom from malice and haughtiness.
> (Chap. 13)

There are two other ethical principles enunciated in the Gita
which are quite interesting. The first is that no matter what we do, it
must be done in a spirit of dedication to the larger whole. The Gita
also says explicitly: "You have rights over only your action. Let not the
fruits of actions inspire you" (2:47). What this means is that in our
commitments to society and community, when we work for a political
cause, for social justice, for philanthropy, etc., it is imperative that we
don't think of personal gains that we should extract from our services
(Raman 1997, 41).

The Code of Manu, often condemned for its caste-based penal
system, gives a most insightful set of ten items that should be our
guiding ethical principles. Three of these are for our physical well-
being: temperance, purity of body and mind, and control over one's
senses; three are for our intellectual well-being: adherence to reason,
pursuit of knowledge, and steadfast pursuit of truth; three are for our
social well-being: forgiving of other's faults, being without anger, and
non-appropriation of what belongs to others. Manu recognized that
the basic laws of the *dharma* (right conduct) he prescribed, however

congenial they may be for ensuring individual and societal happiness, cannot be followed by one and all. It is human nature to give up pursuing a path if there are difficulties and frequent failures. Many potentially significant achievements are nipped in the bud because one does not persevere. So, as a tenth principle, Manu also included perseverance as an important element of ethical conduct.

In the Islamic world, the moral and legal framework is inspired by what is known as the Sharia which is derived from the Holy Qur'an. The traditional Muslim world regards the Sharia as the will of God, which has been described by some Muslim scholars as "the totality of religious, political, social, domestic, and private life" (Kjeilen 2005). Like the Dharmashastras of the Hindu world (which are no longer in vogue in India), the Sharia (which is practiced to varying degrees in many modern Islamic nations) spells out not only what one must do, but also punishments for specific derelictions. There are complex and varied commentaries on it, and also different schools and interpretations of the Sharia. (Bakhtiar and Reinhart 1995). It has been pointed out that in the Islamic worldview:

> God, man, nature, and society are closely intertwined and harmoniously interrelated. Islamic medicine is indeed one of the most important cultural manifestations of the spiritual, moral, and ethical values of Islam. (Bakar 1999, 103)

Though the punishments prescribed for certain offenses do seem rather severe from modern perspectives, it is important to remember that the Shari'a law "recognizes five kinds of actions: obligatory, the meritorious, the neutral, the reprehensible, and the forbidden. While there is broad agreement about the moral character of some activities, there is also wide disagreement about the precise moral nature of other activities, which is discussed within the schools of jurisprudence" (Leaman 1999, 17-18).

> Most of all, equality of all in the presence of God, charity, loyalty to friends and community, gratitude, hospitality,

forgiveness, and subservience to the Almighty are among
the key elements in Islamic ethics. (Esposito 2002)

The Divine is invoked countless times in the Holy Qur'an as *ar-rahïmi*, the most Merciful. Women wearing head-scarfs may seem submissive and oppressed to Westerners, and women in bikinis may seem depraved and exploited to Non-Westerners. Up to a point both these impressions may be right or wrong, but in either case, societal moral values should come from within and not be enforced from the outside.

Thanks largely to world-wide communication systems, the recognition of no longer tolerable values inherent in some traditional systems, as also a growing global trans-religious ethical system, modernists in all traditions are trying to reinterpret, modify, and even discard some of the injunctions in traditional religious frameworks that strike us as anachronistic, unconscionable and unacceptable in our present age. The forces impeding such changes are also growing strong, and time alone will tell which side will eventually assert itself. The Western experience suggests that one can never be totally certain the triumph of Enlightenment is always stable.

Ethics: secular perspectives

All through history there have been thinkers who have argued that moral behavior need not be tied to any religion. One can afford to be good without expecting post-mortem rewards for it, and one can refrain from bad behavior without any threat of severe punishment here or hereafter. Simple as these ideas may seem and even persuasive to many, historically this has not happened, perhaps because one needs to be both intellectually and morally sophisticated to embrace these views. It is true that most normal human beings ordinarily refrain from hurtful actions. It has been said that following the Decalogue and its equivalent may keep us outside the prison walls, but does not elevate us to higher levels. Then again, not lying or stealing or coveting the house or the car in a posh neighborhood occurs primarily when things are fine, and life goes on reasonably comfortably. But this has never been so for the vast majority of humankind all through history. Without fear of punishment, secular or religious, it is difficult for a hungry person to refrain from stealing some food. Likewise, moral restraint, especially of the sexual kind, may be difficult to exercise when one is placed in tempting situations.

Confucius spoke on the basic guidelines for being fully human, without resorting to depictions of rosy heaven and horrible hell. We read in his *Analects* (ca. 479-221 BCE) about benevolence, charity, love, right conduct, duty towards others, selflessness, loyalty, reciprocity, honoring parents, and the like: simple, yet sophisticated virtues with no mumble-jumble about God or after-life or heaven or hell. While stressing self-control, he did not recommend self-denial. He spoke more than 2500 years ago about an empire long gone, probably imaginary, where the spirit of science led to tranquility and happiness.

> Things were investigated, knowledge became complete. Their knowledge became complete, their thoughts were sincere. Their thoughts were sincere, their hearts were then rectified. Their hearts being rectified, their own selves were cultivated. Their own selves being cultivated, their families were regulated. Their families being regulated, their states were rightly governed. Their states being rightly governed, the whole empire was made tranquil and happy. (Legge 1893, 358)

In the seventeenth century, Thomas Hobbes speculated that even the highest moral behavior was ultimately instigated by selfish motives and colored by unhealthy passions. In his view even gratitude is never pure, but tainted by a secret hostility towards the giver. Hobbes, scientific-minded and materialist that he was, believed that man is intrinsically mean and selfish (*Leviathan*, 1651/1668). As the Latin proverb says, "*Homo homini lupus est:* Man is a wolf to other men" (Plautus ca. 190 BCE, 53). This is somewhat in harmony with the Judeo-Christian idea that, because of the misbehavior of Adam and Eve, we are all born as sinners. Largely through the writings of Enlightenment philosophers such as Voltaire, the idea of godless ethics spread.

The thesis of secular ethics is simply this: that most of the civilizing principles inherent in the various traditional religions can be practiced without the metaphysical paraphernalia of religions. In other words, aside from accomplishing the same behavioral goals, secular ethical systems are devoid of beliefs in the supernatural which have no scientific basis, unnecessary fears of punishment from some unseen and overwhelming power, and claims of superiority of denominational religions. But this appeals only to some fairly sophisticated minds. Even while theoretically recognizing its validity, many serious thinkers in the religious traditions are not in favor of it because they feel that belief in God and affiliation to religion do more than make people be nice to others. As they see it, unbelief leads to moral relativism, and opens up possibilities of nihilism. In certain contexts such as sexual morality, it cannot put any rational check on promiscuity and unfaithfulness. They fear that, as Dostoevsky wrote, if God is taken away, then everything would be permitted (1880, 76-77).

Indeed, the fact remains that modern science has had some serious impacts on traditional beliefs and values. To begin with, no matter what theologians say and scriptures declare, the average person in scientifically awakened societies has a sneaking suspicion that science rather than holy books is to be trusted when it comes to explaining and interpreting the world. This shakes the foundations of religious beliefs. When a child gets sick, most parents take it to the doctor or the hospital rather than to the priest or the preacher. Sinner or no sinner, all patients do get cured by the same medications. This casts some doubt on the formerly held notion that we suffer because of our past misbehavior and evil thoughts. The moral constraints of earlier times, which depended largely on threats of unhappy aftermath for proscribed behavior, have also slackened. This leaves greater leeway for religiously discouraged transgressions.

We live at a time when polarization between the secular and the religious is becoming increasingly acute. Proponents of both perspectives are trying to mold the minds and win the hearts of the young. Religious establishments have their schools for guidance and indoctrination, while secular ethics is propagated primarily through books. The media does its own subtle proselytizing of values with its core message that it is okay to erase all boundaries on sexual language, innuendos, and activity. In this context the American Humanist Association recently announced plans to teach non-theistic ethics to all ages.

Gradually, like other long-held prerogatives of religions, ethics began to be usurped by the onward rush of science. With knowledge of the mores in many cultures and the behavior of many species, as also with an understanding of the role of genes in the phenomenon of life, scientists have been analyzing the source and significance of ethical principles, snatching away yet another matter of great significance to the human condition from the purview of religion. Fields like anthropology, biological evolution, and evolutionary psychology have brought down the sources of values from their time-honored pedestal to survival needs, cultural forces, and genetic programming.

Many do's and don'ts of morality are explained as having been prompted by what is conducive to societal survival and healthy propagation of the species. Some are convinced that every impetus to morality may be traced to the DNA; in other words, that morality is another emergent manifestation of molecular matter. Researchers into the behavior of animals have been revealing how non-humans sometimes behave much like us, in morally sound ways.

The pioneering works of Konrad Lorenz (*King Solomon's ring*, 1961) paved the way for the science of ethology (study of animal behavior). The amazing work of primatologists like Frans de Waal (*Primates and philosophers: How morality evolved*, 2006) and others have revealed that many animals are far more evolved in thought and behavior than what we often think. Many ethologists now believe that even such supposedly lowly creatures like rats show empathy. There is an enormous amount of technical research on the behavior of creatures from ants to apes to unravel the complexities of life. Just as the microscope revealed the existence of countless hitherto unknown life-forms, studies of animal behavior are revealing the hidden roots of their behavior.

Anthropologists have been studying different cultures from the outside, not unlike ethologists do with animals, and they draw conclusions about the ethical framework of various cultures. In the process, ethics becomes not a system of values that guide moral conduct, but a pattern of behavior that is instigated by local conditions and presumptions. Such studies, insightful as they are, provide a drastically different perspective on what ethics, understood religiously, is all about. It is not a framework ordained by the Almighty in which we humans need to act because we have been so told. Rather it is the culmination of many generations of trial and error for what is most effective, useful and convenient for a group of people who live together. It is just a tool that has been developed for effective group-living.

In all these efforts one studies, classifies, and explains ethical behavior in the framework of psychology, biology, and evolution, without really providing a convincing answer to the puzzle of how some of the *thou shalts* follow from some of the *thus are*. David Sloan Wilson, a balanced and insightful evolutionist, comments by considering adaptation as the gold standard that:

> Rational thought becomes necessary but not sufficient to explain the length and breadth of human mentality, and the so-called irrational (rationally inexplicable?) features of religions can be studied respectfully as potential adaptations in their own right rather than as idiot relatives of rational thought. (2002, 123)

When subjected to explanation, morality tends to lose its potency as an imperative for action. One can practice much virtue without postulating genetic coding at the root of kindness or compassion. The Samaritan who feeds a hungry stranger accomplishes much of value, even if he has no inkling of DNA and RNA, and has not read erudite philosophers who write books on what makes us moral beings.

Frans De Waal's work (*Our inner ape*, 2005) showed that lowly animals can be mutually friendly, caring, and cooperative also. This is in consonance with the ideas on morality developed by Michael Cavanaugh who starts from the thesis that:

> Inside each of us, as a function of our muscular and nervous and hormonal systems, is a propulsion toward various kinds of actions. We share that propulsion with animals. (1991, 163)

Richard Dawkins developed his thesis of the selfish gene (*The selfish gene*, 1976), which may be regarded as the twentieth-century elaboration of Hobbes's thesis that altruism is no more than camouflaged, self-serving behavior. The idea is that we are just being manipulated by our genes, whose sole goal is to survive. Whether it is bees that kill themselves to protect the hive, jihadists who blow themselves up to protect their land and culture, or Mother Teresa who dedicates her life to serving the wretched, ultimately it is all genes that are at work to propagate themselves. Dawkins also argues that we are unique as a species in that we can refuse to succumb to the selfish gene.

Spinoza, too, had said something similar:

> The very first foundation of virtue is the endeavor to preserve the individual self, and happiness consists in the human capacity to preserve its self. (1677, IV: prop.18:9)

This impressed Antonio Damasio so much that he was prompted to write an insightful book in which, among other things, he shows how:

> The biological reality of self-preservation leads to virtue because in our inalienable need to maintain ourselves we must, of necessity, help other selves.... [So the quote from Spinoza] contains the foundation for a system of ethical behaviors and that foundation is neurobiological. The foundation is the result of a discovery based on the observation of human nature rather than the revelation of a prophet. (2003, 170)

Damasio does not say where Spinoza got his insight from.

Others, however, insist that there is more to kindness, compassion, caring and love than gene-instigated neuron firing. A look into the history of ideas hardly instills confidence that the question will be settled to everybody's satisfaction by debate or even from laboratory revelations. This is the kind of issue that we may not be able to resolve through reason, arguments, measuring devices and mathematics. Endopotent criteria come into play in the acceptance of explanations.

When morality becomes a phenomenon for explanation it tends to lose its potency as an imperative for action. The biologist who seeks kindness or compassion in genes may contribute much to our *understanding* of human behavior, but little to the *practice* of virtue. The Samaritan who feeds a hungry stranger is accomplishing much more of value, even if he has no inkling of genetics and has not read Richard Dawkins.

Explaining morality in scientific terms can also lead to more serious consequences than the conviction that the earth is at the center of it all. We must try to explain all phenomena, of course, but in the view of some it is more important to strive to curtail or cultivate certain modes of behavior. If anger and altruism have genetic or glandular roots, should we condone rage and not commend charities? By laying bare every aspect of human feeling and behavior, some believe that we can curb cruelty and nurture nobility through science and pills. Indeed many scientists now feel that someday drugs will be developed to control ire and prompt more sympathy.

Such understanding will no doubt enable us to tamper with nature's flow and this will affect the free play of culture and history, with no guarantee that this will be in humanity's best interest in the long run. This is a matter of grave concern and heated debate in our own times. Eradication of criminality and (what some may regard as) sexual deviancy may seem to be worthwhile goals from one perspective, but the potential for transforming personhood into a manufactured article as per behavioral specifications sounds ominous to a great many people. James Watson's assertion that "we may need science to save us from our human nature" (2003, 61) may not be altogether correct, if only because partial tuning of a complex whole (human nature) could turn out to be more disastrous than we imagine.

Morality and love are significant dimensions of life, not just phenomena for biologists to explore and alter. Planetary motion has been beautifully explained, but we cannot interfere with celestial orbits (as of now). However, if science can modify human behavior, and if calculations by roboticists and concoctions in laboratories can direct ethical behavior, one never knows what will be the end-result. Policies inspired by mathematical decision theory led to the prolonging of the Viet Nam War. There is more to life than explanation and exploitation of knowledge. As Samuel Butler wrote:

> The foundations of morality are like all other foundations: if you dig too much about them the superstructure will come tumbling down. (1912, 26)

Values

Among the many factors that provoke and guide us in our thoughts, words, and deeds, there is the value system under which we function. Whether for an individual or for a group (society, institution, nation), the weight and significance we attach to what we believe in and choose to do are crucial to us as human beings. The notion of value is complex, and has been discussed extensively by economists and philosophers. Generally, one attaches value to that which one considers to be desirable or worthwhile to hold on to as a guidepost for actions and attitudes as we go through life. There are several sources, overt and subtle, that mold our values. Both science and religion play a role in these. Generally speaking, science contributes in eye-opening ways to the formation of worldviews, and religion contributes in meaningful ways to the formulation of values.

The values inculcated by religion are of two kinds. First there are those which relate to the behavior of people with respect to others in society. These include respect for others, honesty, caring and kindness, not hurting others, and the like. These global ethical principles were discussed in the last section. Then there are values which are specifically affiliated to particular traditions. Such, for instance, are non-attachment to material things in Hinduism, non-injury to living beings in Jainism, moderation in everything in Buddhism, conducting life as per the Ten Commandments in Judaism, acceptance of Jesus as the sole Savior of all humankind in Christianity, making a pilgrimage to Mecca at least once in a lifetime in Islam. In these instances, we see the overlapping of values and belief systems.

Not all the values that were developed in the religious framework are commendable. Many undesirable values, under the impact of science and enlightenment, have been gradually disappearing. Intelligent and enlightened leaders in all religious systems have been making efforts to explain that their respective time-honored holy books do not embody assertions that are inconsistent with the values in the awakened framework of human rights, gender-equality, and the like. Where such interpretations gain acceptance from a large number of the religious fold, society advances in wholesome ways.

Humanists and secularists have been arguing that it is possible to develop value-systems without anchoring oneself to traditional religions. The Charter of the United Nations is based on principles that are not cast in a religious framework. However, one should not forget that in practically all societies some of the finest values in human culture and behavior have come from religious prophets, sages, and poets. Indeed, some hold that without the values that religions try to inculcate, religions would be irrelevant.

It is sometimes said that science is amoral. Like other pithy generalizations, this statement carries only partial validity. It is valid in that what science says is of little help in guiding our individual behavior towards others. Scientific knowledge tells us nothing about what is right and what is wrong, what is good or bad in how we should treat our fellow human beings. Science does not goad us to acts of love or compassion, nor to cruelty or hurt, even if it sometimes makes awkward attempts to explain such behavior. No scientific theory or understanding can tell us if we should wage war, give charity, feed the hungry, or forgive a foe. With scientific knowledge we can cure diseases and devise weapons. But it is not science that tells us to do or not do such things. In this sense, it is appropriate to say that science is morally neutral.

However, science as a body of reliable knowledge is the fruit of human activity. In so far as significant activities occur in a framework that has value-elements in it, the world of science is also imbued in values. These values relate to the overall goals and well-being of the scientific enterprise. If the goal of the scientist is to uncover truths about the phenomenal world (and some regard this as an imperative from the Creator), then search for truth is a fundamental value for the scientist. That search calls for certain attitudes, such as hard work, deep commitment to the discipline, a tinge of skepticism, scrupulous honesty in reporting data and findings to fellow scientists, not assigning weight to propositions on the basis of the authority of the source, and the like. The scientific community expects all its members to embrace and act in accordance with these values, though it does not require a formal oath from its practitioners. Jacob Bronowski stated that what has given science its power and its humanity is that it listens to everyone and silences no one, it honors and promotes those who are right. And he cautioned: "Don't be deceived by those who say that science is narrow; a narrow, bigoted power is as brittle as Himmler's" (1977, 4-5). Here he may have been a little too optimistic. Intolerance, too, can be, and has been, a mighty force that has held sway for long in many regions of the world. It is not always as brittle as Himmler's, especially when there is not a strong enough force to combat it.

Over the centuries, some members of the scientific community have perpetrated fraud on their fellow scientists by fudging data, reporting false observations, even stealing results from others. All this shows that, as with religion, whatever science as an enterprise might stand for, individual scientists are all too human, capable of both sublime and shameful behavior.

Many applications of science have not been happy, not always for the human good. Weapons of mass destruction, pollution, negative side-effects of drugs, and population explosion are among the unwelcome consequences of the rise of modern science.

Ethical questions have come into play even in the context of scientific research, especially on matters relating to the very basis of life and mind: the genome project, molecular biology, eugenics, artificial intelligence, stem cell research, and cloning are among the fields in biology that can have long range and irreversible effects on the human condition, not all for the benefit of the species. In such contexts, it is difficult, indeed irresponsible, for a working scientist, pure or applied, to be indifferent to potential negative impacts of his or her research work.

Science has molded our value system in significant ways. The striving for objectivity is a recognition of the narrowness of prejudices. It is not surprising that the evils of slavery and casteism, the bigotry of religious fanaticism, the presumptuousness of a chosen people, and other stifling perspectives do not appeal to those whose hearts and minds have been touched by the torch of science.

Science has been enriched by its elimination of ethnocentrism, and this enables one to adopt global perspectives. Science seeks universality, and this fosters the values of equality and justice for all. Not surprisingly, though traditional religions embody many noble ethical principles, planetary ethics like racial equality, social justice, human rights and gender respect have arisen after the rise of modern science.

Compassion and Altruism

An ancient Hindu invocation is for happiness to all the people (*loka sanasthà sukhino bhavantu*). The founders of Jainism asked us to treat with reverence all life forms. Gautama Buddha preached compassion towards the suffering. Christ asked us to treat others as we ourselves would like to be treated. Millions of people all over the world try every waking day to do some good to others, even if it involves sacrifice on their part. The urge to care for others and to help others is among the nobler traits of being human. Religions try to cultivate this urge, which is latent in all of us. Science explores the source of this urge.

Richard Dawkins argues that we are unique only in that we can refuse to succumb to the selfish gene. Others, however, insist that there is more to kindness, compassion, caring and love than our genes. Richard Dawkins described humans (and all living organisms) as "survival machines". Our genes do everything in their power for as long as they can to keep us surviving. Nature is/seems to be more interested in the survival of the species than of its component individuals: following a sort of Communist ideology which is more committed to the State than to the predicament of its citizens.

So, through genes or by some other means, Nature instigates us to get interested in finding a mate. To allure the potential mate, we need to show some interest in the person beyond ourselves, sometimes even to the point of paying for the other's dinner on a date. In such contexts, the selfish gene begins to show signs of becoming (overtly at least) less selfish. This replicating behavior is not always perfect. Result: as per the principle of generalized Darwinism, interest in another individual for a very specific purpose (species survival) evolves into like behavior for no such selfish (individual or species-wise) purpose at all, expressing itself as love and altruism. It seems unlikely that amoebas and plants (which do not multiply by mating) will ever become altruistic.

Susan Blackmore (*The meme machine,* 1999), a disciple of Dawkins, suggested that with all their selfish obsession to propagate, memes can also be pictured as being at the root of that commendable (though in some ways paradoxical) quality we call altruism. Simply put, the argument is this: the good guy has more friends than the bad guy whom everyone ignores. The caring and considerate person is therefore more likely to spread memes around than the misanthropic grouch. Hence, memes encourage selfless behavior. People who complain about all the terrible things human beings do to one another may have difficulty understanding, on the basis of this theory, why bad memes seem to be propagating just as well, if not better.

Altruism as a concept has been discussed by scholars over the ages. But in recent years there has been a tremendous surge in the literature on altruism (for example, Stephen G. Post et al., eds., *Altruism and altruistic love: Science, philosophy, and religious dialogue,* 2002).

As has become the practice in neurotheology, people have been experimenting on how various regions of the brain are excited when one engages in altruistic behavior. Not surprisingly, there are specific brain activities when one does some good to others. But one can say this about anything: whether one is watching a game, doing physics, and laughing at a joke, the brain is surely responding in specific ways. For some reason this becomes particularly interesting in the context of yoga, prayer, and God-thought.

Related feelings of compassion and empathy also have religious roots. In Patanjali's *Yogasùtra,* which is the classic treatise on the theory and practice of yoga, we read:

> *Maitrì karunà mudita upekshnàm sukha duhkha punya*
> *apunyà*
> *vishayànam bhàvanàtah citta prasàdanam*
> [Friendliness toward the happy, compassion toward the unhappy, delight at the virtuous, and indifference to the wicked: these attitudes bring calmness to the mind].
> (ca. 2nd century BCE, 1:33)

Compassion has also been studied by philosophers and scientists. There is a huge body of literature on this. Lorne Ladner, for example, discussed this from the Buddhist perspective in *The lost art of compassion: Discovering the practice of happiness in the meeting of Buddhism and psychology* (2004). Though the title and principal theme of the book relate to compassion—the cardinal virtue in the Buddha's teachings—the author, who is a trained psychologist and practitioner of Buddhism, gives his readers many worthy understandings of the human mind and human capacities for good. The connections between Buddhist tenets and findings of current psychology add scientific support to the recommendations in the book. Reminders of eventual death and the ephemeral nature of existence may not be original, but they can inspire restraining reflections on people on the verge of rash or harsh behavior.

Raw aggressiveness and self-centered acts of cruelty and exploitation seem to pervade modern societies, and Ladner's book is meant to transform them to gentler and more civilized modes. However, it is important to remember that our appraisal of the world's moral status is often derived from the daily news. This view of the world is, for most people, very different from the world in which they normally live during their waking hours. When calamities arise, not just in our neighborhood but in distant lands too, the outpouring of caring, compassion, and concrete assistance is generally at more than a modest level. In other words, the art of compassion is not as lost as the title of this book suggests.

Then again, it is not clear that even among peoples where Buddhism is the principal faith, there is the kind of universal compassion that one would imagine in that framework. When one reads about the Sermon on the Mount or the Ten Commandments in Tibet, the reader should not assume that all the people in Judeo-Christian societies put those nuggets of wisdom into practice.

Love in religion and in science

Love is a profound emotion of which most humans are capable. It is experienced in many ways and contexts.

There is love of God: an intense longing for the divine, a spiritual bonding which inspires many on the religious plane. Krishna, in the course of an answer to a question posed by Arjuna, declared that the one who worships the Divine, with mind fully focused on it is truly the best of all aspirants (Bhagavad Gita 6:47). Christ said that the great commandment is that one should love the Lord with all one's heart (Matthew 22:37). In the Hindu world, unadulterated love of God is known as *bhakti*. In Christianity, it is *agapé*. Such love should also lead to caring for fellow humans. Christ says this explicitly, saying that one should not only love one's neighbor but also one's enemies; that one should pray for those who persecute us. Loving those who love us is not a hardship.

Then there is the psychological and emotional love that bonds us to others: There is love for parents and children, love for friends and family, love of community and country. This love gladdens the heart and makes human relations so much richer and more enjoyable. Without it, all transactions would be no more than commercial, official, or legal. It is when interactions transcend law and duty and find joy in giving and in making the other happy that this love blossoms.

Finally, there is love that brings one into intense and intimate physical entanglement with another person, generally with someone of the opposite gender. This could be a climactic expression of psychological and emotional love for one with whom a commitment for life is made, or it could arise quite simply from raw physical attraction, without any emotional entanglement. In such a case, it becomes pure passion, unchecked carnal desire or lust.

From the scientific perspective, love in whatever aspect is another emergence in the complex human brain. There are two levels at which science explains love. Here love is regarded as an aspect of evolution which, with all its blindness, is somehow geared to preserving and propagating the species. Its physiological side is traced to genes and neurotransmitters, relating it to glandular secretions and faster heartbeats. Ultimately, for science, it is all molecular and electro-chemical. Love that is tied to physical attraction is explained as arising from clever DNA programming to assure generational continuance. As to non-carnal love, it too serves survival in some way: Thus, mother's love for child is essential for nourishing the baby. Evolutionary biologists see love as products of a natural process that serves the perpetuation of groups and species. After all, this is enough for bulls and bears. Birds and bees seem to thrive without emotions of love. To some evolutionary biologists, love is the price we pay for having evolved culturally.

Thomas Lewis et al. developed a *General theory of love* (2000), according to which "where intellect and emotion clash, the heart often has the greater wisdom." According to another theory our brains have three levels: the reptilian, which keeps up the vital functions; the (mammalian) limbic aspect, which controls our relationship with other mammals; and the neocortex, which enables us to speak, reason, and do science (MacLean 1990). In this model, there is the primitive urge to feel a fellow-creature's skin and listen to its heartbeat. Love is no more than a sophisticated expression of this level of primitive brain-activity, jazzed up by cultural dressings, of course.

The scientific study of love is not just fancy theorizing. It has revealed that the emotional dimension of life needs to be instilled as much as the rational and the intellectual at a very early stage of development. It is not enough to read stories, recite rhymes and teach children how to count. They must be taught to care and be kind right from year one or earlier, if they are to become well-adjusted adults later. The limbic dimension needs as much early attention as the neocortex.

One may still wonder why more than lust is needed for species-survival. Why romantic poetry, sending flowers, and a twinkle in the eye? The poet Walter Scott wrote:

> True love's the gift that God has given
> To man alone beneath the heaven.
> (from *The Lay of the Last Minstrel*, Canto V, lines 217-18, 1805, 103)

From the religious perspective, love is a reflection of the divine in the human heart. God loves us and fashioned us in His image. His loving nature is implanted in the human heart.

In recent years the notion of *kenosis* from Christian theology has been revived and explored by some scholars. The essence of the concept is that one cleanses oneself of one's own will and receives in its place God's will. In other words, one embraces a moral framework that is out there in the universe. George Ellis, eminent cosmologist, has written and spoken extensively on the subject. In a book he wrote with Nancey Murphy, we read: "The core of the kenotic ethic entails the proscription of violence" (1996, 142), reminding us of the core of Jaina teaching. Also, the notion of a moral universe which Ellis enunciates is very much like the notion of *rta* in the Vedic tradition.

In the Rig Veda, *rta* is both the moral and the physical order that pervades the universe. In a prayer addressed to Indra, the sage poet says: "Lead us on the path of Rta, on the right path over all evils." (10.133:6). What is right is also righteous.

Dharma

In the Hindu world, ethical principles are also conveyed through the concept of *dharma*. We are all members of a group: family, community, nation, and the world at large. In that role we have a responsibility, not unlike the tax we have to pay in most countries, to contribute to the maintenance of the infrastructure of the state. The requirements of social and religious responsibility are referred to as dharma. The word is derived from a root which means to support. Dharma, broadly defined, is that which one must do in order to be at peace with oneself and in harmony with the world around. There are various categories of dharma: *sanàtanadharma* refers to the eternal moral principles to which we are all subject: Such would be, for example, truthfulness, respect for others, the pursuit of knowledge, non-coveting, and other universal ethical principles.

On the other hand, there is also *yugadharma:* duties and responsibilities that are a function of space and time, of region and history. Examples are, what food one takes or avoids, how one greets people, the tax one pays to a government, not violating the laws of a country, etc. Here, as elsewhere, the question is not which is right, science or religion. Rather it is to recognize which is appropriate in which context. This dichotomy resolves the conflict between absolute and relative morality by recognizing that both arise in the course of our lives.

Then again, one talks about *svadharma:* the responsibility of an individual by virtue of his or her station or situation in life: The dharma of a parent, of a teacher, of a lawyer, of a political office-holder, etc. One may contrast this with *paradharma:* the dharma of some other member of the society. A principle enunciated in the Bhagavad Gita is that every individual should adhere to his or her own dharma, and not try to take upon oneself someone else's dharma.

There is an ancient Sanskrit injunction which says:

> *Dharmam carata mA adharmaM*
> *satyaM vadata mA anRtam*
> *dIrghaM paSyata mA hrasvaM*
> *paraM paSyata mA aparam*
> [Follow righteous path and not the unrighteous.
> Speak the truth, and not what is wrong.
> Look from a lofty perspective, and not short-sightedly
> Look beyond, and not just the ordinary]
> (Vasishthasùtra 30.1)

It is important to note the emphasis on the lofty or long-range view, versus the short-sighted one which seeks instant gratification. Wisdom in individuals as well as societies and civilizations is often reflected in whether actions are based on an awareness of the long-range consequences of actions. Furthermore, things are not always what they seem. We should try to look beyond appearances in making decisions and undertaking actions. Note the style here: the contrasting mode adds effectiveness to the injunctions. Hindu thinkers were masters in using such rhetorical devices. Many of the law-givers were also gifted poets.

Is morality innate?

As long as there have been organized societies, there have been codes of behavior. These constitute the ethical systems of the world. The primary goal of most ethical systems is simple: No person should behave in ways that would have unhappy impacts on others. It is surprising that this simple tenet has been elaborated in a thousand ways in various cultures and religions. More remarkably, it has given rise to voluminous debates, discussions, and disagreements. The controversies and confrontations arise, not from the simple tenet, but from its elaborations.

The issues that arise in discussions relating to ethical systems range from the origin of the notion of ethics in the human mind and in nature to the complexity of ethical rules in societies.

But the simple idea that one should not engage in hurtful acts suggests that human beings have a tendency to do just that. Is such a tendency inborn or is it prompted by external circumstances? As often happens, there is no unanimity here, and that is already one cause for debates. Because it led to the coming of Christ to save mankind, Augustine described it as Adam's necessary sin and the Easter Proclamation refers to it as a happy fault. But as John A. Buehrens has pointed out, the third chapter of Genesis gives dramatic form to the awakening of humankind:

> From animality to self-consciousness, symbolized by clothing, sexual self-awareness, and "the knowledge of good and evil." Self-consciousness and moral choice are both founded on a consciousness of facing an objective environment containing both the possibility of death and the inevitability of mortality. (2003, 47-48)

One might also say that it is symbolic of the fact that, as one gains secular knowledge, one loses awareness of spiritual truths.

Mahatma Gandhi, on the other hand, believed in the intrinsic goodness of human beings, even of vicious individuals, and he felt strongly that it is possible to bring about significant positive transformations in the hearts of even the cruelest people. This conviction in the essential goodness of human beings finds expression in many episodes in the mythic literature of India. Even tyrants and evil personages are regarded as going through a passing stage after which they turn good.

Perhaps it is as partial a view to say categorically that humans are intrinsically evil as to affirm that at the core they are truly good and noble. What may be said with some certainty, on the basis of general human history, is that we are, one and all, capable of both good and bad deeds, both kind and cruel behavior.

As William L. Shirer noted:

> The example of his [Gandhi's] life, his search for Truth, as they [Christ and Buddha] sought Truth, his selflessness

which was akin to theirs, his granite integrity, and what he taught and practiced and accomplished were bound to leave an indelible imprint on this earth. (1979, 245)

Ecological ethics

Since ancient times human beings have lived in harmony with the world around: at peace with the surrounding lakes and rivers, mounds and meadows, trees and shrubs, fish and fox.

Most ancient cultures had reverence for nature. They worshiped trees and plants, rain and sky. One of the unfortunate side-effects of scientific technology was the transformation of this worldview to make nature something to be dominated and exploited, both ruthlessly and thoughtlessly. This has led to some perilous consequences for the human condition.

But it is important to remember that the original intention of humanity was certainly not to desecrate, degrade, or disrespect nature. It was merely to make human life less arduous and more comfortable. Then again, humans have also been victimized by diseases and epidemics, and crops have been consumed by pests and parasites. With the rise of modern science, one learned to control the causes of ailments and decimate the pests that destroy the crops. In the process, several lethal chemicals were injected into the soil. These chemicals seeped into ground and air and water. Over the decades a growing number of biologists have been warning that human encroachments into the biosphere have been transgressing the boundaries of safety. More than fifty years ago Norman Berrill compared man to:

> A cancer whose strange cells multiply without restraint, ruthlessly demanding the nourishment that all the body has need of. (1955, 210)

It was in this context that Rachel Carson (*Silent spring*, 1962) brought to the attention of the general public the serious disasters, both actual and potential, that resulted from the reckless use of pesticides such as DDT. Her book brought about an awakening that paved the way for widespread ecological consciousness. She was criticized by the chemical industry and by agro-business, which were solving legitimate problems from purely techno-perspectives. But Carson's book was based on valid data of how chemicals that were meant for pests were also slowly seeping into the food chain. This has led to one of the most difficult ethical questions in human history. Should we abandon chemical means to control plant diseases or use chemicals as we strive for more food production for increasing population?

Less than a decade after Carson's book, Van Rensselaer Potter coined the term bioethics (*Bioethics: bridge to the future*, 1971) in which he gave a bioethical creed for individuals. The subject has grown enormously. With the development of sophisticated medicines and medical technology, prolonged survival of aging people under severe pain or total loss of memory, questions arise about the indefinite continuation of life. Often traditional religious values are at odds with more practical and realistic solutions in such contexts. In an inappropriately titled volume, *Against bioethics* (2006), Jonathan Baron has shown how major bioethical decisions can be made more meaningfully and more effectively by adopting the techniques and fruits of decision theory, which analyzes the utilitarian values inherent in various decisions.

Bioethics and ecology have become important fields where ethics has come to play a major role; in both instances one is striving for codes of behavior that will be in the best interest of individuals and of the species as a whole. In this context, as Ian Barbour reminded us:

> Each of us must make personal decisions about the life-styles we will adopt and the kinds of technology we will seek at home or at work. (1993, 82)

The significance and the urgency of eco-ethics is only slowly beginning to sink into the psyche of people and of governments. It is an irony of human history, indeed a sad reflection on human intelligence, that when problems as grave as deforestations, polar ice-caps melting, impending water shortage, unchecked population growth, and global warming are confronting humanity, so many are bickering and boisterous about which religion is closer to the truth, which race is superior, which nation can build nuclear weapons, and such other ominous trivialities.

In this context we must recall one of the most moving and meaningful books published in recent years on the impending peril for the human race: E. O. Wilson's *The creation: An appeal to save life on earth* (2006). Wilson is a master biologist-writer, and his book is in the format of a letter to a pastor of the denomination from which, touched by scientific worldviews, he had moved away. After seeing many battles between science and religion, instead of calling religion a spell or a delusion, Wilson has realized that we need cooperation between scientists and people of faith in this common threat of total annihilation of terrestrial life.

Wilson gives a bird's eye view of biology and natural history with a lucidity that should make pastors and people with a modicum of education appreciate the richness of life as well as the dangers to it posed by human excesses. He appeals to his readers, whether scientists or Baptists, atheists or believers, to work together *pro bono vitae:* for the good of life. He expounds the basic laws of biology, even while being respectful of religious sentiments. He addresses three issues:

> The decline of the living environment, the inadequacy of scientific education, and the moral confusions caused by the exponential growth of biology....[And he argues that] it will be necessary to find common ground on which the powerful forces of religion and science can be joined. (2006, 165)

Most of all, he assures humanity that it is not yet too late, and that ecology is not incompatible with economy.

On globodium and its roots

Most people like and dislike other people on the basis of their own particular tastes and preferences. This is natural and normal. When these feelings become intense, they become love and hatred. Sometimes, such love or hatred extends to a whole group. Some people like everything about a group. Thus, some love whatever is French and we call them Francophiles. When one likes everything Chinese, one is called a Sinophile. Likewise, we have Anglophiles, Indophiles, etc.

Sometimes people also hate a whole group. One may coin a term to signify hatred of a whole group. Borrowing from two Latin words, we may call this *globodium*. [Latin, *globus:* crowd, cluster; *odium:* hatred.] More exactly, globodium will refer to the blind and intense hatred of a group of people who have a common race, religion, language, nationality, or whatever. Every expression of globodium has one or more target groups. Hitler's *Mein kampf* (1925-1926) was a classic articulation of globodium. It has its countless echoes in today's world on the Internet issuing from the hateful hearts of individuals from most major faith traditions.

Though it is often looked upon as an evil characteristic, globodium is actually a disease of the mind that has been infected by the hate-meme from the powerful media of books and internet postings. It is utterly irrational, but some religious texts have promoted globodium. This infirmity needs to be attended to, rather than frowned upon. The treatment, partial or total, has to be psychological through education and counseling, rather than physical punishment. Love and understanding by members of the target group could also be sometimes helpful.

As with other diseases, physical or mental, it will be useful to identify the causes of globodium. Some of these are obvious, some are hidden; some are real and some are imaginary.

— Severe sense of personal and/or group insecurity. As a character of Bernard Shaw's said: "Hatred is the coward's revenge for being intimidated" (1907, 153). Acute fear that one's own group will lose its identity, as a result of the activities, practices, or existence of the target group(s).

And as Anton Chekhov wrote, "Love, friendship, respect do not unite a people as much as a common hatred for something" (1914, 32).

— A deep conviction that one's own group has the absolute truth and that the target group is completely wrong on fundamental matters.

— The belief that the problems faced by one's own group or by the world can be solved by the elimination of the target group.

— The memory of past (historical) injustices that one's ancestors have suffered at the hands of the ancestors of the target group.

— The conviction that one's own economic security or that of one's group is being jeopardized by the target group.

— A mindless dislike of the appearance or skin color of the target group.

— The certainty that the target group is worshipping a false God.

— The fear that the target group will "pollute" the womenfolk of one's own group.

— An intense and deep-seated envy for the successes of the target group.

Psychologists may tell us that all these are perfectly normal states and reactions. That is why globodium is not as uncommon as one would like it to be, and is even part of certain religious attitudes. However, even in instances where there is provocation for it, by proper training, reflection, and realization, globodium could be averted or cured. One may hope that this would be a goal of enlightened education and religion.

Global ethics

Many roots of ethical injunctions may be traced to religious traditions. There is verse in the Veda wherein we read:

Only lowly minds reckon if one is kin or stranger;
For the noble ones the whole world itself is their family.
(Atharva Veda 10.7: 4-5)

Here occurs the phrase *vasudhà eva kutumbakam:* the whole world itself is a family, which is adopted as a motto in many Hindu temples. Similar lofty visions have been expressed in other traditions.

When one contrasts such formulations with the records of religious history, one wonders if religions have had as much positive impact as one could have hoped. But then it is quite possible that we would have remained more wild and beastly without religions. Who can tell! What we do know is that a great many guideposts for commendable conduct can be found in the teachings of religions.

With the rise of modern science came the emancipation of the mind from many misconceptions about the nature of the physical world and life forms, as also views of our species that transcend culture. So began efforts to formulate frameworks for national and international behavior that would be more humanistic than doctrinal, more global than parochial. During the twentieth century, two world wars were followed by a Cold War, countless local conflicts, and mounting economic, social, and inter-religious problems: the human condition seemed to be fast deteriorating.

So, at the revived Parliament of World Religions in Chicago in 1993, representatives from many groups made a joint "Declaration of the Religions for a Global Ethic." The drafters of the declaration had to be sensitive to all faiths. Since not all religions are theistic, one had to avoid invoking God. Controversial topics like abortion and euthanasia were not even mentioned. No reference was made to prophets and scriptures or to the slaughter of animals for religious festivals. Political tyranny and dictatorship could not be openly condemned, since a number of participants came from nations where these were much in vogue. The notion of human rights was already there in the United Nations.

The global ethic declaration expresses noble sentiments: everyone must be treated humanely; there must be non-violence and respect for life; one must work for a just economic order, for tolerance, truthfulness, equal rights, gender equality and partnership, etc. There was a call for consciousness transformation. The authors of the document expressed the conviction that:

> The new global order will be a better one only in a socially-beneficial and pluralist, partner-sharing and peace-fostering, nature-friendly and ecumenical globe." They committed themselves "to a common Global Ethic" and called upon "all women and men of goodwill to make this Declaration their own. (Küng and Kuschel 1993)

The document is significant in that it was the first ethical proclamation whose signatories come from every religion in the world, and no prophet was involved. However, it is difficult to come up with new ethical criteria beyond the age-old principle of not hurting anyone consciously. What is interesting in this collective effort is that, when people from different religious traditions reflect on values from enlightened humanistic perspectives, they quickly discover that they have much in common, and that everything that is of universal ethical value in the religions can be upheld without doctrinal and metaphysical assertions.

With all that, interfaith conflicts and crimes have continued. The world has witnessed the 9/11 atrocity, the launching of Gulf War II, and countless instances of religious acrimony and sectarian slaughter. No matter how genuine and enlightened our ethical declarations, ultimately group actions are guided by the basic instinct of national self-interest and indoctrinated cultural self-righteousness. Take away the first, and nations may not survive. At the very least, selfishness must be tempered. Take away the second, and there may be no absolute conviction about the mysteries that confound us.

In any event it is unlikely that there will be global peace and harmony until there is economic and social justice, and this calls for unlimited resources.

Chapter 8
Dissimilar Visions on Common Themes

Common themes

There are many matters on which science and religion function independently and meaningfully. For example, science is concerned with measuring the distances of stars, studying the behavior of insects, and the production of very cold temperatures. These have nothing to do with religion. On the other hand in the religious context one sings hymns, observes days of fasting and feasting, and performs sacraments. These have nothing to do with science. But there are also some concepts and principles which are common to both science and religion. Likewise, religion and science both are involved in some societal aspects. In these overlapping contexts, they often have dissimilar visions. If we consider these as different modes of expressions of the human spirit, rather than as competing visions, they become quite interesting. Let us then look into some of these overlapping themes.

Revelation

Revelation is an important idea that needs to be clarified in any discussion of science and religion. In the religious framework, revelation implies communication from supernatural sources, such as non-corporeal voices, visions, angelic beings, (audible) cosmic vibrations, etc. Religions rest upon revelations. Science does not (at least in the sense in which religions do) accept revelation.

In the religious framework, revelation brings some knowledge about Divinity, about the future, or about transcendental truths. That knowledge has been unveiled to select people directly by God or through one of God's agents. Revealed truths are conveyed to the rest of the community, and eventually to large sections of humankind, by the person to whom they were revealed and more often through his disciples. [I say *his* disciples because in most religions God revealed His truths only to men.]

In the Judaic tradition, God is said to have revealed Himself to Moses on Mount Sinai. As we read in the Torah, "God called unto him (Moses) out of the midst of the bush, and said, ... 'I am the God of thy father, the God of Abraham, the God of Isaac, and the God of Jacob'" (Exodus 3:4-6). That revelation is at the root of the three Abrahamic religions. Buddha's enlightenment, which is the fount of Buddhism, is also regarded as a revelation from the Divine. It is reported that the Buddha said, "I directed my mind to the passing away and rebirth of beings. With divine, purified, superhuman vision, I saw beings passing away and being reborn, low and high, of good and bad color, in happy and miserable existences, according to their karma." (Thomas 2000, 67). The source of the revelation is not specified here. The traditional Hindu view is that the hymns of the Vedas were revealed to sage-poets *(rishis)*, and through them they have reached a larger body of humankind. The *Catholic Encyclopedia* states that "The essence of Revelation lies in the fact that it is the direct speech of God to man...The Decree *Lamentabili*...declared that the dogmas which the Church proposes as revealed are 'truths which have come down to us from heaven' (*veritates e coelo delapsoe*) and not 'an interpretation of religious facts which the human mind has acquired by its own strenuous efforts'" (Joyce 1912, par. 2). The Holy Qur'an, per Islamic belief, was revealed to Prophet Mohammed, and is meant to be propagated to the whole world. We read in the introductory chapter of this holy book: "For three and twenty years in patience, conflict, hope, and final triumph, did this man of God receive and teach the message of the Most High" (Ali 1938, 12). In the Tamil Vaishnava tradition of the Hindu world, it is God who spoke to and through the inspired poets of the language. Thus, it has been said that "It is not Nammazvar who sings, but it is God who sings through him" (Nammazar ca. 830, 1.7:7).

In all major religious traditions, revelation refers to truths beyond normal sensory perceptions. Revelation is generally about the nature of God, the origin and purpose of the Universe, ethical principles, heaven, hell, post-mortem states, and the like. Truths are revealed to human beings who seem to be the only ones who possess discursive thought.

Another important aspect of revelation is that it occurs only to a select few in chosen languages. Moses, Vedic rishis, the Buddha, Nammazvar, and Mohammed are among the few personages who are believed to have been so gifted. Because God spoke directly in these cases, Hebrew, Sanskrit, Pali, Arabic and Tamil are regarded as sacred languages by members of the respective traditions. In the Mormon tradition (Shipps 1987), John the Baptist, Saint Paul, Saint Peter, and Saint James appeared before Joseph Smith and Oliver Cowdery in Upstate New York in the 1820s, and invested them with a priesthood. It does not say in which language the saints spoke.

If religions talk to us about truths regarding the human condition, its present and future states, and about God and the worlds beyond, science tells us about the here and the now, and most of all about the physical phenomenal world. And even as religious truths are revealed to but a few, and then shared with others, scientific truths are also revealed to only a few, and soon spread to the world at large, though with relatively less success than religious truths.

But there is a difference. We can count on the fingers of a hand or two the chosen few whom the world recognizes as direct recipients of God's truths, and perhaps a few more who are convinced that God had spoken to them also. However, scientific truths have been revealed to hundreds of people: These are the men and women of science who have made significant scientific discoveries.

Indeed, the recognition of every new law or principle or phenomenon or entity in the physical world may be regarded as a revelation. Scientific revelations generally come to the true seekers.

They may also come as a flash of insight during a waking hour or sometimes in a dream when one is in deep sleep.

Many may recall the story of Archimedes of Syracuse (third century BCE). He had to solve the problem of whether a crown, which had been presented to King Hieron II, was made of pure gold or had been adulterated. He was reflecting on this question and got the answer when he stepped out of a bathtub. The amount of water he had displaced in the bath was equal to the immersed volume of his body. From this and knowing the weight of an object, he could calculate the density and nature of the material. Archimedes was so excited by this principle of buoyancy, which he had understood in a flash, that he is said to have run into the streets stark naked, screaming "Eureka!" (Greek for "I've got it!"). The story may be apocryphal, but it is the quintessential *Aha!* experience of scientific discovery. There have been many in history.

The philosopher Descartes is said to have conceived of an important mathematical idea in a dream. Friedrich Kekulé reported that he got his insight into the nature of the benzene ring through a dream in which he saw a snake biting its own tail (a closed cycle, a ring). The mathematical genius Ramanujan enunciated many complex theorems requiring hours and pages of proof soon after he was up from bed: his village goddess had revealed to him the theorem while he was fast asleep.

Psychologists and philosophers have speculated on the mystery of creativity. Whether in art or music, in science or poetry, some human brains do come up with new knowledge and insights, new visions and compositions that were beyond the reach or understanding of fellow humans. It is fair to say, especially in the field of science, that these are revelations no less. For they tell us about aspects of the world that were, till then, hidden from the rest of humankind.

The revelations in science do not speak to us about worlds beyond Nature or the hereafter. The scientific discoverers are never worshiped. Their works are not held as sacred. There is no place of reverence for Archimedes or Kekulé or Ramanujan.

As to the truth content of the two kinds of revelations, religious revelations are significant and valid for members of a given faith system who may analyze and interpret them in different ways, but not reject them altogether. In some religious systems it is blasphemy to question the veracity of revealed truths, and punishment for that could be severe. It must be remembered that such punishments are meted out by the orthodoxy of a religion, and not by the God who is taken to be the source of the truths. Some may wonder if God would engage in or encourage the kind brutal penalties that His self-proclaimed agents and interpreters inflict in His name. Scientific revelations are verified and built upon by fellow scientists who have no problems rejecting them altogether should new knowledge call for it. It is no offense to challenge scientific revelations, as long as it is done in the framework of scientific methodology.

Sacredness

In the traditional framework, sacredness is related to the divine. The word sacrament, with the same etymology, is an important aspect of traditional religions. Of course, we may describe the breaking of a champagne bottle to launch a ship as a sacrament also, but this is not much different from the book-signing event on the occasion of the publication of a volume: a convention that imitates religious rituals.

In the religious framework, sacredness is often associated with Mystery. It binds us to things that seem to be beyond our cerebral grasp. To the religionist, sacredness is also associated with certain places and prophets, sages and saints, hymns and chants. Every sound and symbol of religion is regarded as sacred. Every thought and word and deed that is disrespectful of that which is held sacred in a religion is viewed as a desecration.

When we unveil any mystery, the associated sacredness is erased. When the rainbow is looked at in terms of the physical properties of light, its magic as the bow of Rama or Indra, as the path of Iris to heaven, or as the bridge between Ásgard and Midgard melts away.

However, because sacredness infuses us with a sense of being more than mere biological creatures, even those who reject religion try to preserve it by modifying its meaning. Religious naturalists implicitly derive a sense of transrational well-being associated with mystery, even after science slowly unveils the layers of wonderment about the physical world. In this effort, they associate sacredness with that which evokes awe, or whatever seems essential to life, and to whatever commands our emotional response by its sheer complexity.

As the religious naturalist Jerome A. Stone points out: "We use the word sacred to describe events, things, and processes that are of overriding importance, and also are not under our control or within our power to manipulate" (2003, 783-800). The sacredness seen by the naturalist is not an inherent aspect of the environment worthy of worship, such as the Moon or Mars are for some religious practitioners. We may shed tears when we are watching a heart-wrenching scene in a play or a movie, but we know that there is really no pain or suffering for the actors. The naturalist's sense of sacredness is somewhat like that. The feeling may be genuine and heart-felt, but it is quite different in its essence and intrinsic significance from the tears one sheds when one sees a near and dear one suffer in pain. Likewise, religious sacredness implies another dimension that is intrinsic to the universe, not just as an imagined property for entertaining us, but for eliciting our awe.

As long as we reduce everything to the concrete and the tangible, to the physical and the calculable, sacredness can at best be only a poetic dimension we attribute to life and nature, if not lip service to a profound dimension of being human. "If any thing is sacred, the human body is sacred," wrote Walt Whitman (1855/1892, 86). That it certainly is, but only for so long as consciousness lingers in it. From the humanistic perspective, one should rather say that if anything is sacred, human dignity is. Those who desecrate it, perpetrate the greatest sacrilege.

The sacredness that physicists and biologists ascribe to Nature, or the compassionate poet sees in humanity, can be meaningful too. In a beautifully crafted book, *The sacred depths of nature* (1998), Ursula Goodenough, a dynamic leader of the Religious Naturalism movement says: "The continuation of life reaches around, grabs its own tail, and forms a sacred circle that requires no further justification, no Creator, no superordinate meaning of meaning, no purpose other than that the continuation continue until the sun collapses or the final meteor collides" (p. 171). But this sacredness is of a very different kind. When an unbelieving scientific humanist describes nature as sacred, one has in mind its magnificence and grandeur, its relevance for our emergence and survival, for it is the environment with its silent laws that sustains all life.

In saying all this, I am not extolling one type of sacredness or diminishing the other, but recognizing the difference between the two.

What a person or a group does with the notion of sacredness of one kind or another, or without recognition of any kind of sacredness anywhere, is like what one does with scientific knowledge and religious faith: it can extend from one extreme to another.

Authorities

When we encounter a proposition about the world, on what basis do we accept or reject it? In most instances, it is on the basis of direct experience: the seeing-is-believing doctrine. On matters that are not directly perceptible, trust in the source is often the reason for acceptance. Trustworthy sources on important matters are called authorities. Now two questions arise. Which sources are trustworthy? How do they become authorities?

There are some important differences between religion and science in this context. In religion, by authority we generally mean the source of a set of propositions that have come to be regarded as sacred and revered in the religion. We refer to them generically as scriptures, though in earlier times, with a capital S, the term was reserved only for the Bible. Scriptures are considered as authorities because they are believed to embody truths that were revealed from a supernatural source.

In the Hindu world, one speaks of *shruti:* spiritual truths which were *heard* by the founding sages. These are the Vedas, which hold an authority that the other texts in the tradition do not enjoy. What this means is that Vedic utterances have to be accepted as such, may be interpreted, or admitted as inscrutable, but they should not be modified or rejected. One modern commentator has extended this even to the Bhagavad Gita, declaring that those not of his subsect do not have the right to comment on the Gita.

The Ten Commandments have supreme authority in the Judeo-Christian tradition because they are taken to have been revealed by God. More generally, any ethical injunction is an affirmation of authority.

In the Roman Catholic tradition, faith in the supernatural is required as per the Church's authority. When Jacques Bossuet wrote a treatise on the knowledge of God (1677), he made it clear that his statements were drawn from the Holy Scriptures. In many respects, Protestants accept the Bible's authority, but allow conscience also to guide. The English-speaking world has an Authorized Version of the Bible.

The Holy Qur'an is held with the highest reverence because it was a revelation of God's word to the Prophet of the faith. Every adherent to Islam is subject to its authority and to the laws that are derived from it. Some Islamic scholars maintain that non-Muslims should not even comment upon any aspect of their religion.

Max Weber pointed out (*Theory of social and economic organization*, 1920) that there are three types of authority: traditional, legal-rational, and charismatic. Sometimes it is difficult to distinguish between the first and the third. The charismatic authority of leaders like Moses, Buddha, Christ, Mohammed, and the Bap (Mirza Ali Mohammad) led to the traditional authority of the religions they founded. Legal-rational authority is often *enforced* by the state. In pre-modern societies, religious authority was/is often inflicted upon one and all, whether they were/are willing to accept it or not. One important feature of modernism is that this is no longer the case. In societies enjoying religious freedom, acceptance of religious authority is generally voluntary. One recognizes it willingly and with submission on the basis of a conviction that its source is Divinity or a spiritually-evolved personage.

No civil society can function without the authority of a recognized government that enforces law and order. Even anarchists do not stand much of a chance of survival if there is no law and order, police and court. This is so in the religious context too. For order and harmony in the practice of faith, there must be a framework that derives its authority from an establishment that is recognized by the members of the fold.

Over 2500 years ago, Gautama Buddha is said to have counseled his disciples: "Do not believe in something simply because it is tradition and old. Do not believe in anything on the mere authority of myself or of any other person" (Kalama Sutta, in the Anguttara Nikaya of the Tipitaka). This injunction was in the context of religious truths and practices, and could be a Protestant principle too. But it also sums up the motto of the scientific community. The suspicion that *what is declared by a higher authority to be true may not necessarily be so* is not a discovery of scientific enlightenment, as we see from the quotation from the Buddha. All through the ages, independent thinkers have expressed this view. Some of them have had to face rather unpleasant consequences by adhering to such a position.

The scientific community is not without its authorities. In every field of science and at every period of history, not one but several authorities hold power in the world of science. These are individuals who, by virtue of detailed study and years of research, have not only mastered all the available information of interest in a particular field, but have also contributed personally and significantly to its advancement. Hence an authority in science is respected and relied upon for depth of knowledge and understanding, but never for infallibility. The potential for erring is considered so human that no one is regarded exempt from it. Authorities in science are generally referred to as *experts*. The real authority (in the sense of one who holds power) in science is not an individual, but a body of experts in the field. This body is not elected, nor vested with special powers, but it forms itself by dint of the efforts and accomplishments of its members. Its members include the peer-reviewers of professional journals. The body of experts does wield power. As in other institutions, the power that comes from being an authority may be, and has been, misused now and again. Scientific authorities are known to have put impediments on the publication of revolutionary ideas, even stood in the way of dissenting scientists from getting positions in academic or research institutions. Sometimes, a younger band of pioneers wait for the older generation to die before new ideas gain ground.

In the world of science, it is not that one rejects what others have said or taught, much less that authorities are necessarily in the wrong. Rather, the view is that nothing is true simply because it originates from a highly respected individual, institution, or text. One is reminded of the lines of the classical Sanskrit dramatist Kalidasa in one of his plays:

> *Purànamityeva na sàdhu sarvam*
> *na càpi kàvyam navamitya vadyam*
> *santah parìkshànyatarad bhajante*
> *màdhah parapratyayaneya buddhih*
> [All that's old is not necessarily good;
> Nor wisdom not to be so called, just because it is new.
> The wise examine both and accept that which is worthy
> Fools accept things on others' understanding and intelligence].
> (from *Malavika and Agnimitra,* ca. 6th century)

Some research programs may be looked upon as openly subversive, for the goal is to substitute currently accepted views and ideas, even paradigms, with newer ones. Understanding often calls for the rejection of old and anachronistic views. Every new thing that we learn is the eradication of something learned before.

The history of science suggests that the longer a scientific personage has held authority over the field, the more vulnerable his or her ideas become. This is because, as the years roll by, the bulk of human knowledge is also steadily increasing. Need for refinement and modification of long-held notions often becomes a matter of routine in the world of science.

Numbers in religions and in science

We tend to associate numbers only with mathematics, or with practical matters like measuring, counting, and accounts. But numbers have also played important roles where there is no immediate use. Every major religion refers to numbers and attaches particular significance to certain numbers.

A hymn in the Leiden Papyrus, dating back to well over 3500 years, reveals number mysticism in Egyptian religion. The Karnak Temple complex is called *Apet-sut* or Enumerator of the Places.

One is an important number in the creed of monotheism. The following verse from the Veda might come as a surprise to those of the Abrahamic faiths who believe Hinduism to be polytheistic:

> Not even eight or nine or ten, He is said to be
> Not even five nor six nor seven, He is said to be
> Not two nor three nor four, He is said to be
> There is but one God for him who knows.
> All are one God, they have with resolution become:
> He watches over everything that breathes
>   and that does not [breathe].
> (Atharva Veda 13.4:15-20)

A book in the Bible presents the results of two censuses, and was translated into Greek as Arithmoi, which means Numbers. Two is an important number in all dichotomies, as in the Yin-Yang principle. Three takes on a special significance in many religious contexts: Anu, Bel, Ea in Mesopotamia; Isis, Osiris, Horus in ancient Egypt; Brahmà, Vishnu, Shiva in the Hindu tradition; Father, Son, Holy Spirit in Christianity; and so on. It also enters into many categorizations in the Hindu framework, such as three *doshas* (blemishes) and three *gunas* (qualities).

The number four was important in ancient recognitions of elements: earth, water, air, and fire. Four is sacred in the Hindu world as the number of Vedas (primary sacred books). The word Yahweh, spelled out in Hebrew, consists of four letters.

In Chinese lore, five is the important number. There are five locations of cardinal directions: east, west, south, north, and center; five principal colors: jade, red, yellow, white, and black; five tastes: sour, bitter, sweet, astringent, and salty; five elements: earth, water, metal, wood, and fire; and five principal tones on the musical scale.

The Pythagoreans regarded six as the perfect number because its factors (1, 2, and 3) also add up to it. Twenty-eight is the next perfect number. Pythagoras also associated properties with numbers; and later, numbers were given to the letters of the alphabet. The combination of these two led to numerology, a system of questionable scientific standing, in which practitioners describe characteristics and predict events on the basis of numbers associated with letters and names. In the Book of Revelation we read that the number associated with Man is Six hundred three score and six (666).

More can be said about six. June 6, 2006 took on the form 06-06-06. This reminded mystery-mongers of a statement in the Book of Revelation: "Let him that hath understanding count the number of the beast: for it is the number of a man; and his number is six hundred threescore and six" (Rev. 13:18). The beast refers to Antichrist. The origin of 666 may be understood if one remembers that in traditional languages (Greek, Hebrew, Tamil) numbers were associated with the letters of the alphabet. Thus, the letters in the names of people add up to a number. From this developed a number mysticism which is known as *gematria* in the Judaic world. Scholars suspect that the beast here refers to the vain-glorious Roman ruler Domitian who fantasized all his family to be divine, cluttered the Capitol with statues of him, and encouraged prayer to Roman gods. He was also known for his ruthless punishment of Christians who repudiated his religious mandates. The number equivalent of his name, written in Hebrew, turns out to be 666, which was why this number was assigned to the Antichrist. As per pseudo-scientific logic, the number 666 thus becomes all the more significant, and the ominous significance of 06-06-06 should therefore be clear to everyone. It does not occur to people who gobble up this kind of fantasy that June as the sixth month is a convention introduced by Julius Caesar, that the number of the year (2006) is only in an era based on a debatable reckoning of the birth of Christ, and that this date, or any date for that matter, has no cosmic significance.

In the Judaic tradition, numbers are associated with Hebrew letters, and this enables experts in *gematria* to uncover esoteric meanings in words. The *gematria* numerology has been traced as far back as Sargon II of Babylonia who lived in the eighth century BCE, and found its way into other cultures as well.

Numerology still persists in this age of science and technology, along with its sister-disciplines of astrology, tarot cards, New Age cults, and such. These products of clouded thinking have been there all through history. About a century ago, there was the flicker of a hope that with the light of the knowledge and understanding gained through a careful and systematic methodology the obscurantism of the distant past would be shelved to the memory of ancient history. But quite the contrary has happened. They have gained currency, if not respectability, from the postmodernist recognition of every ill-informed worldview as truth and knowledge. Anyone who questions the logical coherence or rational basis of ancient belief-systems is likely to be labeled culture-insensitive, arrogant, or slave of scientism.

A lot can be said about the number seven. July 7 of the year 2007 fell on a Saturday. It was abbreviated as 07.07.07. And if one starts from Sunday as the first day of the week, Saturday becomes the seventh day, and this makes it look even more interesting: 07.07.07.07. To the casual observer, and to the scientifically inclined, there may be nothing mysterious about this. But if you have even a touch of poetry in your veins, you cannot avoid being excited about this. There has always been something magical about the number seven over the ages.

After all, the whole thing began with Creation, as any devout reader of the Book of Genesis would remind us. Was not the whole process, including the day of rest, carried out in seven days, causing seven to become special and sacred? No wonder seven occurs 507 times in the Bible. The Book of Revelation mentions seven beatitudes.

It was not for mere convenience that the list of deadly sins came to seven and that there are also seven virtues.

The Greeks had their *hepta sophoi* (seven wise men) as did the Hindus their *sapta rishi* (seven sages). One speaks of the *sapta loka* (Seven Worlds) in Hindu mythic vision.

In Christian mysticism one speaks about the Seven Primordial Spirits, just as in Hindu mysticism one speaks of seven *chakras* in the human body. There are seven apertures on the human face. Judaic scholars talk about the *Sheva Netivot Ha-Torah:* Seven Paths of the Torah. In the Baha'i tradition one speaks about the Seven Valleys. In the thirteenth century, Beatrix of Nazareth wrote on Seven Ways of Holy Love. The medieval Jewish philosopher Maimonides wrote about seven levels of worship of God. In the nineteenth century the theosophist Madame Blavatsky introduced the idea of seven types of substances (matter and spirit) of which the universe is made. One speaks of the seven towers of Mecca, and during *hadj* one is supposed to circumambulate the Kaba seven times. There are seven emblems of the Buddha. Everyone has heard of the seven pillars of wisdom, whatever they are. In Norse legends, the sun's chariot is portrayed as being pulled by seven oxen.

In more realistic terms, one can refer to the seven colors of the rainbow, the seven seas, and the seven continents.

In the literary world, the Brothers Grimm conjured up the story of "Snow White and the Seven Dwarfs," and George Axelrod wrote a play called *Seven Year Itch,* which was immortalized in film by Marilyn Monroe and her air-puffed skirt. One can go on and on: the seven hills of Rome, the seven wonders of the world, and more.

No wonder seven has become the most magical number of all. But how did this come to be? One may trace all this to the fact the ancients did not have a telescope. So the only irregular celestial bodies they detected were the sun, the moon, Mars, Mercury, Jupiter, Venus, and Saturn. These add up to seven, and the Babylonians dedicated a day to each of these bodies (which the Greeks later called planets), thus giving the world the seven-day week. If they had had powerful enough telescopes, they would have discovered Uranus and Neptune also, perhaps even the now degraded Pluto, and we would have a nine or a ten day week. This does not mean there would have been no number mysticism. But it would all be with 9 or 10. In that case, we would have had to wait till September 9, 2009, or October 10, 2010 to fantasize about the numbers.

Does seven have any intrinsic arithmetical properties? One may mention two. It is the largest one-digit prime number. The reciprocal of seven (1/7), written as a decimal is the recurring decimal: 0.142857142857142857....Now, when this is multiplied by 2, 3, 4, etc. we get the same set of six repeated numbers (142857) in the same order: 142857 x 2 = 285714; 142857 x 3 = 428571; 142857 x 4 = 571428; 142857 x 5 = 714285; 142857 x 6 = 857142.

In the Christian tradition, the number eight and the octagon represent resurrection and rebirth, because Christ rose from the grave eight days after his entry into Jerusalem. Eight is thus the symbol of baptism, which is the spiritual rebirth of a person.

Islamic scholars point out that the Qur'an's magic number is nineteen. Its first sura, called *Basmalla,* has nineteen letters (in Arabic). The number of suras in the Qur'an is 114 (= 19 x 6): the number of times *Basmalla* occurs in the Holy Book, etc. The word Allah appears in the Qur'an 2698 (= 19x142) times.

Buddhism speaks of the twelve Golden Rules; Jacob and Ishmael had twelve sons; Elijah built an altar of twelve stones; Christ had twelve apostles, etc.

Thus, numbers come into religion in many contexts. Could this be because numbers are as abstract as God and as relevant to human life as religion?

Sarah Voss (*What number is God?* 1995) examined in scholarly terms some key mathematical notions that are implicit in religious and theological thought, if only as metaphors. She resonates with the revolt against logical consistency which extends beyond romantic reveries and spills into the scientific framework. Her book explores the permeation of mathematical metaphors in the religious context. From Pythagorean mystery-mongering to Plato's view of creation from four elements, from the number symbolism in ancient Middle-Eastern religions to geometrical patterns in Vedic alters, there are many instances where numbers creep into non-mathematical situations. Voss evokes her own imagery and describes the all-embracing Divine as a definite integral.

We can play the game of numbers with the physical world also. There is only one known universe; there are two types of electric charges; space is three-dimensional; there are four fundamental interactions; five outer planets (not counting Pluto); six protons in a carbon nucleus; seven colors of the rainbow, etc.

More relevantly, the world we experience has both qualitative and quantitative aspects. Specific numbers (wavelengths) are associated with light of various colors. Things are heavy or light, and numbers (weights) are associated with things. We associate numbers with the brightness of stars (magnitudes). The number of rings on a tree trunk is related to its age. There are three million DNA nucleotide pairs in the human haploid genome, which are divided among twenty-three chromosomes.

The structure of atoms has to do with how many electrons can be accommodated in each shell enveloping the nucleus, while the chemical properties of elements are governed by how many electrons there are in the outermost shell.

Again, when we say numbers, ordinarily we think of the integers 1, 2, 3, etc., and perhaps of fractions also. One may even consider square roots, cube roots, etc. But there are also numbers that are none of these. Mathematicians call them transcendental numbers. The well-known *pi* (ratio of circumference to diameter of a circle) is an example. Another transcendental number, denoted by the letter *e*, has a role in many natural processes. It comes into play, for example, in the rate of growth of bacteria and the rate of decay of radioactive materials.

The physical universe is also governed by measurable features that are inherent to it. These are known as fundamental constants. Such, for instance, are the speed of light, the electric charge on an electron, the strength of the gravitational attraction, etc. These constants have well-defined values. It is possible to imagine a physical universe with exactly the same laws as govern it now, but with very different values for the fundamental constants. Such a universe would have entirely different properties and quite different things would have emerged in it. For instance, if the value of the gravitational constant had been significantly less, the earth might not have an atmosphere, or if it had been much more, the moon would have one. If the speed of light were enormously less, many galaxies would still be invisible, and so on.

We do not have the faintest idea as to why in our universe the fundamental constants have the particular values they have. For example, why is the speed of light some three hundred million meters per second and not something much more or much less? During the last quarter of the twentieth century it was firmly established that the synthesis of the element carbon in the core of stars could not have occurred if some of the constants had even slightly different values. Knowing that carbon is essential for all life as we know it, it appears that the kind of life there now is would not have come about if the fundamental constants had been even slightly different. This has led to the view that at the beginning of the universe, the constants were fine-tuned so as to make life possible.

There is also the intriguing fact that Eugene Wigner described as "the unreasonable effectiveness of mathematics in the natural sciences" (1960, 1-14). This is a great mystery. The universe itself has been described by some as a mathematical thought. After all, it is possible to reduce a good many fundamental processes and phenomena to mathematical equations. And some laws of physics have essentially mathematical bases. The fact that our space is three dimensional leads to the inverse square law of gravitation. Then there is the question of whether mathematical entities, such as tensors and matrices and transcendental numbers, have an external objective existence or are simply creations of the human brain.

Religion and science in the context of sex

One of the hallmarks of religions is that they all say something about sex and related matters. Bertrand Russell described Communism as a dogmatic religion (1999, 47), but the Communist doctrine says nothing explicit about sex, except perhaps in limiting family size. Religions refer to the abstract and positive significance of sex in human life, and also to its negative sides, which range from excessive indulgence to forbidden sex.

Begetting children was very important in ancient cultures. The Judaic God instructed man to marry and beget children, and He also made a covenant with Abraham that every male child be circumscribed: a practice which Islam adopted, and extended to girls also. There is the story of Abraham, past ninety years old, who sired a son through his maid servant, Hagar, because his wife, Sarah, was infertile. It is also said that later, when he was ninety-nine and Sarah was ninety, God instructed them to have a son. There are numerous references to incest, nudity, and more in the Holy Bible. Noah was seen lying drunken and nude by his son. The Torah refers to certain types of behavior as *to'eva:* abomination. One of these is "lying with another man [homosexuality]" (Leviticus 18:22). Monogamy is praised in Christianity, but Mormons believe that even God enjoys his many wives near the star Kolob.

Qur'anic suras have spoken of *houris* in heaven for the believers pleasure (Bukhari 6:402).

In the Hindu world, *apsaras* are heavenly damsels of ravishing beauty who can seduce the most austere ascetic. However, unlike *houris,* they are not faceless sex-objects, but females with grace, intelligence and personality. In the lore, Indra engages in some lascivious behavior with the wives and daughters of others. In the Brihadaranyaka Upanishad, there are mantras related to the sexual act for producing male progeny. In Tantric mysticism, both sexual act and organs play important roles. The framework of yoga speaks about the retention and sublimation of (male) sexual energy to serve purposes of achieving higher levels of consciousness. Magnificent sculpture, poetry, and devotional music in the Hindu world have sexual themes and undercurrents.

In Buddhism, sexual abstention is very important for monks and nuns, celibacy being one of the more than two hundred vows that *bhikkhus* (Buddhist renunciates) take. This is not unlike the case with their counterparts in Hinduism and Christianity. In some traditions, men are forbidden to have intercourse with their wives during certain days of the month.

Historically, all the rules, injunctions, heaven with seductive women and the like were concocted by men: perhaps by virile men who had difficulty withstanding the lure of the female form, but who recognized that giving free vent to the urge would be undesirable for society. So they transformed their desires into heavenly fantasies and prescribed sexual morality to keep id and libido under check. Yet, in ancient Rome (as elsewhere), though virginity was prized in a bride, prostitutes were prized no less.

In the early phases of religions, sex was regarded in positive terms within the marital context, with no shame or embarrassment associated with mentioning it. Its expressions before and beyond wedlock were generally frowned upon, but this taboo is fast becoming a thing of the past. Obsession with sex as entertainment beyond the bounds of religion is ancient, with the modern world opening it all up in media and magazines. Some scholars believe that the notion of sex as evil may be traced to the Zoroastrian division of everything into black-white, light-darkness, good-evil terms: matter and sex on the negative side, spirit and celibacy at higher levels.

For normal men and women, this is a world with all the joys and frustrations that we bring to one another. The attraction between the sexes adds color and pleasure, fun and fantasies to life, with significant impacts on morals and misbehavior as well.

From the evolutionary perspective, the often intense urge to merge with a member of the opposite sex is a device implanted by nature to assure species preservation through reproduction. If passion became pallid, and love became lust-less that would spell a slow and sure death for the species. Long before Darwin, the misogynist philosopher Arthur Schopenhauer described sexual urges as nothing but a trap that nature had contrived for the continuance of the species. Monks and nuns, adhering to vows of celibacy, and sexual activists who never give up their contraceptive paraphernalia, contribute nothing at all to our continuance.

The precious difference between male and female *(vive la difference!)*, on which our survival depends, results from a single chromosome: the Y-chromosome. Males have an XY pair; whereas, females have an XX pair of chromosomes. To the poet and the lover, woman is an ideal; to the ascetic, she is a temptress; but to the biologist, it is a creature with two X-chromosomes. This difference finds expression in a hundred characteristics that range from ova and sperms to bosoms and beards. Geneticists tell us that many unpleasant characteristics like aggression, greed and promiscuity arise from the Y-chromosome: a scientific way of saying that they are essentially male features. How, some 200-300 million years ago, the Y-chromosome assumed the role as sex-determinant, and how, as a result, it lost its capacity for auto-repairing defects, is a complex and fascinating chapter in evolutionary biology.

We generally tend to associate sex with reproduction, but the two are in fact quite different at the cellular level. Sex involves the fusion of two cells (the sperm and the ovum); whereas, reproduction involves the division of cells and replication. What is important for persistence and propagation is reproduction rather then sex.

This leads to the interesting conclusion that, contrary to what Schopenhauer had surmised from anthropocentric perspectives, sex is not necessary for reproduction in every species. Some species can survive quite well without sex. One may argue about whether there can be as much fun and frolic in such contexts. The whiptail lizard is a unisex species. There are only female whiptails. They lay eggs from which only egg-bearing she-whiptails emerge. This is an example of *parthenogenesis* (Greek for virgin-birth). When progeny can ensue without the benefit of males, there are some advantages, say biologists. For one thing, the population can increase at a faster rate, since 100% of the new generation can reproduce by themselves. It also enables the species to adapt itself much better to new environments. However, in sexual reproduction (which is more general than parthenogenesis) the possibilities of mutation are more limited.

The variety of ways in which males and females play out the song and dance of life are among the wondrous splendors of biology. There are fish species (the wrasse) in which females can change into males, when a he-fish furnishing sperm to a pretty school dies or disappears. There is a marine worm called *Bonellia virdis,* which is said to be 8 to 10 cm. long. Its male partner resides permanently in its womb, nourished by the food the female takes in, and producing sperm for the next generation. The geneticist Bryan Sykes who chronicles all this in his fascinating book, *Adam's curse* (2003), says that on an average a chromosome may contain a thousand different genes; whereas, the Y-chromosome has but a few hundred left! It has lost many genes over the eons, and is destined to vanish. Sykes makes the ominous prediction that some 125,000 years from now, the human world will consist only of women, and the species may well continue through parthenogenesis. Sisters and daughters, wives and lovers will miss their men sorely. Or maybe not.

Food in religion and science

Human experience is enriched by art, music, literature, philosophy, science, religion, and more. But nothing would be possible if the body is not nourished by food. It is, therefore, not surprising that in all religious traditions there are references to food.

Siddhartha fasted for six years, but it was only after taking some food that he attained Enlightenment. The message: food is fundamental for existence and even enlightenment. The Lord's Prayer in the Christian tradition asks for our daily bread, and recognizes that food is a blessing. The Bhagavad Gita declares that those who offer food to the Divine before consuming it are relieved of sins, suggesting that sharing in the intake of food is a meritorious act in the spiritual context. The Tamil poet Tiruvalluvar recognized the importance of food that results from rain, for prayer and worship when he said in a couplet:

> No pompous worship if the skies go dry
> From here below to the gods on high.
> (*Tirukkural* 2.8)

Periodic abstinence from food during certain times is another aspect of religions. The goal is to divert our proclivity for physical satisfactions and direct it to the spiritual. The spirit of sacrifice in an attitude of penance is fostered in the Islamic tradition through daily fasting until sunset during the month of Ramadan. In the Judaic tradition there is the fast of Esther, before Purim. Christianity has its Lent and the Hindu calendar has several dates that are marked as fasting days. The kind of food we eat matters in the religious context. In the Hindu world, there is a classification of foods in terms of their impact on our minds and moods: *satvic* (wholesome for the development of finer qualities), *rajasic* (resulting in aggressive hyperactivity), and *tamasic* (inducing lethargy or inebriation). In the Jewish tradition, the Kushrut prescribes kosher food (often determined by how mammals and birds are slaughtered), and proscribes *treyf* (non-kosher) food. In the Islamic framework, there is *halal* (food that is permitted) and *haram* (food that is not allowed).

Foods also have esoteric dimensions. The ancient Greeks had *ambrosia,* the immortalizing potion, the Romans their nectar, and the Hindus their *amrita.* In the Blessed Sacrament of the Altar (the Eucharist) of the Catholic tradition, there is mystical transubstantiation of bread and wine into the flesh and blood of the Savior. In the Hindu world, ordinary food becomes sanctified as *prasad* by a ritualistic offering to the gods. Food can be made sacred in the religious context.

We live in a world of interreligious sensitivities where it would be inappropriate to attach value judgments to religious practices. But it is not being disrespectful to recall that in more primordial religious systems, human beings were offered as sacrifice to the gods. God's injunction to Abraham (Genesis 22:2) to offer his son in sacrifice reflects this practice. There is a very similar story in the Tamil Shaiva tradition (*Periyapuranam*). Greeks and Romans used to do this routinely. Later, animals were substituted for humans. To this day bleating goats are routinely led to the altar in some places of worship for summary decapitation to propitiate a god or goddess. In one tradition, God is invoked every time creatures are killed in slaughterhouses, as when one commits suicide for a cause.

A goal of religion is to experience the Divine, and this fills the heart and soul of the devout with ecstasy. At the physical level, one of the most universal of such joys derives from the eating of food. From the first suckling of mother's milk to the last gulp before heartbeat ceases, food is not only the ultimate source of our sustenance, but also the provider of pleasure: two great blessings in the human experience. Food is thus the closest to God at the physical level. Starvation can stifle our capacity for love, and bring out the worst in human passion. Continued hunger can blind us to all that is beautiful, including a yearning for God. Food is thus an indispensable factor for religion.

From the perspective of science, living organisms are open systems that are in dynamic equilibrium with their environment. They are continually exchanging matter and energy with their surroundings. Food is a package of mostly energy-containing organic molecules, which are broken up or synthesized into other molecules within the body. During this process, the energy needed for various physiological functions is generated.

Careful observers in all cultures have recognized various kinds of food that serve or deter health and wellbeing. Modern science, with its understandings of elements and compounds, has analyzed molecules that the body needs for sustenance and growth. So we speak of fats, carbohydrates, sugars, proteins, vitamins and the like as the constituents of foods. Science has traced the sources of the essentials for the body: such as Vitamin A in fish liver oil and carrots, Vitamin B6 in eggs and diary products, magnesium in fruits, calcium in milk, chromium in corn oil, etc. When people refer to science glibly as just another mode of perceiving or explaining the world they are usually unaware of, or indifferent to, the enormous data that science through its methodology has been able to gather about so many different aspects of matter and the world.

From an evolutionary perspective, there are two aspects to any life-form: the species and individual. For human beings, nature assures the preservation of the former by making the sexual urge sufficiently strong and quite irresistible; and of the latter by making hunger for food another strong force. As further incentive, it associates intense pleasure when one yields to either of the two forces that help in the survival of the species and of the individual. Physicians tell us that when patients suffer from dysphagia (inability to take in food) they also experience intense psychological trauma, even nightmares. It has been found that when normal food intake is established, there is a simultaneous restoration of mental well-being. Both the extreme aversion for food and the addiction to eating have been studied scientifically. This much seems to be clear: self-discipline, and lack thereof, which seem to be reflected in non-indulgence and over-indulgence, have some genetic and chemical bases. Not everyone who abstains from food is an intentional ascetic, and not all who raid the refrigerator are personifications of greed. Indifference to food may be due to low levels of leptine in the blood stream, and inability to refrain from chocolates could be caused by addictive drugs which are latent in luscious candy bars.

Science has revealed that we need food, not only for muscles and bone strength, but also for the neurotransmitters that govern minds and moods. The brain manufactures opioids, gaba, serotonin, dopamine and norepinepherine whose right amounts in the brain are essential for our sanity, serenity and for not slipping into a stress-cycle.

Science has also given rise to agricultural techniques and fertilizers which have hugely increased the world's food production, preventing mass starvation. Science has assisted in food preparation too: pressure cookers, modern ranges, and microwave ovens. Science has invented ways of preserving food, through vacuum packing and refrigeration. Today we transport food over long distances. Then, there are enriched foods, artificial sugars, low-fat oils, low sodium salt, and so on, which science has introduced in culture and civilization. But science has also enabled the food industry to flood the market with countless pleasurable products, rich in aspartame, caffeine, saccharine, alcohol, and more, which are addictive and potentially harmful. Who can predict the long-term effect of genetically engineered foods?

It is a shame on civilization that there still are countless victims of malnutrition and hunger in our abundant world. The best from religion (compassion, love) and the best from science (knowledge, ingenuity) could converge to serve humanity in this matter.

Magic in religion and science

In everyday parlance the word "magic" is used to refer to tricks or to clever illusions. But it has a more serious connotation also. In its technical sense, magic is a complex set of beliefs and practices whose aim is to influence human beings and events without direct or obvious causal interactions. Anthropologists and psychologists have studied magical practices in different cultures. Theories have been put forward to explain the origins and persistence of magic, which is a powerful element in human culture. As often happens there is not unanimity on the subject. Nor is there agreement among theologians, anthropologists, and scholars on religion as to the difference between magic and religion. Most (religiously inclined) people believe that religion is something noble and lofty whereas magic is something spooky and undesirable.

The assumptions on which magic is based include the following: invisible forces of good and evil permeate the world; they enter into humans and operate through them; objects and persons can be affected by manipulating their images or symbols. The vestiges of this magical worldview may be seen in our language and behavior. When someone acts in a strange way, we ask, "What has gotten into you?" When we have a desire to hurt someone who is much stronger or to control someone beyond our reach, we get some satisfaction by imagining that we are actually harming the person by badly treating an image or a picture. People get considerable emotional satisfaction when they burn flags or leaders in effigy of the country they hate .

In the magical framework, objects, people and events can be influenced through words and gestures. Words are more than a means of communication. They perpetuate knowledge and memory, convey feelings and moods, can evoke love and laughter, tears and fears. The ability to give commands through the use of words (rather than with grunts and grumbles) and see them obeyed, must have given rise to the idea that words can accomplish such effects on things and events as well. Vestiges of this belief are still with us in our practices of saying "Good morning," "Goodbye," and "Go to hell!", which actually mean, "May you have a good morning," "May God be with you," and "May you encounter all sorts of difficulties."

The capacity for symbolism is a powerful human faculty. It is at the root of all human culture. Language itself is the most effective use of symbols. Because of this, human beings in their earliest stage began to see symbols in everything.

Aspects of magic are present in the practice of religions. Some have even argued that there is no difference between magic and religion. Every prayer is a gesture based on the magical tradition, which expects the course of events to be affected by words used appropriately. There are religious rites whose goal is to avert unhappy occurrences. Every gesture of blessing is for causing good things to happen. The candle and the incense, the oil lamp and the tiara, are all magical in that the flame from them is associated with something sacred and potent in the tradition.

There is esoteric significance in magical modes. Even people in the age of science who look upon magic with skepticism, sometimes try to cajole a non-working gadget into action, as with a car key or a non-reactive motor in a lawn mower. Explicit articulation of hope and wish, sprinkling of water in a sacrament, breaking of a champagne bottle to launch a new ship, singing a national anthem, raising and lowering a flag, get-well cards and flowers to a friend in hospital, crossing fingers and touching wood—all these are affirmations of our magical heritage.

Magic is etched, as it were, in the psyche of all cultures. As Lynn Throndike massively documented in his eight volume work, *A history of magic and experimental science* (1923-58), magic has played a powerful role in culture and civilization. How much of magic is related to the objective reality we value in the scientific framework is debatable. All we can say is that magic is endopotent. It transforms the participant in meaningful and significant ways.

The rise of modern science caused a major paradigm shift in our worldview. Science has tended to erase the tenets of the magical framework from our collective consciousness. Sometimes science has discredited the assumptions of magic. Yet, there are interesting parallels between magic and science.

To begin with, both magic and science accept the existence of fundamental entities in the universe that are ultimately responsible for our world of experience. Both consider these entities to be invisible to the naked eye, although one might become aware of their existence in indirect ways. In magic, these are good and evil forces. In science, they are quarks, leptons and other fundamental particles of present day physics. Explanation in terms of the hidden is common to magic and science.

In science, as in magic, one tries to put our knowledge of the fundamental entities and forces to practical use. It is not enough to know that there are good and evil forces, that there are friendly spirits and mischievous agents. One tries to encourage them to act in our interest. Likewise, one of the goals of science is to turn to our advantage our understanding of the laws of physics and chemistry.

To accomplish this, one must adopt well-defined procedures: a condition which, again, is as necessary in magic as in science. In magic, such procedures are referred to as rituals. It is of the utmost importance that rituals be followed meticulously for influencing the magical forces. In science, too, unless one follows the procedures precisely, the facts and fruits of science cannot come under our sway.

Sometimes, even when one carefully follows well-established steps, the expected results do not ensue. In such cases, the validity of the principles is not questioned right away. Rather, one thinks that the fault lies with the practitioner's inadequacy. Indeed, this is why one needs to be trained by an expert, whether in magic or in science. Rigorous training under a specialist is absolutely necessary before one can hope to take full advantage of the knowledge, be it in magic or in modern science.

We may also see a strong parallel between science and magic in the attitude of the public towards the two enterprises. In former times, magicians were held in high esteem, respected and feared also. The reason for this was simple: with the extraordinary powers arising from the esoteric knowledge about the earth and the heavens, magicians could influence people and events in significant ways. In our own times, the same is true of scientists. They are the know-it-alls, and on their expertise depends the foundations of civilization. So, their words must be listened to with interest and attention, even if one does not always understand what they utter.

Finally, both magic and science arise from the capacity of humans to think in symbolic terms. Abstract thought and play with symbols are unique to the human psyche. At the theoretical level, magic presumes unseen and invisible forces reigning supreme in the world. Magicians interact with them through gestures, chants and rituals. They develop instruments which range from twigs and sacred grass to candles and incense. In science, the abstract entities consist of sophisticated conceptual creations bearing such inscrutable (to outsiders) names as Hamiltonian and Lagrangian, while at the concrete level the symbols of science include instruments ranging from thermometers and Geiger counters to such complex systems as radio telescopes and the expansive accelerators of high energy physics.

Poetry in religion and science

Poetry is a pristine manifestation of the human spirit, and is rooted in human culture and civilization. Its impact is inescapable, its ancient vestiges are still powerful, and it resonates with our innermost being. Evocative poems to the Divine are in all cultures. The goal of those literary compositions was perhaps to persuade the deities into propitious actions. We find such appeals in the majestic meters of Vedic verses, in Biblical psalms, in the *divyaprapandam* in the Vaishnava tradition, and in other hymns and prayers in humanity's heritage. The magic of religious poetry touches the soul; it transforms and transports us to realms beyond space and time.

Naïve realism argues that reality is concrete stuff and naught else. But the visions of poets led to the flowering of art, architecture, and music. The fabric of classical Greek society was shaped by Homeric poetry, as that of Indic culture was by Vedic visions. The poet's painting renders more visible what the people already know. A hundred poets have rhymed and sung about the horrors of Hell and the glories of Heaven, about saints and God Himself. Dante's immortal *Commedia* (ca. 1321) is a veritable guided tour of heaven and hell and in-between. Like the *Satya Narayan Katha,* it also describes in spine-chilling triads what await sinners and those who do not bow to a particular God.

In all cultures, poets narrated religion-related stories, cladding them in colorful words. Poetic utterances often passed from age to age through rote repetition. In our own times, not many learn to recite verses of even a dozen lines. But all the lines of the *Ramayana,* the *Mahabharata,* the *Iliad,* the *Odyssey* and the *üligers* of Mongolia were once transmitted from generation to generation through the oral tradition.

Epics played important roles in intertwining religion and culture. Through their noble heroes they conjure up a splendid past when mighty men arose to subdue the agents of mischief, fought valiant battles for truth and honor, and stood tall after virtuous victories. The mind's eye and the heart's throb perceive epic heroes as historical figures, and their accomplishments stir people to cultural pride.

Virgil wrote the *Aeneid* (ca. 29-19 BCE), an epic history of Rome with fantastic encounters between Roman gods, and lifted up the spirit of every responsible Roman. Ferdowsi, the Persian, constructed the immortal *Shahnama* (ca. 1010) in 120,000 lines for his beloved land. He spoke of Gayamurth, Jamshid and Rustam who lived for centuries. The sage-poet Valmiki gave the ideal hero of the *Ramayana* (ca. 400 BCE) a birth date and birth place. The day of Rama's birth is still observed in worship and devotional singing. In the Tamil tradition, we have *Kandapuranam* (ca. twelfth century), leading to the great Tamil festival of Kandasashti.

The grand epics narrate momentous sagas in majestic meters, but they also infused the listeners with a sense of action and participation, sometimes inspiring them to lofty ideals. When the heroic Hector declares in Homer's grand epic (ca. eighth century BCE):

Let me at least not die without a struggle, inglorious,
but do some big thing first, that men to come shall know
     of it.
(*Iliad* 22.304-305)

...a subtle value is imprinted: that we should aspire to something of significance in life. The events and heroes of the classics infuse the epic with historical authenticity.

These hoary narratives, which reflect on life and morals, and refer to divine interventions, have touched the heart and mind of millions. They gave meaning and purpose to generations, engendered feasts and festivals, and are among the cultural treasures of humanity, as precious as pyramids, temples, cathedrals, pagodas and mosques.

Both science and poetry are efforts to cast truth and nature in symmetry and harmony. To the poet, "poetry is truth dwelling in beauty" (attributed to Robert Gilfillan, ca. 1830s), and to the scientist, science is truth dwelling in beautiful principles. Truth is of significance only to the seeker. When Edgar Allen Poe said that, for him, poetry was not a purpose but a passion, he was also expressing the feelings of the true scientist about his own field. In both science and poetry creativity plays an important role. Therefore, while there is difference between poetry and science in the modes of perception and in the framework of the search, there is no difference in the inspiration of the quest.

Sometimes, when a poet speaks out against the scientific worldview, he unwittingly comes closer to the scientist in his description. William Blake, the inspired mystic who regarded Reason as the Devil, and Newton as its high-priest, (see *Milton,* ca. 1804-11, in *Complete Poetry,* 95-146) and who proclaimed that "Art is the Tree of Life...Science the Tree of Death" (from "Laocoon," 1827, 274), echoed powerfully the romantic revolt against a mindless mechanical view of the universe such as was being suggested by eighteenth century physics and astronomy. But when he spoke of the raptures in efforts:

To see the World in a Grain of Sand
And Heaven in a Wild Flower
Hold Infinity in the palm of your Hand
Eternity in an Hour
(from "Auguries of Innocence," lines 1-4, 1805, 490)

...he was putting to rhyme and rhythm the thrills of the scientific pursuit. For when a chemist analyzes a sand grain, or a physicist probes into its atomic structure, they see a world in a grain of sand. When a botanist describes the magic of wild flowers, their forms and their colors, and the plant histologist uncovers the biochemical turbulences that provoke their transformations, they see heaven in action in a wild flower. When the cosmologist talks about the limits of the universe, the astronomer captures electromagnetic subtleties from distant galaxies and the astrophysicist computes the evolution of stars, they hold infinity in their hands.

Imagination is as important in science as it is in poetry. The view of the scientist as a helpless groper chained to the crass world of tangible reality is misleading. When John Tyndal called imagination the architect of physical theories, and when Max Born noted that faith, imagination and intuition are decisive factors in the progress of science, they were not referring to literary imagery. Breaking through the walls of direct perceptions to construct a world of ideas and images, and to infuse that world with the breath of reality, is what the imaginative process is all about. As the physicist conjures up Hamiltonians and entropy, he does precisely that. When Kekulé hit upon the structure of benzene and Van't Hoff conceived the tetrahedral architecture of the carbon atom, imagination played a role.

Poetry is intensely personal and science is intentionally international. Yet, poetic creations are more easily shared than the findings of scientists. True, in order to derive all the joys and meanings of a good poem, one must read it over and over again; yet, most people of reasonable culture can enjoy many good poems. This is not the case when literary intellectuals read technical scientific works.

Tennyson feared the decay of poetry because of the rise of science. "Soon your brilliant towers shall darken with the waving of her [science's] hand" ("Timbuctoo," lines 243-244, 1829), he grimly predicted. If no poet has painted the special theory of relativity or nuclear magnetic resonance in iambic pentameters, neither has Tennyson's fears come true.

Art in religion and science

Art is humanity's creative expression of profoundly experienced truths in ways that are aesthetically fulfilling, spiritually uplifting, and can be easily shared with others. Given that religions also embody deeply felt truths and have a collective dimension, it is not surprising that there have been artistic creations in all religious traditions.

The grand temples beautifying India's religious landscape from Kashmir to Kanya Kumari are magnificent works of art. Their extensions into Laos, Kampuchea and other regions in the classical world, and into Europe and America in modern times show how art, like the religious spirit, can move from land to distant land. The same is true of the awe-inspiring cathedrals of Europe, which are marvels of religious architecture. Their majesty should invoke reverence in all but the most hard-hearted. What is one to say of the magnificent mosques of Islam! The one in Cordoba—now a relic of a by-gone era and tourist site—is but one instance of their breath-taking grandeur. Or consider the glorious Golden Temple of the Sikhs wherein is enshrined the original of the Holy Book of the tradition. One can go on and on, referring to Buddhist pagodas, Jaina temples, Shinto shrines, and more. In all places of worship, the faithful came by the hundreds to pay homage to the Unfathomable.

Innumerable sculptures have been chiseled to transform amorphous alloy and rock into replicas of gods and deities and saints worthy of reverence. Then there are frescoes and paintings, in Ajanta and in the Sistine Chapel, in ancient Egyptian tombs and in countless basilicas, all inspired by religion. Religions have also given rise to individual artistic creations ranging from the colorful patterns of the *rangoli* (Hindu) to the adorning of Christmas trees.

There was/is stringent prohibition of religious figures and figurines in Islam, inspired perhaps by the Jewish commandment against graven images. Some believe that such an inhibition was also there in the early phases of Buddhism. But as geometrical patterns, balanced symmetry, and beautiful calligraphy, in carvings and weaving, magnificent works of art have originated from the Islamic world of Syria, Persia, Iraq, Turkey, and Egypt. Once, they flooded European countries and enriched even church adornments,

In the Christian world, based often on Pope Gregory's idea that the written word is for the learned, and pictures are for the illiterate, religious depictions were the rule. But since Giotto in the fourteenth century and the Renaissance, there came about an outburst of masterpieces of painting that portrayed, with extraordinary depth and color, scenes and personages from the Bible and the saints of the tradition.

In the Hindu world there had been mystical art in various regions, and sculptures of epic episodes for centuries, as in the rock-art in Mahabalipuram. But in the nineteenth century Raja Ravi Varma revolutionized Hindu art by painting epic scenes and divine figures in modes that were not unlike in European paintings. They have had tremendous impact on how modern Hindus visualize Rama and Krishna, Sita and Radha, Sarasvati and Lakshmi.

If religions inspired great works of art, some heinous crimes of art-destruction have also been committed by mindless iconoclasts in the name of their religion. Temples have been destroyed and religious symbols desecrated by true believers who brook no representation of the Divine. The most recent example of this was the destruction of the Hadda sculptures during the civil war in Afghanistan and the Taliban's vandalism of the two tall Bamiyan Buddhas in 2001 in that once-glorious, but now unfortunate, country. Besides bringing discredit to their heritage, such behavior adds to the distortions and prejudices which are on the rise against Islam. It is important not to judge the intrinsic goodness of any religion by the ugly behavior of some of its more ardent and misguided practitioners.

The goal of science may be very different from that of art, but the artistic urge for harmony and symmetry, for aesthetics and balance and the quest for deeper truths are as much factors in the articulations of science as in art. The equations of theoretical physics, the sweeping principles undergirding the natural world, and the laws connecting seemingly dissimilar phenomena have many features of artistic creations, as do the countless measuring and detecting instruments that grace the laboratories and observatories of the world. The mammoth high energy accelerators are no less lofty in goal and great in construction than the grand cathedrals, mosques, and temples of religious traditions. It is not surprising that laboratories have been described as the temples of science.

The principle of perspective, first enunciated by the Arab mathematician Alhazen in about 1000 CE, came to be applied to painting some three centuries later, and has become a primary lesson in any art course.

Technology furnishes material tools for art: alloys, paints, chisels and brushes, canvas and paper: Everything that goes to create sculpture and painting is furnished by chemical and mechanical industries. Their variety and sophistication have been increasing with the march of science. Latex and acrylic products ushered in water-based painting materials. Not all who admire impressionists may be aware of the role of science and technology in their works. New pigments were concocted in the nineteenth century with interesting new chromatic properties, which facilitated the artist's work. New insights were gained into the nature of light and its properties. Then again, the metal paint tube, invented by John Rand in 1840, made paints easily portable. This, too, contributed to the development of the art.

The twentieth century, notorious for its unleashing of chemical toxins into the environment, also made us aware of lead poisoning from traditionally-used paints, and introduced the much less dangerous titanium white and zinc white.

The physics of the twentieth century influenced art in many ways. Historian of science Arthur I. Miller has argued in *Einstein, Picasso: Space, time and the beauty that causes havoc* (2001) that both Einstein's

Relativity and Picasso's Cubism were influenced by the writings of the mathematician Henri Poincaré. Salvador Dali's surrealist masterpiece, "The Persistence of Memory" (1931) is said to have been inspired by Einstein's theory of time. On the other hand, rebelling against the materialist philosophy of science, abstract artists like Wassily Kandinsky argued that their creations would open the door to spiritualism. The artistic veneration of the irrational led to Dadaism, surrealism and the like.

Then again, science has unveiled some great works of beauty that nature has created. We first learnt through X-ray about the geometrical beauty in crystal structure. More recently, X-ray photographs have unveiled aesthetic aspects of the anatomy of plants that are not ordinarily visible to us.

Speaking of X-rays, using a method known as X-ray micro-diffraction, one can identify, as shown by Deborah Lau (Beaumont 2004), the pigments and palettes that artists had used, without adversely affecting the masterpieces. This is a very valuable technique for identifying the authenticity of works of art. Another technique, known as Raman microscopy, has also been used to expose forgeries. Using this method, the so-called Vinland map, which was touted as a map of North America drawn in 1434, has been shown to be a forgery of much more recent vintage.

Thus, if religion inspired art in a hundred contexts, science has influenced art in various other ways. Aside from their intrinsic and different goals, both science and religion have had significant impact on many other aspects of human culture as well.

In this context, one cannot ignore some of the most beautiful formulas of mathematics: for example, infinite series or the famous formula (due to Roger Cotes in the early eighteenth century) that connects e (the base of the natural logarithm), the number pi, the number i (imaginary unit of complex numbers), the number one, and the number zero through what is sometimes called the most beautiful formula of mathematics, referred to as Euler's identity:

$$e^{\pi i} + 1 = 0$$

Then again, some of the geometrical representations of simple algebraic equations are a pure delight to behold.

Celestial world: religious and scientific perspectives

We see around us land and water, hills and meadows, plants, trees, birds, bees and beasts. All this creates empathy for nature in our consciousness. When we look upwards, beyond the passing clouds and high in the sky, we notice the sun and moon rise and set, and countless stars in the celestial dome. They all seem so far, far away, nowhere within our palpable reach.

Our distant ancestors must have wondered about the realm of celestial entities. When spiritual awareness arose in the human heart, one began to feel that the abode of God must be somewhere up there, and that God moved freely in that vast domain, as we do here on earth. That was permanent: the world above. Unlike matter, motion, flowers and creatures here on earth, celestial bodies seem to be forever, and celestial motions seem to have an eternal majesty that is astonishingly predictable.

Yet, now and again, something strange happens up there. A tailed-star blazes in the darkness, or a new star appears all of a sudden. These were interpreted as wanton works of God, perhaps to warn us of something about to happen. That is how new stars, comets, eclipses, even peculiar configurations of planets, were once looked upon.

Every religion has some association or other with celestial bodies. At the birth of the Buddha, a great light is said to have flashed in the sky. Mesopotamian astrologers (the Magi) read in the planetary conjunction of Jupiter and Saturn, which occurred with uncommon frequency in the first decade before the birth of Christ, the announcing of an event of great significance: the birth of Christ. The Star of David, the Crescent of Islam, veneration of Sun-God, not to mention homage to planetary deities, which is implicit in our naming of the days of the week, all reflect connections between religions and the celestial world. A good many religious observances are marked in relation to the phases of the moon. In some languages, such as French and German, the word for sky is the same as the word for heaven *(ciel* and *Himmel).*

The darkening of the sun in broad daylight, or of the moon on a full moon night, must have been frightening to the first humans who noticed them. The Chinese spoke of Hsi and Ho, semi-divine guardians who were derelict in their duties and caused disharmony between sun and moon. Ancient Hindu myths pictured eclipses as the sun (or the moon) being eaten up by a monster, periodically maiming the heavenly bodies. Amerindians fantasized a gigantic jaguar doing the job. In the *Odyssey,* there is reference to a day when the sun perished, spreading an evil mist. The Bible says God once warned He would "make the sun go down at noon, and darken the earth in broad daylight" (Amos 8:9).

In the framework of the fear and mythology of ages past, comets were expressions of divine wrath to warn us of an impending disaster: the demise of a king, the onset of a plague, or the invasion of an alien horde. A sixteenth century author wrote, perhaps tongue in cheek, that comets "are formed by the ascending from the earth of human sins and wickedness, formed into a kind of gas, and ignited by the anger of God. This poisonous stuff falls down again on peoples' heads, and causes all kinds of mischief, such as pestilence, Frenchmen, sudden death, and bad weather" (Dreyer 2004, 64). The 1456 comet was taken as presaging the onslaught of the marauding Turks. The Pope promptly excommunicated this celestial anomaly, which (in later visits) came to be called Halley's Comet.

In ancient science, there was a clear demarcation between the celestial world and the sub-lunar. We live and die in this world of decaying matter where nothing seems as perfect as the silent stars, the majestic moon and the brilliant sun. The world up there is visibly way beyond our reach. Aristotle taught in no uncertain terms that, whereas everything in our mundane field is decaying and imperfect, in the celestial world there was only incorruptible permanence and grand motions in perfect circles.

This neat dichotomy was ruined when the Copernican hypothesis of a sun-centered universe gained ground, making the earth another speck among the planets that orbit our central star. When Kepler discovered the planetary paths, even the perfect circles were flattened into ellipses. And when Galileo's peering lenses revealed that the lunar surface is rugged and wrought with enormous potholes, the rotund smoothness of celestial bodies was transformed like the wrinkled cheek of an aging beauty that had once impressed the admiring beholder as soft loveliness.

In due course, more discoveries came, sharpened by Galileo's application of mathematics to physical phenomena, facilitated by instruments of increasing range and probing depth. Astronomers spotted double stars and clusters, and entities like planetary satellites, new planets, novas and asteroids. With the power of spectroscopy, even the composition of stars has been revealed. They are not made up of incorruptible unearthly heavenly substance, as the great Aristotle had led us to believe, but of hydrogen, calcium, iron, helium and the like. In composition, all heaven was uncovered to be no different than the crass earth that harbors us. It was a rude awakening, like the truth about Santa Claus: the celestial world crumbled like the fantasies of mythology. Modern astronomy and astrophysics have unveiled the nature of comets as chunks of dirt and ice, novas as flare-ups in double star systems, asteroids as amorphous rocky chunks, and flashing meteors as cosmic debris burnt to smithereens in the enveloping air of our planet.

There is nothing special about the extra-atmospheric realm, except perhaps for the current suspicion that there might be inquisitive minds amidst the stellar billions. Even of this, one cannot be quite certain. It may well be, as those engaged in the SETI (Search for Extraterrestrial Intelligence) project are convinced, that some sophisticated techno-creatures are watching us at this very minute with radio telescopes and all.

The ancients had imagined that events in the heavens affect us. Modern science has exploded that myth, but not entirely. We do know, on the weight of current astrophysics, that a mammoth cosmic event determined our fate. All the complex elements that form our solar system were synthesized in a supernova of unknown history. In the beginning, there were only electrons and protons, from which were born all the atoms of hydrogen in the world. Then, after many eons, the first hydrogen-helium stars came to be. After eons more, some of the gigantic stars grew so dense that heavier elements were synthesized at their core. One of these super-hot stars blew up as a supernova, spewing heavy elements. These became the materials of our solar system.

Religions say our material bodies formed on this earth and our spiritual aspect came from heaven. Science says that the material constituents that ignited life were made in the heavens, but our spiritual dimensions emerged on earth. Religion is soothing to the soul; science is respectful of the mind. One is as necessary as the other. Religions should become more respectful of the mind and science more soothing to the soul.

Politics in religion and science

Politics involves the acquiring or grabbing, wielding and sharing of power. Though generally associated with governments, it is part of any institutionalized system. So it is not surprising that institutionalized religions have also had a political side. Sometimes they have usurped from, sometimes competed with, governments for power over the people. Religions regard laws as coming directly from God. That is why a government that is based on such laws (the Ten Commandments, the Bible, the Sharia, etc.) is described as a theocracy (rule by God).

The classic trial of Socrates in ancient Greece was an early instance of confrontation between state and a religious leader. Until the Middle Ages, the Roman Catholic Church wielded power over European kings and lords. Derelictions from the Church's pronouncements were not brooked. The practice led to the notorious Inquisition. In some cases, representatives of the Church had to choose between the Pope and the King as the higher authority. Thomas Becket's decision to put Pope Alexander III on a higher pedestal over King Henry II of England cost him his life. Protestant monarchs who broke away from Papal authority, established their own versions of the church and made themselves head of the church, also, often, assuming a Divine Right of kings.

The establishment of the caliphate after Prophet Mohammed's death saw the emergence of a vast empire which divided the world into Dar-al-Islam (where the Sharia ruled) and Dar-al-Kufr (where unbelievers ruled). The Caliphs were Commanders of the Faithful.

There was a time when Christians and Jews enjoyed full religious freedom in Islamic countries. In our own times there are some theocratic states are not tolerant of other religions. Some countries blatantly violate basic human rights by banning Hindus, Baha'is, Zoroastrians, and others.

In classical times, Hindu kings had religious men as their counselors: the illustrious Vasishtha and Vishvamitra were among them. The works of a Tamil poet-minister changed the realm from Jaina to Hindu. Councils to formally promulgate the teachings of the Buddha have been formed since ancient times in the Buddhist world. Tibet was once a theocratic state under the Dalai Lama; however, it was tolerant of others religions in its midst.

The United States was one of the first countries to incorporate the principle of separation of church and state in its constitution. The secularist principle is that no religion, ruled by scripture or dharmashastra, acharya or bishop or ayatollah or any religious head will have authority in the governance of the nation. However, some traditional religious values and perspectives are implicit in the laws and ideals of secularist countries. All beliefs and non-hurtful practices of religions (and of non-religious and anti-religious views) are given equal rights in secularist nations.

In modern times, there have been instances where the government's ideology was imposed on science. For example, in Nazi Germany the government ordained what was good science (Aryan) and what was bad science (Jewish). Therefore, the theory of relativity was banned. At about the same time, the Soviet Union was directing its scientists to make their theories conform to the doctrines of Marxism-Leninism. Therefore, the Copenhagen interpretation of quantum mechanics was banned there. Attempts to impose creationism in schools and restrict research on stem-cells come close to governmental interference with science.

In recent decades, even in secular countries, ardent religious enthusiasts have been trying to insinuate themselves and their doctrines into governmental affairs. They are not content with providing a spiritual anchor to the faithful. Chris Mooney, in *The Republican war on science* (2005), discusses with numerous examples how the religious right has acquired or manipulated political power in the United States to distort or curb whatever science was disturbing or inconvenient for them. Perhaps the book is wrongly titled. It could more appropriately be called *Right-Wing machinations against science,* because, though it is presented as an indictment of a political party in one country, the book tellingly illustrates what can happen in any society when religion and politics get control over science. The phenomenon is not unique to the United States.

Mooney does not give the background for this unfortunate development. When science was neutral, it received little attention. Not many in the eighteenth century were interested in whether light was wave or particle. In the nineteenth century, only scientists cared for thermodynamics and electromagnetism. When science began to bear fruit through countless gadgets, the public and the government became enthusiastic about it. However, when science seemed to undermine religion through Darwinism and tended to foster atheistic worldviews, and some scientists engaged in virulent attacks on the religious view of life, it upset many religiously-inclined people. Also, when scientists revealed that technology was injurious, industrialists became unhappy. Since they could do little to curb Darwinian biology or the warnings of global warming, the forces joined hands, resulting in this unfortunate attack on the integrity of science.

It is difficult for those who live in free societies to imagine the plight of individuals in nations where thoughts and words against the government result in imprisonment, torture, or exile. Yuri Orlov, in *Dangerous thoughts: Memoirs of a Russian life* (1991), has reminisced on his own misadventures under a system that for decades fooled many intellectuals abroad into believing that it alone stood for the well-being of the common man. From the now-distant atrocities of Stalinist ruthlessness to more recent outrages of Siberian seclusion and psychiatric indignities, much mischief was wrought in the Soviet Union on those who clamored for freedom and spoke out against hypocrisy and corruption. When Yuri Orlov, once a devotee of Saint Joseph (Stalin) and ardent member of the Communist Party, deviated from the party line, his troubles began. But he continued to question the system, while practicing physics, and went on to found the *Helsinki Watch* to keep an eye on the Soviets' promise to the international community to respect the human rights of its citizens. For this he was condemned as a CIA spy, interned in labor camps, constrained from scientific research, and barred from writing letters to the outside world. Thanks to support from abroad, the dogged determination of others (like Sakharov), and to the transformations within the Soviet Union, Orlov was finally let go.

Scientific materialists have often been looked down upon or even ostracized by religious establishments since ancient times. For example, the Epicureans of ancient Greece and the Charvakas of ancient India suffered such fate. Scientifically held truths which run contrary to the worldview of the ruling orthodoxy, whether religious or secular, have often been condemned. When Copernicus published his earth-moving hypothesis about the solar system, he unleashed the anger of religionists: not just the Pope of the Catholic Church, but also Martin Luther, an initiator of Protestantism, was vehemently against it. Many early modern scientists, though deeply religious, never suspected that their findings would offend those wielding power to the degree that politics would influence, impede or distort the progress of science. But this has happened. It is mainly the politicians of religion who react to fossil interpretation and biological evolution.

In modern secular democracies one often thinks of the linking of religion and politics as an unhealthy mixture. But this depends on time and place and context. In the first half of the nineteenth century, William Wilberforce, a renowned religious conservative was very involved with the Anti-Slavery Society. He authored *Appeal to the religion, justice and humanity of the inhabitants of the British Empire: In behalf of the Negro slaves in the West Indies* (1823), in which he condemned the institution of slavery as a national crime and called for legislation to abolish the ignoble practice and to actively enforce the already existing laws against slave trade (Pollock 1977).

Towards the end of the nineteenth century, Lokamanya Tilak, a fiery patriot in India united his people in their freedom fight against the British occupation of their country by transforming a low-key domestic religious observance of the deity Ganesha into an annual public event of grand proportions in which Hindus of all castes mingled (Thapan 1997).

Science and politics have interacted in other ways. From the time science became dependent on government funds for research projects, which were becoming more and more expensive, it was not scientific results, but scientific goals which came under increasing governmental scrutiny. In some countries, like the former Soviet Union and some newly emerging nations, science was/is generously supported, not so much for its own sake, as for catching up with the West, and for its usefulness in technology. In the United States, there was ample funding for science and technology in the decade following the Sputnik triumph of the Soviet Union. After the end of the cold war, support for research in fundamental physics dwindled.

As research funds gradually diminished because of competing demands from other more socially urgent and practical projects, politics began to influence the course of science. The American Supercollider, which would have played a role in confirming some esoteric speculations of theoretical physics, had to be scrapped because of limited funds and the assessment by congressmen of the value of the research. In this context, some scientists have not shirked from distorting or exaggerating the relevance of their research for practical energy and defense needs, promise of cures for diseases, etc. in their application for grant-money. A good deal of highly sophisticated and utterly useless theoretical research work has been generously funded on the basis of such pretenses. Scientists have also received support based on the general proposition that one can never tell what benefits even purely scientific research might lead to.

We live in an age that is both secular and religious. It is secular where the power and prestige of science have overshadowed the other dimensions of human culture to the point of marginalizing the ontological claims and explanatory models of traditional religions. It is religious in that vast numbers of people in a great many nations have been stirred as never before to reaffirm their religious traditions which have been diluted or debilitated by the onward march of science and secularist values.

Today, secularism is a grave threat to religion mainly in the Western Christian world where science and the Enlightenment have taken deep roots. It is no threat in nations where theocracy is strong and supreme, and secular calls are condemned and punished. Secularism is also decried in some nations as culture-destructive, because it is regarded as an import from erstwhile colonialists.

When secularism is rejected, the mind-freeing potencies of science and Enlightenment become beyond the reach of people who, inspired largely by post-modern Western scholars, have been denigrating science as formulations of an arrogant minority from a civilization that perpetrated aggression, exploitation, and oppression on militarily weaker peoples during the past four centuries.

This simplistic caricature does not understand that secularism is perhaps the most civilized principle of government in all of history. In nations where secularism is derided and devalued, the medieval mind-set still lingers, in which the religion of the wielders of political power alone is true, and which disallows religious expressions of others.

Secularism in the modern world is not a rejection of religion, nor the denial of religious rights. It is rather a framework in which every citizen can exercise his or her chosen mode of spiritual fulfillment, whether it is traditional or modern, theistic, pantheistic, or atheistic; and where the laws of the land will not be dictated by the rules set forth in any particular holy book.

On the other hand, the theoretical successes and practical benefits of science sometimes so seduce a people that they totalize all human experience under a science that can offer no guidance in a moral dilemma, set no bounds on instinctive self-serving behavior, nor provide comfort and solace in times of emotional crisis. And in the name of law and of separation of church and state, secularist-atheists protest when believers pray or express their faith in God in public places, in however harmless a manner. Ridiculing, condemning, or constraining public religious expressions in the name of secularism achieves little more than causing emotional hurt to believers.

Humanity is facing many challenges: diminution of resources, growing population, deteriorating environment, and more. In this context, the wisdom in religious traditions can be of much help. Periodic meditation with wholesome thoughts could help us curb our more hurtful instincts. But it is equally important to curb the religious zeal that can cause pain and persecution as it did in ages past.

It may not be in our best interest to try to snuff all religious dimensions of society and culture. And it is neither intellectually possible nor socially appropriate to continue with many aspects of the religions of our ancestors. In a secular world, religions need to formulate worldviews and visions that are informed by the results of science and strengthened by the values that are prompted by the sages of the traditions. Religions have to attend to the needs of the poor and the sick, as preached and practiced by Christ. They must reinstate the kinds of ethical values that were conveyed by the Ten Commandments through Moses. They must foster the compassion of the Buddha, the principle of non-injury of Mahavira, the egalitarian principles implicit in Islam and Sikhism. As in Hinduism, religions must teach that there are multiple paths to religious fulfillment. Religions ought to guide people to meaningful spiritual experiences which will elevate their thoughts and inspire them to helpful and productive behavior.

Technology in religion and science

How did the major religions spread in the ancient world? This was achieved by the inspired devotees of the various prophets and pioneers of the spiritual quest. No religion could have gone beyond the hearing range of its originators were it not for the more ardent disciples who took it upon themselves to propagate what the Master had declared to be transcendental truths. The propagation of religious systems via tireless missionaries, and of scriptural passages through the oral tradition are among the marvels of humanity's cultural continuity, for it all happened ages before the modern technologies of communication came into existence.

But religions have also been affected in many ways by technological inventions. The printing press was probably the most far-reaching of them all. In 1455, Johannes Gutenberg, the inventor of the printing press and movable type, produced some 180 copies of the Bible whose single-manuscript version had taken two full years to complete. Since then, millions of copies of the Bible have been printed and distributed in different countries in different languages. Likewise, we now have countless copies of the Qur'an, the Bhagavad Gita and all the scriptures of the world's religions.

With the invention of the microphone and speakers, preachers could address larger audiences, and with radio sermons began to reach millions of people in distant places. With television, the messages of religions are spread with even greater ease and frequency.

It was thanks to the audiocassette that Ayatollah Khomeini smuggled his message from Paris to his native country, and thus succeeded in re-establishing Shiite theocracy in Iran. Evangelists like Pat Robertson and Jerry Falwell have imitators in spreading the Word, both within the Christian world and in other religions also. It is very unlikely that the teachings of Ramakrishna or the ISKCON (International Society for Krishna Consciousness) movement would have spread all over the world without the ships and the planes that carry their messengers with ease to the five continents.

Now, with the internet, all this has taken a quantum leap, with enormous potential for both good and bad. Wise and enlightened religious visions and information can be spread effectively. But given that anyone with any credentials can also mouth off to the world at large, vast amounts of religious misinformation, fanatical nonsense, and hate propaganda are also warping the minds of millions of gullible minds.

There are other ways in which technology has had impacts on religion. Consider the case of the shroud of Turin. Since the Middle

Ages the shroud was believed to be part of the cloth that had covered the body of Christ after the crucifixion. With carbon dating and microscopic analysis of the pigments, serious doubt has been cast on this claim. The tug of war on this issue between science and religion has not quieted down since it first broke out in the 1980s (Gove 1996). Technology has enabled us to dig deep into the ground and unearth the remains of the past, enabling one to recover or study the historical roots of religions. Not everyone can understand how the sanctity of Christ is enhanced or diminished by dating a piece of cloth which is presumed to have been touched by Christ's body.

Then again, antibiotics, planes, telephones, television and other technological wonders accomplish with a hundred-fold effectiveness what used to be regarded as miracles by a saintly few: curing the sick, seeing and hearing distant events, speedy transportation of bodies, etc. Indeed, some scholars have argued that technology would eventually replace religion as the immense source of power that one often attributes to God.

Technology may be looked upon as human ingenuity to harness matter and energy in the service of human beings, especially to reduce muscular effort, to make life's chores less arduous, to enhance comfort and conveniences, and to facilitate human interactions. From the first flints and arrows at the dawn of civilization to stun game animals, and wheels and pulleys to move and lift, technology has steadily grown over the centuries. With the industrial revolution in the eighteenth and nineteenth centuries, it began to take giant strides, and its achievements in the twentieth century can be described only as spectacular. However, unlike ancient and classical technology, a good deal of modern technology has developed from precise understandings of natural processes. Thermodynamics served the cause of steam engines, and electromagnetism has led to countless electro-mechanical gadgets that have become ubiquitous in the modern world. Much of twentieth century technology—though not all—has resulted from deep and detailed knowledge of atoms and nuclei, as also discoveries in quantum physics. Computers and the Internet would have been impossible without that understanding.

If science has contributed much to advances in technology, technology has also helped science in countless ways. The Copernican hypothesis of a sun-centered solar system would not have gone much beyond being an interesting speculation without the invention of a simple gadget—the telescope—in early seventeenth century. In its various modifications and improvements, the telescope has literally opened our eyes to the very limits of the universe. Likewise, the invention of the microscope (a simple combination of tiny lenses) in that same century opened up rich and new aspects of the world around us. This instrument, in myriad modifications, has revealed to us the existence of countless microorganisms, as also the structure and composition of cells and other entities too minute to be visible to the naked eye. And then there is the radio telescope—pure technology in construction—which has brought us knowledge about pulsars and quasars, and might some day tell us about distant, and as yet unknown, civilizations in the universe.

The spectroscope has brought to us knowledge about the stars: their chemical composition, as well as the motions of galaxies. Other instruments have made us aware of ultraviolet and infrared radiations, argon, helium and much more. Many instruments enable us to measure various quantitative features of the physical world.

Crude versions of the steam engine prompted the scientific field of thermodynamics, and led to the formulation of the principle of energy conservation.

Balloon flights and airplanes contributed much to cosmic ray physics. Many of the discoveries in high-energy physics, and the verification of some of its theories, call for very sophisticated technology and paraphernalia, such as giant accelerators and colliders. One can go on and on with examples. A peep into any laboratory will show how much pure science is dependent on technology. Every item there, from beakers and faucets to oscilloscopes and meters and practically everything in between, comes from some manufacturing center or another.

Thus, technology has contributed to the propagation of religions without itself benefiting from the latter; whereas, the impacts and influences of technology and science have been mutual. Technology without science would have remained far less sophisticated, and science without technology would not have been as refined and advanced as it is today.

Music in religion and science

The aesthetic dimension of religion often finds expression through music. The Hindu Vedas are said to be the earliest religious hymns in humanity's cultural history. And they are chants: verses sung, often in groups, as per canonically prescribed intonations. The Sama Veda is entirely musical in construction. In Hindu mythopoeia, there are said to be minstrels in Heaven (the *gandharvas*). In the Vaishnava tradition, Sri Chaitanya sang exhilarating melodies dedicated to the Divine, which sent him into a trance. The composer-saint Thyagaraja, like his counterpart Johann Sebastian Bach in the Christian tradition, carved out the *gana-marga* or musical path for spiritual fulfillment. Collective devotional singing called *bhajans* and *divya-nama-sankirtanam* induce ecstatic experience.

In a Buddhist treatise on the *Perfection of great wisdom* (ca. 100 BCE), we read: "the Bodhisattvas make use of beautiful music to soften people's hearts. With their hearts softened, people's minds are more receptive, and thus easier to educate and transform through the teachings" (Stowe 2004, 146). In the Buddhist tradition, music is part of ceremonial offerings. In the Chinese Buddhist tradition, Emperor Wu of Liang Dynasty composed musical pieces to propagate *dharma.* He also initiated choirs for children. We are reminded of the medieval Pope Innocent VI who composed the Eucharistic hymn *Ave verum corpus* (ca. 1360).

In the Judaic tradition, music is given a high place. Its role in spiritual experience is fully recognized. Jewish prophets and mystics sang inspired tunes, called *nigunim*. Already in ancient Jerusalem music was part of the worship service in Jewish temples. One of the psalms in the Old Testament says: "Praise the Lord with harp: Sing unto him with the psaltery and an instrument of ten strings. Sing unto him a new song…" (Psalms 33:2-3).

The Christian tradition has some of the most beautiful music in humanity's heritage. Not just the Gregorian chants, which have their counterparts elsewhere, but pieces like Bach's *Passion* (1727), which movingly conveys Christ's suffering; *Exultate, Jubilate* (1773), which Mozart wrote when he was barely seventeen and whose printed words "Rejoice, shout, o you blessed souls, singing sweet hymns; responding to your song the skies sing psalms with me!" do little justice to the joy that comes from listening to the lines; and the *Messiah* (1741), during whose composition, Handel said, "I think I did see all Heaven before me and the great God himself." Non-Christians can exclaim that the birth and crucifixion of Christ was something they can appreciate because those events gave rise to music of such magnificence.

In religious traditions, one sometimes makes a distinction between acceptable and unacceptable music, often depending on the theme in a song or in the use of instrument. There is often the fear that certain types of music might corrupt the mind. As late as in the nineteenth century, some churches did not allow instrumental music in their services, except perhaps for the organ. Nowhere is this attitude more explicit than in traditional Islam. And yet, according to one Muslim scholar, "Among the entertainments which may comfort the soul, please the heart, and refresh the ear is singing. Islam permits singing under the condition that it not be in any way obscene or harmful to Islamic morals. There is no harm in it being accompanied by music which is not exciting" (Al-Qaradawi 1960, 300). But others have maintained that music is *taboo,* though songs without music are okay if the words are not sinful. Indeed, it is/was believed by some that Satan inspires the composition of certain types of music. The famous violinist and composer Paganini was suspected of having made a pact with the devil to enable him to write his tempestuous music (Sugden 1980). For this alleged offence his bones were removed from his grave. By and large, Christianity and Judaism have overcome such negative attitudes, but some orthodox Jews are still touchy about the themes of songs.

Music is certainly one of the most pleasing of art forms. Singing, however crudely, is within reach of everyone. Besides the auditory pleasure it gives, music stirs the soul, be it a national anthem or a religious invocation. So it has played a role in religious traditions.

The recognition of mathematical proportions in musical notes by Pythagoras was perhaps the first link between music and science, for through this recognition one realized that there was more to music than pleasurable experience. The Pythagorean discovery, along with the observation of periodicities in the motions of stars and planets, led to the ancient notion of music of the spheres, which was invoked even in the seventeenth century by Johannes Kepler in the context of his laws of planetary motion.

Music has inspired the science of acoustics, an important branch of physics. Over the ages, musical sounds have been analyzed in terms of pitch, loudness, and quality, using such concepts from physics as frequency, amplitude, and wave form. Careful study of musical notes have unveiled that multiplicities in the frequencies of notes correspond to octaves. The differences in sound waves corresponding to a note in a flute and the same one in a violin have also been studied. The systematic theoretical analysis of the vibrations of a string in the eighteenth century by the likes of Daniel Bernoulli and Jean le Rond D'Alembert led to one of the most fertile branches of mathematics, known as Fourier series. This, in turn, has been abundantly valuable in understanding many other natural phenomena as well.

Science, through technology, has contributed immensely to the propagation of music. Until the close of the nineteenth century, live music could be appreciated only by a small number of listeners in a hall. With the invention of the microphone and the speaker, live music is heard loud and clear by large numbers of people in large halls. Recorded music first began with the label "His Master's Voice," and was once a wonder. Now, with far greater fidelity, it has found countless modes: in cassette tapes, CD recording, MP3, iPod and more. In the world of Internet, music has come within reach of anyone with a computer. With access to The World Wide Web, one can listen to any music: grand symphonies, pop tunes, or recitations from the sacred scriptures. The Vedas and the Bhagavad Gita, the

Torah and the Qur'an, Buddhist and Gregorian chants, have come within reach of one and all.

Science, through its recording devices, has enabled the music of one generation to be etched for future generations. There have been thousands of singers and performers prior to the twentieth century. But all the musical sounds they produced vanished in the air that surrounded them. But not so with recorded music of the more modern period, for they have been made permanent in various media. With YouTube, even the dance and live performances of artists long gone can be recalled on the computer monitor. With the development of digital technology *(Musical Instrument Digital Interface)*, the entire transmission system for music has been revolutionized. Aside from assisting in the propagation and preservation of music, science has also been musically creative. Today computers can generate (compose) music.

Neuroscientists have been studying the impact of music on brain development. In the 1990s, scientists began talking about the *Mozart Effect:* When infants listen regularly to good quality classical music (like Mozart's) it makes them brighter. One effect of this news item was that many parents began to play Mozart and other classical music in the rooms of their children. This may not be different from the claim that children who recite the Gayatri Mantra or Pater Noster or Qur'anic suras develop into finer human beings. What can be said with some certainty is that such practices tend to enrich the child, aesthetically or spiritually, with no guarantee of higher intelligence quotient or necessarily more kindness and compassion.

History in religion and science

Every religion has a history, in so far as the origin of religion is a human event. How old that history is depends on whether one approaches the question from an inquiring perspective or on the basis of ancient writings and cultural inspiration.

The sacred books of every major religion contain references that sound historical. The Old Testament has names of kings and dynasties and chronologies, specifying how many years they ruled. Abraham and Moses are regarded as historical figures. Some allow the same historical authenticity to Adam and Eve, as well as to the story of Noah and his ark. The New Testament speaks about the birth of Jesus, the places where he traveled and preached, as well as specific episodes in his life, including miracles, all of which read much like historical texts. But they are not as convincing from detached historical perspectives.

If the spiritual framework of Hinduism rests on Vedic hymns, Upanishadic writings, and the *agamas,* the tradition itself relies on the grand epics of the *Ramayana,* the *Mahabharata,* and the *Kanda Puranam* of the Tamil world. All these are regarded by many Hindus as reporting on historical personages and events. Some scholars have gone so far as to calculate the years and dates when some of the major events in the lore, such as the Kurukshetra Battle, occurred; this, notwithstanding the temporal framework in which the epics are believed to have occurred (i.e., in different *yugas,* hundreds of thousands of years ago). To a degree, the various Sanskritic Puranas are also given historical weight by many practicing Hindus.

The *Jatakas* of Buddhism and the stories associated with the Jaina *Thirtankaras* are also regarded as historical verities by the followers of those faiths. The statement to the effect that the Prophet of Islam received messages from Archangel Gabriel is taken as historically true by the followers of that religion, as are the events recorded in the Hadith. And all these have sacred significance.

In other words, there is more to religions than doctrinal assertions and spiritual experiences. Every religion is linked to personages, episodes and places that not only carry the weight of tradition, but also the affirmation and appearance of factuality. But many such claims collapse upon historical scrutiny.

Normally, there are discernable dividing lines between fact and fantasy, but this is often not the case in the religious context. Those who are faithfully affiliated to specific religions take most of the scriptural narratives to be literally true. The sacred history of other religions may seem obviously non-factual in their view; whereas, they see their own as a true representation of historical events.

Some people in all traditions recognize the difference between parable and moral, between symbol and substance. But it can be a sensitive matter when an outsider tries to point out which elements of the religious narratives are plausible and which are clearly not.

In ancient times, history was invariably oral in transmission, and as with translation, something was always lost or added in oral transmission too. Combined with this was the fact that in the framework of magic—in which the ancient world functioned—many things that may seem strange or impossible to us were considered perfectly normal. As a result, history blended with fantasy in enriching in imperceptible ways. For example, from the orthodox perspective in Judaism, the world had its origin a few thousand years ago. In some traditions it is believed that the value of a work and of a tradition is directly proportional to its antiquity. Thus, for example, some Jaina scholars state that Thirthankara Rishabha, who was the founder of their religion, lived "a few billion years ago."

In the eighteenth century some inquiring minds began to question the authenticity of generally accepted versions of the past. Thus began the enterprise of modern historical research, in which one tries to probe into the sources of statements whose validity had been taken for granted in the past, for they had relied solely on the authority of tradition. Since much of what passed for ancient history is enshrined in religious texts, careful examination into such matters was often interpreted as religious skepticism: something not always regarded as a good trait. Because modern science first emerged in Western Europe, the first examinations about the historical basis of a religion involved Christianity. Questions relating to the historicity of the personages and episodes mentioned in religious literature have been vexing scholars for at least two centuries. It is difficult to take as a historical fact that Moses met with God and received the Ten Commandments personally. Many papers and volumes have been written on the historical Jesus. Such inquiries cast some doubt on the miracles and magical feats associated with the religious personages mentioned in sacred texts, leading to the so-called documentary hypothesis, according to which anonymous scribes put together much of the Old Testament, basing themselves on a long oral tradition. This view was refuted by Umberto Cassuto (*The documentary hypothesis and the composition of the Pentateuch*, 1941). The historicity of Jesus has been questioned and re-examined also (see, for example, Tabor, *The Jesus dynasty*, 2006).

Dispassionate scholars, even with great reverence for the *Ramayana* and the *Mahabharata*, have explored the genesis of these marvelous works, which strike them as impressive poetic creations of the human spirit (see for example, Gupta and Ramachandran, *Mahabharata: Myth and reality*, 1976). Serious questions have been raised about the dates of the Buddha (see for example, Bechert, *When did the Buddha live?* 1996).

When history is undertaken as a scientific inquiry, one applies principles of rigorous methodology for accepting what is true. One also adopts the tenet that the world is ruled by immutable laws that make no exception for events to make them favorable or special for human consumption. Thus the idea of the waters of the sea separating at the command of a prestigious personage, of stars leading wise men to Bethlehem, of special celestial spectacles when the Buddha was born, the virgin birth of Christ, the emergence of Sita from furrowed ground, angels whispering to a man in seclusion: these become matters of questionable authenticity. All the miracles associated with ancient religious heroes and heroines are called into question by scientifically-guided historians. As a result, major cracks have developed in the grand structures of traditional religions which had been accepted as the truth for centuries. Science-based history has not been helpful to deeply felt religious belief.

On the other hand, science also began to give altogether new perspectives on religious truths. It made people (at least those who are conditioned by rationality and coherence and full faith in the laws of nature) aware that religious truths lie deeper than ancient tales of mythopoeia, and are meant to reveal aspects of the human condition, rather than historical facts and figures of cosmic significance. The perennial truths of religions are meant to give meaning and purpose to life, and to enhance the significance of human interactions and culture. They are not to be measured with the yardsticks of empiricism and Euclidean proofs.

Science has also served the cause of history in other important ways. Through the development of archaeology, science has unearthed civilizations that had been buried for centuries by the sands of time and soil. Who would have known about the Indus Valley civilizations or ancient Egypt or Ashoka's missions to Sri Lanka, for example, without the aid of science? It required scientific investigators to decipher Babylonian cuneiform tablets and Egyptian hieroglyphics.

And yet, it is precisely in the interpretation of ancient relics that controversies and misunderstandings have arisen. When these relate to current civilizations, interpretations have emotional and psychological impact, especially on those that take pride and cultural sustenance from distant ancestors. In such cases, any interpretation that is unfavorable or puts one's civilization at a chronologically later stage of development becomes unacceptable to many, and tends to be looked upon as arising from sinister motives.

The upholders of orthodoxy, let alone the common people, find scholarly stances impertinent, perhaps even disrespectful. Some of them fear, not without reason, that the knowledge unraveled by scholarship might shake the stability of ancient icons and practices. There is, therefore, derision on the part of traditionalists for no-nonsense cold-blooded scholars whose concern is for solid facts more than for soothing feelings.

This is a cultural manifestation of the perennial conflict between the head and the heart. All through human history, in practically every society the behavior and beliefs of traditionalists have been challenged by inquiring minds. This has resulted in new understanding of the past for an elite minority. But they tend to cause discomfort, even pain and shock, to many people. The conquests of the mind in religious matters may upset a joyful heart. An impeccable proof to the effect that no almighty God lovingly keeps watch on us when we go to sleep could cause worrisome insomnia in some.

Whether one should accept the evidence of carefully gathered data and the logic of arguments, or respond to the call of a deeper faith that endows us with peace and spiritual ecstasy is the dilemma that we sometimes face. Some make a decision, and claim their preference to be the right one. There is perhaps no right or wrong choice in this matter, if only because one is as human as the other and both have contextual significance.

This dichotomy is an illustration of what is called the *principle of complementarity:* reality is recognized as consisting of apparently contradictory, but in fact mutually complementing, features. Niels Bohr used to say that there are two kinds of truths: small and great ones. A small truth is one whose contrary is false. That milk is white is a small truth, because to say that milk is black is clearly wrong. But a great truth is one whose contrary is no less true. To say religions have done much good is as true as stating that religions have done much harm. That the electron is a particle is as true as that it is a wave.

As long as we are experiencing one side of a coin, we cannot perceive the other. But it would be simplistic, if not a grave error, to imagine that the coin has only one side. For the analytical scholar to maintain that the spiritual dimension of the *Ramayana* is without significance would be as partial a vision as the claim of the religious devotee who does not realize that *bhajans* and *mûrties* have evolved over the ages in human culture, and are meaningful modes towards a greater goal, rather than reflections of objective truths.

The charm of Aesop's *Fables* (ca. sixth century BCE) lies, not in the conversations of animals but in the morals they spell out. It is possible to drink deep of the spiritual fountain of religious narratives and also look into those works as creations of inspired poets.

One meaningful compromise may be affected in this context by separating sacred history from secular history. Whereas secular history is based primarily on relics, verifiable facts, and rational interpretations of ancient documents, sacred history is the history based on sacred writings and religious narratives which provide meaningful enrichment. The fact that the story in an opera is highly improbable does not take away the charm and the aesthetic enjoyment the opera itself can and does provide, which is considerably more than what a factually correct news report of a local event might provide.

In other words, by evaluating matters in terms of their cultural enrichment rather than factual content, it is possible to accommodate both factual accounts and sacred narratives in the scheme of things. History offers exopotent truths, whereas sacred history offers endopotent truths.

Philosophy in religion and science

Philosophers are keen and prolific thinkers who reflect, both rationally and speculatively, on important issues. Many of these issues relate to human life and existence and all that is associated with it. In ancient Greece, there were many philosophers who had little to say about any particular religion. The Pre-Socratics like Thales and Anaximander, Anaxagoras and Heraclitus spoke little about religion. This was true of Plato and Aristotle too. This was also the case in China. Confucius, Laozi, and Mo-Ti were not exactly religious philosophers. However, after the rise of the major religions, practically every great philosopher was affiliated with one religion or another.

One generally thinks of religion in terms of God and prayer, rites and rituals, worship and devotional songs. But religions have also produced some of the greatest philosophical thinkers in humanity's intellectual heritage. Since religion and faith in God are significant aspects of human life, philosophers have often been drawn to these matters in all religious traditions. Therefore, it is not surprising that many of them have been influenced by the religions in which they were born and grew up. The Upanishadic thinkers were essentially connected to the visions of Vedic sage-poets, as were later philosophers like Abhinavagupta (Shaivism). Philo of Alexandria was wedded to Judaism and Augustine to Christianity. The Buddhist world can also boast of a good many philosophers, from Nagarjuna to Dogen Zenji, the founder of the Japanese Soto Zen school of Buddhism.

Religious philosophers have influenced and shaped the corresponding religion. Shankara and Ramanuja, for example, have changed the course of Hinduism, as Al Gazali did for Islam, Maimonides did for Judaism, and Aquinas did for Christianity.

Often philosophers in the religious context attempt to argue for the tenets of their religion in the framework of science and rationality. This practice goes back to Philo of Alexandria, who incorporated Greek thought into Judaism, and even earlier in other traditions. But Philo was overshadowed as the preeminent Judaic philosopher by the twelfth century Maimonides, who likewise tried to reconcile Aristotle's physics with the Talmud. In the Islamic world, the brilliant thinker Al Gazali started as a skeptic, preceding Descartes by a few centuries, but argued that there was something incoherent in philosophers who tried to challenge the truths of the (Islamic) scripture. He also propounded the principle that, in the explanation of events, God plays a more important role than causal connections. He became an effective spokesperson for (Islamic) religious truths. It may be recalled that another keen philosopher of the Islamic world, Averroes, who emerged a century later, tried to refute the perspectives of Al Gazali, but not very effectively. The works of such philosophers serve as models for integrating religion with rational philosophical (scientific) thinking. This enterprise continues down to our own times. When philosophers are essentially interpreters of sacred texts in a rational framework, they are theologians.

After the rise of modern science, there have continued to be many philosophers in the Western tradition who are/were affiliated with Christianity. In this lineage we have thinkers like Descartes (skepticism), Berkeley (idealism), Spinoza (ethics), and Kierkegaard (existentialism). These were not theologians, but philosophers. S. Radhakrishnan, Sri Aurobindo and S. N. Das Gupta in the Hindu world may be regarded as philosophers in their own right. We see from all these instances the enormous contributions that religions have made to the development of philosophical thought.

In the ancient Greek world, a number of philosophers from Thales to the likes of Aristotle and Democritus were also engaged in explaining the natural world, albeit largely speculatively. In classical India philosophical schools like Nyaya, Vaiseshika, and Charvaka were also of this kind. This type of philosophy re-emerged in association with empirical science after the rise of modern science.

Philosophers like René Descartes, David Hume and Immanuel Kant set the stage for John Locke's (eighteenth century) idea of philosophy being the hand-maiden of science. What this meant was that philosophers—or at least a good number of them—were interested not so much in reflecting on the human condition, matters of religious import, or the nature of metaphysical reality, as on probing into the source, nature and validity of human knowledge. In other words, epistemology became the primary concern of many philosophers.

While empirical scientists were accumulating more and more knowledge about the physical world, and theoreticians were building explanatory structures to put the results of observation in rational and consistent frameworks, philosophers began to investigate the logical legitimacy of the modes by which human beings acquire knowledge. Such inquiries served sometimes to elucidate some of the key ideas upon which the scientific methodology rests: such as the principle of causality and conservation, the rigor in mathematical analysis, the nature of logical reasoning, the limits of empiricism, and the like. These thorough looks into the foundations of knowledge and belief have had two significant impacts. The first was to put science itself on more reliable and rigorous grounds. The other was to sow seeds of doubt on some of the fundamental tenets and assumptions of science. While this type of philosophical analysis often strengthened the roots of science, it also tended to weaken the roots of religion.

Scientific philosophy reached a climax in the 1920s through an agenda formulated by a group of philosophers in Vienna. Their tenet was that all (valid) human knowledge has its source in experience and must be logically consistent. Mauritz Schlick, Rudolf Carnap, and Kurt Gödel were among the eminent members of the Viennese Circle whose influence spread far and wide. A natural extension of their ideas was logical positivism, which went on to reject any other system that claimed truth (such as metaphysics, theology, or ethics) that served no function but to provide emotional satisfaction.

Later philosophers have disagreed, and in due course other perspectives emerged challenging the claims of science and reason.

These include thinkers like Thomas Kuhn (*The structure of scientific revolution*, 1962), who argued that scientific truths are subject to paradigm shifts, Karl Popper (*The logic of scientific discovery*, 1934), who developed the thesis that one can only falsify, never verify, scientific theories, and Paul Feyerabend (*Against method*, 1975), whose works were meant to dethrone science, at least among philosophers, from its hegemonic status in the world of truths. Thus, one impact of post-modernist epistemologies has been to propagate the view that science is no more than a useful enterprise, with little relation to any absolute or objective truths. To the extent that such perspectives, formulated in logical and coherent terms, dilute the narrowness and arrogance of some scientists, these have been healthy new moves. To the extent that they also fuel, sometimes venerate, irrationality and outworn beliefs that constrain humanity to pre-scientific worldviews, one may say that they ill-serve civilization.

Aesthetics in religion and science

Aesthetics is related to the appreciation of beauty. Beauty is generally associated with form and shape, color and face. In an extended sense one can speak of beauty in thoughts and ideas too. Ultimately, beauty is a dimension of human experience. Whether a painting or a flower is beautiful per se, independently of humans, it is difficult to say, for it is not unlike the rustle of leaves where no human ear is present. But we do know that beauty is recognized as such by a conscious entity. We, as thinking and feeling humans, know that there is much evil in the world, and there is also much good; there is cruelty and callousness in the world, and also kindness and compassion. In brief, there are many things wrong and negative in the world, but there are also many things right and positive. All that is good and positive may be described as beautiful, and all that is bad and negative as ugly.

In principle, religions enable us to choose, cultivate, and experience whatever is good and right and positive, and therefore, whatever is beautiful. As Paul Carr points out, "Beauty is also a delicate dance between mystical subjective revelations and mathematical and objective processes that maintain the universe and life" (2006, 6). This goal of religion is reflected in the symbols of religions. And these symbols are invariably beautiful.

The Hindu symbol for *aum* has a unique curved majesty:

Its sonic serenity is said to represent the essence of the Cosmic vibration that sustains the universe. It has other esoteric significance as well.

The Tai-chi symbol from the *I Ching* (a circle divided into two halves by a curve, with a small circle in each half) stands for *yin* (moon) and *yang* (sun), which represent the complementing principles behind the phenomenal world, and also the solstices. The Judaic Star of David has a wonderful geometric symmetry. Though regarded as a relatively recent symbol of the much older tradition, it has become a beautiful emblem for the Jewish faith.

The Christian Cross which symbolizes how the sin and ugliness of human actions are absorbed by a caring and compassionate Divine has a universal beauty all its own. In the view of many Muslim scholars, it is pure white, the symbol of purity, which represents Islam. The star and crescent, like the Star of David, is of more recent vintage. It gained popularity in the Islamic world only since the Ottomans overthrew Byzantium and changed Constantinople into Istanbul.

Aside from all these symbols, who can fail to see beauty in the Cosmic Joy represented in the *Nataraja,* in the sublime peace that the Buddha in clay and stone exudes, in the *Pietà* of Michelangelo, revealing the love of Mother and Child, and in countless religious icons, especially in the Hindu, Buddhist, and Christian world? The calligraphy and intricate mosaic in Islamic domes and mosques also contribute immensely to religious aesthetics. So do the beautifully lit lamps and statues in temples, candles and immense stained-glass works in magnificent cathedrals.

Ultimately, one derives aesthetic experience in religion through prayers and singing. These are not mere words and tunes, but invocations that fill the heart of the devout with the kind of inner satisfaction that a lover of art gets upon seeing a masterpiece. There is beauty in butterfly wings and in clouds, in rainbows and in stars, but the contemplation of the Divine, in whatever name or form or symbol, confers one of the most abstract aesthetic joys that human beings are capable of deriving. This is as important a component of religions as any other, and it is beyond the grasp of those who approach religions only as systems of ancient beliefs. This is why critical analysis is critical analysis, and religious experience is religious experience, and the twain can seldom meet. One who has never been to an opera cannot really enjoy it on an old, scratched record, much less from the libretto alone.

Unlike the Western tradition, where aesthetics and ethics may sometimes come into opposition (Hitler was a connoisseur of art and enjoyed classical music), in the Indian traditions of art, as Kapil Kapoor points out, "there is no opposition between beauty and welfare, between aesthetics and ethics" (2003, 11-19).

Science, like religion, has many dimensions, and one of them is the aesthetic. The aesthetic dimension of science has at least three components. The first may be described as revelatory, in that it reveals certain aesthetic aspects of the phenomenal world that are not ordinarily perceived in everyday life. Such, for instance, are the symmetries in snowflakes, the geometry of crystals revealed by X-rays, the tetrahedral architecture of the carbon atom, and the molecular structure of the benzene ring. The zoomorphic configuration of some constellations had been fantasized by ancient cultures, but it was not until after the rise of modern science that the majesty of Saturn's rings and the grandeur of spiral nebulas were recognized. The elliptical orbits of planetary motion has been known since the time of Kepler, but Sommerfeld et al. in the early decades of the twentieth century modeled elliptical atomic orbits. These are among the beautiful aspects of nature that science has revealed.

Then there are the abstract aesthetics of science, especially of physics, reflected in the concepts, theories and equations of physics. Thus, for example, the concepts of invariance, entropy and parity, all have an intrinsic beauty that physicists experience and appreciate. Most of these concepts are not only beautiful but turn out to be extremely useful, and often indispensable in the understanding and interpretation of the physical world. Consider, for example, the notion of symmetry. The symmetry of geometrical figures such as squares, isosceles triangles and circles is obvious. But there are other types of abstract symmetries also. These play significant roles in the theories of current physics. Many of the conceptual bases of physics have mathematical bases, which are at the core of their beauty.

There is an endless variety of equations in physics that portray various physical laws and phenomena, each with considerable aesthetic appeal. Such, for instance, are the mathematical formulations of the laws of motion (Newton's $F = ma$), the superposition of the vibratory modes of strings (Fourier's series), the laws of electromagnetism (Maxwell's equations), the wave equation for a particle (the Schrödinger equation), the relativistic aspect of the wave-particle (the Dirac equation), and the curvature of space-time due to mass in the universe (Einstein's gravitational equation).

Theories in science are also appreciated for their aesthetic value. Recall T. H. Huxley's famous phrase to the effect that a beautiful theory can be slain by an ugly fact. The physicist H. A. Lorentz once said he hoped Einstein's theory would turn out to be true because it is so beautiful, reminding us of Keats' famous line: "Beauty is truth, truth beauty" (from "Ode on a Grecian Urn," line 49, 1819, 234). Just as the spiritual elevation that only the truly religious can experience, and as the opera connoisseur alone can appreciate a complex aria at a more sophisticated level, those who have delved into the technical aspects of physics alone enjoy their beauty-content to a heightened degree.

Finally, we come to the tangible aesthetics that have flowed from science. Many technological inventions, be it car or camera, wrist watch or electric fan or whatever, are designed to be beautiful. In other words, the world of technology and manufacturing has created a wondrous range of beautiful things. The mammoth structures of the modern era, like skyscrapers, suspension bridges, and the Eiffel tower have their aesthetic sides too. Giant scientific instruments, from high energy accelerators to radio telescope, are wonderfully beautiful also.

Thus we see that, like religions, science too has its aesthetic dimensions. These are as important and intrinsic features of the scientific enterprise as its explanatory power and practical applications. The aesthetic dimensions of science, like that of great classical music, are evident to the aficionado.

Chapter 9

Origins and Ends

Cosmogenesis: religious and scientific perspectives

Perhaps the most intriguing phenomenon in the physical world is its very existence. So is the presence of human beings, not simply as biological entities that come and go, but as feeling and reflecting creatures that engage in love and hate, create and destroy, formulate and follow moral injunctions, seem to know the difference between right and wrong, beauty and ugliness... and then are transformed into cold and inert bodies, bereft of the consciousness that kept them alive and kicking.

Religions attempt to explain these interesting phenomena: cosmogenesis, biogenesis, and ethico-genesis. Their answers, though seldom described as such, may well be looked upon as theories also. For example, the Vedas, the Bible, and the Koran—all revered texts in major religious traditions—tell us about the creation of Man. From an epistemic perspective, these are different theories to explain the presence of humans on the planet.

In cultural history, these theories are embodied in texts that have acquired sanctity. As a result, they have a degree of invulnerability and infallibility within a given religious framework. One important difference between scientific and religious theories consists in how they are evaluated. The successes of religious theories are judged, not so much by their resilience in the face of logical and empirical scrutiny, but by the reverence associated with their sources. Since religious theories do not depend on verification of their logical consequences, competing and mutually contradictory religions have flourished all through history. In other words, scientific and religious theories differ, not in the goal of their proponents, but in the attitude of their adherents. It is important to recognize (assuming human and historical origins to scriptural writings) that their authors were keen intellects who sought to solve the perennial mystery of origins in what seemed to them at the time to be the most reasonable terms. It is quite possible that if the thinkers who wrote those texts were to come back in our midst, they would be the first to want revised editions of their theories in the light of current knowledge and understanding, for they were extraordinarily intelligent people.

According to ancient Babylonians (Dalley 1991), first there was only a primeval deep consisting of nothingness. From this arose the gods of Light. But there was also a dragon of Chaos, known as Tiamat. Tiamat set out on a rampage to subdue and destroy the gods and take control of everything. This provoked a battle with the great god Marduk. When Tiamat opened her mouth to swallow Marduk, a raging hurricane was thrust into her mouth. Tiamat swelled, and Marduk killed her by piercing her with a lance. Then he rent her asunder. One half of Tiamat was hung up above as the skies, and the other was cast below for Marduk to stand on. This became our earth. After this, Marduk created the stars, the sun, and the moon. He imposed inexorable laws on them. Then he made plants and animals, and finally Man. The first man was called Adapa [Adam].

There are different visions of cosmogenesis in the Hindu world. According to one (Rig Veda 10.121), the undiscerned universe was rendered discernible from a *hiranya garbha* (golden egg), which arose from a seed in cosmic waters. Later works of the tradition (the Upanishads and the Puranas) elaborated on this idea, naming the Creator Brahmà. This gave rise to the manifested world. However, in another creation hymn we read the following:

> Not even nothing existed then
> No air, and yet no heaven.

Who encased and kept it where?
Was water in that darkness there?

Neither deathlessness nor decay
Nor the rhythm of night and day.
The self-existent, with breath sans air:
That, and that alone was there.

Darkness was in darkness found
Like light-less water all around.
One emerged, with nothing on
It was from heat that this was born.

In it Desire its way did find:
The primordial seed born of mind
Sages do know deep in the heart
That what is, is kin to what is not.
(Rig Veda 10.129, trans. V. V. Raman)

A Chinese legend recalls that the cosmic architect, P'an Ku, worked hard for 18,000 years to accomplish the task. The ripples of the primordial event have not died out. P'an Ku's breath and sighs are today's winds and rising clouds. The roaring majesty of his voice still resounds as thunder. His flesh congealed as earth: green grass and tall trees are vestiges of his lush hair. Metals and minerals are P'an Ku's bones, while the sweat of his lasting labors continues to drip down as rain. Finally, the lice and insects that clung to his body are now seen as the swarms of humans that populate the planet (Carus 1974).

According to an Iroquois view, once a woman was ejected from heaven. She fell on a turtle from which the world was formed.

Australian myths talk about an avian creator (Mountford 1973).

In the Norse framework, the world was pictured as a tree called Yggdrasil. The earth is at its stem, and its branches reach the heavens (Lindow 2001).

In the Abrahamic tradition, the Book of Genesis speaks of Light as being the first of God's creation, for there is nothing in the universe more encompassing than light. This insight has been elaborated on by many theologians over the centuries.

In the Jaina worldview, the universe has always existed (without a beginning, perhaps in interminable cycles), so there is no birth moment or cosmic end for the universe (Gopani and Bothara 1989).

These are some of the ways in which ancient thinkers and founders of religions pictured the genesis of the Cosmos. The poetry and insight in the religious visions of cosmogenesis are astounding. Notwithstanding their variety, all the traditional interpretations, save the Buddhist and Jaina visions, take for granted some supernatural principle in accounting for the emergence of the physical world. All make humans primary in the cosmos, for it was difficult in ancient thought to picture a world where humans were absent and where humans played no role. In these two respects—the origination from a supernatural factor and the centrality of humans in the universe—modern scientific theories of cosmogony differ radically from the religious. Nevertheless, many theologians try to blend the religious and the scientific modes when considering cosmogony. This is no easy task.

Since the most ancient times, parallel to the religious modes, there have also been efforts to account for the emergence of the world in purely naturalistic terms (i.e., without a divine agency). Some Upanishadic thinkers of ancient India, as also Thales of Miletus of the Greek tradition, seem to have been among the first to consider the origin of the world in this way. Pre-Socratic philosophers like Anaximander imagined principles like heat and cold, and other mutually opposing entities as having given rise to the world. Later, Epicurus thought that an initial chaos eventually settled down to an orderly world: a rather keen insight that saw the universe as a transformation of disorder into order. But until the twentieth century, not many scientific thinkers took up the question of the genesis of the cosmos as religious visionaries did.

It is interesting, and perhaps a little ironic, that though the telescope was in hand since the beginning of the seventeenth century, while observational and theoretical astronomy advanced at an impressive pace for at least four hundred years, not many scientists wondered about the origin of the universe until the twentieth century. There are reasons for this. First, it was necessary to know something about the constitution of planets and stars before one could speculate about their formation. There still lingered the impression that celestial bodies were made up of materials quite different from earthly ones. It was not until a deeper understanding of the nature of light and the invention of the spectroscope in the nineteenth century that one began to gain knowledge about this. Next, one had to have some estimate of the age of the earth before considering the age of the universe. Though there had been informed guesses, it was not until the discovery of radioactivity in the last decade of the nineteenth century that astronomers began to recognize that billions of years were involved. Finally, we needed to know that stars are born, grow and die. This required the emergence of astrophysics and a good deal of theoretical physics: all fruits of twentieth century science. Two more major breakthroughs—one theoretical and one observational—ultimately led to modern cosmogony. These were Einstein's general relativity and Hubble's discovery of the recession of galaxies. They are the foundations on which science proposed the now well-known big-bang model for the birth of the cosmos (Singh 2005). This view was not—and still is not—universally accepted. There has been a competing world picture (not unlike the Jaina view) to the effect that the universe has been in a steady state forever and forever. In any event, at least one extremely creative and extraordinary physicist, Stephen W. Hawking, wrote a best seller on the subject (*A brief history of time,* 1988) in which he suggested, perhaps metaphorically, that physics was reading the mind of God. This claim was looked upon as an arrogant assertion by some traditional theologians. Nevertheless, aside from the $250,000 Hawking received as advance for his book, the book is said to have sold some nine million copies in a decade. One may wonder how many who bought the book read it from cover to cover, and what percentage of them understood even a fraction of its contents. In recent years, even the big-bang has been undergoing refinements and modifications (see, for example, Steinhardt and

Turok, *Endless universe: Beyond the big bang,* 2007). No one can predict what scientific cosmogony will say a century from now.

Carefully chiseled scientific cosmogonic theories have been subjected to modifications in less than fifty years, whereas the ancient scriptural visions have stayed steady for millennia. This is the price science pays for basing its worldviews on acquired and accumulated knowledge. Religious worldviews, hinging on God-given knowledge, enjoy enviable permanence. It has been said that science is proof without certainty, whereas religion is certainty without proof. Indeed, proof is more important than certainty for scientific worldviews. In religion, it is the opposite. When it comes to the origin of the universe, no matter what science suggests or what religions assert, the Vedic sage-poet was most insightful indeed:

> When and how did creation start?
> Did He do it? Or did He not?
> Only He up there knows, maybe.
> Or perhaps, not even He.
> (Rig Veda 10:129)

The anthropic principle and skeptical views

In the 1970s, the attention of physicists was drawn to some perplexing coincidences that exist in the quantitative features in the world. This gave rise to the formulation of what is known as the anthropic principle, a term that was coined in 1973 by Brandon Carter (Barrow and Tipler 1986).

The essence of this rather technical doctrine may be presented by means of an analogy. Suppose that one kicks a ball from some point in a field. The path followed by the ball in the air as it rises and falls back to the ground will be a parabola. This path is the result of the basic laws of motion in the earth's gravitational field. Where precisely the ball will land will depend on the initial speed and angle of projection. There are countless spots where the ball could hit the ground, depending on how fast it was kicked and along which direction. Suppose that of all the available spots, the ball enters smack into the center of the goalpost. It is difficult to believe that this happened by pure chance. It seems far more probable that it was projected by an intelligent player with a specific goal in mind [no pun intended].

Likewise, the current phase of the universe depends as much on the physical laws governing it as on the initial conditions. It is possible to imagine a perfectly consistent, coherent, and ordered universe, but very different from our own, if the fundamental constants molding its overall features had taken on different permanent values. Indeed, it turns out that if the initial values of some of the constants had been different ever so slightly, nuclear synthesis in the core of supernovas would not have resulted in carbon atoms. The generation of carbon is crucial for the emergence of any form of life such as we know.

Intriguing coincidences in the values of the so-called fundamental constants, which are ultimately responsible for the kind of world we experience, raise profound questions. In particular, carbon-based life (and its long-range offshoot, the human mind) would be impossible if some of the constants had even slightly different values. This has led to the fascinating conjecture that the specific values were *intended* to give rise to quantum physicists and cosmologists.

No serious physicist can afford to be indifferent to the remarkable coincidence of numbers that could be interpreted in terms of some hidden intention at the very birth of the universe to make the eventual emergence of humans possible, whether or not one agrees with an anthropocentric interpretation of the fact. Not surprisingly, the physicist-celebrity Stephen Hawking wrote:

> It would be very difficult to explain why the universe should have begun in just this way, except as the act of a God who intended to create beings like us (1988, 127).

On the other hand, Freeman Dyson declared more cautiously:

> As we look out into the universe and identify the many accidents of physics and astronomy that have worked together to our benefit, it almost seems as if the universe must in some sense have known that we were coming (1979, 59).

Die-hard skeptics may wonder why so many silent eons were frittered away in the lighting and snuffing of stupendously vast stars before *Homo sapiens* could come to the fore. An all-powerful Designer could surely have come up with the appropriate combination of constants to manufacture an Einstein and a Feynman in short order and in a smaller span of space, without the tortuous and time-consuming route of supernova furnaces for synthesizing heavier elements. While correctly recognizing that the universe is not anthropocentric, many scientists fail to see that science is, in its very mode, anthropic. Take away the human mind, and there can be no description of the world in terms of concepts like momentum and energy, let alone *visible* light, *short-lived* particles, and *audible* sound.

In any event, there are thinkers who seem to be conditioned to be averse to any mention of God. They are convinced there is nothing beyond matter and energy in space and time. In their opinion, those who speak of God and salvation are soft-hearted, misguided souls, unable to cope with the tribulations of life, people who naively continue to believe in a loftier version of the fairy tales of their infancy. The unswerving commitment of unbending materialists to the causal and the spatio-temporal, and their uncompromising rejection of anything spiritual can only be described, (in terms of its deeply-felt attachment), as religious, much as they would abhor the epithet. Their understandable conviction about the physical world is perhaps indispensable for advances in science, but in its absolute certainty it is no less religious than the one which affirms that sooner or later we will all be saved.

Laplace and the God hypothesis

W. W. Rouse Ball (1888, 417-418) reported on reliable grounds that when the great mathematician Pierre Simone de Laplace went to present his magnum opus entitled *La mécanique céleste [Celestial mechanics]* (1799-1825) to Napoleon Bonaparte, the latter taunted him by asking how he managed to write such a massive work on the system of the world without mentioning the Creator. To this Laplace famously replied: *"Je n'avais pas besoin de cette hypothèse-là* [I had no need for that particular hypothesis]." According to the story, when Napoleon mentioned this reply to the no less great mathematician Lagrange, the latter said, *"Ah! C'est une belle hypothèse; ça explique beaucoup de choses* [Ah! It is a beautiful hypothesis; it explains many things]."

Atheists have sometimes gloated over Laplace's answer, and theists have found it to be somewhat arrogant. The fact of the matter is, Laplace was not making any statement on the existence or otherwise of a Creator. He was absolutely right in saying that for describing, analyzing, and explaining astronomical phenomena, one simply does not need to consider the existence or otherwise of a God. Indeed, science explores and tries to explain the world such as it is, and does not, perhaps cannot, address the question of the ultimate cause of it all. It is religion that concerns itself with the authorship and purpose of the universe. The literary critic is interested in analyzing a literary work, and need not be worried about who wrote the work or why. So it is with science and religion.

On the other hand, Lagrange's answer was very pertinent also. He simply said that the God hypothesis was beautiful—certainly from a poetic point of view—and that it explains "many things." There is no question but that the perplexing questions pertaining to the why and the wherefore of the universe, its existence and purpose, cannot be explained adequately by scientific methodology. But it is all answered quite simply by accepting the existence of God.

The Biogenesis

As to science's view of biogenesis (Luisi, *The emergence of life*, 2006), with which not all scientists concur, it was only billions of years after cosmogenesis that biogenesis occurred. In the remote past, more than three billion years ago, and barely a billion years after the formation of our planet, there were lands barren and waste, volcanoes steaming and puffing sulfuric fumes, and oceans of salt-free waters. The earth's atmosphere consisted then largely of hydrogen, ammonia, methane, and a few other gases. Gigantic clouds and torrential rains rose and fell, seeping salts from land to pristine sea. In the mammoth laboratories of the earth's oceans and airs, kindled by heat and lightning, by radiations from the sun and other excitants, the turbulent chemistry of the early molecules churned out the first organic structures. Carbohydrates and amino acids were thus concocted. These increased in complexity as further reactions took place. The waters of the period constituted what has been described as a primordial soup in which mutual interactions of the components gave rise to molecules of ever increasing size and intricacy. Energy trapping mechanisms came into play. After myriad patterns and permutations, mysterious entities with the property of self-replication emerged. These again grew in numbers and variety, until at last nucleic acids and proteins were formed. The wonder of life had begun.

Such seem to have been the consequences of the physiochemical context in which the earth found itself at that time. Whatever the ultimate cause of it all, the end result, Life, was truly magnificent. But this was only an inkling of grander glories yet to come.

One can understand how some simple proteins may be synthesized from amino acids, but there is no understandable model for self-replication of proteins. Then again, all amino acids in organisms are invariably left-handed, and one sees here the need for ribosomal RNA and transfer RNA. That is why RNA becomes more fundamental.

During the past several decades, experimentalists have been trying to replicate the process by simulating a primordial soup subjected to early atmospheric conditions, but we are far from synthesizing anything like DNA. The reason is not far to seek. The mycoplasma genitalium which is one of the simplest living organisms has some 570,000 base pairs in its DNA, and it depends on other organisms for its survival. The blue-green algae which is some 3.5 billion years old has 3.6 billion base pairs. It may be argued that synthesizing a few organic molecules from appropriate physiochemical conditions and concluding from this that this is how life began would be like saying that because we found patterns in sand dunes which resemble alphabets, that is how *La divina commedia* came to be written.

It has also been suggested that perhaps there once were much simpler organisms which have now disappeared altogether, and from which all the life we know now, including the ones in fossils, came to be: except that thus far there has not been the slightest observational evidence for this. According to one model, there once was a prebiotic evolutionary process in which a community of informational molecules participated. In the course of this process, the symbolization/encoding of interactions resulted in permanent information processes, which led in turn to the cell which involved essentially autonomously duplicating chemistry.

Fred Hoyle is among many respected scientists who disagree with this view. He asked rhetorically:

> Life as we know it is, among other things, dependent on at least 2000 different enzymes. How could the blind forces of the primal sea manage to put together the correct chemical elements to build enzymes? (1981, 105)

He was a staunch supporter of the *panspermia* hypothesis. According to this idea, in the version first suggested by Svante Arrhenius (*Worlds in the making,* 1908), life did not originate on earth, but elsewhere in the universe. Perhaps some frozen spores of organisms clung to splintered rocks from an exploding planet, and these reached the earth as meteorites. According to some NASA scientists, DNA from fossilized bacterial remains, some 200 million years old, have been detected in meteorites. In purely scientific terms, the *panspermia* theory gives us a grander vision of life in the universe. It suggests that life is not unique to any particular planetary system, and may well be a universal phenomenon in the literal sense of the term. Of course it is difficult to imagine how such organisms could have survived for thousands of years in the cold of space, incessantly subjected to cosmic ray particles. The *panspermia* theory may be taken as a non-romantic version of the idea that we are all descendents of creatures from another planetary system, and that those creatures landed here in the remote past. Robert Shapiro (*Planetary dreams,*

1999) argues that the laws of nature favor the generation of life everywhere in the universe.

Anthropogenesis

As science gains more and more understanding of the ultimate constituents of life (i.e. genes), it also tracks down the biological origin of humans. According to one estimate, based on genetic analysis, we are all descendents of a single human being—the Adam of our species, one might say—who lived some 270,000 to 400,000 years ago. This ancient ancestor of ours, some evolutionary biologists tell us, had ancestors who lived a few million years ago. They and mice had one common ancestor 50 million years ago, and so on. These, in turn came from the very first self-replicating molecules which were formed some three and a half billions years ago.

In the midst of all the data, complex theories, and shifting ideas as to how life began, some have argued that corresponding to the mystery of the Big Bang for the physical universe, there was a biological Big-Bang whose cause and purpose may never be known. Whether human beings began in one particular continent (Africa) or simultaneously developed in different regions of the world is another question on which there is no unanimity (Leakey, *The origin of humankind,* 1994).

Evolution

Once the spark of life was lit, the self-replicating systems began to multiply in number and variety. The nucleic acids embodying the subtle coding that preserves life patterns slipped now and then. These changes in structures were the mutations which may be looked upon either as responses to the unceasing turmoil in the earth's environmental features, or as alterations resulting from changing conditions.

First formally formulated and systematically developed by Charles Darwin (*On the origin of species,* 1859), the idea of biological evolution is revolutionary, and has turned out to be one of the most successful scientific theories to account for the richness and diversity of life forms. The first palpitations of life began to evolve along countless directions. As ages rolled by, and grand upheavals shook the planet's crust, ever newer kinds of plants and creatures shaped themselves. Both land and sea became homes for innumerable life forms. Amphibians, insects, reptiles, and mammals, all evolved along with a picturesque plethora of plants and trees. After well over a billion years of such experimentation, the evolving principles brought forth the product we call the human race.

Mind-boggling time scales are involved in all of this. Changing scales and assuming that the earth was formed a hundred years ago— which we take to represent four and a half billion years—humanoids began to emerge barely three weeks ago, and the Christian era is only some twenty minutes old. Astrophysicists assure us that on this time-scale in another hundred or so years the sun would extinguish itself, probably after an orgy of conflagration during which it would mercilessly swallow up Mercury and Venus, and perhaps even our dear Earth.

Some find this account to be quite interesting and also persuasive because it is fortified by charts and data and mathematical theories. It is a conjectural *conclusion* rather than a solemn proclamation or intelligent speculation. Those who adopt scientific cosmology grant that there is, as there always will be, something tentative in any scientific vision of biogenesis. Only its reasonableness and coherence at any given time make a scientific picture of origins appealing to working scientists. Unfortunately, it is viewed as going against the version of biogenesis of some traditional religions and the beautiful scientific framework has become a matter for intense controversy. As David Sloan Wilson noted:

> Evolutionary Theory is a ship that has weathered many storms. Lately it has been buffeted by the winds of creationism and its born-again cousin, Intelligent Design (ID), but the enemies of evolution are tame compared to its friends (2007, 11).

Eruption and emergence; creation and co-creation

When there is a sudden spewing of matter or passion, of disease or destruction, we call it an eruption. Volcanoes erupt, as do anger, fury and an epidemic of plague. Eruptions are usually unwelcome occurrences which have impact on the surroundings, short-lived or lasting, but the eruptions themselves fade into memory.

When that which appears retains its integrity in form and substance, it is an emergence. Arthur Peacocke defined emergence as:

> That general feature of natural processes wherein complex structures, especially in living organisms, develop distinctly new capabilities and functions at levels of greater complexity (2003, 188).

More generally, a flower emerges as does a sonnet. Emergence also refers to a property of a system that is absent in its components. The letters m, a, and n have their specific roles in the alphabet, but when put together we get the word *man* whose meaning is not there in the component letters. Hydrogen and oxygen have properties, but when they combine in proportion they become water whose properties are very different from those of its constituent atoms. Generally speaking,

> If a and b yield C,
> but C is not equal to a + b,
> then we have emergence.

In other words, when the whole is not equal to the sum of the parts, there is emergence. In current scientific paradigm one tries to account for thought, mind, consciousness, etc. as emergent properties of the brain, related to complexity.

Sometimes, what emerges might be governed by law and principle, and it evolves. We may refer to an emergence of this kind as creation. Creation launches something that never existed before and that does not remain the same. Thus, a child is a creation, as also a city that is founded or a religion that is established.

In this terminology, though the Big Bang resembled an enormous eruption, it was in fact much more. The universe was not just an emergence either. The cosmos was a creation. What is created has an existence of its own. More importantly, others things appear from it. The theologian Phil Hefner spoke of human beings as:

> God's created co-creator whose purpose is to be the agency, acting in freedom, to birth the future that is most wholesome for the nature that has birthed us—the nature that is not only our own genetic heritage, but also the entire human community and the evolutionary and ecological reality in which and to which we belong (1993, 27).

In other words, he describes us as co-creators with God. We create ideas and things, values and works of art, and more. Hefner's idea is insightful, for there certainly is an element of what we regard as the divine in each one of us: not just in our capacities for goodness, justice, compassion and mercy, but in our creative faculties also. When the Upanishadic seers declare "Thou are That," or the Bible says we were created in "God's image," this is what may have been meant.

This notion may be extended further. We are conscious co-creators, for there are unconscious and semiconscious co-creators as well. The matter and energy that were created from the Big Bang were unconscious co-creators, for they led to the formation of atoms and molecules, to elements and compounds, to planets and stars: each is a created entity in its own right, for each new level is different from its initial components.

When self-replicating macro-molecules of life arose, there was another level of co-creation: for evolution is a creative process too. Biological evolution is different from the unconscious formation of atoms and stars, and it may be described as semi-conscious co-creation, for there is a fine difference between crystal growth and cell-division.

With the onset of mind, creation leaped to the higher level of self-awareness. Self-awareness creates ideas and ideals, values and morals, rather than just machines and bridges. This constitutes conscious co-creation. As the universe unfolds, there continue to be eruptions, as with novas and supernovas; emergences, as when quantum entities are observed and measured or when works of art and music are produced; and creation, as when a child is born or a new system of thought is formulated.

All this has been possible because the Big Bang was a creation and not just an eruption.

Origin of languages

One of the most powerful modes of communication among creatures may be found in human languages. There is ample scientific evidence that other creatures communicate too in subtle and sophisticated ways, through bark and roar, through bird songs and ultrasound. Human languages have gone beyond vocal sounds into symbolic representations in writing. That we are essentially symbolic creatures has been recognized for a long time (Deacon, *The symbolic species,* 1997).

But it is yet a puzzle as to when and how human languages actually came to be. In the *Mahabharata* there are episodes wherein human beings communicate with animals and birds, or rather those creatures could speak and communicate with us. There are similar mythic views of language. Whether this was an inspiration for or an interpretation of ancient fables in which animals talk, it is difficult to say. According to the biblical story of the Tower of Babel, there once was a time when "... the whole earth was of one language, and of one speech" (Genesis 11:1). And when some people began to build a tower brick by brick, the Lord decided to come down and confound the common language so that "... they may not understand one another's speech" (Genesis 11:7). It sounds as though the divisions among people resulted from God's will. One may give meaningful interpretations to this alleged act of God to sow disunity among people. But it is difficult to imagine what was to be accomplished by this, except perhaps to generate a variety that has indeed enriched humanity's culture.

That children naturally acquire the ability to speak languages to which they are exposed led Noam Chomsky (*Aspects of theory of syntax,* 1966) to suggest that the human brain is hard-wired to learn languages. In other words, there is a Universal Grammar which is inherent in all normal human brains.

On goal and purpose

A question that sometimes crops up in reflective minds is whether the universe has any goal or purpose. We may make a distinction between goal and purpose. A goal is a point or a state towards which the activities of an individual or system seem to tend. In living organisms, goals are learnt or are fixed in the mind of the being. Purpose, on the other hand, is the reason why a system functions to reach a goal. The scientific study of the physical world does not seem to indicate that the universe as a whole is functioning with any goal in mind, or that it has come to be formed for any particular purpose.

Already in the seventeenth century, philosophers were using the watchmaker analogy to argue for the existence of an intelligent creator. In *A treatise on metaphysics* (1736), Voltaire developed this idea cautiously as follows:

> When I see a watch with a hand marking the hours, I conclude that an intelligent being has designed the springs of this mechanism, so that the hand would mark the hours. So, when I see the springs of the human body, I conclude that an intelligent being has designed these organs to be received and nourished within the womb for nine months; for eyes to be given for seeing; hands for grasping, and so on. But from this one argument, I cannot conclude anything more, except that it is probable that an intelligent and superior being has prepared and shaped matter with dexterity; I cannot conclude from this argument alone that this being has made the matter out of nothing or that he is infinite in any sense. (quoted in Randall 1926, 296).

William Paley (*Natural theology,* 1802) used this argument as the foundation for his proof of God.

Richard Dawkins wrote a whole book (*The blind watchmaker,* 1986) to demolish this idea. He emphatically asserted that natural selection has neither a mind nor a mind's eye. His goal in this book (though he repudiates a goal in the universe) is to demonstrate that science can explain biological phenomena, even those that are apparently goal-driven.

A basic problem associated with attributing or discovering goal and purpose is this: a careful external observer may be able to infer the goal of a system from its behavior. But an outsider can never fathom its purpose. As Shakespeare's Cicero said:

> Men may construe things after their fashion,
> Clean from the purpose of the things themselves.
> (in *Julius Caesar,* Act 1, Scene 3)

This is a very important point in discussions on goals and purposes. Only the system itself is aware of them, if such exist, because purpose implies conscious thought. This is obvious in human activity. The goal of a student may be to graduate with a degree. The purpose may be to get a good job, to impress her parents, or to satisfy a longing. Only the student knows this. If getting a good job is the goal, the purpose of that goal may be to lead a good life, to repay a loan, to raise a family, etc. These correspond to Aristotle's final causes: goals towards which specific phenomena occur.

There may be goal without purpose, but there cannot be purpose without goal. For example, the goal of a body thrown in a field of force is to occupy the state of minimum potential energy, but there may be no purpose to it. On the other hand, if the goal of a plant is to grow towards sunlight, the purpose may be to continue to live. Purposeful activity is more sophisticated than goal-directed activity, because it implies awareness.

The factors enabling a system to achieve its goal(s) are of two kinds:

(a) Extrinsic, i.e., in the world beyond its own control;
(b) Intrinsic, i.e., within itself: internal elements may modify the course of action.

A difference between animate and inanimate is that in the inanimate world, the extrinsic factors alone count; whereas in the animate world, intrinsic factors also come into play. Intrinsic factors are more dominant in more sophisticated bio-entities. And yet, as may be seen in the political arena, many heads of states are constrained by external (international) forces in the decisions they make to protect or aggrandize their own country.

The goal of every life form seems to be its own continuation for the maximum possible length of time. The purpose for this goal may be related to the conscious or unconscious satisfaction the entity experiences in living.

What about the universe? Science suggests that the cosmos functions on the basis of laws. The goal of phenomena seems to be the stability of the universe for an extended period of time, and incessant increase of its overall entropy. Since an external observer cannot know the purpose, human minds have not been able to discern purpose in the universe by their analysis. It is doubtful they ever can. We may hypothesize some goal to the universe, such as, for example, the emergence of the human species, but its purpose is not for us to know. Most religions affirm a purpose to the universe. Abraham Lincoln once observed, "The Almighty has his own purposes" (1865, 44). This can at best be poetry; at worst, a proposition that cannot be established through scientific methodology.

Some spokespersons for science say with definiteness the universe has no purpose. Yet, the purposefulness of the universe, enunciated by religions may, but need not, be correct. It would seem that neither science with its observationally acquired data, nor any reasoning, will be able to unravel any such purpose which only a conscious universe can know. The difference arises because science sees no cosmic consciousness, but religion does (in God, Brahman, etc.).

The cautious contention of science that there seems to be no purpose does not minimize the firm conviction of religion that there is a purpose in the world.

On designer cosmology
Recall the opening lines of Alfred Tennyson's poem:

> SEE what a lovely shell,
> Small and pure as a pearl,
> Lying close to my foot,
> Frail, but a work divine,
> Made so fairily well
> With delicate spire and whorl,
> How exquisitely minute,
> A miracle of design!
> (from "The Shell" in *Maud,* 1855, 82)

It is difficult not to be awed by the shell and the pearl, the butterfly and the bird, and all the beauteous wonders we see in the world around. From atomic orbits to galactic spirals and everything in between, Nature's creativity strikes us as much by the aesthetic joy it provides as by its variety. And when we reflect on living organisms, from the minute amoeba to the mammoth whale, their delicate anatomy and the precise functioning of their parts do incline us to imagine that these must have been carefully designed and crafted by some super intelligence. To posit such a designer cosmologist is surely not contrary to reason or clear thinking. A systematic formulation of this ancient suspicion constitutes what is sometimes called natural theology.

It was/is a beautiful and quite harmless way of picturing how it all came to be: not by random chance but by the intention and intelligence of a Supermind that decided to create a magnificent work of art that was, at the same time, complex clockwork with countless mini-machines routinely ticking away in it. The general belief that all this must be the work of a grand Divinity, endowed with the qualities of omniscience and omnipotence has therefore been implicit or explicit in practically all the cultures and religious systems of humankind.

But this pleasing picture was wrecked in the nineteenth century with the ushering of Darwin's idea of biological evolution, and in the twentieth century by the notion of chemical evolution and the utterly blind big bang which is believed to have started it all. Now science is able to account for the emergence of stars and planets, bees and birds, and everything, as resulting from chance, physical laws, natural selection and adaptation. What Laplace had called the God hypothesis in the context of physics now seemed to be stricken off the worldview of science. Even life and Man are seen as products of complex physics and chemistry.

Though the rise of science was a welcome enrichment to human culture, from religious perspectives it has had unwelcome consequences, not unlike the fact that, though logs and oil burning add to our creature comforts, deforestation and global warming have also ensued from technology. Furthermore, little by little, science has been eroding belief in a personal God and faith in religious matters. This has not been without social and ethical consequences.

The reaction to the negative side-effects of science has been twofold. The first relates to the Enlightenment mode which strives to guard all the positive dimensions of religion without those that are untenable in the scientific framework; and to improve the basic ethical, humanistic, and aesthetic contributions of religions.

The second reaction to the iconoclastic onslaught of science has been to try to cast traditional theistic modes of understanding the natural world in a scientific garb. The discomfort and anger generated by the dilution of religious beliefs as a direct consequence of Darwinian evolution had been simmering for a long time. They came to a head in the infamous Scopes Trial in the United States in 1920. There, William Jennings Bryan, antievolutionist and lawyer for the fundamentalist school of thought, stated succinctly what it was all about:

> I accept the Bible absolutely. I believe it was inspired by the Almighty, and he may have used language that could be understood at that time instead of using language that could not be understood until Darrow was born (quoted in Larson 1997, 4).

John Scopes was found guilty of violating a law that forbade the teaching of evolution, and fined a hundred dollars. This court-room victory was an echo of the hearts of millions for whom religion is a powerful fount of meaning and shared joy, sacrament and solace. Few people give up their religion because courts declare that Darwin's theory is science. According to a news report:

> Two-thirds in a poll said creationism, the idea that God created humans in their present form within the past 10,000 years, is definitely or probably true (Lawrence, *USA Today,* June 7, 2007).

Yet, it is difficult to say if the outcome of that trial was a victory for religion. Darwinian evolution, as the only valid scientific view of anthropogenesis, continues to be taught in colleges and universities in the United States and in many other countries all over the world. Traditional religious accounts of anthropogenesis are not taken literally by most thinking and well-informed people.

To counteract this, some other scientific theory was needed. In its absence, at least the complexity of the problem had to be presented in scientific terms. This was the goal of Charles B. Thaxton et al. when they published *The mystery of life's origin* (1984). The power of books cannot be underestimated, and does not always depend on their intrinsic worth or value. Karl Marx's *Das kapital* (1867) led to the Communist movement. Sayyid Qutb's *Ma'alim fi'l-Tariq [Milestones]* (1964), which called for Islamic nations to embrace the Sharia, ignited the Al-Queda explosion. Likewise, this book led to a new movement which has come to be called *Intelligent Design* or ID.

Another such book was Michael Denton's *Evolution: A theory in crisis* (1985). The book and its author were mercilessly castigated by the scientific establishment, in which such epithets as dishonest, incompetent, and misrepresenting were used, though Denton himself was by no means a creationist. But that did not deter others from taking inspiration from his book.

It drew Michael Behe, another biochemist with academic credentials from reputable universities, to take up the question and propound the thesis that at the most basic level of biological systems there is a complexity that simply cannot be reduced to molecules and valence bonds. True or not, Behe's claim does not mean that the as-yet-nebulous connections between pure chemistry and fundamental biology cannot be cleared up some day. Behe asserted:

> The impotence in Darwinian theory in accounting for the molecular basis of life is evident … from the complete absence of the professional scientific literature of any detailed models by which complex biochemical systems could have been produced (*Darwin's black box,* 1996, 187).

He went on to propose, as a solution, that there is an *intelligent design* (ID) behind it all, arguing that: "the conclusion of intelligent design flows naturally from the data itself [sic]—not from sacred books or sectarian beliefs" (p. 193). By this statement he made the ID thesis scientific and non-religious. Yet, he has received much support and acclaim from certain religion-friendly groups, but from hardly any scientists.

Behe and his supporters have been attempting, through books, conferences, public lectures, and organizations, to propagate the idea that at the core all natural phenomena are caused by a silent and invisible intelligent principle without which the world would have been a chaos of grand proportions. The thesis is not new in the world of ideas, and is more kin to religions than any science-sounding theory of biogenesis. Behe's thesis seems hardly threatening: the world and life, and Man most of all, came to be created by an intelligent principle. Behe and his supporters do not explicitly use the term God.

Among the ID proponents are keen thinkers from a variety of fields such as law, biology, physics, theology, and mathematics.

Nevertheless, Behe has been roundly criticized and condemned by the scientific establishment, and publicly ostracized by his academic department and university which disclaimed any affiliation with his ideas. All this, because it is feared that he is surreptitiously bringing in the science-rejected notion that God is behind all natural phenomena. Many religiously inclined scientists and avowed atheists, as also a vast number of reasonably educated citizens, have resisted attempts to theologize science.

The scientific establishment regards any suggestion of the supernatural as anathema, not only because there is not a shred of scientific evidence to that effect, but also because the basic assumptions of science are that nature can be fully accounted for in terms of scientific laws and principles, and that the supernatural belongs to the realm of poetry and fantasy.

It has been said that ID propagandists in the United States have two layers of intentions. The first is to re-establish a Christian world in those countries where Christianity is still a majority religion. Some can empathize with this goal, but using science for this purpose simply will not succeed because science is based, by definition and practice, on a methodology that transcends race, religion, nationality and other cultural boundaries. The other goal of the ID movement is to reinstate religious perspectives, which are quickly losing their significance in human culture. One may regard this as a commendable project in so far as one wishes to preserve the best aspects of religions. But here again, the injection of even such a seemingly worthwhile goal into technical science and science education may not be the best way to accomplish it.

On the other hand, many scientists, in their explicit commitment, not to say zeal, to explain everything within the naturalistic framework and in their insensitivity to the religious longings of vast numbers of people, have been going overboard in their condemnation and caricature of religion and religiously-inclined thinkers. When a scientist of the stature of Dawkins writes, "It is absolutely safe to say that if you meet somebody who claims not to believe in evolution, that person is ignorant, stupid, or insane (or wicked, but I'd rather not consider that)" (1989, 34), irrespective of the truth-content of the statement, it does little service to the image of science among the general public. In the view of more tolerant observers, conceding that one may look upon the universe as having originated from an intelligent cosmic principle in no significant way affects the intellectual development of children or even the progress of science.

The ID hypothesis is in some ways not unlike the puzzle of consciousness and thought from the neuron-structured brain. That puzzle may someday be solved by technical science, and has already been solved to the satisfaction of many by the introduction of the technical term *emergence*. If someone had called this *intelligent emergence*, the term might have become anathema to its own proponents.

Thoughts on death: theist and atheist

Nothing that is born lives on for ever. Life, as someone quipped, is a terminal disease: sooner or later, we all must cease in our current bodies and minds. Death is a curious puzzle in one's youthful days, and the recognition of an impending event in one's graying phase. Different people react to the thought of death in different ways.

For the theist, irrespective of one's religion, there is the hope of a more glorious life in the hereafter. Even with threat of punishment by a severe God for sins slight and serious, there is a feeling that, with repentance and after payment of dues, one will enter a state of eternal peace in the region of an all-merciful Almighty. Even when there is the requirement of revisiting earth to reap the consequences of conscious actions, the cycle will end sooner or later, and ultimate liberation with merger with the Universal Spirit is a cheerful and uplifting possibility.

When a near and dear one breathes no more, there is the conviction in the heart of the believer that he or she is safe and secure in a world beyond, away from the rough and tumble of this arduous life with its fears and fury, residing with the certainty of our own eventual arrival there. What can be more promising than the thought that after all is said and done, there will be a joyous eternity in the realm and reflection of the Creator!

Thus the person who lives in faith and conforms to the norms of ethics has little to fear about death, for it escorts one to a place non-existent for doubters. Contrary to what some atheists say, death is not, or should not be, ugly or intimidating to religious people.

However, it is important for the theist to know that atheists are generally not disturbed by the thought that in due course they will be turned to dust or debris, pulverized beyond recognition, lingering perhaps in the fading memory of some who, too, will some day mingle with the molecules in lumps of mud and slime. The awakened atheist rejoices in life while it lasts, and feels that life's splendor is intense and exhausted in lived moments, focused only here below in this insignificant niche in the cosmic stretch. Life is like reading a fascinating novel without wanting the narrative to go on forever, or sipping a fine glass of Bordeaux without craving for the glass to be an endless fount. Be born, be well for a while, then be gone for good, is the commandment of blind biology.

To the atheist, death is simply the inevitable cessation of the vital functions of a living entity. Sure, it is a threatening idea to some; it is intense pain for the loving ones who are left behind, and a mystery to some thoughtful people. Even atheists sometimes toy with a "what if…" question in this context, for it is not easy for everyone to imagine that the thoughts, feelings, ideas and experiences accumulated and encapsulated in a brain and body for years vanish into void with an interruption of oxygen-intake. It is as if, when the covers of a book are closed, all its contents are erased in a jiffy.

Since ancient times, people have argued about death and beyond. Even with all the progress in science, wonderment about death persists at the philosophical level, and firm convictions about it persist at doctrinal levels. These are likely to continue for as long as we shed tears, eulogize, write epitaphs, and wish or pray for the peace of the departed.

There have also been numerous anecdotal reports of what has come to be known as NDE: *Near-Death-Experience.* This term was coined by Raymond Moody (*Reflections on life after life*, 1977), who presented evidence to the effect that many individuals experienced a variety of intense and meaningful, often enriching and sometimes frightful visions when they were almost going to die. Moody's book prompted great interest, both scientific and popular, on the question. As may be expected, scientists by and large believe that it is all related to the messing up of the brain prior to its imminent end, whereas religiously inclined people take NDE as an affirmation of the existence of something beyond.

In Hindu esoteric literature (Katha Upanishad 1.1:20-21) there is a dialogue between an aspirant Nachiketas and Yama, the God of Death. Nachiketas tells Yama of the doubt that people have about the post-mortem continuance or otherwise of one who has died. And he wishes to clarify that doubt. To this Yama replies that even the ancient gods had doubts on this question, for it was a difficult and subtle truth to comprehend. Perhaps everything about death is stated succinctly here. The ancient gods should be taken to mean the various religions. That they had doubts on this means they can in no way be certain about what they proclaim on the question. That the truth about death is too subtle to be understood simply means that the human mind can never find an absolute answer for this mystery.

One may react to the thought of death meaningfully, whether one is a believer or not. However, what matters now is not if we will live disembodied forever, or if we will become unrecognizable bits scattered on earth's mantle, but how we spread joy, alleviate suffering, serve others, and strive to make this a better world while we are alive. Atheists and theists of goodwill can join hands and work together as fleeting earthlings for the good of all.

End of the world, as seen by physics

From the sixteenth to the middle of the nineteenth century, during which period modern science made enormous strides, there was little talk of the end of the world from any serious scientific perspective. William Thomson was perhaps the first physicist to use the word death in a scientific work. After considering the possibility of universal death, he said:

> But it is impossible to conceive a limit to the extent of matter in the universe; and therefore science points...to an endless progress, through an endless space, of action involving the transformation of potential energy into palpable motion and hence into heat (Thomson and Tait 1867, 2:485).

Rudolf Clausius' formulation of the second law of thermodynamics also led to the prediction of an eventual Heat-Death for the entire Universe. No matter how reasoned or reasonable, an announcement of mass extinction of the human race is never welcome news. Scientists began to consider other possibilities, and sure enough scientists like Pierre Duhem (1906, 287ff) gave arguments that the heat-death prediction was based on certain unwarranted assumptions.

But then, developments in astrophysics and cosmology were not helpful in these efforts. Calculations show beyond a reasonable doubt (Zeilik and Gregory 1998) that in about four to five billion years the sun will transform into a phase where it will gobble up the earth, since its humungous radius will be far greater than where the earth is in orbit.

We were almost reconciled to this dire scientific prediction, with the consolation that the ultimate conflagration was not going to come about in the conceivable future.

Since the last quarter of the twentieth century, our hopes were raised again. Freeman Dyson (*Infinite in all directions,* 1988) proposed that life will adapt itself to changing conditions as the universe gets to be more and more difficult to live in. With only a finite amount of energy, life can manage to continue indefinitely in time, if the energy is expended at an appropriately slow rate. Frank Tippler (*The physics of immortality,* 1994) proposed that when contraction occurs in a closed universe, information processing will speed up towards an Omega Point, assuring immortality. Andrei Linde has suggested in some of his writings (*Inflation and quantum cosmology*, 1990), that eventually baby universes will emerge into which life forms from the current universe will seep, and thus life will always be there in the cosmos. Modern mythologies are mathematics-minded, but that alone does not make them any more valid than ancient ones.

This new field of immortality-physics has brought in technical terms like aleph: a state in which infinite information is stored and processed; angel plasma: a very, very hot state in which superintelligences "exist as computational systems in particle interactions" (Sandberg 1999). Those who regret that marginalization of metaphysics with Baconian-Galilean-Cartesian physics may take comfort from these developments. When it comes to ultimate questions, scientists can be as naïvely serious with their conceptual and jargon-toys as medieval scholastics.

Speaking in less ethereal and more relevant terms, Martin Rees warns us (*Our final hour*, 2003), there are any number of forces that could terminate human life on the planet within the next century. These include the eruption of a super-volcano raising immense dust clouds, nuclear terrorism, a devastating virus and global warming.

Planetary disasters spelling the extinction of *Homo sapiens* are not impossible, but they are highly unlikely within the next few centuries. But before such a catastrophe comes to pass, one may expect more strife from increasing population and decreasing resources. Environmental discomfort, disease and devastation could stem from technological pollution. The devastating potential in our increasing knowledge of the genome is unclear. More acts of terrorism, instigated by frustration, envy, oppression, religious fanaticism, and aided by easy availability of destructive means may be expected, unless injustices are removed and religious spokespeople are weaned from medieval mindset. At the same time, the internet ease of spreading hate and lies can do more harm than good, but it is difficult to arrest this.

An asteroid might land in the midst of our concerts, prayers, politics, wars, jealousies, religions, sciences, and all the rest. Then, after shrieks in every tongue and nation, the noise of human voice and the magic of subtle thought will be erased forever. History, philosophy, culture and science will all be gone for good, even their memories will disappear, for there will be no brain to recall. The earth will continue its routine swing for more eons, letting perhaps some birds to coo, frogs to croak, insects and microbes to survive. In the end, when even the sun's last embers simmer down, the mute silence of a mindless, pristine world without a living cell will revert to way back when. But, humanity may survive for a much longer time than seems probable now.

On the end of civilization

A running theme in the past few decades has been something we used to read only on the screen at the conclusion of movies: The End.

In recent years, we have had books and articles on the End of the World, the End of Physics, the End of Time, the End of History, the End of Communism, and the End of Civilization. There seems to be no end to publications of this kind, fueled by the Internet free-for-all and the flourishing market for sensationalist publications.

A couple of generations ago, monster movies and murder mysteries used to sell well too. Now these types of frightful prognostications seem to be the fad. Unfortunately, the ends predicted by current Nostradamuses are not the fantasy-calculations of star-mongers and soothsayers of a by-gone era, but serious predictions by well-read scholars and well-informed scientists. But they do remind us of the Biblical book of *Revelation* and the Puranic *Kalki Avatara*: both of which were inconvenient truths of ages past, but those projected unhappy endings were to be followed by happy beginnings, for in the end Almighty God would establish harmony and bliss.

But the ends foreseen by current diviners are dismal beyond compare. These days we are heading to a kind of thermodynamic disaster which, in its entropic fury, is leading us along a path of no return, and no chance of a cyclic reinstatement of an Arthurian Utopia.

Most people who are counting on more years of planetary residence for themselves and their progeny are disturbed by all this. Our only hope seems to lie in the scientists being dead wrong, but that does not seem very likely. Some of us are frantically looking for some loophole in the arguments that prophesy inevitable catastrophe.

But then when these pundits talk of civilization they are primarily thinking of the indulgent lifestyle of abundant creature-comforts, consuming the products of a highly industrialized and voraciously energy-devouring system, which happens to be the current goal of billions all over the world.

Then again vast numbers of people of the world are in blissful ignorance of these projected perils, and are looking forward to the mid-twenty-first century when, per economic forecasters, India and China would have equaled, perhaps surpassed, the United States in Gross National Product. They are thinking, not about the end, but about the beginning of a new era when it will be their turn to lead the world.

There are also billions living in many villages in Africa and Asia and South America right now where people live fairly peacefully as all our ancestors did centuries ago, making do with whatever is available, sitting around for chats and songs and folktales, listening to ancient stories narrated by elders, laughing and merry-making, and above all, being quite content, even if the average life-span is not considerable. One wonders if those civilizations will also come to an end because of the unintended catastrophic forces that scientific knowledge, industrial pollution and ecological rampage are all unleashing.

In the midst of these pessimistic predictions, we may tell ourselves that, like individual death, the end of civilization will also be but a sad and passing phase of history. When it is all over, the surviving few will manage somehow or other, perhaps sitting in groups and recalling how their more mindless ancestors lived and enjoyed and ruined it all.

But there are perennial technological optimists. Perhaps the foremost among them is Ray Kurzweil. He predicts (*The singularity is near,* 2005) that in the not-distant-future technology would have become as sophisticated as biology and result in the creation of newer forms of life and intelligence. Before the end of this century, we will be harnessing solar energy for all our needs, our life-span will have increased significantly, every human being will have a most powerful computer, probably built into the body, and the most fantastic things will happen to human civilization. The inconvenient truth of global warming and deforestations will have all become fears of the past. The least one can say about Kurzweil's vision is that when one merges into that yet-to-be-born era of future history, one is removed for a moment from the hugely depressing state of the world and heartened by a hope for future generations.

Chapter 10
Concluding Thoughts

What began as visions of the beyond grew into the rich variety of religions. Revelations about the human spirit were given to the sage-poets of religious traditions. They have provided humanity with a rich backdrop which transforms mechanical existence into meaningful life. Choirs in churches, chants in temples, readings in synagogues, calls from minarets and other invocations bring joy and enrichment to the humdrum of night and day. Religions bring out our relevance in the cold of the cosmic grandeur, and speak of our destiny, individual and collective, in the saga of the world.

Religions bring communities together. They offer satisfying answers to complex questions regarding the meaning and purpose of existence, and present a coherent worldview to the practitioners. They rest on thoughts and insights that have acquired weight and sanctity by virtue of their age. Religions present us with opportunities for recognizing transcendental reality, whether real or imagined, through various modes, and are meant to induce us to actualize our potential for the good and the noble. Most importantly, religions enable us to build enriching bridges between the genders and between generations, mark life stages through sacraments, and establish bonds, not just among the members of a community, but also between us as humans and the cosmos at large. We are enriched by the emotional, spiritual, ethical, and inspirational nourishment that all the religions of the human family provide. No wonder religions appeal to vast numbers of people.

Every believer proclaims his or her religious heritage with love, commitment, and pride. However, the dogma that the message of one's faith system is the only divine voice must be reconsidered. We attach primacy to our sun, but we also acknowledge countless other suns, each central in its locality. We love our parents, but also allow that others love theirs. Religions are like optical telescopes that can be directed only to a particular star. But even as one gazes through an eyepiece, one should not think there are no other stars up there in the sky. Religious leaders must stress that no one faith system is final and for all. We cannot, with moral uprightness or rational legitimacy, proclaim one religion as inferior to another. But we may affirm that those aspects of religion that respect human dignity and mutual respect are superior to those that do not. As we read in my poem:

> If religious frogs just jump out
> Into the big, big sea,
> They'll know there's much more
> To religious ecstasy!
>
> Religions are like volcanoes:
> Powerful sure they are.
> But they come from a deeper Source
> That's grander, oh by far.
> (Raman 2002)

In the modern interconnected world where the vast majority adhere to one religion or another, we have no choice but to respect all religions. But when religions become belligerent, it is incumbent upon those who speak for religion to call for the arrest of inter-religious hate and hurt.

When it comes to fundamental guideposts for actions and attitudes, such as love, compassion, caring, humility, respect for others, and reverence for the sacred, the religions of the world are bound in commonality rather than shorn in animosity. Even in worship modes and prayerful postures for lauding the unseen glory or surrendering to the cosmic principle, religions resemble rather than reject one another. Religions differ in their historical roots, not in the spiritual sensibilities they evoke. Every view of the Divine is partial. As a Vedic sage poet proclaimed, we articulate our visions in different ways. It is as enriching to see a facet of the Divine in the Star of David as in the Cross, in the Crescent inspired by the Qur'an as in the abstract sound of the sacred *Aum*. Religious pluralism does not mean abandonment of one's faith, nor naïve embrace of all, but the recognition that other religions also enshrine the wisdom of the ages in their own ways, other faiths rest upon supreme spiritual experiences, and other traditions offer fulfillment in the yearning to connect with the Cosmic Mystery.

The persistence of religious diversity is understandable, even commendable. It has its cultural roots and aesthetic richness too. The core of the problem is not the local practices of religions, but their doctrinal and condescending confrontation with one another. The situation is crying for fresh perspectives. Ours has become an interwoven world with complex interactions between peoples. It is not a world where religious birds of the same feather always flock together. There are inevitable global exchanges between people of different faith systems: Hindus work in Dubai, Sikhs in Canada, Muslims in France, Jews in Argentina, Buddhists in America, and so on. Yet, in such a world there are some nations that are firm in their anchor to a single religious loyalty, and demand the same of all their citizens, prohibiting other worship modes, while others foster religious pluralism.

But ours is also a world where economic injustices, political squabbles, and asymmetry in religious freedom disfigure human societies. In such a world, it is urgent that enlightened religious leaders from every faith and intellectuals from every culture inspire men and women of goodwill to complement their local loyalties with a global vision of trans-denominational prayer and cooperation. This would not only enhance their own sensitivities for the sacred and the spiritual, but also serve to lessen tensions and mistrust among the more ardent true believers. In this effort, we need to extract from all religions whatever is best and overlapping in values and perspectives.

At this point in history, there is still hope that the hate and intolerance lurking in traditional religions may be subdued, tamed, and transformed. Yes, there are still pockets of religious animosity and persecution, but there are also places where enlightened laws restrain self-righteous passions. We must strive for the day when sectarian cleansing, witch hunting, and infidel-cursing will become mere embarrassments of a buried past, and the religions of the world will coexist in harmony. Our challenge is to bring about a balance between amoral, no-nonsense science, and trans-rational, enlightened religious visions. Whether this can be achieved in the current rigidity of billions who are wedded to the mine-alone-is-the-Truth mentality, is the fundamental question of the day. No matter what, it is imperative that in this new century, we create a synthesis of worldviews and values.

We can draw the worldview components from whatever is reasonable, rational, and verifiable in the scientific perspective, and derive the value components from whatever is ennobling, meaningful, and fulfilling in traditional religions.

When it comes to explaining any aspect of perceived reality in the phenomenal world, one will have to embrace the scientific mode, not because this is the truth, but because, based on the weight of all available evidence at a given time, it is the most persuasive interpretation. Science will readily discard the theory of yester-century if it fails in the scientific criteria for truth content in the face of newly acquired data. This springs not from disrespect for investigators of former generations, but because newly gathered data sometimes make older views untenable. The insights and understanding, the visions and profound worldviews that modern science has brought to humanity by adhering to its methodology are unparalleled in the millennia of human history.

In addition to bringing to us all the knowledge that has enlarged our appreciation of the physical and biological world, science has eradicated countless fears and superstitions that used to haunt millions in generations past. Moreover, science has also enabled us to apply that knowledge and understanding for eliminating much poverty and hunger, and for the betterment of the human condition.

It has contributed immeasurably to the quality of life of countless people all over the world, increased physical health, extended longevity, produced more food, made communication and transportation unimaginably easy, and accomplished a thousand other things that were only in the fantasy world of our distant ancestors.

With all that, like many other initially benign forces in human culture including religion, scientific knowledge and science-based technology have also had their negative impacts. They have wrought ominous changes that are posing grave dangers to the human condition and to our bio-friendly planet. It is, therefore, not surprising that, like rationality-intoxicated thinkers who decry, denounce, and denigrate religions with little appreciation for what religions are, many sensitive thinkers have become science-phobic. Even philosophers have questioned the claims of science in unscrambling the mysteries of nature, naively equating the efforts of science in this regard with the speculative, mythic, and poetic reflections of other keen thinkers. Some have tried to trivialize scientific knowledge and equate it with ancient interpretations of cosmogenesis and biogenesis. Attacks and subversion of science can only be detrimental to culture and civilization. If anti-science forces, armed with science-generated technology, stifle free inquiry, curb scientific research, and persecute liberated theology, culture and civilization will stagnate then and there. When technology is blindly adopted in the absence of a scientific spirit and associated enlightenment values, society can become as brutal as a mindless, manipulating monster.

More than for its extraordinary breakthroughs, the twentieth century will be remembered for consciousness-raising. That century made racism a bad word and shameful practice; recognized gender oppression as social evil and began to redress it; proclaimed human rights as transcending race, caste, and religion; pleaded for international economic justice; condemned the exploitation of the young; began to celebrate diversity; and initiated care for the disabled. It released millions from centuries of colonial shackle, and it established world organizations in which free nations come together to solve their problems of food and health, trade and education, and to resolve their political differences through debates and discussions. The twenty-first century will perhaps eradicate the evils of religious bigotry, fanaticism, and exclusivism from all religious frameworks.

It is paradoxical that with all the spiritual, cultural, and knowledge enrichment that religion and science have given us, and with all the social progress we have made on so many fronts, the saga of our species is still sullied with countless episodes of conflict and confrontation, animosity and aggression. Internal peace and external harmony seem to be all too elusive. We are tormented by hate and wars even as threats of doom hang as dark clouds over human destiny. We feel collectively insecure about our future, and yet quarrel on how God is to be addressed.

One major cause of wars and conflicts is related to matters of social and global justice. Nature has distributed material resources— fertile lands, fresh water, rainfall, minerals and such—as unevenly as God has endowed intelligence and good fortune among His creatures. Human ingenuity has exploited these in different regions of the world with varying degrees of efficiency and success. Human beings have also been exploiting fellow humans of other races and religions. This has happened within every society, and beyond as well. The greed and callousness implicit in this last aspect of economic development and the resentment it has provoked are among the roots of much international bitterness.

It is a Biblical saying that man does not live by bread alone, but this is true only as long as the oft-derided material needs are satisfied. Economic exploitation, social injustice, and misdistribution of wealth are all hallmarks of civilizations that have historically ignored the basic necessities of life of many people. But now, thanks to communication technology, this historical truth has been brought into the open and to the attention of the victims. Perhaps the have-nots will thus have enough power to fight nationally and internationally for economic justice.

What all this means is that two conditions are essential for national stability, international peace and universal harmony:

— the religions of the world should wake up to enlightened visions of tolerance and service to the needy;
— and global economic systems should deal equitably with all the peoples of the world.

There never will be peace and goodwill in the world as long as there are unconscionable disparities between the rich and the poor within and among countries, mindless fanatics out to destroy those who think differently about God and religious truth, and heartless exploiters of the weak for their own self-interests.

Now, as never before in human history, we have come to realize that we are all co-passengers in the only spaceship that is ours to share. Fortified by the knowledge that comes from the sciences and enriched by the values and wisdom that come from traditions, we must make every effort to forget the antagonisms and animosities of the past, and strive to build a world civilization that will make this our planet a more rewarding place to live. One may hope that religious leaders will spread the message that one can achieve mature religious experience through the complex world-pictures of science, for science, too, is revelation. It is revelation of the ultimate roots of perceived reality, unveiling to the human spirit occult truths about the microcosm and the macrocosm, about life and brain and mind. Just as science without religion is simply heartless and unpoetic information, religion without scientific awakening could remain fantasy-based fulfillment.

John Comenius, a Moravian Bishop, wrote in the early seventeenth century:

> We are all citizens of one world, we are all of one blood. To hate a man because he was born in another country, because he speaks a different language, or because he takes a different view of this subject or that, is a great folly. Deists, I implore you, for we are all equally human.... Let us have but one view, the welfare of humanity; and let us put aside all selfishness in considerations of language, nationality, or religion (quoted in Durant 1961, 582).

Hermann Hess expressed a similar idea in the first stanza of his poem, *Allein* [Alone]:

> *Es führen über die Erde*
> *Strassen und Wege viel.*
> *Aber alle haben*
> *Dasselbe Ziel.*
> [Many paths and ways on earth there are:
> And they all do lead.
> But the goal they all do have
> Is the same indeed.]

Or again, recall the words of the poet Samuel Longfellow:

> Light of ages and of nations,
> Every race and every time
> Has received your inspirations,
> Glimpses of your truth sublime.
> ("Light of Ages and of Nations," lines 1-4, from *Hymns of the Spirit*, 1864, 438)

Long before the emergence of multiple faith systems in the world, a sage poet of the ancient Hindu world had pithily formulated what could well serve as the motto for the Parliament of World Religions:

> *Ákáshád patitantoyam*
> *yathá gacchati ságaram*
> *sarvadeva namaskárah*
> *shri kesavam pratigacchati*
> [As waters falling from the skies
> Return to the self-same sea,
> Prayers to all the deities.
> Go back to the same divinity].
> (Lines from "*Suryanarayana vandanam* [Prostration to the Source of All Light]" from the Sanskrit epic *Mahabharata*)

340 *Truth and Tension in Science and Religion*

REFERENCES

Abdelhadi, Magdi. 2008. Muslim call to adopt Mecca time. *BBC News,* April 21.

Addison, Joseph. 1694. *The Works of the Right Honorable Joseph Addison.* Reprinted, ed. Richard Hurd, Vol. 1, London: Bell & Daldy, 1885.

Agrippa, Cornelius. 1526. *De incertitudine et vanitate scientiarum atque artium declamatio invectiva* [*Declamation attacking the uncertainty and vanity of the sciences and arts*]. Cologne. Reprinted as excerpts in Henry Morley, *Cornelius Agrippa: The life of Henry Cornelius Agrippa von Nettesheim, doctor and knight, commonly known as a magician,* Chap. 8-9, 2:151-209. London: Chapman and Hall. (1856)

Ali, Abdullah Yusuf. 1938. *The meaning of the glorious Qur'an.* Cairo, Egypt: Dar al-Kitab al-Masri.

Al-Qaradawi, Yusuf. 1960. *The lawful and the prohibited in Islam.* Indianapolis, IN: American Trust Co.

Antony, Louise M., ed. 2007. *Philosophers without Gods: Meditations on atheism and the secular life.* New York: Oxford Univ. Press.

Aquinas, Thomas. 1264. *Summa contra gentiles.* Reprint, English Dominican Fathers, trans. 5 vols. London: Burns Oates and Washbourne, 1924.

Aristotle. 350 BCE. *Metaphysica.* Reprint, *Metaphysics,* W. D. Ross, trans. Oxford: Carendon Press. 1924.

Arrhenius, Svante. 1908. *Das Werden der Welten.* Leipzig: Academic Publishing. Reprint, *Worlds in the making: The evolution of the universe,* H. Borns, trans. New York: Harper & Row, 1908.

Atkins, Peter. 1993. *Creation revisited.* New York: W. H. Freeman & Co.

———. 1997. Religion—the antithesis to science. *Chemistry and Industry* 20, January: comment section. Also online at *Transtopia,* http://www.transtopia.org/antithesis.html.

Augustine of Hippo, Saint. 394. *De sermone Domini in monte.* [*Our Lord's sermon on the mount*]. Reprinted in *A select library of the Nicene and Post-Nicene fathers of the Christian Church,* Vol. 7, edited by Phillip Schaff, trans. by John Gibb and James Innes, 3-33. Buffalo, NY: The Christian Literature Co., 1888.

———. ca. 400. *Joannis Evangelium, Tractate xl.* [*On the Gospel of St. John, Homily 40*]. Reprinted in *A select library of the Nicene and Post-Nicene fathers of the Christian Church,* Vol. 7, edited by Phillip Schaff, trans. by John Gibb and James Innes, 225-29. Buffalo, NY: The Christian Literature Co., 1888.

———. ca. 416. *De trinitate* [*On the Holy Trinity*]. Reprinted in *A select library of the Nicene and Post-Nicene fathers of the Christian Church,* Vol. 3, edited by Phillip Schaff, trans. Arthur West Haddan, 1-228. Buffalo, NY: The Christian Literature Co., 1887.

Aurobindo. See Sri Aurobindo.

Bakar, Osman. 1999. *The history and philosophy of Islamic science.* Cambridge, UK: Islamic Texts Society.

Bakhtiar, Laleh and Kevin Reinhart. 1995. *Encyclopedia of Islamic law: A compendium of the major schools.* Chicago: Kazi Publications, Library of Islam Series.

Ball, W. W. Rouse. 1908. *A short account of the history of mathematics.* 4th ed. Reprint, New York: Dover, 1960.

Barbour, Ian. 1993. *Ethics in an age of technology.* San Francisco: Harper Collins.

Barker, Dan. 1993. Evangelistic atheism: Leading believers astray. *Freethought Today,* Jan/Feb.

Baron, Jonathan. 2006. *Against bioethics.* Cambridge, MA: MIT Press.

Barrow, John D. and Frank J. Tipler. 1986. *The anthropic cosmological principle.* New York: Oxford Univ. Press.

Barrow, John D. 1990. *The world within the world.* New York: Oxford Univ. Press.

Bayle, Pierre. 1695. *Dictionnaire historique et critique* [*Historical and critical dictionary*]. 12th ed. Reprint, Paris, C. V. Duriez, 1830.

Beaumont, Lucy. 2004. A New Look at Art with X-ray Vision. *Health and Science,* August 15.

Bechert, Heinz, ed. 1996. *When did the Buddha live? The controversy on the dating of the historical Buddha.* Delhi: Sri Satguru.

Behe, Michael J. 1996. *Darwin's black box: The biochemical challenge to evolution.* New York: Touchstone.

Bernard, Claude. 1865. *Introduction à la médecine expérimentale* [*An introduction to the study of experimental medicine*]. Reprint, trans. H. C. Greene, New York: Dover, 1957.

Berrill, Norman J. 1955. *Man's emerging mind; Man's progress through time—trees, ice, flood, atoms, and the universe.* New York: Dodd, Mead, & Co.

Bharati, Agehananda. 1976. *The light at the center: Context and pretext of modern mysticism.* Santa Barbara, CA: Ross-Erikson.

Bibby, Cyril, ed. 1967. *The essence of T. H. Huxley: Selections from his writings.* New York: St. Martins Press.

Blackmore, Susan. 1999. *The meme machine.* New York: Oxford Univ. Press.

Blake, William. 1982. *Complete poetry and prose of William Blake.* Ed. David V. Erdman. Berkely, CA: Univer. of California Press

Bodhi, Bhikkhu. 1995. *In the Buddha's words: An anthology of discourses from the Pali Canon.* London: Wisdom Publications.

Bose, D. M., S. N. Sen and B. V. Subbarayyappa, eds. 1971. *A concise history of science in India*. New Delhi: Indian National Science Academy.

Bossuet, Jacques Bénigne. 1677. *De la connaissance de dieu et de soi-même: traité du libre arbitre*. Reprint, Paris: Librairie monarchique de N. Pichard, 1821

Boyer, Pascal. 2001. *Religion explained: The evolutionary origins of religious thought*. New York: Basic Books.

Braun, Theodore, and John B. Radner, eds. 2005. *The Lisbon earthquake of 1755: Representations and reactions*. Oxford: Voltaire Foundation.

Bronowski, Jacob. 1977. *A sense of the future: Essays in natural philosophy*. Cambridge, MA: MIT Press.

Brown, Norman. 1953. Introduction to *Hesiod: Theogony*. New York: Liberal Arts Press.

Browning, Elizabeth Barrett. 1856. *Aurora Leigh*. Reprinted in The *Complete poetical works of Elizabeth Barrett Browning*. Whitefish, MT: Kessinger Publishing, 2005.

Buehrens, John A. 2003. *Understanding the Bible: An introduction for skeptics, seekers, and religious liberals*. Boston: Beacon Press, 2003.

Burton, Richard F. 1880. *The Kasidah of Haji Abdu El-Yezdi*. Reprint, London: Octagon Press, 1991.

Butler, Samuel. 1912. *Note-books of Samuel Butler*. London: A. C. Fifield.

Cantore, Enrico. 1977. *Scientific man: The humanistic significance of science*. New York: ISH Publications.

Carr, Paul H. 2006. *Beauty in science and spirit*. Center Ossipee, NH: Beech River Books.

Carson, Rachel. 1962. *Silent spring*. Reprint, Boston: Houghton Mifflin, 1990.

Carus, Paul. 1974. *Chinese astrology, early Chinese occultism.* LaSalle, IL: Open Court Books.

Cassuto, Umberto. 1941. *Torat HaTeudot.* Reprint, *The documentary hypothesis and the composition of the Pentateuch,* Israel Abrahams, trans. Jerusalem: Magnes Press/The Hebrew Univ., 1983.

Cavanaugh, Michael. 1995. *Biotheology: A new synthesis of science and religion.* Lanham, MD: University Press of America.

Chalmers, David. 1996. *The conscious mind: In search of a fundamental theory.* New York: Oxford Univ. Press.

Chekhov, Anton. 1914. *Notebooks of Anton Chekhov.* Reprint, trans. S. S. Koteliansky and Leonard Woolf, New York: B. W. Huebsch. 1921.

Chomsky, Noam. 1965. *Aspects of the theory of syntax.* Reprint, Cambridge, MA: MIT Press, 1966.

Clooney S.J., Francis F. 2001. *Hindu God, Christian God: How reason helps break down the boundaries between religions.* New York: Oxford Univ. Press.

Comfort, Alex. 1984. *Reality and empathy: Physics, mind, and science in the 21st century.* Buffalo: State Univ. of New York Press.

Copernicus, Nicolaus. 1543. *De revolutionibis orbium coelestium.* Nuremberg: Johannes Petreius. Reprint, *On the revolutions of the heavenly spheres,* trans. and commentary by Edward Rosen. Baltimore: Johns Hopkins Univ. Press, 1992.

Corey, Michael. 1993. *God and the new cosmology: The anthropic design argument.* Lanham, MD: Rowman & Littlefield.

Corfield, Penelope. 1995. Georgian England: one state, many faiths. *History Today,* 45.4: 14-21, April.

Coyne, Jerry. 2006. [Letter to the editor]. *Playboy,* August.

Crick, Francis. 1994. *The astonishing hypothesis: The scientific search for the soul.* New York: Charles Scribner's Sons.

Dalley, Stephanie, ed. and trans. 1989. *Myths from Mesopotamia.* New York: Oxford Univ. Press.

Damasio, Antonio. 2003. *Looking for Spinoza: Joy, sorrow, and the feeling brain.* New York: Harcourt.

Daniélou, Alain. 1964. *The myths and Gods of India.* Rochester, VT: Inner Traditions Intnatl.

D'Aquili, Eugene and Andrew B. Newberg. 1999. *Mystical mind: Probing the biology of religious experience.* Minneapolis: Fortress Press.

Darwin, Charles. 1859. *On the origin of species.* Reprint, Rockville, MD: Wildside Press, 2003.

Davies, Paul, and J. Brown, eds. 1988. *Superstrings: A theory of everything?* Cambridge: Cambridge Univ. Press.

Davies, Paul. 1992. *The mind of God: Science and the search for ultimate meaning.* New York: Simon and Schuster.

Dawkins, Richard. 1976. *The selfish gene.* (New York: Oxford Univ. Press, 1976).

———. 1986. *The blind watchmaker.* New York: W. W. Norton.

———. 1989. Book Review. *The New York Times,* April 9, sec. 7: 34.

———. 1998. *Unweaving the rainbow: Science, delusion and the appetite for wonder.* Boston: Houghton Mifflin.

———. 2002. Religion's Real Child Abuse. *Free Inquiry* 22.4: 9-12.

———. 2003. *A devil's chaplain: Reflections on hope, lies, science, and love.* Boston: Houghton Mifflin.

———. 2006. *The God delusion.* Boston: Houghton Mifflin.

Dawson, Ernest Rumley. 1917. *The secret of sex: The discovery of a new law of nature, how sex is caused.* Reprinted, Whitefish, MT: Kessinger Publications, 2004.

Deacon, Terrence William. 1997. *The symbolic species: The co-evolution of language and the brain.* New York: W. W. Norton.

Dehejia, Harsha V. and Makarand Paranjape, eds. 2003. *Saundarya: The perception and practice of beauty in India.* New Delhi: Samvad India Foundation.

De Morgan, Augustus. 1872. *A budget of paradoxes.* Reprint, LaSalle, IL: Open Court Books, 1915.

Dennett, Daniel C. 1991. *Consciousness explained.* Boston: Little, Brown, & Co.

———. 2006. *Breaking the spell: Religion as a natural phenomenon.* New York: Viking.

Denton, Michael. 1985. *Evolution: A theory in crisis.* Bethesda, MD: Adler & Adler.

De Waal, Frans. 2005. *Our inner ape: Power, sex, violence, kindness, and the evolution of human nature.* New York: Riverhead Books.

———. 2006. *Primates and philosophers: How morality evolved.* Princeton, NJ: Princeton Univ. Press.

Diamond, Jared M. 1997. *Guns, germs, and steel: The fates of human societies.* New York: W. W. Norton.

Dijksterhuis, Eduard J. 1950-1961. *The mechanization of the world picture.* London: Oxford Univ. Press.

Dirac, P. A. M. 1930. *The principles of quantum mechanics.* Oxford: Clarendon Press.

Donald, Merlin. 2001. *A mind so rare: The evolution of human consciousness.* New York: W. W. Norton.

Dostoevsky, Fyodor. 1880. *The brothers Karamasov.* Reprint, trans. Constance Garnett, New York: Signet Classics, 1999.

Dreyer, J. L. E. 1890. *Tycho Brahe: A picture of scientific life and work in the sixteenth century.* Reprinted, Whitefish, MT: Kessinger Publications, 2004.

Duhem, Pierre. 1906. *La théorie physique son objet et sa structure* [*The aim and structure of physical theory*]. Reprint, Phillip P. Wiener, trans. Princeton, NJ: Princeton Univ. Press, 1954.

————. 1915. *La science allemande* [*German science*]. Paris: A. Hermann et Fils. Reprint, John Lyon, trans., La Salle, IL: Open Court, 1991.

————. 1913-1959. *Le système du monde. histoire des doctrines cosmologiques de Platon à Copernic* [*The system of the world: A history of cosmological doctrines from Plato to Copernicus*]. 10 vols. Paris: A. Hermann et Fils.

Durant, Will and Ariel Durant. 1961. *The age of reason begins.* New York: Simon & Schuster.

Dyson, Freeman. 1979. *Disturbing the universe.* New York: Basic Books.

————. 1988. *Infinite in all directions.* New York: Harper & Row.

————. 1995. The Scientist As Rebel. In *Nature's imagination: The frontiers of scientific vision.* ed. John Cornwell, 1-11. New York: Oxford Univ. Press. Reprint, in *The scientist as rebel,* 3-18. New York: New York Review Book Collection. 2006.

Eccles, John Carew. 1984. *Evolution of the brain: Creation of the self.* London: Routledge.

Edelman, Gerald, and Giulio Tononi. 2000. *A universe of consciousness: How matter becomes imagination.* New York: Basic Books.

Efron, Noah J. 2007. *Judaism and science: A historical introduction.* Westport, CT: Greenwood Press.

Einstein, Albert. 1940. Science and Religion. *Nature,* vol. 146.

Esposito, John L. 2002. *What everyone needs to know about Islam.* New York: Oxford Univ. Press.

Festinger, Leon. 1957. *A theory of cognitive dissonance.* Evanston, IL: Row, Peterson.

Feyerabend, Paul. 1975. *Against method: Outline of an anarchistic theory of knowledge.* London: New Left, 1975.

Fitzgerald, Edward, trans. 1859. *Rubaiyat of Omar Khayyàm.* Reprint, London, Penguin, 1989.

Frank, Philipp. 1957. *Philosophy of science: The link between science and philosophy.* Englewood Cliffs, NJ: Prentice-Hall.

Frawley, David. 1990. *Astrology of the seers: A guide to Vedic/Hindu astrology.* Twin Lakes, WI: Lotus Press.

Freud, Sigmund. 1927. *The future of an illusion.* Reprint, James Stachey, trans., New York: W. W. Norton, 1989.

Gaukroger, Stephen. 1978. *Explanatory structures: Concepts of explanation in early physics and philosphy.* Atlantic Highlands, NJ: Humanities Press.

Gell-Mann, Murray. 1994. *The quark and the jaguar: Adventures in the simple and the complex.* New York: W. H. Freeman & Co.

Gödel, Kurt. 1995. Ontological Proof. In *Collected works. III: Unpublished essays and lectures,* eds. S. Feferman, S. Kleene, G. Moore, R. Solovay, and J. van Heijenoort, 403-404. New York: Oxford Univ. Press,

Goethe, Wolfgang Johann von. 1811-33. *Aus meinem Leben: Dichtung und Wahrheit* [*Out of my life: Poetry and truth*]. Reprint, *Autobiography of Goethe: Truth and poetry: From my life.* Parke Godwin ed., John Henry Hopkins, Charles Anderson Dana, and John Sullivan Dwight trans., 2 vol. New York: John Wiley, 1849.

Goodenough, Ursula. 1998. *The sacred depths of nature.* New York: Oxford Univ. Press.

Gopalakrishnan, G. P. 1991. *Periyar: Father of the Tamil race.* Chennai, India: Emerald Publishers.

Gopani, A. S., and Surendra Bothara, eds. 1989. *Yogaúâstra (Sanskrit) of Âcârya Hemacandra.* Jaipur, India: Prakrit Bharti Academy.

Gould, Stephen. 1999. *Rock of the ages: Science and religion in the fullness of life.* New York: Ballantine.

Gove, Harry. 1996. *Relic, icon or hoax? Carbon dating the Turin shroud.* Philadelphia: Institute of Phyiscs Publishing.

Grant, Edward. 2004. *Science and religion, 400 BC-AD 1550: From Aristotle to Copernicus.* Baltimore, MD: Johns Hopkins Univ. Press.

Green, William Scott. 2003. Introduction to *God's rule: The politics of world religions,* ed. Jacob Neusner. Washington, DC: Georgetown Univ. Press.

Greenspan, Louis, and Stefan Andersson, eds. 2003. *Russell on religion: Selections from the writings of Bertrand Russell.* New York: Routledge, 2003.

Gregory the Great, Pope St. ca. 591. *Homiliarum in evangelia,* 26. In *Patrologia Latina,* edited by J. P. Migne, 76, 1197c, 1844-45.

Gribbin, John, and Stephen Plagemann. 1974. *The Jupiter effect.* New York: Walker & Co.

Gribbin, John. 1977. *White holes: Cosmic gushers in the universe.* New York: Delacorte/Delta.

Grotius, Hugo. 1625-46. *De jure belli ac pacis libri tres* [*The law of war and peace*]. Reprint, Francis Kelsey, trans., Washington, DC: Carnegie Institution, 1925.

Gupta, S. P., and K. S. Ramachandran, ed. 1976. *Mahabharata: Myth and reality.* New Delhi: Agam Prakashan.

Hameroff, Stuart. 2006. Consciousness, neurobiology and quantum mechanics: The case for a connection. In *The emerging physics of consciousness,* ed. Jack A. Tuszynski, chap. 6, 193-244. Berlin: Springer.

Haught, John F. 1995. *Science and religion: From conflict to conversation.* New York: Paulist Press.

———. 2006. *Is nature enough?: Meaning and truth in the age of science.* Cambridge: Cambridge Univ. Press.

Hawking, Stephen W. 1988. *A brief history of time.* New York: Bantam.

Hefner, Philip. 1993. *The human factor: Evolution, culture, and religion.* Minneapolis: Fortress Press.

Herbermann, Charles G., et al, eds. 1913. *The [original] Catholic encyclopedia.* New York: Robert Appleton Co.

Hiebert, Erwin. 1970. Mach's philosophical use of the history of science. In *Historical and philosophical perspectives in science,* ed. Roger H. Stuewer, 184-204. Minneapolis: Univ. of Minnesota Press.

Hill, Christopher. 1965. *Intellectual origins of the English revolution.* Oxford: Clarendon Press.

Hitchens, Christopher. 2007. *God is not great: How religion poisons everything.* New York: Twelve Books.

Hitler, Adolf. 1925-26. *Mein kampf [My struggle].* Reprint, trans. Ralph Manheim, New York: Houghton Mifflin, 1962.

Hobbes, Thomas. 1642. *De cive [On the citizen].* Reprint, Richard Tuck and Michael Silverthorne, ed. and trans., London: Oxford Univ. Press, 1998.

———. 1651/1668. *Leviathan.* Reprint, Michael Oakeshott, ed. New York: Oxford Univ. Press, 1998.

Hook, Sidney, ed. 1961. *Determinism and freedom in the age of modern science.* New York: Collier.

Hoyle, Fred. 1981. Hoyle on evolution. *Nature* 294, Nov. 12: 105.

Huizinga, Johan. 1938. *Homo ludens [Man the player].* Reprint, R. F. C Hull, trans., Boston: Beacon Press, 1955.

Huxley, Thomas Henry. 1889. "Agnosticsim" In *The Nineteenth Century* 25: 169-94, February.

Ingersoll, Rober G. 1877. The liberty of man, woman and child [Lecture]. Reprinted in *The complete works of Robert G. Ingersoll.* 12 vols. New York: The Dresden Pub. Co., C. P. Farrell. 1902.

Iyer, K. A. Krishnaswamy. 1930. *Vedanta or the science of reality.* Madras: Ganesh & Co.

Jaki, Stanley. 2000. *The savior of science.* Grand Rapids, MI: Eerdmans.

James, William. 1890. *Principles of psychology,* vol. 1. New York: Henry Holt & Co.

Johnson, Phillip E. 1995. *Reason in the balance: The case against naturalism in science, law and education.* Downers Grove, IL: InterVarsity Press.

Joyce, G. 1912. Revelation. In *The Catholic Encyclopedia.* New York: Robert Appleton Company. Retrieved March 1, 2009 from New Advent: http://www.newadvent.org/cathen/13001a.htm.

Kalidasa. ca. 6th century. *Malavikagnimitram [Malavika and Agnimitra].* Reprint, Ramji Thakur, ed. New Delhi: Global Vision, 2004.

Kapoor, Kapil. 2003. Saundarya and Indian aesthetics. *Evam: Forum on Indian representations* 2.1: 11-19.

Kauffman, Stuart. 2008. *Reinventing the sacred: A new view of science, reason, and religion.* New York: Basic Books.

Kearney, Hugh. 1971. *Science and change 1500-1700.* New York: McGraw-Hill.

Keats, John. 1907. *The Complete Poetical Works of John Keats.* Ed. H. Buxton Forman. New York: Oxford Univ. Press.

King Jr., Martin Luther. 1959. *The measure of a man.* Philadelphia: Fortress Press.

Kjeilen, Tore. 2005. Sharia [Internet article]. Retrieved March 1, 2009 from *Looklex Encyclopaedia*, http://lexicorient.com/e.o/sharia.htm

Kline, Morris. 1985. *Mathematics and the search for knowledge.* New York: Oxord Univ. Press.

Koenig, Harold. 2000. The healing power of faith. In *God for the 21st century,* ed. Russell Stannard. Radnor, PA: Templeton Foundation Press.

Koestler, Arthur. 1972. *Roots of coincidence.* New York: Random House.

Kuhn, Thomas. 1962. *The structure of scientific revolution.* Chicago: Univ. of Chicago Press.

Kumar, Sehdev, trans. 1996. *The vision of Kabir: Love poems of a 15th century weaver-sage.* London, Ontario: Third Eye Pub.

Küng, Hans and Karl Joef Kuschel, eds. 1993. A global ethic: The declaration of the Parliament of the World's Religions. New York: Continuum. Full text of declaration also posted at http://www.weltethos.org/dat-english/03-declaration.htm.

Kurzweil, Ray. 2005. *The singularity is near: When humans transcend biology.* New York: Viking Penguin.

Ladner, Lorne. 2004. *The lost art of compassion: Discovering the practice of happiness in the meeting of Buddhism and psychology.* New York: Harper Collins.

La Mettrie, Julien Offray de. 1748. *L'homme machine.* Leyde: Elie Luzac, Fils. Reprint, *Man: A machine,* Gertrude C. Bussey and M. W. Calkins, trans, La Salle, IL: Open Court. 1961.

Lamotte, Étienne. 1984. Mahäyäna Buddhism. In *The world of Buddhism: Buddhist monks and nuns in society and culture,* eds. Heinz Bechert and Richard Gombrich, 90-93. New York: Facts on File Publications.

Laplace, Pierre Simon de. 1840. *Essaie philosophique sur les probabilities* [*Philosophical essay on probabilities*], 6th ed. Reprint, F. W. Truscott and F. L. Emory, trans., New York: Dover, 1951.

Larson, Edward J. 1997. *Summer for the words: The Scopes trial and America's continuing debate over science and religion.* Reprint, New York: Basic Books, 2006.

Laughlin, Robert B. 2005. *A different universe: Reinventing physics from the bottom down.* New York: Perseus Books.

Lawrence, Jill. 2007. Poll shows belief in evolution, creationism. *USA Today,* June 7.

Leaman, Oliver. 1999. *A brief introduction to Islamic philosophy.* Cambridge, UK: Polity Press.

Leakey, Richard. 1994. *The origin of humankind.* New York: Perseus Books.

Leary, Timothy, Ralph Metzner, and Richard Alpert. 1964. *The psychedelic experience: A manual based on the Tibetan Book of the Dead.* Reprint, New York: Citadel Press, 1992.

Legge, James, trans. 1893. *Confucius: Confucian analects, the great learning, and the doctrine of the mean.* Reprint, New York: Dover, 1971.

Leibniz, Gottfried. 1710. *Essays on theodicy, on the goodness of God, human liberty and the origin of evil.* Reprint, Austin Farrer, ed. and E. M. Huggard, trans., La Salle, IL: Open Court, 1985.

Leoni, Edgar. 1982. *Nostradamus and his prophecies.* New York: Wing Books.

Lewinsohn, Richard. 1958. *Science, prophecy and prediction: Man's efforts to foretell the future—from Babylon to Wall Street.* Originally published in German as *Die enthullung der zukunft* [*The unveiling of the future*]. Reprint Arnold J. Pomerans, trans., New York: Bell, 1961.

Lewis, Clarence I. 1929. *Mind and the world order: Outline of a theory of knowledge.* 1929, Reprint, New York: Dover.

Lewis, Thomas, Fari Amini and Richard Lannon. 2000. *General theory of love.* New York: Random House.

Li, David H., trans. *Dao De Jing: A new millennium translation.* Bethesda, MD: Premier Publications, 2001.

Libet, S. Benjamin. 2004. *Mind time: The temporal factor in consciousness.* Cambridge, MA: Harvard Univ. Press.

Lincoln, Abraham. 1865. Second Inaugural address. Reprinted in *Lincoln's Gettysburg oration and first and second inaugural addresses,* 26-45. New York: Duffield & Co., 1907.

Linde, Andrei. 1990. *Inflation and quantum cosmology.* Boston: Academic Press.

Lindow, John. 2001. *Norse mythology: A guide to the gods, heroes, rituals, and beliefs.* London: Oxford Univ. Press.

Lindsay, Hal. 1981. *The 1980s: Countdown to armageddon.* New York: Bantam.

Longfellow, Samuel. 1864. *Hymns of the spirit.* Reprint, Houghton, Mifflin and Co., 1889.

Lorenz, Konrad. 1949. *King Solomon's ring: New light on animal ways.* Reprint, M. K. Wilson, trans., New York: Thomas Y. Crowell, 1961.

Lovelock, James. 1979. *The ages of Gaia: A biography of our living earth.* Reprint, 3rd ed., New York: Oxford Univ. Press, 2000.

Luisi, Pier Luigi. 2006. *The emergence of life: From chemical origins to synthetic biology.* Cambridge: Cambridge Univ. Press.

MacLean, Paul D. 1990. *The triune brain in evolution: Role in paleocerebral functions.* New York: Plenum.

Maher, Bill. 2008. *Religulous.* [Documentary film/DVD]. Directed by Larry Charles. Produced by Thousand Words.

Margulis, Lynn. 1998. *Symbiotic planet: A new look at evolution.* New York: Basic Books.

Martin, David. 1997. *Does Christianity cause war?* New York: Oxford Univ. Press.

Martin, T. T. 1923. In *God and nature: Historical essays on the encounter between Christianity and science,* edited by David C. Linberg and Ronald L Numbers. Berkley, CA: Univ. of Calf. Press. 1986.

Marx, Karl. 1867. *Das Kapital.* Ed. Friedrich Engels. Reprint, *Das Kapital: A Critique of Political Economy,* Serge L. Levitsky, ed., abridged, Washington: Regnery Gateway, 1996.

McKinney, Laurence O. 1994. *Neurotheology: Virtual religion in the 21st century.* Cambridge, MA: American. Inst. for Mindfulness.

Merton, Robert K. 1973. *The sociology of science: Theoretical and empirical investigations.* Chicago: Univ. of Chicago Press.

Midgley, Mary. 2003. *The myths we live by.* New York: Routledge.

Miles, Jack. 1995. *God: A biography.* New York: Vintage Boks.

Miller, Arthur I. 2001. *Einstein, Picasso: Space, time and the beauty that causes havoc.* New York: Basic Books.

Moaddel, Mansoor. 2005. *Islamic modernism, nationalism, and fundamentalism: Episode and discourse.* Chicago: Univ. of Chicago Press.

Moody, Raymond. 1977. *Reflections on life after life.* Harrisburg, PA: Stackpole Books, 1977.

Mooney, Chris. 2005. *The Republican war on science.* New York: Basic Books.

Mountford, C. P. 1973. *The dreamtime book: Australian aboriginal myths in paintings by Ainslie Roberts.* Englewood Cliffs, NJ: Prentice-Hall.

Muggeridge, Malcolm. 1970. The great liberal death wish. [Essay] Reprint, in *The portable conservative reader,* Russel T. Kirk, ed. New York: Penguin, 1982.

Murphy, Nancey. 1990. *Theology in the age of scientific reasoning.* Ithaca, NY: Cornell Univ. Press.

———— and George F. R. Ellis. 1996. *On the moral nature of the universe: Theology, cosmology, and ethics.* Minneapolis: Fortress Press.

———— and William R. Stoeger SJ. 2007. *Evolution and emergence: Systems, organisms, persons.* London: Oxford Univ. Press.

Myre, Ernst. 2001. *What evolution is.* New York: Basic Books.

Namazhar. ca. 830. *Thiruvaimozhi.* In *For the love of God: Selections from Nalayira Divya Prabandham.* Hawthorn, VIC: Penguin Books Australia Ltd., 1996.

Nanda, Meera. 2003. *Prophets looking backwards: Postmodern critiques of science and Hindu nationalism in India.* New Brunswick, NJ: Rutgers Univ. Press.

Nasr, Seyyed Hossein. 1968. *Science and civilization in Islam.* New York: New American Library. Reprint, 2nd ed., Cambridge: Islamic Text Society, 1987.

Needham, Joseph, Ling Wang, and Peter J. Golas. 1954-59. *Science and civilization in China.* Cambridge, Cambridge Univ. Press.

Newman, John Henry. 1891. *Apologia pro vita sua: Being a history of his religious opinions.* London: Longmans, Green, & Co.

Nielson, Kjeld. 1984. *Incense in ancient Israel.* Leiden: E. J. Brill.

Nietzsche, Friedrich. 1883-85. *Also sprach Zarathustra [Thus spoke Zarathustra].* Reprint, Graham Parkes, trans., New York: Oxford Univ. Press, 2005.

Nostradamus, Michel de. 1555. *Prophecies.* Also available online at www.scribd.com/doc/6391081/Nostradamus-Prophecies.

Orlov, Yuri. 1991. *Dangerous thoughts: Memoirs of a Russian life.* Trans. Thomas P. Whitney. New York: William Morrow & Co.

Osiander, Andreas. 1543. Foreword to *De revolutionibis orbium coelestium.* Nuremberg: Johannes Petreius. In reprint, *On the revolutions of the heavenly spheres,* Edward Rosen, trans., xx. Baltimore: Johns Hopkins Univ. Press, 1992.

Pagels, Heinz. 1982. *The cosmic code: Quantum physics as the language of nature.* New York: Simon & Schuster.

Pais, Abraham. 1982. *Subtle is the Lord: The science and the life of Albert Einstein.* London, Oxford Univ. Press.

Paley, William. 1802. *Natural theology, or evidences of the existence and attributes of the Deity collected from the appearances of nature.* Reprint, 6th ed. London: Baldwin & Co., 1819.

Park, Robert. 2000. *Voodoo science, the road from foolishness to fraud.* New York: Oxford Univ. Press.

Pascal, Blaise. 1670. *Pensées.* Reprint, A. J. Krailsheimer, trans., New York: Penguin Classics, 1995.

Peacocke, Arthur. 2001. *Paths from science towards God: End of all our exploring.* Oxford: One World.

———. 2003. The significance of the DNA structure: Reductionism and emergence. In *From complexity to life: On the emergence of life and meaning,* ed. Niels Henrik Gregersen, as Chap. 10: Complexity, Emergence, and Divine Creativity: 187-205. New York: Oxford Univ. Press.

Pearson, Karl. 1892. *The grammar of science.* Reprint, New York: Cosimo, 2007.

Peierls, Rudolf. *Atomic histories: A walk through the beginnings of the Atomic Age with one of its true pioneers.* (New York: American Institute of Physics, 1996).

Pelikan, Jaroslav. 2000. *Divine rhetoric: the Sermon on the Mount as message and as model in Augustine, Chrysostom, and Luther.* Crestwood, NY: St Vladimir's Seminary Press.

Penrose, Roger. 1994. *Shadows of the mind: A search for the missing science of consciousness.* New York: Oxford Univ. Press.

Peters, Karl. 2002. *Dancing with the sacred: Evolution, ecology, and God.* Harrisburg, PA: Trinity Press Intl.

Pickover, Clifford A. 1976. *Wonder of numbers: Adventures in mathematics, mind, and meaning.* New York: Oxford Univ. Press.

Plantinga, Alvin. 2000. *Warranted Christian belief.* New York: Oxford Univ. Press.

Plautus, Titus Maccius. ca. 190 BCE. *Asinaria.* Reprinted *Asinaria: The one about the asses.* trans. John Henderson. Madison: Univ of Wisconsin Press, 2006.

Plessner, Martin. 1973. Abu 'Uthman 'Amr ibn Bakr al-Jahiz. In *Dictionary of Scientific Biography,* ed. Charles Coulston Gillispie, 7: 63-65. New York: Charles Scribners's Sons.

Polkinghorne, John. 1998. From physicist to priest. In *Science and theology: The new consonance,* ed. Ted Peters, 56-64. Boulder, CO: Westview Press.

Pollock, John. 1977. *William Wilberforce.* New York: St. Martin's Press.

Popper, Karl. 1934. *Logik der Forschung* [*The logic of scientific discovery*]. Reprint, Karl Popper, trans., London: Hutchinson, 1959).

Post, Stephen G., Lynn G. Underwood, Jeffrey P. Schloss and William B. Hurlbut, eds. 2002. *Altruism and altruistic love: Science, philosophy, and religious dialogue.* New York: Oxford Univ. Press.

Potter, Van Rensselaer. 1971. *Bioethics: Bridge to the future.* Englewood Cliffs, NJ: Prentice-Hall.

Power, Eileen. 1924. *Medieval people.* London: Methuen.

Prabhupada, Bhaktivedanta, trans. 1968. *Bhagavad Gita as it is.* Reprint, New York: Bhativedanta Book Trust, 1972.

Qutb, Sayyid. 1964. *Milestones.* Reprint, Indianapolis, IN: American Trust Co., 1990.

Radhakrishnan, Sarvapalli, ed. and trans. 1953. *The principal Upanishads.* London: Oxford Univ. Press.

Ramachandran, V. S., and Sandra Blakeslee. 1998. *Phantoms in the brain: Probing the mysteries of the human brain.* New York: William Morrow.

Raman, V. V. 1997. *Nuggets from the Gita.* Mumbai, India: Bharatiya Vidya Bhavan.

———. 2002. *Random rhymes and various verses.* Philadelphia: Xlibris.

Randall, John Herman. 1926. *The making of the modern mind: A survey of the intellectual background of the present age.* Reprint, New York: Columbia Univ. Press, 1976.

Randi, James and Arthur C. Clarke. 1995. *An encyclopedia of claims, frauds, and hoaxes of the occult and supernatural.* New York: St. Martin's Griffin.

Randi, James. 1992. Help stamp out absurd beliefs. *Time Magazine,* April 13.

Rankin, Aidan. 2006. *The Jain path: Ancient wisdom for the West.* Ropley, UK: John Hunt - O Books.

Ravindra, Ravi. 2004. Yoga, physics, and consciousness. In ed. David Lorimer, Denis Alexander, Scientific & Medical Network. *Science, consciousness, ultimate reality: Exploration of the interface between science, religion, and consciousness,* 93-108. Charlottesville, VA: Imprint Academic.

Rees, Martin. 2003. *Our final hour: A scientist's warning.* New York: Basic Books.

Reich, Helmut. 2002. *Developing the horizons of the mind: Relational and contextual reasoning and the resolution of cognitive conflict.* Cambridge: Cambridge Univ. Press.

Rheingold, Howard. 1991. *Virtual reality: Exploring the brave new technologies of artificial experience and interactive worlds—from cyberspace to teledildonics.* New York: Touchstone.

Richter, Johann Paul. 1807. *Levana oder Erziehlehre* [*Levana or the doctrine of education*]. Reprinted, trans. AH, London: Longman. 1848.

Rolston III, Holmes. 1987. *Science and religion: A critical survey.* New York: Random House.

Rosen, Edward, trans. 1939. *Three Copernican treatises: The commentariolus of Copernicus; the letter against Werner; the narratio prima of rheticus.* Reprint, New York: Dover, 2004).

Rue, Loyal. 1994. *By the grace of guile: The role of deception in natural history and human affairs.* New York: Oxford Univ. Press.

Ruse, Michael. 2000. *Can a Darwinian be a Christian? The relationship between science and religion.* New York: Cambridge Univ. Press.

Russell, Bertrand. 1999. *Russell on religion: Selections from the writings of Bertrand Russell.* Ed. Louis I. Greenspan, Stefan Andersson. New York: Routledge.

Rhys Davids, T. W., and C. A. F. Rhys Davids, trans. 1923. *Dialogues of the Buddha: Translated from the Pali of the Digha Nikaya.* London: Oxford Univ. Press.

Sagan, Carl and Ann Druyan. 1995. *The demon haunted world: Science as a candle in the dark.* New York: Random House.

Sandberg, Anders. 1999. Terminology from the Omega Point Theory List. Retrieved March 1, 2009 from http://www.aleph.se/Trans/Global/Omega/omeg_term.html.

Saxe, John Godrey. 1873. *Poems of John Godrey Saxe*. Boston: James R. Osgood & Company.

Schopenhauer, Arthur. 1839. On the freedom of the will. [Essay] Reprint, [Book] K. Kolenda, trans., Oxford: Basil Blackwell, 1985.

Scott, Walter. 1805. *The lay of the last minstrel*. Reprinted, ed. Margaret Andrews Allen, Boston: Ginn and Co., 1897

Shah, Nagin J., ed. 2000. *Jaina theory of multiple facets of reality and truth (Anekantavada)*. New Delhi: Motilal Banarsidass.

Shapiro, Robert. 1999. *Planetary dreams: The quest to discover life beyond Earth*. London: Wiley.

Sharpe, Kevin. 2006. *The science of God: Truth in the age of science*. Lanham, MD: Rowman & Littlefield.

Shaw, George Bernard. 1907. *Major Barbara*. Reprinted, *Major Barbara: With an essay as first aid to critics*. New York: Brentanos, 1917.

Sheen, Fulton J. 1958. *Life of Christ*. New York: McGraw-Hill.

Sherbourne, Donald A. 1981. *A key to (Whitehead's) process and reality*. Chicago: Univ. of Chicago Press.

Shipps, Jan. 1985. *Mormonism: The story of a new religious tradition*. Chicago: Univ. of Illinois Press.

Shirer, William L. 1979. *Gandhi: A memoir*. New York: Simon & Schuster.

Singh, Simon. 2005. *Big bang: The most important scientific discovery of all time and why you need to know about it*. New York: Fourth Estate.

Smith, George Hamilton. 1974. *Atheism: The case against God*. New York: Nash.

Smith, Huston. 2001. *Why religion matters: The fate of the human spirit in an age of disbelief*. London: HarperCollins.

Smuts, Jan Christiaan. 1926. *Holism and evolution*. New York: Macmillan.

Sorenson, Dane C. 2005. Atheists from around the world: E. V. Ramasami Naicker. Retrieved March 1, 2009 from http://www.conservativehumanism.com/Naicker.htm.

Spinoza, Benedict de. 1677. Ethica ordine geometrico demonstrata. Reprint, *The Ethics of Benedict de Spinoza: Demonstrated after the method of geometers*, trans. Daniel Drake Smith, New York: D. Van Nostrand, 1888.

Sri Aurobindo. 1914-1920. *The life divine*. First serialized in *Arya*, a monthly review, Pondicherry, India. Reprint, Twin Lakes, WI: Lotus Press, 2000 ed).

———. 1920. The nature of the Supermind. First published in *Arya*, a monthly review, Pondicherry, India. Reprint, in *The synthesis of yoga*, chap. 19, 754-768. Twin Lakes, WI: Lotus Press, 1992.

Stannard, Russell. 2000. *The God experiment: Can science prove the existence of God*. London: Faber and Faber, 2000).

Steinhardt, Paul J., and Neil Turok. 2007. *Endless universe: Beyond the big bang*. New York: Doubleday.

Stenmark, Mikael. 2001. *Scientism: Science, ethics, and religion*. Aldershot, UK: Ashgate.

Stone, Darwell. 1903. *Outlines of Christian dogma*. New York: Longmans, Green.

Stone, Jerome. 2003. Is nature enough? Yes. *Zygon: Journal of Religion and Science*, 38.4 December: 821–37.

Stowe, David. 2004. *How sweet the sound: Music in the spiritual lives of Americans*. Cambridge, MA: Harvard Univ. Press.

Stuart, Nancy Rubin. 2005. *The reluctant spiritualist: The life of Maggie Fox*. New York: Harcourt.

Sugden, John. 1989. *Niccolo Paganini: Supreme violinist or devil's fiddler?* Cincinnati, OH: Seven Hills Books.

Sykes, Bryan. 2003. *Adam's curse: A future without men.* London: Bantam Press.

Tabor, James D. 2006. *The Jesus dynasty: The history of Jesus, his royal family, and the birth of Christianity.* New York: Simon & Schuster.

Teilhard de Chardin, Pierre. 1955. *Le phénomène humain* [*The phenomenon of man*]. Reprint, Bernard Wall, trans., New York: Harper Torchbooks, 1966.

Tennyson, Alfred. 1829. *Timbuctoo: A poem, which obtained the Chancellor's medal at the Cambridge commencement, 1829.* Cambridge: J. Smith.

———. 1855. *Maud, and other poems.* Boston: Ticknor & Fields.

Thapan, Anita Raina. 1997. *Understanding Ganapati: Insights into the dynamics of a cult.* New Delhi: Manohar Publishers.

Thaxton, Charles B., Walter L. Bradley, and Roger L. Olsen. 1984. *The mystery of life's origin: Reassessing current theories.* New York: Philosophical Library.

Thomas, E. J. 2000. *The Life of the Buddha as Legend and History.* New York, Dover.

Thompson, Richard L. 2003. *Maya: The world as virtual reality.* Alachua, FL: Govardhan Hill Publishing.

Thomson, Sir William, and Peter Guthrie Tait. 1867. *Principles of mechanics and dynamics.* Reprint, New York: Dover, 2004.

Throndike, Lynn. 1923-58. *A history of magic and experimental science during the first thirteen centuries of our era.* 8 vols. New York: Macmillan.

Tillich, Paul. 1951. *Systematic theology,* vol. 1. Chicago, Univ. of Chicago.

Tippler, Frank. 1994. *The physics of immortality: Modern cosmology, God and the resurrection of the dead* . New York: Doubleday.

Tiruvalluvar. 2000. *Tirukkural.* Trans. V. V. Raman. Chennai, India: Manimekalai Prasuram, 2000.

Valmiki. ca. 500-100 BCE. *The Ramayana.* Trans. Sri Desiraju Hanumantu Rao and Sri K. M. K. Murthy [Online Version with Sanskrit and English] http://www.valmikiramayan.net/Ramayana1.htm. 1998-2008.

Vasudev, Gayatri Devi. 2001. *The art of matching charts.* Delhi: Motilal Banarsidass.

Vogt, Eric W., ed. 1996. *The complete poetry of St. Teresa of Avila: Bilingual edition.* New Orleans: Univ. Press of the South.

Voltaire [pen name of François-Marie Arouet]. 1756. *Poème sur le désastre de Lisbonne et sur La Loi Naturelle avec des Prefaces, des Notes etc., [Poem on the Lisbon Disaster].* Genève. Reprint, in *Toleration and Other Essays,* Joseph McCabe, trans., 255-258. New York: G.P. Putnam, 1912.

Voss, Sarah. 1995. *What number is God?: Metaphors, metaphysics, mathematics, and the nature of things.* Albany, NY: State Univ. of New York Press.

Vukanovic, Vladimir. 1995. *Science and faith: Well-known scientists talk about God.* Minneapolis: Light & Life Pub Co.

Vulliaud, Paul. 1952. *La fin du monde.* Paris: Payot.

Waldrop, Mitchell M. 1992. *Complexity: The emerging science of order and chaos.* New York: Simon & Schuster.

Wallace, B. Alan. 1996. *Choosing reality: A Buddhist view of physics and the mind.* 2nd ed. Ithaca, NY: Snow Lion.

Ward, Keith. 2006. *Is religion dangerous?* London: Lion Hudson Plc.

Watson, James. 2003. Future visions. *Time Magazine,* February 17.

Watson, William. 1895. *The father of the forest and other poems.* Chicago: Stone.

Watts, Fraser, and Kevin Dutton, eds. 2006. *Why the science and religion dialogue matters.* Philadelphia: Templeton Foundation Press.

Weber, Max. 1915. *Theory of social and economic organization.* Reprint, A M Henderson, ed. and Talcott Parsons, trans., New York: The Free Press, 1947.

Weinberg, Steven. 1977. *The first three minutes: A modern view of the origin of the universe.* New York: Basic Books.

———. 2001. *Facing up: Science and its cultural adversaries.* Cambridge, MA: Harvard Univ. Press.

Wheeler, John. 1979. Drive the pseudos out of science. [Appendix to an paper presented at the annual meeting of the American Association for the Advancement of Science: Not consciousness but the distinction between the probe and the probed as central to the elemental quantum act of observation]. Included in Martin Gardner and John Wheeler, 1979, Quantum Theory and Quack Theory [Article] in *New York Review of Books,* 26.8 May 17: 39-40. Reprint, [Chapter] in *Science: Good, bad, and bogus,* ed. Martin Gardner, 185ff. Buffalo, NY: Prometheus Books, 1981.

Whewell, William. 1857. *History of the inductive sciences.* London: John W. Parker & Son.

White, Andrew Dixon. 1896. *A history of the warfare of science with theology in Christendom.* 2 vols. London: Macmillan & Co.

Whitehead, Alfred North. 1929. *Process and reality: An essay in cosmology.* New York: MacMillan. Reprinted, corrected edition, ed. David Ray Griffin, Donald W. Sherburne. New York: Simon & Schuster. 1979.

Whitman, Walt. 1855/1892. *Leaves of grass.* Philadelphia: David McCay.

Whittaker, Sir Edmund. 1951. *A history of the theories of aether and electricity,* 2nd ed., vol. 1. London: Nelson.

Wigner, Eugene. 1960. The unreasonable effectiveness of mathematics in the natural sciences. *Communications in Pure and Applied Mathematics,* 13.1 February: 1-14.

Wilber, Ken. 1997. An integral theory of consciousness. *Journal of Consciousness Studies,* 4.1: 71-92. February.

Wilberforce, William. 1823. *An appeal to the religion, justice, and humanity of the inhabitants of the British Empire: In behalf of the Negro slaves in the West Indies.* London: J. Hatchard and Son.

Wilson, David Sloan. 2002. *Darwin's cathedral: Evolution, religion, and the nature of society.* Chicago: Univ. of Chicago Press.

———. 2007. *Evolution for everyone: How Darwin's theory can change the way we think about our lives.* New York: Delacorte Press.

———. 2008. Atheism as a stealth religion V: ineffective, silly, or worse. Feb. 27. Retrieved March 1, 2009 from http://www.huffingtonpost.com/david-sloan-wilson/atheism-as-a-stealth-reli_b_88795.html.

Wilson, E. O. 2006. *The creation: An appeal to save life on Earth.* New York: W. W. Norton.

Wilson, Horace Hayman, trans. 1840. *Vishnu purana.* Reprint, [Facsimile edition] London: Ganesha Publishing, 2001.

Yao, Xinzhong. 2000. *An introduction to Confucianism.* Cambridge: Cambridge Univ. Press.

Zeilik, Michael A., and Stephen A. Gregory. 1998. *Introductory astronomy and astrophysics,* 4th ed. Fort Worth, TX: Saunders College Publ.

INDEX

A

Dr. V. V. Raman, recipient of the Raja Rao Award (2006), is a philosopher, physicist, writer, and a man distinguished by a sense of humor and cultural wisdom. Raman was born into a Tamil family who had resettled in Bengal. He received his Bachelor's and Master's degrees in physics and mathematics from the University of Calcutta. His doctoral work in Paris, under the supervision of the Nobel laureate Louis de Broglie, was in theoretical physics,  specifically on the mathematical underpinning of quantum mechanics.

As a youth, Raman was drawn to poetry and philosophy, to mathematics and music, to languages and literature. He was fascinated by the depth and scope of meaningful knowledge that science has brought to humanity, and impressed by the power and coherence of scientific methodology. He grew up reading and reflecting on humanity's heritage. With strong links to his own tradition, he now regards himself as a human being most of all, with respect and sympathy for all that is enriching, ennobling, and enlightening in human culture.

After obtaining his doctorate from the Sorbonne, he returned to India and worked at the Saha Institute of Nuclear Physics. Then he served UNESCO for a few years, during which time he became more interested in the history and philosophy of science. Eventually, he settled at the Rochester Institute of Technology in the United States as a professor of Physics and Humanities. He went on to publish extensively on the historical, philosophical, and social aspects of science. His scholarly papers on those matters have been on the history of thermodynamics, the origins of physical chemistry, the genesis of the Schrödinger equation, the early reactions to Einstein's theory of relativity, the impact of the Copernican revolution, and on the Euler-D'Alembert controversy in eighteenth century mathematical physics. He has also written on such topics as the history of the theory of gravitation, of the energy conservation principle, and of acoustics.

He has lectured on many aspects of Indian heritage and culture and is the author of several books on that theme: *Glimpses of Indian Heritage, Satanama: Hundred Names from India's Past, Nuggets from the Gita* and *Reflections from Alien Shores*.

Since the 1990s Professor Raman has been very involved with the emerging academic field of Science and Religion. In this field he has published papers in *Zygon: Journal on Science and Religion,* as well as in *Science and Spirit.* He was elected the 2004-2005 Senior Metanexus Fellow on Science and Religion.

Dr. Raman has been a member of the Calcutta Mathematical Society, American Physical Society, American Association of Physics Teachers, Philosophy of Science Association, History of Science Society, the Institute on Religion in an Age of Science. He has served on the Editorial Board of The (American) Physics Teacher. He has served as the President of various cultural/social organizations, including the Interfaith Forum of Rochester, the India Community Center of Rochester, the Bengali Association of Rochester, the Rochester Tamil Sangam (which he founded and served on the board of), the Martin Luther King Commission of Rochester, the Metanexus Institute on Science and Religion, and the Institute on Religion in an Age of Science. He is an elected member of the International Society for Science and Religion.

—Professor Nitant Kenkre
University of New Mexico